# Teaching with Charisma

LLOYD DUCK  *George Mason University*

ALLYN AND BACON, INC.  *Boston • London • Sydney • Toronto*

Copyright © 1981 by Allyn and Bacon, Inc.
470 Atlantic Avenue, Boston, Massachusetts 02210

*Series editor:* Margaret Quinlin

**Library of Congress Cataloging in Publication Data**

Duck, Lloyd.
   Teaching with charisma.

   Bibliography:　p.
   Includes index.
   1. Teaching.　2. Education—Philosophy.　I. Title.
LB1025.2.D84　　371.1′02　　　80-19777
ISBN 0-205-07257-7 (pbk.)

10　9　8　7　6　5　4　3　2　1　86　85　84　83　82　81

Printed in the United States of America

*For all my family, who continue to teach me at home
with unfailing patience and good humor.*

*And for E.B.R., one of the best among many inspirational
educators who taught me at school.*

# CONTENTS

## *Chapter Four*

THE RECONSTRUCTIONIST TEACHER AS
"EXPERIMENTALIST-TURNED-REFORMER"     **99**

## *Chapter Five*

THE EXISTENTIALIST TEACHER AS INQUIRER INTO
HUMAN NATURE     **129**

# PREFACE

## A FEW WORDS ABOUT INTENT

This book offers a unique approach to teacher preparation which looks first at current classroom practice and then analyzes history, philosophy, and curriculum issues responsible for the evolution of five very different ways to teach. *Teaching with Charisma* focuses on the teacher's power as an instructional decision-maker and enlarges that power through an exploration of how certain instructional behaviors cluster naturally within five different role models for teaching. As one teacher remarked recently, the approach contained here involves learning how to "pull your own strings." You become aware of the possibilities for thoughtful selection among teaching behaviors. And once you have selected them thoughtfully, you get a newfound power to convince learners that your motives have merit. Most of this power comes from a self-assessment emphasis that helps you investigate practical linkages between classroom behaviors and a personal set of assumptions about learning that you have been formulating throughout all your educational experiences. I am certain, in short, that an intimate knowledge of one's philosophy of teaching can and does produce the inspirational quality we sometimes describe as "charismatic."

The key advantage of the *Teaching with Charisma* approach involves development of your own personality-tailored style of teaching. You learn how to build a repertoire of teaching behaviors that are effective because they complement your personality. You learn to convince students they can succeed by responding to your preferred set of teaching behaviors. You learn how to select behaviors that will not send out conflicting messages to students. You learn to test using techniques that match your teaching behaviors. All these features help enhance the credibility of teachers and allow them to be perceived as "whole" persons. They become more genuinely convincing, enthusiastic, and self-confident.

## A FEW WORDS ABOUT FORMAT

*Teaching with Charisma* offers the means for self-assessment in ways of educating. It overcomes the problem of random observation of teaching behaviors by using classroom vignettes to illustrate five very different ways to teach. This is a noteworthy advantage, since most of us proceed through our entire schooling careers and get exposed only to two variations on a single role model for teaching. The format here allows an in-depth look at five role models and makes these role models understandable through the application of an easy-to-use analytical tool. This analytical tool, which comes from trends in educational history and philosophy, is set forth in Chapter One. The next five chapters begin with lessons illustrating each of the five role models, explore the philosophy, history, and curriculum issues underlying the role models, and conclude with personal considerations about choices for. pre-service and in-service educators. Every role model is shown to have advantages and disadvantages for instruction that must be taken into account. Chapter Seven gives guidance for applying the five role models to *all* subject matter areas and *all* age groups. There are assessment guidelines for observing the styles of other teachers and self-assessment guidelines for analyzing one's own classroom behaviors. There are also several personal self-assessment devices for exploring one's attitudes about teaching and learning.

The blend of methodology, history, philosophy, and curriculum issues contained here asks the reader to be involved first as an adult learner. Just as I am sure that gaining awareness about linkages between classroom behaviors and philosophy can spark charisma, I am equally certain that every reader of this volume is an adult learner. Pardon me for stating what is so mundanely obvious. I simply want to say that I will not be asking you to attempt an impossible re-creation of yourselves before you can participate in the classroom vignettes that begin these chapters. Because you are adult learners, you cannot turn yourselves back into smaller beings with those lower levels of awareness you had in grade six or three or one. And by saying this I am assuming no lack of dedication on your part.

I also do not mean to indicate that the lesson vignettes are applicable only to adult learners. In fact, they are exceedingly effective from middle school through college age groups, with minor adjustments in vocabulary. However, they are deliberately constructed around issues that give you an opportunity for sincere involvement as an adult first. This procedure allows you to get the true flavor of a role model before applying it to *all* subject areas and *all* age levels. Though examples for translating these instructional ideas into classrooms from primary level through college abound throughout the volume, the most concentrated summaries and guidelines for this have been placed in Chapter Seven.

Perhaps the most useful quality about this format is its unique applicability to two levels of teacher preparation. For those who, like myself, prefer to seek dominant trends in teacher behaviors and use them to reveal preferences for a role model, it offers a device for self-assessment and a means for becoming more "charismatic" in the classroom. For those who emphasize the degree to which we are all eclectics in that we all borrow from every role model, it becomes an approach that can help teachers adapt the same curriculum material for an Essentialist lesson, an Experimentalist lesson, an Existentialist lesson, and so on. Whichever of these positions one takes, I have found *Teaching with Charisma* a most powerful vehicle for teacher education during the past seven years. Its unique synthesis of methodology, curriculum, philosophy, and history has helped in-service teachers become more "charismatic" by aiding them in defining new patterns of growth. It has also been used very successfully in self-assessment activities with master's and doctoral students and in preparation for comprehensive examinations. The book's bibliographic essay has been particularly useful in guiding in-service teachers and advanced students to investigate additional sources, while at the same time not cluttering the main points of exposition in the first seven chapters with weighty references. The approach has also proven exceedingly valuable in helping undergraduates become familiar with the choices available to them for constructing a "charismatic" teaching style.

As the book now stands, it is the result of efforts (1) to convince students that there is a definite link between a teacher's classroom behaviors and philosophy, (2) to provide a manageable analytical tool by which it is possible to sample a set of behaviors and "work backwards" toward a philosophy, and (3) to demonstrate that philosophical labels are not to be used as mutually exclusive categories, some of which are inherently "good" and some of which are inherently "bad." In truth, teachers within any one of the five major role models to be considered here have a definitely productive and beneficial task to perform for youngsters.

## A FINAL WORD ABOUT BEGINNINGS

One caution as you begin. The analytical tool may seem deceptively straightforward at first. Refinements occur as the reader proceeds, however, so that with a combination of continua and indicators the full richness and complexity of that intricate art we call teaching ultimately emerge.

## ACKNOWLEDGMENTS

In addition to the beneficial insights pre-service and in-service teachers have given me in classroom and workshop settings, there are many others—and it is impossible to mention everyone—without whose help this effort could not have been completed. First of all, there is my wife Betty, who knows all the right questions to ask and all the best ways to be supportive. Then there are those colleagues whose conversation has never failed to fascinate and stimulate me as well as refine my thinking about this project: Dr. Jerry Moore of University of Virginia; Drs. Marjory Brown-Azarowicz, Hank Bindel, Gloria Chernay, Harold Chu, Clark Dobson, Mary Ann Dzama, Robert Gilstrap, Robert Gray, Judith Jacobs, Jack Levy, Don Smith, and Betty J. Schuchman of George Mason University; Drs. Larry Bowen and Mark Spikell, who have been supremely supportive of my attempts to complete this task in their roles of dean and department chairman respectively.

I am greately indebted to Professors Harold Shane of Indiana University, George F. Kneller of University of California at Los Angeles, and Marie Wirsing of University of Colorado at Denver who gave superbly constructive advice on portions of the manuscript. To Professors Glorianne Leck of Youngstown State University, James Hart of University of Maine, and Jesus Garcia of Texas A&M University goes my special gratitude for having analyzed the entire manuscript and provided supremely useful insights about the relationships among topics in each chapter. For their services in examining the manuscript for its usefulness with undergraduates and graduates in foundations, methodology, philosophy, and curriculum courses, special thanks are due to Sr. Shirley Schmitz of the College of St. Teresa and to Professors Barbara Bontempo of West Virginia University, T. F. McLaughlin of Gonzaga University, S. Marilynn Hofer of Marian College, and William Beck of Southern Methodist University. I was also supremely fortunate to have the expert advice of the following colleagues who reviewed the manuscript after participating with me in a workshop in Oregon: Professors Lawrence Bagford of East Stroudsburg State College, James Parsons of The University of Alberta, Martha Murray of Campbell University, Patricia Baker of SUNY at Brockport, Roger Zimmerman of Mankato State University, Thomas Turner of The University of Tennessee at Knoxville, and Walter Parker of University of Washington at Seattle. And the manuscript would never have been typed so well without the expert skills of May Thompson, Joan Thomassy, and Virginia Berry. To Christopher and Joanna I am indebted for what could turn out to be the most constructive of all hints. They wondered why their dad didn't decide to do a book of ghost stories instead of one about teaching.

I am also extremely indebted to Margaret Quinlin, Jack Peters, and Sig Hermansen of Allyn and Bacon for their excellent insights. I will be eternally grateful to Susanne Canavan, Shirley Davis, and Anne Kilbride for their superb editing skills and their unfailing good humor in coordinating the efforts of so many so that this project could become reality.

# THE HEART OF THE MATTER:
## An Analytical Tool

# CHAPTER ONE

## *The Need for Fusion:*
## METHODOLOGY, PHILOSOPHY, HISTORY, AND CURRICULUM ISSUES

An eleventh grade United States history class has completed a study of the effects of industrialization on minority ethnic groups. The teacher has just shown the film *Geronimo Jones*, in which a white man at a local trading post cons a twelve-year-old Indian lad out of a highly prized amulet presented to him by his grandfather. Students have been asked to describe what they consider to be the three most important choices this Indian youngster will face in life and advise him about those choices on the basis of what they have just learned during their study of industrialization's effects on minority ethnic groups. Students have been told that they will write brief responses for this assignment as part of their preparation for a general class discussion on the topic.

Ask a group of students who have just finished a course in educational philosophy to apply a philosophical label to the instructor described in the previous situation. Have students assume that this situation represents the typical teaching style for this instructor. Responses are likely to occur as follows:

"I think this teacher is a Progressive because kids are being asked to solve a problem."

"But what about the information that has already been given out? You can tell she has taught a great deal about minority groups, so I think she is an Essentialist."

"Wait. We're overlooking the emphasis on personal choice for the Indian lad and how kids are supposed to give him advice. That sounds Existentialist to me."

"I've just heard people apply three different terms to this teacher. Since she seems to borrow from three different philosophies, she must be an eclectic. That's what I consider myself."

Thus, we arrive at the ultimately safe answer: an eclectic. How can one go wrong with this answer if, by definition, an eclectic borrows from several different philosophies? Who does not borrow? Who would expect to see a teacher whose methods completely represent only one philosophical position? Therefore, the term eclectic would seem almost universally applicable.

Classroom teachers do borrow from different philosophical systems, primarily as a means to assure variety in methods of instruction. However, a philosophical position is actually indicated by emphases and preferences which translate themselves into behavior. Thus, it is the behavioral emphasis or preference which should be identified to reveal the underlying set of philosophical assumptions. Despite the tendency of many students when they have just completed an academic study of educational philosophy to rely on the term "eclectic," it seems highly unlikely that many educators are true eclectics. In fact, few, if any, teachers would apply all methodologies with equal degrees of enthusiasm. The behavioral emphases and preferences for a certain cluster of methodologies are keys to determining a philosophical position. Probably no other circumstance could exist, unless philosophical labels were viewed as indicators of separate, distinct, and mutually exclusive categories.

## HOW TO STUDY TEACHING BEHAVIOR FOR TRENDS AND PREFERENCES

To identify a series of preferences, as opposed to a set of behaviors that belong to mutually exclusive categories, any beneficial analytical tool should have more than one indicator. The analytical tool we will use has indicators dealing with the following four questions:

1. What is the nature of the learner?
2. What is the nature of the subject matter?
3. How should one use the subject matter to guide students toward meaningful learning activities?
4. What behavior trend should one exhibit in order to carry out one's philosophical position?

In using this analytical tool we actually will be collecting data regarding the last question, which deals with behavior trends. In addition, that data will be used to infer how the teacher who is being observed might answer the three previous questions. Most importantly, after identifying a particular trend, we will attempt to infer how we think a given teacher might answer the first three questions. Once the behavior trend has been identified, and we have attempted to infer answers to the three previous questions, there will be a total of four indicators that, viewed as a whole, should quite accurately reveal a philosophical position.

Let us imagine that each one of these four questions presents us with an indicator. On the indicator there exists an infinite variety of possible answers to each question. Imagine, then, a continuum of possible answers for which two extremes have been clearly delineated.

## Finding Locke and Plato in Today's Classroom

For the question about the nature of the learner, I have defined the extremes of the continuum by using the terms "Lockean" (passive) and "Platonic" (active).

1. What is the nature of the learner?

Lockean                                     Platonic
(Passive)                                   (Active)

    I am sure everyone, at some point during his or her educational career, has met teachers who appeared to like youngsters and who sincerely enjoyed working with them. I am equally certain that everyone has known a few teachers who seemed not to like children or at least appeared to be indifferent. For instance, there's the teacher who says, "I'm with kids all day, so I really don't want to be bothered with their questions after 3:00 P.M.!" Or, there's the teacher who has become so tired and "burned out" that he decides to look for another job, after noting that every "chomp" of some kid's gum seemed to pierce his bone marrow.

    Suppose we select the latter position, the extreme in which a teacher may be too "burned out" to cope with classroom interaction any more and just wishes the kids would come, listen, remain perfectly silent, and "absorb the material presented." I have applied the term "Lockean" to that position because it was John Locke, in his *Essay Concerning Human Understanding*, who first wrote about mind as *tabula rasa*. He envisioned the operation of mind as similar to a blank wax tablet on which data taken in through the senses would make "impressions." Sensory data which a learner absorbed formed the true source of knowledge. Any complex mental operations involving association, interpretation, or evaluation of sensory data led to the formulation of increasingly complex knowledge.

    Of course, some teachers may feel that in particlular subject areas the principal business of learners ought to be absorption, because they do not bring with them into the classroom items about that subject which they can contribute to the learning environment. Such teachers may like kids immensely and may thoroughly enjoy classroom interaction. Remember that it is the extreme position regarding "absorption" of prescribed subject matter which is implied by the term Lockean, as we have used it here. The milder position of the Latin teacher who wants youngsters to absorb knowledge about the Latin language but who finds classroom interaction very pleasantly stimulating simply belongs further down the continuum for this question about the nature of the learner.

Let us now look all the way down the continuum to the extreme which has been labeled "Platonic." Imagine the teacher who has so much respect for what learners can contribute to the learning environment that he or she definitely does not want them to "absorb" prescribed subject matter, as the teacher sees that subject matter. Under such circumstances learners are viewed as the most important ingredient of the classroom enviroment be-cause they teach each other and their teacher through interaction, while they are "inquiring" about problems which are meaningful to them. It is almost as if learners have knowledge locked inside them which they can then release through interaction. The term Platonic seems appropriate for this view of learners because of the Platonic concept of the *doctrine of reminis-cence.*

Both Plato and Socrates saw learning as a process of remembering or "reminiscing" about that knowledge which one's soul had possessed directly before the soul had been tied to a body. Plato envisioned birth as a trauma so great that it caused the soul to forget its pure knowledge. He envisioned all subsequent learning as a lifelong struggle to remember that direct and pure knowledge; this process supposedly was aided by interaction with others or with one's inner nature by a style of questioning known as the dialectic. Bronson Alcott, the American Transcendentalist, poetically expressed a simi-lar idea: "There is in man a star of whose rising he retains a dim remem-brance."

This "dim remembrance," as Plato saw it, was rekindled by a special kind of questioning—namely, the dialectic. In Socratic dialogues Plato pre-sented Socrates as the master of *eristic,* the game which consisted of asking a number of "yes" and "no" questions until a pupil reached a point of perplex-ity in which he realized his answers had led him to an illogical position. It was at this point of perplexity, called the *elenchus,* that Plato envisioned the beginning of thinking, or the beginning of a process by which one would remember the "pure" knowledge lost at birth. In the *Meno* Socrates has a conversation or dialectic with a slave boy about the Pythagorean theorem. The youngster insists that he is totally unfamiliar with the Pythagorean theorem. Furthermore, the student claims that he is unaware of any geomet-ric principle which states that the square of the hypotenuse equals the sum of the squares of the other two sides of a right triangle. By a series of skillful questions the lad derives the formula $c^2 = a^2 + b^2$. The feeling Socrates presents is something like, "See, you knew this all along, but you had to be stimulated to remember it through the dialectic."

In Plato's philosophy the dialectic provided the means by which men could travel back to the "world of forms" or "world of universals" which held the exact concepts of Truth, Beauty, and Goodness. Since these concepts were seen as more real than the tangible world in which men existed, everyone, after using the dialectic, would agree about principles of Truth, Beauty, and Goodness, because these concepts were eternal—valid for all people in any time period. The dialectic was viewed as ultimately effective in bringing humans from their imperfect ideas about the "world of forms" back into direct knowledge of that world, because an idea (thesis) and its opposite (antithesis) could be analyzed until a more comprehensive idea (synthesis) was attained. By using the dialectic process, people would weave a chain of analysis to establish increasingly "pure" syntheses of ideas, until those people most skilled in dialectic once again attained direct communication with the "world of forms."

Few educators today are as certain of their faith in the dialectic as were Socrates and Plato. However, many do feel that learners bring extremely valuable contributions to the classroom environment: these contributions are even more important than those supplied by experts in the subject matter. Thus, students' perceptions and contributions are viewed as being of paramount importance, because it is through these perceptions and contributions that generalizations within a subject matter area will become meaningful to students. Such a position about the value of student contributions we shall call Platonic.

## Teaching to Emphasize Structure

To analyze the philosophical assumptions underlying a teacher's classroom behaviors, the second most important question to consider, after answering the one about the learner's nature, is the question concerning the teacher's views toward the subject matter. No matter what miraculous claims teachers may make about the benefits of some areas of the curriculum, it is highly unlikely that a certain body of knowledge will feed youngsters when they are hungry, or provide love when they need to be loved. Because teachers are so often encouraged to look at the prodigious capacities of subject matter, however, they seem particularly prone to emphasize its delights and make fantastic claims for its benefits. It is precisely for this reason that I feel no one should teach within any subject area until he or she has been encouraged to think realistically about what that subject matter can and cannot accomplish. Therefore, the next question in our tool for analysis is the one concerning the nature of subject matter; for this question I have used the terms "amorphous" and "structured" to delineate extremes on the indicator's continuum.

**1.** What is the nature of the learner?

Lockean                                    Platonic

**2.** What is the nature of the subject matter?

Amorphous                                    Structured

Recently Allen Funt, renowned for the "Candid Camera" television show, filmed a skit in which he asked primary school youngsters to explain excerpts from the "Pledge of Allegiance" to the United States' flag. The children who were interviewed and filmed had memorized the "Pledge of Allegiance" very carefully and were delighted to have an opportunity to talk about what they had learned. The answers they gave could not have been more charming and ingenuous, but none of their remarks seemed to follow logic understandable to adults. As refreshing and humorous as the youngsters' responses were, it was obvious that they had not really understood what they had memorized, although they were very successful at imitating the sounds of the "Pledge of Allegiance." It is this extreme of the continuum which has been labeled "amorphous." This extreme denotes the ability to repeat items and details, without any corresponding capacity to demonstrate insights about relationships among separate items.

The "amorphous" label has been reserved for rote learning which emphasizes that each item to be learned is equal in importance to every other item which has to be learned; hence, youngsters are not encouraged to find relationships among items, and no item is seen as being more important than others. It is as if the teacher who would teach history with this approach were to assume that facts of history are always inherently good, and one must improve oneself by learning as many of these bits and pieces of information as possible. Without considering the actual effects a certain subject area can achieve, some teachers give the impression that the more bits and pieces of the subject kids learn, the more benefits they will derive. In truly extreme examples of this variety of learning, the teacher may feel so satisfied to hear kids recite details verbatim that there is no attempt to check their actual comprehension.

In *Goose-Step*, a provocative study of education in the United States during the early 1920s, Upton Sinclair recounted his early experiences in religious education. He had carefully memorized the line "and thence He shall come to judge the quick and the dead," but it took him some years to decide whether "Thency" were a person, place, or thing. Another example of the kind of learning which results from an "amorphous" view of subject matter is that of the youngster who learned to sing "the consecrated cross I'd bear," although he could never quite understand why there would be a hymn about a "consecrated cross-eyed bear."

One of the most delightful examples of an "amorphous" view of subject matter has been recounted in *The Water Is Wide* by Pat Conroy. In the excerpt below Conroy has been trying to give youngsters on remote Yamacraw Island a better image of themselves by having them memorize the names of musical selections on a recording. It is obvious, however, that they really do not understand what they are learning.

---

"Gang, we are going to learn all the songs on this record," I said. "And I just thought of a good reason for doing it. Because you are going to look like geniuses when you know these songs. People are going to come to this island to revel in stupidity and poverty. I am going to switch on the record player and you are going to look at these people and exclaim with British accents, 'Pahdon me, suh. Are you perchance familiar with Rimsky-Korsakov?' We can knock their behinds off. Now, an important question: do you guys and gals think you can learn these songs and who wrote them? You already know three of them. You know Beethoven's Fifth, 'The Flight of the Bumblebee' by Rimsky-Korsakov, and Brahms' Lullaby. You learned three of them without even trying. Can you learn a whole mess of them?"

"Yeah," everyone shouted.

"I believe you."

So we did it. That night I chose twenty of the most impressive titles written by the most impressive composers. For the next two months a portion of each day was set aside for the consumption, memorization, and enjoyment of this top twenty. On a weekend I purchased a huge poster of Beethoven, and hung his shaggy-maned visage on the bulletin board. It tickled me to think of Big B's reaction to his celebration on an island as remote as Yamacraw. In a short time he became "Bay-Toven the Fifth" and no matter how earnestly I tried to explain that the Fifth was not an addendum to his name, so it remained. It gave an incredible feeling to put the needle down, to hear Tchaikovsky swell into the room, then watch the hands shoot up. . . ."*

---

If we look all the way along the continuum to the extreme labeled "structured," we may expect to find a position represented by those who have quite a realistic view of what subject matter can never accomplish for youngsters, as well as a practical assessment of its benefits. The term "structured," as used in this context, implies a view of subject matter expressed by Jerome Bruner, when he emphasized the "natural structure of a discipline." To be considered a "discipline" any subject matter should be viewed as having a natural structure which can help to explain relationships among its components and which can also be used to find out new information within that subject matter area. For example, the historical or scientific method may be described as consisting of the following elements: (1) presentation of a problem; (2) preliminary investigation of the problem; (3) formulation of an hypothesis; (4) completion of in-depth research about the problem; (5) checking results of the research against the hypothesis; and, (6) formulation of a conclusion. To an historian the historical method is a convenient way to explain relationships among facts, because events are viewed in terms of their relevance to specific hypotheses or conclusions. But the historian will also probably use this method while investigating a new problem which he or she finds meaningful and which no one in the discipline has previously investigated. Of course, this historian might "skip" the use of the historical method and find a solution to his new problem in a flash if insight, but such a case does not discount the validity of the more typical use of the historical method, which is an embodiment of the "natural structure" of history.

The continuum we have just examined concerning the subject matter embraces a broad spectrum, ranging from the position which regards subject matter as a series of items to be known (approaching the "amorphous" extreme) to the position which views subject matter as a method for finding out new things (approaching the "structured" extreme). For example, we could formulate the question more directly for the term *science*. Is science primarily a collection of things to be known or a way of knowing? Is science an end in itself or is it a means to attain new knowledge?

A teacher who assumed the extreme "amorphous" position might teach biology as the memorization of unrelated vocabulary items, or English literature as the memorization of poetry and literary terminology, or history as a collection of events to be learned on a time line. However, it is highly unlikely that any observer would find many examples today of teachers who adopt an "amorphous" position, except those who may be working with very young students who are attempting to master basic skills of vocabulary. This is due primarily, of course, to the widespread influence of Bruner's "structure-of-the-discipline" concept and to the curriculum materials which have been produced containing a problem-solving emphasis.

If a teacher moves away from the "amorphous" end of the continuum toward the "structured" extreme, however, there are two basic ways in which his or her behavior might manifest the new preference. To emphasize "structure" the teacher might tell students to learn major ideas in a lesson, as well as items which relate to these main ideas; in fact, a teacher could have students deal with this kind of "structure" by having them memorize ideas, and then check to be sure youngsters were comprehending relationships among ideas. However, a teacher might also emphasize "structure" by asking students to solve a problem through which they would be hypothesizing and creating their own structure, then relating details they uncover to the hypotheses they have formulated. This latter method of emphasizing "structure" has been overwhelmingly popular, especially in the physical and social sciences, since the various curriculum projects of the early 1960s.

In conjunction with the question concerning the nature of subject matter, we are also dealing with a host of popular attitudes about the relative merits or demerits of disciplines. I suppose most students at the college level are more or less familiar with wars fought in academia over which degrees will be awarded first during a graduation ceremony. Such debates about graduation ceremonies usually hinge on the amount of prestige which the public chooses to place on the various disciplines. All one has to do to understand feelings involved in such debates is to consider the job market rewards which might be available to those graduating with degrees in the following disciplines: social sciences, sciences, mathematics, history, literature, languages, fine arts, physical education. Those in academia who organize graduation ceremonies are, of course, totally aware of job market rewards attached to certain disciplines and of the relative prestige indicated thereby. Sometimes they bow to popular notions and first award professional degrees in the physical sciences, but sometimes they use university tradition as a guide and first award degrees in older fields, such as classical languages, philosophy, and theology. Of course, it is possible to side step this issue entirely and award degrees alphabetically by colleges within a university, or each college could be permitted to have its own separate graduation ceremony.

Nevertheless, the scholarly world in general remains influenced by popular notions of prestige, as is evident in the evolution of social science disciplines in the twentieth century. As Lord Kenneth Clark pointed out in the final installment of his *Civilisation* series, twentieth century Western man has shown unbounded fascination for technology, science, and engineering. To enhance prestige for their own disciplines, social scientists increasingly drew from the physical sciences for their methodology. Methods within the social sciences—particularly in sociology, economics, political science, archaeology, and history—began to resemble the scientific method; moreover, these methods adopted mathematics, the language of the physical sciences, in their reliance on statistical analyses. Even in the discipline of history, many works rely heavily on statistical analysis. For example, in *A New England Town in the First Hundred Years,* Lockridge applied contemporary methods in sociology and in statistical analysis to study town records from the colonial period of American history. This propensity to borrow from the physical sciences and mathematics to enhance the prestige of social science disciplines has served to underscore Lord Clark's point about the twentieth century's worship of technology, science, and engineering.

It is often difficult to avoid an exposure to these attitudes about prestige among disciplines when choosing a major in undergraduate school. Some academicians never tire of extolling the merits of a major in the humanities as opposed to one in business administration or education. Many students learn to say with pride that their majors are in chemistry, while others who major in physical education speak in more muted tones about the virtues of their field. Furthermore, in professional schools many students have been encouraged to become lawyers or doctors, instead of teachers or theologians.

An acquaintance recently related the frustrations of her brother who had completed a Ph.D. in English literature, then was unable to secure a teaching position. He finally took a job in the construction industry and found it was delightful to have evenings free for working on a novel. Physical labors of the day relaxed him for intellectual labors in the evening. How long he found this arrangement satisfying is difficult to imagine.

The same consideration of deferred professional aspirations is inescapable in the sad plight of one of our recent teacher education graduates. When I contacted her as part of some research on job market "success," she seemed very pleased to tell me she had a job. I was also pleased, assuming she had found a secondary school teaching position, until she told me she was working as a waitress. It became apparent that the enjoyment she found in this position emerged only because everyone she worked with had a master's degree, and they had formed a discussion group to analyze the most interesting and most recent literary works.

Both of these examples offer unfortunate commentaries on the exclusiveness of the teaching profession. They emphasize the cruel irony of having to adopt temporary measures for earning a living while professional dreams wither. Those who feel too constrained by the demands of a professional role might well ponder the alternatives. However, many traditionally prepared professionals who feel overwhelmed by paperwork often desire more freedom to read and to discuss ideas. Thus, the value of a liberal arts education is being reexamined, at least in terms of its rich potential for self-edification.

Everyone has been influenced, to some degree, by popular notions about the worth of certain disciplines. Consequently, each teacher's view of subject matter has been in the process of being shaped during his or her entire educational career. Similar to other questions in our tool for analysis, feelings about the nature of subject matter constitute a philosophical position toward which a teacher has been moving for years. These feelings remain powerful guides for future decisions about classroom behavior, despite the teacher's conscious or unconscious examination of those feelings. Perhaps such feelings are even more powerful as determinants of behavior if the teacher does not examine them.

## To Be or Not to Be Controversial?

A third question—applicable to those in Kanawah County, West Virginia, who worry about the content of textbooks, and to those in Montgomery County, Maryland, who were upset about showing the film *The Lottery* to their youngsters—concerns the use of subject matter.

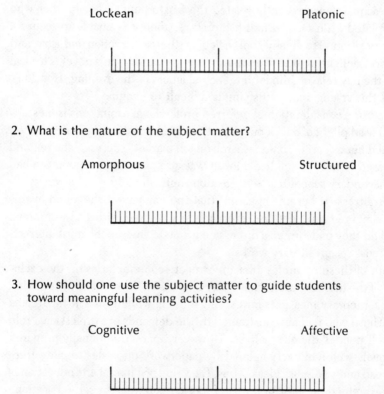

1. What is the nature of the learner?

           Lockean                                    Platonic

2. What is the nature of the subject matter?

           Amorphous                                  Structured

3. How should one use the subject matter to guide students toward meaningful learning activities?

           Cognitive                                  Affective

For this indicator's continuum I have used the terms "cognitive" and "affective" as end points; these terms were immortalized in Bloom's and Krathwohl's *Taxonomies of Educational Objetives.* I have deliberately chosen the phrase "end points," because the concepts deal not with mutually exclusive categories, but rather with matters of emphasis and preference. If cognitive learning emphasizes intellectual skills devoid of emotion, and affective learning emphasizes feelings and emotions, then it is obvious that both cognitive and affective learning can be, and usually are, closely linked. Thus, the decision revolves around which of the two to emphasize. Since any responsible assumption of the teacher's role involves some degree of skill development and information-giving among students, the question concerns the best way to develop skills and give information—either by emphasizing the cognitive or by stressing the affective domain. Selecting between these two approaches is each teacher's personal decision, which can involve a great deal of controversy.

To highlight the potential for controversy, I'd like to cite an incident from my own professional preparation. I had been given the assignment of devising an effective means for teaching youngsters the concept *revolution,* while using what Edgar Dale has called "direct experience,"—a concept within his "cone of experience" which usually translates, in practical terminology, into a learning activity which takes place outside the confines of classroom walls. After lengthy consideration, I decided it would be most appropriate and effective to have youngsters replicate in a local shopping center the experiment discussed in the newspaper article reprinted below. Kids could then compare responses from local citizens to responses reported in the article; thus, they would make a rather informal comparative analysis of awareness about the concept *revolution* for participants dealt with in the article and for participants in their own experiment.

---

### Independence Document 'Subversive'*

Senator Mark Hatfield, addressing the Senate of the United States recently, informed his colleagues of the results of a "very revealing survey." Students in a class of American Government and Politics at the University of Maryland, European Division, circulated a portion of the preamble of the *Declaration of Independence* among a cross section of Americans at an Air Force base in Germany. The survey was designed to see how many of the country's citizens would actually recognize their own *Declaration of Independence.* The students also wished to know how many of the individuals interviewed would support the document and, if necessary, sign it as evidence of their convictions.

The results, printed in the *Congressional Record,* are as follows:

Preamble of the *Declaration of Independence*

'When, in the course of human events, it becomes necessary for one people to dissolve the political bands which have connected them with another, and to assume, among the powers of the earth, the separate and equal station to which the laws of nature and of nature's God entitle them, a decent respect to the opinions of mankind requires that they should declare the causes which impel them to the separation.

'We hold these truths to be self-evident, that all men are created equal; that they are endowed by their Creator with certain unalienable rights; that among these, are life, liberty, and the pursuit of happiness. That to secure these rights, governments are instituted among men, deriving their just powers from the consent of the governed; that, whenever any form of government becomes destructive of these ends, it is the right of the people to alter or to abolish it, and to institute a new government, laying its foundations on such principles, and organizing its powers in such form, as to them shall seem most likely to effect their safety and happiness. Prudence, indeed, will dictate that governments long established, should not be changed for light and transient causes; and, accordingly, all experience hath shown, that mankind are more disposed to suffer, while evils are sufferable, than to right themselves by abolishing the forms to which they are accustomed. But, when a long train of abuses and usurpations, pursuing invariably the same object, evinces a design to reduce them under absolute despotism, it is their right, it is their duty to throw off such government and to provide new guards for their future security.'

*Tabulations*

I.  Direct totals:

    a.  Total number interviewed—252
    b.  Total number who signed document—68
    c.  Total number who would not sign document—148
    d.  Total number who agreed with the document but would not sign it—36
    e.  Total number who realized exactly what the document really was —41

II. Direct percentages to part I:
    a.  Percentage of base population interviewed—11
    b.  Percentage of those who would sign the document—27
    c.  Percentage of those who would not sign the document—73
       1.  Percentage of those who agreed with the document but would not sign it—14
       2.  Percentage of those who absolutely would not sign the document —59
    d.  Percentage of those who realized exactly what the document really was—16

*Statements of People Interviewed*

(These are just some of the statements that were given, but they are a good sample of many responses received.)

1.  Some called it a lot of trash.

2. Many felt that the document is advocating a *coup d'etat.*

3. Many did not believe in the principles stated in the document.

4. Some felt that the document is very vague and left a lot to be desired.

5. Many felt it was a direct rebuttal of the government.

6. One teacher at a local junior high school, after reading it stated: "Do you really believe in this document?" When the man replied with a definite YES, the teacher shouted: "You believe in what you want to, you dirty Communist."

7. Many would not sign the document for fear of repercussion.

8. Some would not sign the document because it failed to clarify how the government would be replaced, and had there been any mention of elections they would have signed it.

9. Four individuals accused the surveyor (a Negro) of trying to develop his own black state.

10. This document is "advocating the abolishing of our government and the possible establishment of a dictatorship."

11. One individual refused to sign the document and called it a very radical document; he also thought it was poorly written.

12. A few felt it was an outdated document and left too much for interpretation.

13. An individual felt it was not necessary to reaffirm the principles to which he has dedicated his life and had sworn to uphold when he took the Oath of Allegiance.

14. One man said the document was "basically stupid and a lot of trash." Also, this same individual felt people should not have the right to abolish the government.

15. Some individuals would not sign it because they wanted to know what it would be used for.

16. Another individual stated: "Who wasted an afternoon writing this?"

17. Another man felt that the government should not be changed by the "little people."

18. Too much "legal talk."

19. Doesn't give enough to the majority class.

20. One individual left the room and refused to even talk about the document again.

21. One individual didn't like the word prudence in the document.

22. Many thought this document to be too radical.

23. Another individual thought the document was "pretty," but not workable.

24. One gentlemen asked if the document had anything to do with the "Communist Party of America."

25. One individual said that "it sounds like that long haired kid stuff."

*Reprinted with permission from "Independence Document 'Subversive,'" Cavalier Daily, Vol. 79, April 28, 1969.*

I was somewhat naively pleased with this lesson and eager to report about it to other students in the seminar. The young lady whose presentation immediately preceded mine, however, explained that she would teach the concept *revolution* by placing students in a "survival situation" during which they would be taught how to use techniques of guerrilla warfare against each other. Right away I made two decisions: (1) that I was a hopeless "hidebound" conservative; and (2) that the administration at the local high school where I taught would frown upon my helping students learn techniques of guerrilla warfare, especially since conditions at the school were in such a confused state that one might suspect that the kids already knew a great deal about guerrilla warfare.

The lesson involving techniques of guerrilla warfare was probably more affectively based than mine. There are, however, a host of other examples which could also be cited. What about the "Right to Life" proponent so intent on shocking students into an awareness of the abortion problem that he uses slides showing pails of aborted human fetuses when he gives a "guest lecture" to a local high school sociology class? Needless to say, parents complained about the guest speaker's techniques.

In my own work with secondary students during a unit on industrialization's effects on minority ethnic groups within the United States, I asked youngsters to consider the pervasive influence Charles Darwin's ideas had had on social and economic thought. To introduce the topic I assigned an article about this country's version of the "Abominable Snowman," sometimes called "Bigfoot" or "Sasquatch." After youngsters had talked animatedly about the pros and cons of the possibilities that this creature existed, they were asked if their opinions of themselves as human beings would change if they found out for certain that Bigfoot really did exist. When they seemed puzzled about the reason for this question, I explained that some people might use Bigfoot as Darwin's missing (evolutionary) link between ape and man, and as evidence that none of us has a soul. Two years later I received a note from one of our graduates saying that she had seen a recent "short subject" on Bigfoot at a local movie theater and that she still refused to believe any of those things Charles Darwin had to say.

Kids do exhibit, of course, effective self-corrective techniques, whenever subject matter is presented in what they consider to be too emotional or too personal a manner. I was working with one of our student teachers whose cooperating teacher was allowing her to teach a major segment of a mini-course on "Death in Literature." The student teacher had asked youngsters to read excerpts from Elisabeth Kubler-Ross's *On Death and Dying* and apply Kubler-Ross's "stages of dying" to the main character in John Gunther's *Death Be Not Proud*. After visiting one of her classes, I was moved by the seriousness with which youngsters seemed to identify with the main character in Gunther's play—a phenomenon that wasn't surprising, since the main character was, like themselves, a high school student struggling with all the usual problems of adolescence, plus the additional burden of knowing that he was terminally ill. On this particular day's visit I was emotionally caught up in the mood of the first class, when two students from the second class began to ready themselves for that day's activity. After placing a newly opened package of Kleenex tissues on her desk, one student remarked to the other, with some degree of mock impatience, "I'm so tired of having to get ready to cry every day when I come to this class!"

Examples like these, of course, lead some teachers to adopt what they consider the ultimately "safe" position of emphasizing only cognitive learning activities. They occasionally forget that, even though they may plan their instruction to emphasize the cognitive, their students are perfectly capable and adept when it comes to thinking of emotion-packed questions and examples. Such teachers, especially if they are working with classes in the humanities or social sciences, may find themselves dealing with disturbingly affective issues which they had not previously planned to include.

I can remember one occasion early in my own teaching career, when I had decided to play safe with one of my classes and deal only with strictly controlled cognitive learning. During the innocuous discussion, one in which the topic was unimportant enough to have made no lasting impression on my own memory, one student in this class interupted another. Immediately there was a taunting cry, "He just interrupted her 'cause she's Black!" With that comment several young men were ready to shed each other's blood. Even though I don't remember the "safe" topic for discussion that day, I will never forget the lesson the kids taught me about affective education. It is difficult now to reconstruct the chain of events, but at least no blood was shed. I had been using recorded music as a reward for getting the day's task done—a technique frequently used by teachers who have been influenced by behavior modification techniques. As a result, things resolved themselves quite well amid the strains of stimulating martial and ragtime music.

Although there are teachers who can use a strictly cognitive approach and still maintain the interest level of students, these teachers are rarely dealing with the physical sciences (although it is becoming increasingly hard to outdo Jacques Cousteau or *Jaws* in the capacity to sustain interest); they may be helping young children acquire basic skills; or they could be helping adolescents become proficient in skill-oriented subjects for which there is a high demand in the job market. I do remember one particularly effective government teacher whose approach was strictly cognitive. She taught how bills became laws, without giving examples to stimulate any interest in social issues. She taught about the three branches of government, with the emphasis placed on abstractions. Whenever questions that were particularly relevant to kids in the community and that were particularly controversial reared themselves during class discussion, she changed the subject with these simple but potent words: "I'm sorry we can't discuss that; it's under litigation." This was her way of avoiding an "emotionally blocked" topic, as Maurice Hunt and Lawrence Metcalf have used the phrase in *Teaching High School Social Studies.* Her credibility was helped because there were, indeed, a number of "hot" issues in the community which were "under litigation." She relied heavily on memory-oriented tests and a series of carefully planned "small successes" to maintain student interest, but the approach was effective because her students did learn a great deal about the organization and function of government in this country. It would be unfair, however, not to mention that, as a teacher, she was respected and honored among the students largely because she had served so conscientiously in this school setting for a number of years.

In order to illuminate factors involved in any teacher's decision to emphasize cognitive or affective learning activities it might be helpful to consider the following addendum to our indicator for the question about the use of subject matter.

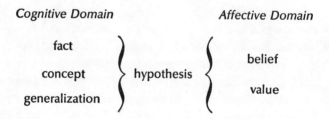

*Cognitive Domain*                    *Affective Domain*

fact

concept        }  hypothesis  {        belief

generalization                        value

## Practical Definitions

**fact**   a verifiable truth. (e.g., A certain priest sold an indulgence as indicated by church records.)

**concept**   a word or phrase containing at least one noun. (e.g., indulgence, river, favorable balance of trade.)

**generalization**   a statement about facts or concepts, or both facts and concepts. (e.g., Indulgences were sold in German principalities during the fifteenth century.)

**belief**   a statement which is assumed to be true, often uncritically (e.g., I believe in God [when "meaningful" others believe in God and the speaker has not examined his position critically]. I believe it is going to rain.)

**value**  a belief about which someone cares deeply and which has been examined critically (e.g., I believe in God.)

**hypothesis**  a statement which is assumed to be true for the purpose of critical examination. (e.g., Any one of the following statements in which one is uncertain about their validity and wishes to examine relevant evidence: (1) Indulgences were sold in German principalities during the fifteenth century. (2) I believe it is going to rain. (3) I believe in God.

Let us assume that all subject matter areas or disciplines are composed of three basic raw materials: facts, concepts, and generalizations. Let us also assume that youngsters bring to the classroom certain attitudes, which involve the emotions and which can be stated as beliefs and values. These beliefs and values are especially powerful in their capacities to influence the way youngsters perceive facts, concepts, and generalizations within any discipline.

Evidence abounds that kids bring to the classroom attitudes which influence the way they perceive facts, concepts, and generalizations. A few pertinent examples, however, may help to underscore this point about attitudes and perception. During my fourth year of public school teaching a small group of professional actors and actresses decided to offer a series of dramatic poetry readings for our English classes. The administration scheduled these events in the media center and invited a few classes to each session. During one particularly moving rendition of the works of Langston Hughes, one group of students sprang up and shouted, "See, that's why we hate you!"

They were promptly answered with equal vehemence by another group, "Yeah, and that's the reason we hate you!"

Unfortunately, just at that point, the period bell sounded and kids groped their way out into the halls and back to their lockers. Items previously cited—for example, one student's reaction to Charles Darwin or another youngster's readiness to place what he considered a rude interruption into the context of racial conflict— serve equally well to stress the same idea. Have you ever been with a friend while witnessing an exciting event and wonder, as you hear the event described by that other person, how anyone could possibly have watched what you saw and then come up with such a bizarre, inaccurate description? This is another illustration of how differing attitudes and emotional states of two people influence perceptions.

Some teachers are fortunate to have youngsters who come to their classes with fairly positive attitudes toward the subject matter at hand. In such cases the teacher may be able to proceed with a cognitive emphasis and find that youngsters continue to maintain a high interest level. However, there are obviously many situations in which students' attitudes toward subject matter vary from lukewarm to openly hostile. If the teacher is attempting to help youngsters think critically by transforming generalizations, beliefs, and values into hypotheses which can be tested, then perhaps the only way to stimulate these mental processes in a hostile setting is to emphasize the "affective domain." Will the teacher feel comfortable, however, in dealing with the affective? Can he or she refuse to be initimidated when asked by a parent, administrator, or student, "Why are you using this material about the Hanafi Muslims in your class?" The best answer to such a question is, of course, a calm and direct statement of one's philosophical rationale. If, instead of swallowing hard and stammering through an answer which sounds absurdly close to an admission of using material about the Hanafis for its shock value, the teacher can produce a direct response, the results may seem like a gigantic "daily double" in their power to repay all efforts at philosophical soul-searching.

Philosophical soul-searching about the three questions we have just considered in our simple analytical tool has definite advantages. There is, except in very rare cases, at least one bleak day during the first year of a teacher's career when he or she will feel that slitting the wrists and slowly bleeding to death in the middle of the classroom would attract no notice from the students. On that day one youngster will probably ask pointedly and quite loudly, so that everyone can hear, "*Why* are we doing this?" This is the moment when a teacher's future success with any student in the room will depend on the skill with which an answer to that all-important question is given. It is, indeed, infinitely more crucial to be able to answer this question adroitly and convincingly for a student than for either an administrator or a parent. When students are convinced that any teacher is together enough to decide what is beneficial about the subject matter he is selling, how he wants to sell it, and how he would like to use student contributions to the learning environment, only then will the teacher be perceived as being sincere in his desire to help students. More importantly, the teacher must feel secure enough to talk openly and directly with students about elements he or she considered in making decisions about these first three questions in the analytical tool.

The following excerpt from a teacher's planning notebook provides an example of ways to examine evidence about decisions concerning the nature of the learner, the nature of the subject matter, and the use of subject matter. I have chosen an excerpt involving the colonial period of our history to be taught to eleventh grade students, who frequently think of colonial history in terms of a "Betsy-Ross-and-the-Father-of-our-Country" approach and turn off or become somewhat sullen and hostile at the thought of learning more of the same information. In other words, we are looking at a setting in which kids are likely to ask, "*Why* are we doing this *again*?" Of course, such a question provides an ideal opportunity to discuss one's philosophical position in clear, direct terms.

*Excerpt from a Planning Notebook (Two Major Ideas for a Unit in Colonial American History)*

I.  A.  Teacher's values: They ought to know something about economics, instead of emphasizing dates of colonies which they've had so much.

    B.  Generalization and chronology of major understandings: Under the mercantilist system a government tries to regulate its economy to obtain a *favorable balance of trade*.

    C.  Popular issues, kids' values, and psychology: Ask why we didn't exchange our money for gold on the world market during the wage-price freeze or similar questions leading to concept-formation for *favorable balance of trade*.

Possible sources for selection of objectives, content, strategies:
—textbook has already selected content
—generalizations
—chronology of major understandings
—teacher's values
—kids' values
—popular issues
—method of the discipline
—psychology

II. A.  Teacher's values: They ought to be aware that Puritans felt responsible for each other morally and believed that the "Devil made work for idle hands." (Puritan ethic)

    B.  Method of discipline and kids' values: Have a better student use deductive reasoning with the historical method as it relates to *Witchcraft at Salem* by Chadwick Hansen.

    C.  Popular issues and teacher's values: Show extremes of which the Puritan mind was capable by having a student read and report on Emory Battis' *Saints and Sectaries: Ann Hutchinson and the Antinomian Controversy in the Massachusetts Bay Colony* (story similar to *Rosemary's Baby*).

It should be obvious from items in the planning notebook that this teacher does feel kids can bring some valuable, or at least useful, contributions to the learning environment. The teacher also views history as having a natural structure which can be used to illuminate relationships among facts, concepts, and generalizations. He or she, by choosing to stress economics and sociology within a course labeled history, is also employing an interdisciplinary approach. A mild affective emphasis may be indicated, but that is impossible to determine solely by examining this one excerpt from a notebook. The actual classroom behaviors—strategies used to implement answers which the excerpt implies regarding our first three questions—must be observed before other insights can be gained.

### To Converge or Diverge—That Is the Question

This brings us to the final, and perhaps the most crucial, question in our analytical tool. The question about behavior is especially critical because it is not uncommon for an observer to hear a teacher voice one set of philosophical assumptions, yet find that the teacher's behavior seems to support an entirely different set of philosophical assumptions. This fourth question is also crucial because we must always begin with observable classroom behaviors before any answers may be inferred about a teacher's position regarding the other three questions.

I have chosen the terms "authoritarian" and "non-authoritarian" for extremes on this continuum, despite the fact that I intend the discussion to go beyond what is usually called "classroom management." Although these two terms may seem to imply "strict," as opposed to "permissive" classroom management, the intention is to emphasize a more inclusive approach to classroom management than merely dealing with discipline problems. Thus, it is an overall view in regard to the student and the subject matter which this indicator has been designed to examine.

For instance, suppose some teachers encourage students to view subject matter only as experts in that field might view it; hence, these teachers habitually accept for each major question under examination only one right answer which all students are expected to adopt and understand. In terms of Ned Flanders' system of analyzing classroom behaviors such teachers would be said to encourage convergent thinking. For the purpose of our own analytical tool we shall say that such a teacher exhibits an authoritarian behavior trend.

Part of this tendency toward an authoritarian behavior trend is indicated by the subject matter with which a teacher is dealing. For instance, a chemistry teacher might set up a laboratory "experiment" in which the students are asked to determine if Boyle's law regarding the nature of gasses still holds. In such a situation all answers to the "experiment" should look alike no matter which student or group of students derived them. No

## Analytical Tool

**1.** What is the nature of the learner?

        Lockean                                 Platonic

**2.** What is the nature of the subject matter?

        Amorphous                           Structured

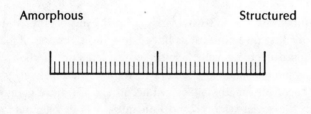

**3.** How should one use the subject matter to guide students toward meaningful learning activities?

        Cognitive                             Affective

**4.** What behavior trend should one exhibit in order to carry out one's philosophical position?

    Authoritarian World View        Non-authoritarian World View
      (Convergent Thinking)             (Divergent Thinking)

alternate answers would be accepted as "true" because all students are supposed to discover that, indeed, Boyle's law still holds. However, there are options to the use of convergent thinking even in introductory courses in physical sciences. Suppose, for instance, that the instructor wanted students to "measure" pollution within the local school district. Some youngsters will devise means to measure pollution in the atmosphere, others may examine water pollution, and some may look at impurities in foods. Several answers to this question about pollution are possible, and the teacher would probably be expected to encourage alternate plans of action to get rid of pollutants.

This second example in which kids measure pollutants would involve what Flanders has called "divergent thinking" because more than one answer is encouraged for the question at hand. For the purposes of our analytical tool we shall call this behavior trend "non-authoritarian." Although one might correctly expect the non-authoritarian trend to be most frequently associated with the humanities and the social sciences, there is some evidence of its use with the physical sciences, as the previous example from an ecology class points out.

Remember that we have stressed earlier in this chapter the fact that answers to our first three questions have been in the process of formulation throughout a prospective teacher's entire educational preparation. What is it that causes some prospective teachers to want to deal primarily with the physical sciences and mathematics, while others are more comfortable in dealing with the social sciences and humanities? Is it that some are more adept with convergent thinking, while others are more adept with divergent thinking? If so, we would expect these feeling, or philosophical assumptions, which have been in the process of formulation for years to manifest themselves quite clearly in a teacher's classroom behavior.

There is only one other caveat before we look at a chart summarizing our analytical tool and the philosophical divisions indicated by classroom behavior trends. Do not assume that the terms "authoritarian" and "non-authoritarian," when applied to a behavior trend, connote "strictness" or "permissiveness" of classroom management. Everyone who responsibly assumes the teacher's role—whether he or she is an Essentialist Experimentalist, Existentialist, Reconstructionalist, Perennialist, or Behaviorist —expects and must receive enough cooperation from students so that learning can occur. This minimal amount of cooperation is necessary for every learning environment; hence, a dichotomy between autocracy and chaos is definitely not the extent to which we envision the continuum for the last question in our analytical tool.

Now let us take a brief look at the chart below because it will serve as the basis for refined use of our analytical tool. As the chart indicates, an "authoritarian" behavior trend places one within the broad philosophical category of Essentialist/Perennialist, while a non-authoritarian behavior trend is indicative of the broad category of Experimentalist/Existentialist.

## Overview of Terminology
### I. Analytical Tool

1. What is the nature of the learner?

Lockean         Platonic

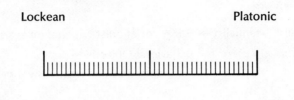

2. What is the nature of the subject matter?

Amorphous        Structured

3. How should one use the subject matter to guide students toward meaningful learning activities?

Cognitive         Affective

4. What behavior trend should one exhibit in order to carry out one's philosophical position?

Authoritarian World View   Non-authoritarian World View
(Convergent Thinking)     (Divergent Thinking)

Curriculum Design Continuum: Core ———— Subject ———— Great Books
                                  Curriculum    Curriculum      Curriculum

<————————————————————————————————>

(least structured        most structured)

**II.  *Two Broad Philosophical Categories Which are Most Easily Recognizable by Teaching Styles***

Perennialist/Essentialist → S-R Associationist Theories of Learning

Behavioral Objectives

Assumption of one right answer per problem.

Experimentalist/Existentialist → Gestalt Theories of Learning

Cognitive — Affective Objectives

Assumption of alternative appropriate answers for each problem.

**III.  *Further Differentiation of Philosophies***

*Perennialism*—emphasis on humanities as presented in great books; assumption that there are absolute truths and standards more real than the physical world.

*Essentialism*—emphasis on physical sciences as used by authorities; assumption that there are no absolute truths and that success is based on absorption of knowledge about the physical world.

*Experimentalism*—emphasis on social sciences as a framework for problem-solving; assumption that physical world is constantly changing.

*Existentialism*—emphasis on problem-solving about highly controversial and emotional issues in any subject matter area; assumption that learners "define" themselves and their relationships to the environment by their choices.

*Reconstructionism*—implies one has decided what the "perfect" form of society is and seeks to reach that society through teaching techniques associated with Experimentalism/Existentialism.

*Behaviorism*—implies that one has decided what the "perfect" form of society is and seeks to reach that society through teaching techniques associated with Essentialism.

The next chapter explores specific examples of teaching styles and reveals how those styles indicate preferences for certain sets of philosophical assumptions.

# The Essentialist Teacher
## as Problem-Solver

# CHAPTER TWO

## *The Setting:*

## MS. CHRONICLER AND THE VIKINGS

Ms. Chronicler asked her eleventh grade students to read the folowing article about the Kensington Rune Stone and to concentrate on the main ideas which caused two investigators to hold different opinions about the stone. She knew students would find the problem of the rune stone appealing, and she was careful to provide vocabulary listings at the end of the article so that everyone would understand the issues. She was also quite pleased with herself for conceiving a lesson plan which would help youngsters understand the finer points of historical scholarship.

---

### The Riddle of the Kensington Stone*

#### *Thomas R. Henry*

Did a group of Scandinavians reach this country—and perish under Indian tomahawks—130 years before Columbus came? Once denounced as a fraud, the message they left for posterity is now called "the most important archaeological object yet found in North America."

A challenging enigma confronts American historians. Did a Norwegian knight named Paul Knutson lead an ill-fated band of forty armored soldier-missionaries to the headwaters of the Red River in West Central Minnesota 130 years before the first voyage of Columbus? Evidence of such an expedition, accumulating through half a century, is now so substantial that some of this country's foremost archaeologists consider the case nearly proved. A few hard facts jut like mountain crags out of the clouds of New World antiquity.

The first of these facts: Late in the autumn of 1354 King Magnus Erikson, first ruler of the combined realms of Norway and Sweden, commissioned Knutson, a "law speaker"—or judge—and one of the most prominent men of his court, to recruit an expedition to rescue the souls of a vanished Norwegian colony on the west coast of Greenland. Presumably the party sailed early the next spring. It was never heard of again.

The second fact: Fifty years ago a stone slab was found clutched in the roots of a tree by a Swedish homesteader near Kensington, Minnesota. It bore what purported to be a message to posterity, carved in runic letters. It recorded an Indian massacre of a group of explorers. Assuming the relic is genuine, these explorers must have been members of Knutson's expedition. The inscription's date was 1362.

The third fact: A few weeks ago the slab was placed in the great hall of the Smithsonian Institution, in Washington. Dr. Matthew W. Stirling, chief of the Government's Bureau of American Ethnology, called it "probably the most important archaeological object yet found in North America."

When it was first discovered, the stone was denounced generally as a naive fraud. In the half century that has elapsed since its discovery, the major objections have been met with corroborating evidence. For more than ten years, discarded and discredited by scholars, the relic had been a flagstone in a farmer's muddy barnyard. The very features which once caused experts to denounce it are now cited as bearing witness to its genuineness.

The whole case rests, of course, on the authenticity of this blue-gray slab which the highly conservative Smithsonian has just placed among its greatest treasures. It was back in the summer of 1898 that Olof Ohman, young Swedish immigrant and homesteader near the village of Kensington, in Douglas County, Minnesota, grubbed up the stump of an aspen tree at the edge of a marsh. Clutched in its roots was a flat, gravestone-shaped piece of graywacke, one of the hard glacial sandstone rocks of the region. It was about the size of a headstone in a Swedish country cemetery. Carved on one face and one edge of this slab were strange letters.

All this had no meaning and little interest to Farmer Ohman. He was a stolid, unimaginative man. The character of Ohman is significant in the effort to validate the relic. The circumstances of the stone's discovery are recorded in a sworn affidavit which Ohman made before a local justice of the peace. If Ohman had been a glib talker or student of history—especially if he ever had tried to make any money out of his find—there might be grounds for suspicion. But he was the kind of man who had no inclination—and even less capacity—to perpetrate a fraud.

He told some neighbors about the queer stone. At their suggestion he delivered it to the local bank on his next trip to the county seat for supplies. The banker had a keen interest in local antiquities, and he, in turn, sent the relic to the University of Minnesota, at Minneapolis. There Prof. O. J. Breda, one of the foremost Scandinavian scholars in America, found little difficulty in deciphering most of the inscription. The letters were Norse runes, the curious first alphabet of the Germanic peoples derived in some roundabout way from the letters of the Greeks and Romans. Some of these symbols meant nothing to Breda. In his translation, he left blank spaces where they occurred. It now is known that they represent numbers.

This is the translation as now accepted: [We are] 8 Goths [Swedes] and 22 Norwegians on (an) exploration journey from Vinland through (or across) the West. We had camp by (a lake with) two skerries [rocky islands] one day's journey north from this stone. We were [out] and fished one day. After we came home [we] found 10 [of our] men red with blood and dead. AV[e] M[aria], Save [us] from evil. [We] have 10 of (our party) by the sea to look after our ships (or ship) 14 days' journey from this island. Year 1362.

Professor Breda was not at all impressed. It was such an obvious hoax, he said, that it was not worthy of further attention from anybody. The language itself was a dead giveaway. It was a mixture of Norwegian, Swedish and what looked like old English. In the days of runic writings Swedes and Norwegians had been bitter enemies and it was incredible that they could have been partners on an expedition. The three letters AVM were Latin, not runic. The Roman alphabet had not been introduced into Scandinavia until early in the Middle Ages.

The learned runologist missed the date—1362. The figures representing it were not in the early runic alphabet. Breda quite naturally assumed that any

Norseman who could have reached central Minnesota must have come from the Greenland colonies of Eric the Red sometime in the twelfth century. There was no room here for any argument. The Kensington Stone could not have been carved by any such Greenlander. It was all a crude and silly fraud perpetrated by somebody with a superficial knowledge of runes together with a gross ignorance of Scandinavian history. The hoaxer, whoever he was, hardly could have expected to be taken seriously. He had said that the stone was carved on an island in a lake. There was no lake within twenty miles of Ohman's homestead.

Nevertheless, the relic was sent to Northwestern University, at Evanston, Illinois, for a further check by runic experts. They agreed with Breda, and the slab was sent back to the country bank, which returned it to Farmer Ohman.

What is "probably the most important archaeological object yet found in North America" very likely still would be in that barnyard had it not been for the interest of an outstanding Norse-American historian, Hjalmar R. Holand of Ephraim, Wisconsin. For thirty years he has given most of his spare time to its study in every aspect—geological, archaeological, geographic, linguistic, and historical. He has taken it to twenty-three European universities for consultation with experts. One after another, the most serious objections to its authenticity have proved the strongest points in its favor. First was the discovery of the meanings of the runic number symbols and the determination of the date. These particular runes were of late origin and local usage in Norway. In the fourteenth century the Latin alphabet had been introduced, and its letters were intermingled quite often with the ancient Germanic symbols. That disposed of the apparent incongruity of the Roman letters AVM for AV(e) M(aria). This was a well-understood symbol, easy to write. It would have required a lot of space to have produced it in runes.

The biggest break, however, came about twenty years ago with the publication in a Danish archaeological journal of a copy, found by chance in the royal library at Copenhagen, of King Magnus' order to Knutson. It was translated as follows:

"Magnus, by the grace of God king of Norway, Sweden and Skaane, sends to all men who see or hear this letter good health and happiness.

"We desire to make known that you, [Paul Knutson], are to take the men who are to go in the Knorr [the royal trading vessel] whether they be named or not named, from my bodyguard and also from among the retainers of other men whom you may wish to take on the voyage, and that Paul Knutson, who shall be the commandant upon the Knorr, shall have full authority to select the men who are best suited either as officers or men. We ask you to accept this, our command, with a right good will for the cause, inasmuch as we do it for the honor of God and for the sake of our soul, and for the sake of our predecessors, who in Greenland established Christianity and have maintained it to this time, and we will not let it perish in our days. Know this for truth, that whoever defies this, our command, shall meet with our serious displeasure and thereupon receive full punishment.

"Executed at Bergen, Monday after Simon and Judah's day in the six and XXX year of our reign (1354). By Orm Ostenson, our regent, sealed."

Thus it was established that a few years before the date found on the Kensington Stone a certain Paul Knutson, one of the most prominent citizens of Magnus' kingdom, had been ordered to recruit and lead an expedition across the Atlantic. Certainly no hoaxer of the nineteenth century could have known this. The date on the stone, eight years after the issuance of the order, would have been a remarkable coincidence with history. Eight years was a reasonable time to have allowed Knutson to have come from Bergen to the headwaters of the Red River.

There can hardly be any question but that the crusade left Norway. Mr. Holand ventures a tentative reconstruction of what happened. Presumably, Knutson, guided by vague descriptions in the Icelandic sagas, proceeded to some point on the New England coast, established a base camp, and made a systematic search for the lost colony. Failing to find any trace of the Greenlanders, he must have turned northward with a considerable number of his party—perhaps leaving a small rear guard in what is now Massachusetts or Rhode Island—and finally sailed into the iceberg-filled Hudson Bay. Still there was no trace of the men he sought. And very likely his instructions from King Magnus had been quite peremptory: If you don't find them you needn't come back.

He came to the mouth of the great Nelson River, followed it southward to Lake Winnipeg, and thence by a series of lakes and portages to the Red River country, whose waters flow into the Mississippi and the Gulf of Mexico. Even today there is an almost continuous waterway from the ice-filled sea to the Minnesota lakeland where the Kensington Stone was found. This, the explorer probably thought, would have been a natural route from Greenland for the lost colonists. Also, Mr. Holand conjectures, he thought he was following the easiest route back to his base in Vinland. He did not picture North America as a continent but as a group of large islands

This, of course, is all highly speculative. But one fact remains: If the Kensington Stone is genuine, Paul Knutson and his crusading knights were in Central Minnesota in 1362. Evidence increases for the authenticity of the relic. If Farmer Ohman told the truth about the circumstances of the stone's discovery—and this stolid, hard working, unlettered immigrant must have been leading an extraordinary sort of double life if he concocted the story—the tablet had been in the spot where he found it for at least as long as the aspen tree had been growing. Archaeologists have a reasonably accurate means of dating trees and timbers from the rings in the wood; examination of similar trees in the neighborhood has led to the conservative assumption that the tree in whose roots the rune stone was found was at least forty years old in 1898. This means that, if the relic had been "planted," the attempted deception must have taken place in the 1850's. There were then few white men in that part of Minnesota. It was inhabited by savage and hostile Sioux.

The conglomeration of languages alone was enough to convince Professor Breda that the stone was a fake. But he was thinking in terms of the language of the sagas in which had been related the exploits of Eric the Red and Leif the Lucky. This stone had been inscribed more than three centuries later. Norway then was in contact with all Europe. Some English words had been introduced into the vulgar speech. Both Swedes and Norwegians participated in the expedition. Magnus was king of both countries. It was natural enough that the "crusaders" should have spoken a slight mixture of tongues. Furthermore, these men were not scribes or scholars. Very likely their priests had been left in Vinland. But they were reasonably intelligent, literate young men. Mr. Holand's researches in the popular literature of fourteenth-century Scandinavia convince him that the words of his despairing note on stone are just about the words to be expected of such a man, especially when he was under emotional stress. Whoever carved these runes may hardly have expected to live to finish the job.

Why did he use runes at all? By that time the Latin alphabet was well known in Norway and was used in most documents. For the simple reason, Mr. Sarff explains, that runic characters had been especially adapted for carving on gravestones. They were used for that purpose in both Iceland and Norway long after they had been abandoned in ordinary writing. It was easier to carve in hard stone the straight-lined runic symbols than the roman letters with curved lines. Whoever inscribed these letters was in a hurry to finish his job. He was working on the edge of eternity.

The message stated that some of the party had been left behind to look after the boats by the sea, "14 days' journey from this island." It has been found that the expression "day's journey" was a conventional term of the time, meaning approximately seventy-five miles, or the distance which a vessel could sail in a day with a fair wind. This would be just about the correct distance to the mouth of the Nelson River. The journey probably had taken Knutson's men at least a year.

The inscription indicates that the party was encamped on an island in a lake, seventy-five miles away from another lake containing two rocky islands, on the shore of which their comrades had been massacred. It is to be assumed that they had come there for temporary security from the Indians. Ohman found the stone at the edge of a marsh. This now is dry land. Geological surveys show that the slightly elevated, rocky land from which the farmer grubbed the aspen stump was almost certainly an island in 1362. The countryside has been getting progressively drier for the past century.

Just about seventy-five miles away is the only lake with two "skerries," or rocky islands. It is Cormorant Lake, in Becker county. On its shore are large glacial boulders with triangular holes drilled in three of them. This was a common device for mooring boats along the fiords of fourteenth-century Norway. Beside one of these rocks a fourteenth century Norwegian fire steel was recently picked up. Several other such mooring rocks have been found in this section of Minnesota. The implication is that the explorers continued their journey eastward for a time, probably seeking a waterway back to Vinland. Along the course of the Nelson during the past half century various Norwegian implements have been picked up—three battle-axes, a fire steel and a spearhead. This may indicate the route followed by Knutson's men southward from Hudson Bay.

There is only a vague suggestion that some of the men left at Vinland, or with the ships at the mouth of the Nelson, returned to Norway: It is said that, in the midst of the great plague, King Magnus received news that his Greenland colony was lost without trace. Who could have been the bearer of these bad tidings? There still remains a faint possibility that among age-yellowed manuscripts in some European archives there may be found a full account of the expedition by somebody who accompanied Knutson.

## Classroom Dialogue for the Essentialist Role Model

*Ms. Chronicler:*   Can anyone tell me what question the men in the article were investigating?

*Rowena:*   They wanted to find out if Vikings came to America in the 1300s.

*Ms. Chronicler:*   Yes, but let's focus on the specific problem they were trying to deal with. Can you put this problem in the form of a question?

*Charles:*   Weren't they trying to find out if the stone was real?

*Ms. Chronicler:*   I agree, but maybe "real" is not the most appropriate word.

*Charles:*   They really wanted to know if it was a fake or if it was genuine.

*Ms. Chronicler:*   That's right! Let's also use one of the new words you've met recently—the word "artifact." Suppose we put the question this way: Is the Kensington Stone a genuine artifact? That lets us know we're dealing with what is written on the stone because the writing is what makes the stone an artifact.

Now, can you tell me who was trying to answer this question, and what answers they gave?

*Rowena:*   I'm not sure about how to pronounce their names, but Breda said the stone was a fake, and Holand said it wasn't a fake.

*Ms. Chronicler:*   O.K.! What were some points Breda used to say the stone was not a genuine artifact?

*Merrill:*   He didn't think it made any sense that Swedes and Norwegians were together, did he?

*Ms. Chronicler:*   That's right! He didn't. Why not?

*Merrill:*   Because they were supposed to be enemies.

*David:*   But he had the wrong date. He didn't know what the time period really was, so he made a big mistake.

*Ms. Chronicler:*   Good point, David! But we will try to deal with the problem of dates in a few moments. Can we focus first on Breda's arguments?

*Harper:*   Didn't he also talk about the distance these people had traveled? He said they couldn't have come so far in fourteen days.

*Thomas:*   He also didn't think the tree was old enough.

*Ms. Chronicler:*   What tree, Thomas?

*Thomas:*   The one the farmer was pulling out when he found the stone. If the tree was forty years old when the stone was found, the stone was at least that old, but maybe not old enough to be anything but a fake.

*Ms. Chronicler:*   You mean the writing on the stone was not old because of the age of the tree?

*Thomas:*   Yes, I think that's right.

*Ms. Chronicler:* Well, I think I know what you're saying, but I'm not sure Breda gave so much emphasis to the tree's age. The tree could have grown up at any time after the stone was carved, but we would be dealing with a time span of only forty or fifty years, rather than several hundred years. As Holand said, if someone were playing a trick with the stone, it would have had to be carved before about 1850, and that was a time when warlike Sioux lived in the area. But right now, let's go ahead and add "age of the tree" to our list of points. Although it is an idea to be considered, we should also remember that, just because the tree was only forty years old in 1898 when the stone was discovered, this is not an indication in and of itself that the stone was carved fairly recently.

*David:* We haven't talked about the letters "AVM." Breda didn't think it made sense that these Latin letters would be mixed with runes.

*Ms. Chronicler:* Good! Let's add that item to the list. Any others?

*Harper:* He did say that the writing on the stone mentioned an island and a lake and that there was no island or lake nearby.

*Ms. Chronicler:* I can see you've all read fairly carefully. So let's talk about how Holand answered the question we're discussing, and see why he answered the way he did.

*David:* It seems his most important reason for thinking the stone was real was the copy of the king's order about an expedition. That gave him some new ideas about the date.

*Ms. Chronicler:* Yes, that really goes back to something you said earlier about dates. This is a very important point, so we need to list it under Holand's reasons for his answer to the question. Remember, everybody, that these men knew the stone was real but they were trying to decide if it was a genuine artifact.

*Merrill:* The date helped him understand that Norwegians and Swedes would be on the expedition together because Magnus was king of both countries then.

*Ms. Chronicler:* Yes, and that means their languages might logically be mixed on the stone. Let's list those points. Any more?

*Rowena:* He did figure out that "day's journey" is an idiom.

*Ms. Chronicler:* That's right, and what do we mean by an "idiom?"

*Rowena:* It's like a short way of saying something. It was supposed to mean how far you could sail in a day's journey, not how far you could walk.

*Harper:* He did talk about the age of the tree too, but I think you've already said something about that. He knew there were hostile Sioux Indians around during the 1850s, so nobody was likely to have "planted" the stone then.

*Ms. Chronicler:* That's true, so let's list that last point.

*Charles:* What about "AVM"? He said that in the 1350s, Swedes and Norwegians would have known those letters and that they were just as easy to carve as runes because they all had straight lines.

*Merrill:* And he found out that geologists had said the land around Ohman's farm had been drying out for a long time, so there really could have been a lake. It did say Ohman found this thing "at the edge of a marsh."

*Ms. Chronicler:* O.K.! Good job! I think we're now ready for our analysis and summary. Do you notice in looking at our lists of reasons that both men used almost all the same points, except one, in their arguments? They both used points about mixture of languages, about Norwegians and Swedes being together, about the phrase "day's journey," the age of the tree, the letters "AVM," and the fact that no lake or island existed when the stone was discovered. The only point in our lists which differs is the one about King Magnus' order to Paul Knutson. Please explain this for me. How can both men have used all the same points except one and have ended with opposite answers to their question about the stone?

*Thomas:* One knew more about dates than the other one did.

*Ms. Chronicler:* O.K. But how can you explain that with some of the new terms we've met recently?

*Thomas:* What about "frame of reference"?

*Ms. Chronicler:* Yes, what about "frame of reference"? Does it fit here? Both of these men were interested in history, so in a sense they had similar frames of reference.

*Thomas:* But one thought this stone would have to be carved about 1000, and the other thought it could have been carved in the 1360s.

*Ms. Chronicler:* So you're saying that different assumptions about dates made their "frames of reference" differ and also affected the way they used "clues" when they were solving this puzzle.

*Thomas:* Well, it certainly made a big difference.

*Ms. Chronicler:* O.K.! Do you have any questions about this operation of "frame of reference?" I'm glad you've thought about how to apply it here.

If there are no questions, let's look at one final point. I want you to remember that whenever historians or social scientists have a problem like this to investigate they try to use steps in their investigation similar to the ones Breda and Holand used. Now I want you to think about what steps these two men went through in their work and describe those steps in general terms so that we could apply them to some other kinds of investigations.

*David:* I don't think I understand what you're asking.

*Ms. Chronicler:* Breda and Holand went through specific steps as they tried to answer their question. I want you to tell me what those steps were in general terms that would fit other investigations. Let's try it. We can think of Breda and Holand as "minding their own business" or pursuing their careers quietly until something happened. What was that "something?"

*David:* Farmer Ohman found his rock.

*Ms. Chronicler:* That's right! But how would you say that *in general terms?*

*Rowena:* Somebody gave him a problem.

*Ms. Chronicler:* O.K., but when this problem was "given" to them, they decided they wanted to work on it. Right? Let's list the first step, then, as "Presentation of a Problem."

What's our next step? What did Breda and Holand do next?

*Rowena:*   They formed a "hypothesis" about the stone.

*Ms. Chronicler:*   True, they did form an "hypothesis" or "guess" as to whether the stone was a genuine artifact. But didn't they do something else first?

*Charles:*   They translated the carving.

*Ms. Chronicler:*   Exactly! And for our purposes we'll call that step the "Preliminary Research." They did just enough investigating to help themselves "guess" about whether this was a genuine artifact. Remember that they didn't have to do much preliminary research, because they already knew a great deal about Scandinavian history.

    Now we have three steps: (1) "Presentation of a Problem"; (2) "Preliminary Research"; and, (3) "Hypothesis." What is the next step?

*Harper:*   They have to check the hypothesis.

*Ms. Chronicler:*   That's right, but we are going to break that process down into two steps. They did "in-depth research," so every time they uncovered a point of evidence related to the question, they checked that bit of evidence against the hypothesis. Therefore, we have the next two steps: (4) "In-depth Research"; and (5) "Checking the Hypothesis." But what is our final step?

*Thomas:*   They reached conclusions.

*Ms. Chronicler:*   Good! And that step completes our list describing in general terms what Breda and Holand did.

    What might be another name for this series of steps?

*Thomas:*   It looks like the scientific method to me.

*Ms. Chronicler:*   Great! But historians and social scientists also use these steps, and in this class we'll be referring to the process as the "historical method." In fact, if I wanted to restate the historical method in a form shorter than actually listing the six steps, I could say this: Historians try to validate hypotheses. Do you remember that the word "validate" was in your vocabulary list at the end of the article you read for today?

    Any questions?

## Role Model Analysis: Ms. Chronicler Stands Alone

Ms. Chronicler was indeed fortunate to have accomplished so propitiously all she set out to do regarding the "finer points" of historical investigation. Obviously not all classroom dialogue generally goes so smoothly; however, for the sake of brevity we have taken a bit of literary license and presented Ms. Chronicler on one of her inimitable good days.

    Remember, however, that as we begin the analysis of this teacher role model, we will follow the usual procedure of working first with the final question in our analytical tool—the question concerning behavior trends. We can only start with Ms. Chronicler's behavior, because we certainly cannot look directly into her thoughts to determine her position regarding our questions about learners and subject matter. In addition, we also will be focusing on what Ms. Chronicler—or any teacher serving as a role model—

plans to accomplish. Obviously many surprises could occur, such as the one mentioned in the previous chapter in which youngsters took an opportunity to scream at their classmates, "That's why we hate you!" Nevertheless, we are dealing here with how the teacher *plans* to put philosophical assumptions into action, and not how he or she reacts to a stressful situation by adopting one of a number of survival strategies.

Ms. Chronicler felt justified in being pleased with her skill and good fortune in carrying out her plans for teaching about use of the historical method. Her techniques and materials were adapted from suggestions made by Edwin Fenton in *Teaching the New Social Studies in Secondary Schools: An Inductive Approach.* She decided her students might indeed "get hooked" on the intriguing Kensington Stone question and that she could use that interest to teach them about the historical method.

Let us look again at the question concerning behavior in reference to Ms. Chronicler's instruction about historical methodology.

4. What behavior trend should one exhibit in order to carry out one's philosophical position?

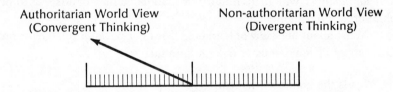

Authoritarian World View
(Convergent Thinking)

Non-authoritarian World View
(Divergent Thinking)

Remember that our first query concerns what Ms. Chronicler plans as the ultimate outcome of her lesson. Did she encourage and accept alternate logical answers about the nature of historical methodology? Or did she plan for everyone to leave the classroom with one particular answer about the historical method? If we examine the last segment of dialogue, noting such words and phrases as "summary," description *"in general terms"* so as to be applicable to other situations, and "historians try to validate hypotheses," it should be apparent that she expected all students to leave with the same answer about the historical method. The planned answer did not include recognition of the power of a flash of insight which might allow an historian to skip several steps in the method; moreover, it did not include the acknowledgment that students might never again want to be bothered with the historical method because it is too tedious to be worth the effort, especially if they could never know for certain whether medieval Scandinavians left the graywacke stone or not. There was only one planned answer: Historians try to validate hypotheses.

Note that the single acceptable answer is based on the way historians, especially Edwin Fenton, see the historical method, but it does not ask students what they feel about historical methodology in general. Also note that Ms. Chronicler never asked kids what they felt about the stone's genuineness as an artifact. In other words, the planned outcome for this series of teacher behaviors represents what we have called an "authoritarian" position on this question's continuum. Ms. Chronicler was emphasizing "convergent" thinking: namely, leading students through a long process of analysis to one answer. She seems to have a world view in regard to the student and the subject matter which means that she sells kids an expert's view of that subject matter. This philosophical position can be an extremely useful one because kids can begin to feel comfortable with problem-solving skills and can emerge from the process feeling that they have been rewarded by finding a correct answer; thus, they are not frustrated by playing with several different possibilities which are dependent on the whims of time and place.

Moreover, according to our analytical tool, described in the previous chapter, a determination of "authoritarian behavior trends" places the teacher role model within a broad philosophical category labeled "Perennialist/Essentialist." Consideration of the three other questions in our tool for analysis will help refine our understanding of Ms. Chronicler's philosophical position.

What about her view of learners? Does her position come closer to the Lockean or Platonic ends of the continuum?

**1.** What is the nature of the learner?

Lockean                                              Platonic

She included many questions, which fortunately generated considerable response from the students. How does the presence of student participation in this lesson fit with what we discovered previously about Ms. Chronicler's plan to have her instruction lead kids to one acceptable answer? Did she look for answers only she wanted to hear, or did she listen to answers students wanted to give, or did these two possibilities mesh "happily" in the segment of dialogue presented? A close examination of that dialogue should reveal extended use of phrases like the following:

"Yes, but let's focus on . . . "

"I agree, but maybe 'real' is not the most appropriate . . . "

'That's right!"

She was also quick to remind David that the question of dates would be more appropriate to consider at a later time in the discussion. In other words, she most clearly rewarded kids for answers which fitted her plans exactly; for those answers approaching the phrases she had in mind, her reinforcement consisted of a qualifying, "Yes, but . . ." She apparently perfected her skill of "keeping students on the track" during the discussion by giving her strongest rewards to answers which would lead ultimately to the precise goal she had planned for the lesson. Although there was considerable student participation, the scale for this indicator's continuum would tip slightly toward the "Lockean" position, because students were expected to absorb prescribed information about the use of historical methodology.

During the dialogue which began this chapter, Ms. Chronicler showed in several ways an awareness of possible pitfalls for discussions in which a teacher "guides" students to preconceived answers and prescribed information. She was careful not to squelch comments with a forthright "No!", if students were not following the desired pattern. To Thomas, who focused on the age of the tree in a way she considered inappropriate, Ms. Chronicler did not say, "But what does that really have to do with the matter at hand?" Instead, she questioned him matter-of-factly to learn about his reasoning process; then, after making several qualifying statements, she concluded the interchange by listing his point. This technique buffered her use of convergent thinking so that Thomas would not feel his comments were so far off base that he would be tempted to stare blankly into space for the remainder of the session. In fact, he did comment again on the question of dates and helped Ms. Chronicler bring her lesson to a successful resolution.

Teachers who are not as careful as Ms. Chronicler about their use of the word "no" during discussions based on convergent thinking can quite effectively squelch dialogue based on students' sincere efforts to advance an investigation. When such teachers reward only the answers they had planned to hear, they send out a subtle message which students eventually understand quite clearly; in other words, the message says: "Unless you're sure you can read this teacher's mind, it's better not to risk giving an answer." Such a teacher may be left wondering why it's so hard to get a discussion going.

Despite Ms. Chronicler's skill at buffering the possible pitfalls of convergent thinking during discusssion, however, the scale points toward a Lockean position. She moved her students inexorably toward the absorption of prescribed subject matter. Consequently, the students probably felt satisfied that they had achieved a correct answer for their efforts.

What did this example reveal about Ms. Chronicler's views of "prescribed" subject matter? The essence of her lesson, with its emphasis on historical methodology, offers a definitive position concerning history as a discipline.

2. What is the nature of the subject matter?

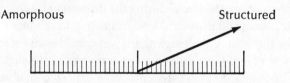

Amorphous                                                    Structured

She asked youngsters to analyze the approaches of Breda and Holand to a specific problem. In fact, she asked kids to solve the problem of deciding how the tasks of Breda and Holand could be described in general terms so that the resulting description could appropriately be used as guidelines for other investigations. When youngsters are asked to solve a problem dealing with subject matter, they are, in effect, creating a "structure" because each point or each piece of evidence is either used or discarded in light of its relevance to the problem. Therefore, the task of problem-solving itself causes youngsters to sort through data and select items on the basis of their relevance to a larger idea. Ms. Chronicler has placed kids in a situation requiring them to discover concepts about the natural structure of history and the social sciences. Kids learned that the historical method is a tool whereby researchers get new information about problems and analyze the usefulness of each piece of information for furthering the investigation.

Although in Ms. Chronicler's lesson the topic focused directly on a discipline's structure, every situation in which youngsters engage in problem-solving requires them to learn concepts about structure and about how facts relate to a larger idea. Ms. Chronicler definitely intended for her students to understand that history and the social sciences have a natural structure; therefore, the scale for this indicator should point to the area which we have labeled "structured" on the continuum.

Did Ms. Chronicler intend to emphasize the cognitive domain or the affective domain? She certainly expected that kids would find it at least mildly entertaining to contemplate the Kensington Rune Stone's authenticity.

3. How should one use the subject matter to guide students toward meaningful learning activities?

Cognitive                                                    Affective

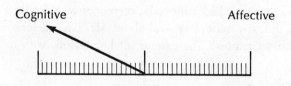

Please note that, although Ms. Chronicler expected students to be enthralled by her problem in archaeology, she did not ask them directly how they felt about the stone's genuineness as an artifact. In addition, questions similar to the following are also noticeably absent from the dialogue:

1. How would you feel about this discovery if you were Farmer Ohman? Why?

2. If you were Farmer Ohman, would you have trusted Breda or Holand? Would you have trusted both men or neither man? Would you have felt duped and cheated because fame and fortune seemed to be pointing in Holand's direction? Why or why not?

3. Do you, as a reader, trust Holand? Is his evidence really sound? Could he be letting his imagination run away with him because he wanted to believe the stone was a genuine relic? Why or why not?

4. If you were of Scandinavian descent, how would the Kensington Stone make you feel about your place in the history of this country? Why?

Imagine, for instance, that Ms. Chronicler were teaching her lesson in a Minnesota community where many people of Scandinavian descent took special pride in emphasizing their ethnicity. Asking questions like those listed above would then personalize the lesson in such a way that kids might be expected to have their consciences piqued about Ohman's role in this discovery. They might even become angry about his victimization by Holand or they might feel indignant toward a fate which denied him the potential honor reserved for the Kensington Stone's discoverer. Some kids might even see this chain of events as a slur against themselves as people of Scandinavian descent.

Indeed, Ms. Chronicler's lesson did not contain any overt elements that might personalize the effects of the Kensington Stone's discovery. She wanted students to be interested in the stone because she could then more effectively use the material to get them to understand the historical method as historical experts, rather than youngsters, understand it. If she had asked students for their own interpretations about the stone and had deliberately tried to involve their emotions about an injustice suffered by Ohman, then she would have been emphasizing the affective domain. However, since she seemed determined to have kids understand the historical method as she and Fenton perceived it, this indicator's scale should tip toward the cognitive end of the continuum.

Analyzing Ms. Chronicler's lesson according to our four indicators should clarify the significance of her role as Essentialist problem-solver. The brand of problem-solving which she used led students to one answer: namely, an answer which most experts in the field have accepted. Thus, her technique caused kids to discover what experts in the discipline already know. Often such a technique is referred to as the  discovery" method, a name which seems especially appropriate for the Essentialist problem-solver's approach.

Perhaps the most dominant of all teacher role models today is that of the Essentialist problem-solver. Since Sputnik's launching in 1957, as well as the Wood's Hole Conference in 1959 which spawned Bruner's *Process of Education,* curriculum-makers have displayed almost unflagging fascination for techniques associated with "discovery." National Science Foundation Curriculum Projects—from "Chem Study" to "Harvard Project Physics" to "Physical Sciences Study Course"—have emphasized that kids will use laboratory experiments to discover the "laws of science." A similar emphasis on discovery took hold in education in the social sciences. The lesson which begins this chapter is notable in its adaptation of the scientific method and discovery to history, archaeology, and the social sciences in general. From "Man: A course of Study" to the SRSS (Sociological Resources for the Secondary School) curriculum materials, social studies educators have attached themselves to the discovery emphasis in an effort to make their commercially produced curriculum packages imminently salable.

However, one does not have to make predominant use of the discovery problem-solving techniques to follow the Essentialist Role Model. One could be a lecturer/information-giver and could still, quite accurately, exemplify the Essentialist Role Model. It is even possible to assume aspects of this role model in an extreme form, as in the case of my own sixth grade teacher. She seemed to delight in drills of every kind, especially for studying mathematics and English grammar. These were not just "practice exercises," in which kids were expected to improve their skills in settings that were mildly competitive, but actual DRILLS, in which anxiety levels soared unbearably high. It was a common practice for each kid to count the number of students who must recite before him during a drill in parsing sentences, and silently rehearse to himself the name for the part of speech each word in his sentence had assumed. But, despite all this rehearsing, there was something about the teacher's manner which made it devilishly likely that you would be sure to say "noun" when you really meant to say "coordinate conjunction."

Mrs. Précis (a fictitious name, of course) had a profoundly effective way of implementing her physical education curriculum. If your team happened to be unlucky enough to lose the day's game of softball, there was a potent motivating device which Mrs. Précis used liberally. The defeated teammates were required to squat in a circle and walk on haunches like Cossacks under her direction; presumably, this technique was devised to ensure that, for the next game of softball, team members would have stronger physiques and, as a result, would be less likely to lose. Mrs. Précis was in the habit of administering this technique under her own careful supervision.

She also taught a particularly unforgettable lesson on patriotism. Our entire elementary school student body was rehearsing for its annual May Day celebration in commemoration of spring. Unlike the May Day famous to the Communist bloc or the rather risqué seventeenth century English holiday which featured countryfolk traipsing into the forest to pick flowers, our particular celebration presented young ladies dressed in crinoline dancing around a May Pole and entwining the pole with brightly colored streamers. After the dance with the colored streamers our class, the sixth grade, was scheduled to perform a skit in which all the flags of the United Nations were displayed. During this skit's finale someone unfortunately dropped the United States' flag. That ended the rehearsal! Everyone was marched back to the classroom, where Mrs. Précis launched into a diatribe about patriotism in which she indicated that only if wounded in battle would a person be forgiven for dropping the flag. It was a stirring, but frightening, lecture on patriotism, particularly since she concluded with the remark that those who fought for their country must be willing to die for its preservation and welfare.

Her approach to moral uprightness was basically the same as her approach to the concept of patriotism; that is, she set a forceful example and expected students to conform. And nothing less than conformity was expected in standards of behavior; students knew that lack of conformity could and did lead to corporal punishment. Hence, one never disparaged the cafeteria fare because four very dedicated ladies worked extremely hard to prepare nourishing meals. One unfortunate young man was so unwise as to make a reference to the "slop in the lunchroom," while the lunch money was being collected. There is no better way to describe what happened to this fellow than to use a very old-fashioned phrase: he "got his ears boxed." The general atmosphere of misery over the incident was increased because, in the process of "boxing" the young man's ears, Mrs. Précis upset a vase of flowers on her desk and spilled water on her grade book.

This portrait of Mrs. Précis is worthy of extra attention because it embodies a principle we addressed in the last chapter. Indeed, it is possible to assume, responsibly and moderately, any one of the role models we will study so that beneficial results occur for youngsters. It is also possible to implement any one of the role models in such an extreme manner that results for kids may be anything but positive. Let us look, then, at possible variations for the Essentialist Role Model from problem-solver to lecturer/information-giver. Of course, the problem-solver or lecturer/information-giver aspects of the role may be assumed either responsibly and moderately

### Essentialist Role Model
### (Ms. Chronicler and Ms. Précis)*

1. What is the nature of the learner?

Lockean                                          Platonic

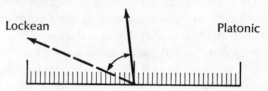

2. What is the nature of the subject matter?

Amorphous                                    Structured

3. How should one use the subject matter to guide students toward meaningful learning activities?

Cognitive                                      Affective

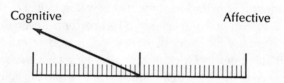

4. What behavior trend should one exhibit in order to carry out one's philosophical position?

Authoritarian World View               Non-authoritarian World View
(Convergent Thinking)                     (Divergent Thinking)

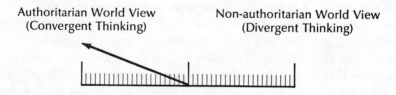

*Ms. Chronicler's position is shown with solid lines. The more extreme position toward which Ms. Précis was moving is shown with broken lines.

*Please note that as indicated in Chapter Two, pp. 36–46, variations from Ms. Chronicler's style are possible within Essentialism.

or irresponsibly and immoderately.

Because the Essentialist Role Model embodies both problem-solver and lecturer/information-giver aspects, it is especially important to note potential shifts in the "scales" as indicated on page 44.

In the case of the Essentialist Role Model, indicators on the scale for the first two questions in our analytical tool are noteworthy because of the subtleties they indicate regarding the problem-solver and lecturer/information-giver aspects. During Ms. Chronicler's discovery lesson, youngsters were led inexorably toward a preconceived right answer, but, at the same time, they were participating in a lively discussion. Therefore, it seems appropriate to indicate a slightly Lockean propensity for this question's continuum. However, in the example of Mrs. Précis's sentence-parsing drill students were expected to repeat, on cue, the correct definition for the part of speech assumed by each word. Students had been given a body of information about functional English grammar which they were expected to memorize and repeat under proper circumstances. Therefore, it seems appropriate to indicate a strictly Lockean position in regard to this example. Such a strict Lockean adherence indicates any situation in which the learner is required to memorize, imbibe, or absorb basic information that must be reproduced verbatim. The material to be mastered may be vocabulary and rules about grammatical structures, notes on various historical events, excerpts from poetry, or other specific and technical bodies of information.

In regard to the second question in our analytical tool both Ms. Chronicler and Mrs. Précis emphasized the structure of their particular disciplines. However, imagine a situation in which the anxiety level is so extreme that students decide to memorize, without attempting to understand the material they are memorizing. Through rote memorization, these students would please the teacher and avoid punishment by reciting perfectly and verbatim whenever the need arose. Suppose, for instance, a youngster succeeded in memorizing all of William Cullen Bryant's *Thanatopsis* so that he could repeat it perfectly for his teacher, although he did not comprehend sufficiently to paraphrase even one stanza. The result of this effort in poetry would be similar to the situation Allen Funt found when he interviewed six-year-olds who had memorized the *Pledge of Allegiance* to the U.S. flag, but whose charming and candidly entertaining explanations bore no resemblance to any form of logic understandable to adults. In other words, learners in such situations behave as if it were inherently good to absorb as many details of the subject matter as possible and seem to assume that no item within that subject matter is more important than any other item.

Similar situations, in which there is an amorphous position regarding subject matter, are rarely seen today, although it does occasionally appear in some teaching situations. An amorphous emphasis may be viewed as somewhat more typical of education in the last century. Almost all teachers— whether they are Essentialist problem-solvers, or Essentialist lecturer/ information-givers, or any of the other role models we will be discussing— want students to relate details to a broader perspective. Therefore, they emphasize structure either by having kids associate facts and generalizations as they solve problems or by having kids absorb and understand how details relate to principles in a set of lecture notes or in a textbook chapter.

Whether the Essentialist Role Model is assumed by a problem-solver or a lecturer/information-giver, however, the "scales" on our last two indicators do not vary. In either aspect of this role model a teacher emphasizes *cognitive* elements of the subject matter and promotes the *authoritarian* view which represents an expert's opinion of what is worthy of attention within a given discipline.

In addition to this overview of the continuum, a summary of the principles underlying the Essentialist philosophy should provide deeper insights into the assumptions which help determine behaviors for those teachers who have chosen the Essentialist Role Model.

## PHILOSOPHIC PRINCIPLES SUPPORTING THE ESSENTIALIST ROLE MODEL

Although the analytical tool and the four "scales" we have been using provide basic characteristics for an Essentialist problem-solver and an Essentialist lecturer/information-giver, we would be remiss if we did not examine additional details about this role model. These additional insights have been adapted basically from a series of interrelated principles outlined by George Kneller in *Introduction to the Philosophy of Education*. Kneller's principles have here been embellished and linked to examples of teacher behaviors previously discussed in this chapter.

(1) *Learning, due to its nature, involves hard work and often unwilling application.* If we examine this principle for extremes, we would perhaps find, on the one hand, belief in the pseudo-science of phrenology and the "mind-as-muscle" concept and, on the other hand, a mild faith in the adage that "practice makes perfect"—or at least that "practice makes better." In fact, I can remember very distinctly being "sold" the Latin language on the basis of its painful difficulty and its unquestionable capacity to give me

new insight into the merits of English grammar. For me the sales pitch really worked, but then I was one of those kids who became quite excited about many items in the curriculum that no one else seemed to care a great deal about. I truly enjoyed reading about the Helvetians from Caesar's *Commentaries on the Gallic Wars* and was intrigued that so much information had been passed down about that troublesome little tribe and that I could actually read it *in the original language.* Most other kids bought Latin because the pain was supposedly good for mental muscles.

The idea about developing mental muscles may seem to belong most appropriately to the last century and to the fad of phrenology charts showing which part of the brain managed each faculty, and how you could be sure that the shape of your skull destined you to be a great mesmerist or a poet or an astute criminal. After all, nineteenth century literary works are replete with detailed descriptions of the face and head which evidence a certain fascination for phrenology. However, today we see diagrams in psychology textbooks which show the different segments of the brain that manage certain functions; moreover, we speak of forming mental associations among specific details within a body of information to be learned. And, by the way, I do think Latin taught me something about languaging—to use a current term—and about the structure of languages in general. Moreover, I am not at all convinced that we have given up on the idea of practicing to improve our mental faculties. Ms. Chronicler seemed to feel that practice with the application of historical method had its merits, and Mrs. Précis was certain about the benefits of drill in parsing sentences.

There is also another dimension to the "*often* unwilling application" phrase in this principle. Many Essentialists assume that a hearty initial effort at a task will create the interest and motivation for mastering the task, or that interest grows with effort. One should ideally feel a certain amount of intellectual pleasure at increased proficiency in analyzing use of the historical method or at parsing sentences. Such efforts should be viewed as inherently good, because they accustom youngsters to subordinate fleeting desires in order to obtain worthy but distant goals. In other words, learning should be used as a vehicle for the development of self-discipline. And who would be better equipped to guide youngsters in their development of self-discipline than a skillful teacher?

(2) *The initiative in education should lie with the teacher rather than with the pupil.* The teacher is that special expert who serves as mediator between the adult world and the world of children. The teacher knows how to give the necessary guidance if kids are to attain "full potential" when they

are physically mature. There is no attempt at pupil-teacher planning in developing units of study. Essentialists' advice to teachers might be something like this: Don't ask kids whether they want to learn about the historical method or about parsing sentences, and don't inquire about their feelings regarding these two topics. The teacher must decide what is worthy to be taught and how to teach it; however, one should be able to construct interesting lessons with at least some power to motivate. Ms. Chronicler counted on the natural appeal a lesson on the Kensington Stone problem would have for students. She suspected that a lesson built around investigation of this relic would have greater chances for success than a prosaic recounting of steps in the historical method with no concrete example attached to the list of steps.

(3) *The heart of the educational process is the absorption of prescribed subject matter.* No matter how often students might like to think otherwise, the environment does not change itself in order to meet the needs of learners more adequately. On the contrary, to obtain intellectual and social skills prerequisite to survival and to the hope of success, students must learn as much about this environment as possible. Since the environment cannot be assumed to adapt to individual needs and since individuals can best prepare themselves for life by learning about this environment, it is best to learn how experts view the world as presented through the logical organization of subject matter. Supporting the individual learner by giving him investigative tools to help him "make his own sense of the environment" can be wasteful, if not dangerous. The wisdom of many experts is considerably more trustworthy than any one individual's knowledge.

This wisdom of the experts includes knowledge about the physical universe and does not directly address the question of spiritual realities. In fact, the material and social environment largely determines how a person shall live, since the environment does not adapt to humanity's needs. Since realization of one's potential must take place in a world which operates independently from the individual, the quest for knowledge and understanding about this world is quite an all-encompassing task. There really is no time left for asking open-ended questions about truth, beauty, and spiritual qualities. "Absolute truth" in the physical world is worthy of pursuit; but, "absolute truths" in the spiritual and moral realms cannot be ascertained by the use of human reason and, thus, are not dealt with directly. The most adequate preparation for the future comes not from contemplation of spiritual reality but in mastery of information about one's heritage and about the physical world. In a society so complex as ours this information about the heritage and the contemporary environment can best be presented within a highly structured educational system.

(4) *The school should retain traditional methods of mental discipline.* Perhaps the best way to underscore this principle is to review a list of concrete recommendations made to educators and parents by Max Rafferty in his 1963 publication, *What They Are Doing to Your Children.**

1. Get a state board of education that believes in the primacy of subject matter.
2. Get a state superintendent of schools who does the same.
3. Change the state's requirements for teaching credentials, stressing more "what" and less "how" in teacher-training courses.
4. See that local school boards are advised that primary reading and spelling should be taught through a predominantly phonetic approach and supply them with materials needed to make this possible.
5. Adopt a recommended list of children's classics in prose and poetry and make it available to all elementary and junior high schools, urging that books on the list be given priority for outside reading and book reports.
6. Have your state department of education call things by their right names, thinking and speaking always of history as history, geography as geography, and civics as civics. Forget "social studies" and "social living" and "language arts." Adopt textbooks that stress this same approach.
7. Require all schools to give standardized achievement tests each year, and make the results public.
8. Demand from the great publishing houses textbooks that are packed with vital and interesting factual material instead of with fuzzy, bland, easy platitudes.
   There is no trend in existence better than this one.

Although Mr. Rafferty's views are certainly not shared by all Essentialists, his efforts as Superintendent of Public Instruction for California to rid school divisions of "Progressive" educators did address, perhaps in an extreme way, some major misgivings shared by many Essentialists about the benefits of problem-solving, especially "open-ended" problem-solving that allows alternative answers to be acceptable. He reported in *What They Are Doing to Your Children* his reactions to the "Progressive" teacher whose unit on Eskimos consisted mostly of teaching kids how to make igloos out of ice cubes. Rafferty's rage stemmed largely from the fact that these youngsters might learn a good bit about techniques of fitting ice cubes together (for whatever real or imagined purpose, it would probably take someone like

*Reprinted with permission from Max Rafferty, *What They Are Doing to Your Children.* New York: New American Library, 1963.

Plato to justify), but students learned virtually nothing about Eskimos. Ms. Wolynski, who wrote the article, "Confessions of a Misspent Youth," for *Newsweek* magazine, could certainly understand Rafferty's wrath and his insistence that carefully delineated traditional subject matter categories should form the basis for every school's curriculum.

---

### Confessions of a Misspent Youth*
#### Mara Wolynski

The idea of permissive education appealed to my mother in 1956 when she was a Bohemian and I was 4. In Greenwich Village, she found a small private school whose beliefs were hers and happily enrolled me. I know it was an act of motherly love but it might have been the worst thing she ever did to me. This school—I'll call it Sand and Sea—attracted other such parents, upper-middle-class professionals who were determined not to have their children pressured the way they had been. Sand and Sea was the school without pain. And it was the kind of school that the back-to-basics people rightly fear most. At Sand and Sea, I soon became an exemplar of educational freedom—the freedom not to learn.

Sand and Sea was run by fifteen women and one man who taught "science." They were decent people, some old, some young, and all devoted to cultivating the innate creativity they were convinced we had. There was a tremendous emphasis on the arts. We weren't taught techniques, however, because any kind of organization stunted creativity.

#### Happiness and Hieroglyphics

We had certain hours allotted to various subjects but we were free to dismiss anything that bored us. In fact, it was school policy that we were forbidden to be bored or miserable or made to compete with one another. There were no tests and no hard times. When I was bored with math, I was excused and allowed to write short stories in the library. The way we learned history was by trying to re-create its least important elements. One year, we pounded corn, made tepees, ate buffalo meat, and learned two Indian words. That was early American history. Another year we made elaborate costumes, clay pots, and papier-mâché gods. That was Greek culture. Another year we were all maidens and knights in armor because it was time to learn about the Middle Ages. We drank our orange juice from tinfoil goblets but never found out what the Middle Ages were. They were just "The Middle Ages."

I knew that the Huns pegged their horses and drank a quart of blood before going to war but no one ever told us who the Huns were or why we should know who they were. And one year, the year of ancient Egypt, when we were building our pyramids, I did a 30-foot-long mural for which I laboriously copied hieroglyphics onto the sheet of brown paper. But no one ever told me what they stood for. They were just there and beautiful.

## Ignorance is Not Bliss

We spent great amounts of time being creative because we had been told by our incurably optimistic mentors that the way to be happy in life was to create. Thus, we didn't learn to read until we were in the third grade because early reading was thought to discourage creative spontaneity. The one thing they taught us very well was to hate intellectuality and anything connected with it. Accordingly, we were forced to be creative for nine years. And yet Sand and Sea has failed to turn out a good artist. What we did do was to continually form and reform interpersonal relationships and that's what we thought learning was all about and we were happy. At 10, for example, most of us were functionally illiterate but we could tell that Raymond was "acting out" when, in the middle of what passed for English, he did the twist on top of his desk. Or that Nina was "introverted" because she always cowered in the corner.

When we finally were graduated from Canaan, however, all the happy little children fell down the hill. We felt a profound sense of abandonment. So did our parents. After all that tuition money, let alone the loving freedom, their children faced high school with all the glorious prospects of the poorest slum-school kids. And so it came to be. No matter what school we went to, we were the underachievers and the culturally disadvantaged.

For some of us, real life was too much—one of my oldest friends from Sand and Sea killed himself two years ago after flunking out of the worst high school in New York at 20. Various others have put in time in mental institutions where they were free, once again, to create during occupational therapy.

During my own high-school years, the school psychologist was baffled by my lack of substantive knowledge. He suggested to my mother that I be given a battery of psychological tests to find out why I was blocking out information. The thing was, I wasn't blocking because I had no information to block. Most of my Sand and Sea classmates were also enduring the same kinds of hardships. My own reading comprehension was in the lowest eighth percentile, not surprisingly. I was often asked by teachers how I had gotten into high school. However, I did manage to stumble *not* only through high school but also through college (first junior college—rejected by all four-year colleges, and then New York University), hating it all the way as I had been taught to. I am still amazed that I have a B.A., but think of it as a B.S.

## The Lure of Learning

The parents of my former classmates can't figure out what went wrong. They had sent in bright curious children and gotten back, nine years later, helpless adolescents. Some might say that those of us who freaked out would have freaked out anywhere, but when you see the same bizarre behavior pattern in succeeding graduating classes, you can draw certain terrifying conclusions.

Now I see my 12-year-old brother (who is in a traditional school) doing college-level math and I know that he knows more about many other things besides math than I do. And I also see traditional education working in the case of my 15-year-old brother (who was summarily yanked from Sand and Sea, by my reformed mother, when he was 8 so that he wouldn't become like me). Now after seven years of real education, he is making impressive film documentaries for a project on the Bicentennial. A better learning experience than playing Pilgrim for four and a half months, which is how I imagine they spent this year at Sand and Sea.

And now I've come to see that the real job of school is to entice the student into the web of knowledge and then, if he's not enticed, to drag him in. I wish I had been.

*Reprinted from *Newsweek*, August 30, 1976.

---

I am deeply sympathetic with the wrath both Rafferty and Wolynski voiced. In fact, I sense more than a little indignation rising within me over the plight of youngsters who are exposed to what Rafferty and Wolynski experienced. However, I submit that they did not witness the Progressive (Experimentalist) Role Model at all. What they did see was irresponsibility carried out under the guise of "teaching." What they saw, in fact, can serve very well as object lessons for a point we have been examining—that anyone can assume responsibly any of the models presented here and expect kids to benefit and that anyone can assume any of these role models irresponsibly and expect results to be anything but positive for youngsters and teachers alike. Although a clearly categorized subject-oriented curriculum may seem "safest" to Essentialists because they are so concerned about the information-giving function, problem-solving—whether of the "discovery" variety or of the "open-ended" inquiry variety—can be an extremely effective vehicle for relaying information.

Essentialist skepticism about problem-solving tends to center basically around difficulties of time and variations in learning styles. Some Essentialists object to problem-solving as a major mode of learning. They feel that, although there is value in problem-solving techniques, so much knowledge is too abstract to be taught by such methods. As a case in point, such educators might say that Ms. Chronicler could have taught her abstractions about the historical method in much less time by a clearly composed lecture or through a practice exercise, rather than in the context of a discovery-oriented discussion. In any event, they feel that all children should not be expected to learn through problem-solving just because some kids find it difficult to deal with abstractions. When youngsters can easily and quickly conceptualize abstractly, teachers can then see merit in presenting information directly through a lecture or through "programmed" text materials.

In addition to Rafferty's strong statement in support of "traditional methods of mental discipline" mentioned in our fourth principle, his recent position on the teacher's exemplary behavior highlights another tendency in Essentialism. I had, until quite recently, lost track of Mr. Rafferty's career since his days as Superintendent of Instruction in California. When I was on the brink of finishing my Ph.D. requirements, however, I attempted to "crash" into the job world by blanketing university campuses with letters of application. Practically all responses contained subtle remarks to the effect that no current vacancy was open in my field of preparation, nor was one anticipated during the remainder of this century. Determined to soothe my crumpled ego by filing the rejection letters in the trash can, I stopped long enough to spot an interesting signature from the Dean of the School of Education at Troy State University in Alabama: Max Rafferty. I decided immediately to save my refusal from Mr. Rafferty. He was still active at Troy State when he penned an article, "Should Gays Teach School?" for *Phi Delta Kappan* (October, 1977). As one might suspect, he had no difficulty giving an emphatic "No!" in reply to this question, because he was convinced of the power of any teacher to persuade kids to emulate the teacher's behavior patterns. Although several generations ago, single school teachers in this country did not succeed in producing an epidemic of single adults, there is an obvious possibility that what a teacher is, as exemplified by behavior, may speak to kids more forcefully than what the teacher says about subject matter.

Since Essentialists insist that teachers should emphasize "traditional methods of mental discipline" as the curriculum and since they do not deal directly with a quest for "absolute truths" regarding spiritual reality, in the realm of controversial issues they are left only with the moral influence a teacher may wield by his or her own standards of personal conduct. In other words, Essentialists seem to place their hope in the adage, "values are caught, not taught." Their curriculum does not include asking open-ended questions about the possibility of widespread use of abortion as a method of birth control, for instance. They tend to rely, instead, on the teacher's ability to respond with acceptable rationales for traditional Judaic-Christian mores whenever an unsettling question about diverse life styles "happens to come up." Or, as in the case of Mrs. Précis, a stirring lecture on patriotism might be what is in order.

As one attempts to understand how implications of these four principles for the Essentialist Role Model affect practice, remember to consider the examples of Ms. Chronicler, Mrs. Précis, and Max Rafferty. It is really impossible, as well as useless, to presume that these principles can be divorced from classroom practice. The Essentialist proclivity for relying on an expert to provide one acceptable answer per question tends to evidence more respect for the exactness of the physical sciences in the classroom than for the social and behavioral sciences, where ambiguities can seem rampant. Often Essentialists see themselves as devoted mainly to examining and reexamining curricular matters in order to separate the essential from the nonessential. Since their emphasis is on information presented through a subject-oriented curriculum, it is typical for Essentialists to worry about maintaining, or even raising, intellectual standards. They may also strive to reduce the number of professional education courses in teacher preparation programs, apparently under the assumption that the more knowledge one has gleaned, the more information one can give.

## HISTORICAL ANTECEDENTS: SHOULD BEETHOVEN TEACH MUSIC IN THE FIFTH GRADE?

In regard to this tendency to de-emphasize professional education courses it may be helpful to look briefly at some historical antecedents for the Essentialist position. If a person had been studying educational philosophies during the early 1950s, for instance, he or she might have been exposed to ideas encapsulated by the hypothetical title, "They Wouldn't Let Beethoven Teach Music in the Fifth Grade." I suppose it is, in a way, shocking that Beethoven, a musical genius, would not have qualified during the1950s—or now, for that matter—to receive an elementary school teaching certificate. An author of such an article would obviously intend for taxpayers to be dismayed by the constraints of an overbearing and sometimes illogical educational bureaucracy. Surely Beethoven, if resurrected, could teach music to fifth graders; thus, some people might assume that the certification requirements must be absurd, since knowledge of the subject matter should be the major, if not the only, prerequisite for teacher certification. However, even though I would applaud Beethoven's occasional appearance before fifth graders as a guest lecturer/performer, I am not at all sure he should be certified to work with elementary kids on a day-to-day basis. The emotional turmoil and changes in moods that he experienced in attempting to deal with his hearing loss do not constitute the kind of learning environment I would want my fifth grade youngsters to experience regularly. I want the teacher in grade five, and in all other grades, to be thoroughly prepared with knowledge about physical and mental development, as well as in appropriate methodological techniques. Yet, it is characteristic of "back-to-basics" movements to adopt the Essentialist position regarding professional teacher preparation courses.

Ideas expressed in the title "They Wouldn't Let Beethoven Teach

Music in the Fifth Grade" had already attained wide acceptance before the U.S.S.R. launched Sputnik I in 1957. Subsequently there was a rush of titles similar to the following that expressed great trepidation about the failure of U.S. public schools to provide adequate knowledge or to help kids build appropriate skills: Rudolph Flesch, *Why Johnny Can't Read;* Arthur Trace, *What Ivan Knows That Johnny Doesn't;* Mortimer Smith, *The Diminished Mind: A Study of Planned Mediocrity in Our Schools.* We have already mentioned the subsequent fascination of curriculum-makers for "discovery" approaches, especially in the physical sciences, as well as the "Chem Study," "Harvard Project Physics," and "PSSC" materials which were supposed to "catch us up" with the Russians. We have also looked at the work of Max Rafferty, whose suspicions about all problem-solving approaches were supposed to encourage proper "corrective" measures which would reestablish a subject-oriented curriculum in its proper purity. As educators and taxpayers worry about declining SAT scores and the failures of some educational innovations which had been widely adopted during the 1960s, the Essentialist brand of "back-to-basics" is taking on a new familiarity.

There are antecedents to the current Essentialist position, however, which go much further back in time than three decades ago—in fact, all the way back to fifth century B.C. Greece. When Protagoras (481–411 B.C.) and Isocrates (436–338 B.C.) plied their educational wares to Athenians, they claimed to teach practical knowledge, as opposed to those like Socrates (470?–399 B.C.) and Plato (427?–347 B.C.) who stressed the search for eternal truths. The attractiveness of Protagoras's and Isocrates's pronouncements, as well as those of other Sophists, hinged on the nature of a society in which aristocratic ideals had been largely eclipsed by democratic ideals. In a "direct" democracy in which all citizens participated in the legislative process, it was easy for young men to see that the best lawmakers had rhetorical training—the exact kind of training which Sophists insisted that any young man could receive. In order to be convincing in legislative debates one needed to know how to speak and write artfully, how to "pepper" one's discourse with illustrations from history and literature, and how to manage oneself skillfully in disputation. All these skills were what Sophists promised (for a substantial fee, of course) to young men who would study with them.

Sophists tended to disparage the silly pursuits of those in philosophy, when it was so obvious that the skills of rhetoric made men truly successful and admired by Athenians. Why, then, should one worry about contemplating the afterlife, the gods, or universal truths? In any case, life seemed too short to investigate things which man could not know through the use of his reason, when it was quite apparent that men needed to study rhetoric in order to live effectively in the existing world.

What was the world, as it existed then? Athens was a direct democracy, so practical knowledge consisted almost entirely of verbal skills: in other words, the transformation of reading, writing, and speechmaking into highly polished arts. When this ideal of the Sophists' practical learning was copied by others, the emphasis on verbal skills remained, though there have been imminently few direct democracies in which rhetorical skills could be termed strictly practical. In order to understand some implications of copying the Sophists' practical model for learning, however, it is noteworthy to remember the current emphasis on verbal, not vocational or professional, skills among Essentialists and throughout our public schools today.

## THE ESSENTIALIST ROLE MODEL AND THE TEACHER

The fact that Essentialism provides the dominant role model for education worldwide will undoubtedly exert a powerful influence on teachers as they consider the behaviors they wish to adopt or to preserve. When we are examining role models and the philosophies underlying them, we are talking about clusters of behavior preferences, rather than mutually exclusive categories of behavior which are adhered to religiously. We are also dealing with an analysis of an individual's learning styles and habits which have been in the process of formulation during an entire educational career. For instance, some students find that they like to operate as convergent thinkers and that they enjoy the exactness which one usually associates with the physical sciences and mathematics. Such students, then, would probably not be surprised to find themselves leaning toward the philosophical position of the Essentialist Role Model. But, such students who are serious about wanting to be teachers will still have a basic decision to make—whether to emphasize the aspect of "discovery" problem-solver or of lecturer/information-giver. For those who already are practicing members of the profession and who wish to continue to use the Essentialist Role Model, periodic re-examination of their behaviors regarding the two major aspects of that role model may offer powerful stimuli for increased classroom effectiveness.

### Natural Strengths and Weaknesses of Essentialist Teaching

Again, one must remember that every role model has potential major weaknesses and traps. In other words, it is possible to assume a role model responsibly, as well as with awareness and insight, and expect kids to benefit. It is also possible to assume a role model irresponsibly, as well as with a lack of awareness and few insights, and achieve less than desirable results. We have just looked at a model in which the most glaring weaknesses can center around giving kids the feeling that the only way to win is to read the teacher's mind. These weaknesses are concomitant with convergent thinking activities which always lead kids inexorably to one right answer per problem. Unless teachers who emphasize convergent thinking learn ways to buffer this mind-reading syndrome, as Ms. Chronicler did, they can unintentionally squelch student contributions and stifle creativity. One would generally expect, because of tendencies inherent within the subject matter, to see a predominance of the Essentialist Role Model in the physical sciences and in mathematics. One also would ordinarily assume that teaching the basics of languaging to young children would usually occur under the Essentialist Role Model, as would courses in the performing arts and those vocational or professional courses which involve mastery of specific, refined skills. Teachers working with kids in any of these subject matter areas, then, may need to be especially aware of the long-range difficulties which can come from rewarding only those answers which one plans to hear, but squelching, rather than helping, youngsters to analyze the answers one did not expect to hear. Attention to this special potential problem is even more important, however, for those in the social sciences and humanities who wish to adopt the Essentialist Role Model.

## What Should Students Learn?

One other caveat is particularly appropriate to this role model. If Essentialists tend to see themselves as continuously scrutinizing the curriculum in order to distinguish essential from non-essential elements, it is important to remind ourselves of the implications of this process. The solemnity of the process is underscored when you realize that nothing less than an accurate prediction of what kids will need to know to make it through the next twenty-five to fifty years is a necessary condition for the curriculum decision-maker's success. That can be an awesome responsibility.

Let us suppose, for instance, that one could list on half of a tally sheet a number of adjectives which would adequately describe kids in a particular school division. On the other half of the tally sheet one could describe the environment of the twenty-first century, since we all hope these kids are going to be active, intelligent, decision-making citizens for sometime beyond the beginning of the twenty-first century. None of us needs to be reminded of the kinds of descriptions one would get by projecting problems of pollution, overpopulation, and all those predictions of Club Rome scientists about declining supply "curves" and rising demand "curves" into the mid-twenty-first century. The question for the reverse side of our tally sheet then would be clear as ice crystals: What should one teach kids so that they will make it in the twenty-first-century environment? The question becomes truly staggering only after one gets beyond the basic skill levels in reading, writing, and computation and beyond foundational competencies in vocational/ professional subject areas. Are we sure, for example, that students must have proficiencies in foreign languages, in trigonometry, in Shakespeare, in Middle Eastern history? Indeed, I am not against any of those elements of the curriculum; I simply want to emphasize the responsibility of a process which purports to separate essential from non-essential elements of a curriculum.

## How Well Can Students Read the Teacher's Mind?

Every role model does have its flaws and potential weaknesses. Just as in the case of Essentialism our next role model for consideration, Experimentalism, also has some possible concomitant infirmities. In Essentialism the infirmities gravitate around the mind-reading syndrome, but for Experimentalism kids could, if one is not careful, get the feeling that all learning is so relativistic that it is hardly worth the trouble. However, the purpose of our investigation is to increase awareness of role model options in order to give teachers a greater opportunity for success in selecting classroom behaviors. Along with that broadened awareness needs to go some insights about potential pitfalls, as well as obvious strengths, of each role model.

# The Experimentalist Teacher
## as Problem-Solver

# CHAPTER THREE

*The Setting:*

## MS. PROGRESSO'S CATALOGUE JOURNEY BACK TO 1908

Ms. Progresso wanted her seventh graders to investigate the effects of advertising on industrial development in the United States at the beginning of the twentieth century. She decided to construct an activity which would allow her to assess their level of understanding about industrialization, as well as encourage kids to gain new insights concerning relationships between producers and consumers. Her method was sure-fire, she thought, because it involved just the material which would fascinate her youngsters—excerpts from a *Sears, Roebuck Catalogue* first printed in 1908. She distributed copies of the following pages to all her students and carefully explained that the entire reprint volume from which those pages had been taken was available for examination. Youngsters were told that they would be working in groups of five students each while examining the catalogue pages. Each group was required to write down two statements about industry in the United States in 1908 which they had learned while reviewing the catalogue. They were cautioned to formulate only those statements they could justify from the catalogue reprint. Each group had the task of selecting a recorder for its statements, as well as a spokesperson to report findings to the class, after thirty minutes of investigation.

Ms. Progresso knew that some kids would find out how very difficult it is to construct generalizations based on limited amounts of evidence. She intended, however, to help students sharpen their skills of investigation and to ask questions that would really challenge youngsters' abilities to support the generalizations they would formulate on the basis of data taken solely from the catalogue pages.* She also planned to determine how well her students could work together to complete a task; in fact, she decided to give both "group" and "individual" grades and informed the class about her system of evaluation.

### Classroom Dialogue for the Experimentalist Role Model

*Ms. Progresso:*  What did you find out? Who's going to be our first reporter for a group?

*Julia:*  We couldn't believe how cheap everything was back then, so both our statements were about that, Ms. Progresso.

*Ms. Progresso:*  O.K.! Let's hear your first statement.

*Julia:*  We just said that things in the 1908 *Sears Catalogue* were less expensive than things in a *Sears Catalogue* today.

*Catalogue pages reprinted from Sears, Roebuck, and Company *Catalogue No. 117.* Copyright © 1969 Digest Books, Inc. Used with permission.

*Ms. Progresso:*   Good, Julia. Now, could you and your group tell me how you justified that statement?

*Georgia:*   Well, if you put one of today's catalogues next to these pages from 1908, everybody would see that things in 1908 cost less.

*Ms. Progresso:*   When you said "less expensive," did you mean that things "cost less?"

*Julia:*   Yes. All of us were surprised at the difference in prices.

*Ms. Progresso:*   Do you think, then, that it was easier for someone in 1908 to have his eyes examined, take his prescription to be ground, and buy a pair of glasses than it would be to get those things done today?

*Julia:*   It certainly did cost less then, if that's what you mean.

*Georgia:*   But we don't really know how much people got paid then. Maybe they made less money.

*Julia:*   If they did make less money, it might not have been any easier for them to buy glasses than it is for us.

*Harold:*   It couldn't have been too hard for them to scrape together $2.14 for a pair of glasses, though. Today you can't even get sunglasses in the dime store for that price!

*Julia:*   But we really don't know for sure that it was so easy for them to pay $2.14, because we don't know their salaries in 1908.

*Ms. Progresso:*   Can anybody help us with this problem? Is there a way we could help Julia's group reword its statement so thay we could justify it from the catalogue pages?

*Bill:*   Why didn't they just say that things were priced lower in 1908, and let it go at that?

*Ms. Progresso:*   You mean we should just get rid of the words "less expensive" and have it read that things in a 1908 *Sears Catalogue* were priced lower than things in today's *Sears Catalogue*?

*Bill:*   Yes. You could tell that by putting two catalogues side by side.

*Ms. Progresso:*   Is that all right with your group, Julia?

*Julia:*   Yes! That way we wouldn't have to worry about the question of salaries, because we can't answer that question from looking at the catalogue pages.

*Ms. Progresso:*   That's a good point, Julia. The words "less expensive" imply that it would have been easier to buy these items in 1908 than it is now. But we really don't know that, because we can't compare salaries. It might have been harder for someone in 1908 to pay $2.14 for a pair of glasses than it would be for us to pay $100 today. Remember the word "inflation" in your reading list? We can assume that if prices go up, then wages will go up too. But in this case we don't have the information in our catalogue that would tell us whether wages were higher compared to prices in 1908 than wages are now compared to today's prices. And the assignment was to write only statements you could "prove" by using the catalogue. We do know something about what prices are like today, though, so Bill's suggestion has been a big help.

Harold, what about your group?

*Harold:*   We kept thinking about how many words there were on each page. The print was so small.

*Ms. Progresso:*   I'm glad you brought that up, Harold. What did your group

say about the small print and the number of words per page?

*Harold:* We thought they really must like to read if the catalogues contained so many words. Today's catalogues have mostly pictures.

(A few chuckles can be heard.)

*Ms. Progresso:* Wait, class. There's something very important about what Harold is saying. Harold's group has just indicated that people liked to read long descriptions in their catalogues. If the Sears Company printed such long descriptions, they probably did assume people would like this quality about their catalogue. It also means they assumed what about the abilities of the public?

*Harold:* That they could read, I guess.

*Ms. Progresso:* O.K.! I'm especially glad you brought this up. As a matter of fact, I had not realized our class would think of examining this point, but it is one of tremendous importance when you study industrial development in any country. Our nation in 1908 was made up of what we would call a "highly literate" population. That's one reason why mail-order businesses could work. What else could we say about the lengthy descriptions in the catalogue?

*Harold:* Maybe they wanted you to know a lot about what you were buying. I'd really rather see what I'm getting, though, instead of ordering it from a catalogue.

*John:* But what if you were far away from the stores and couldn't see these things? And what if something you bought broke down?

*Bill:* It does really say you could fix the cream separator yourself. "With a screwdriver and wrench a boy can take the entire machine apart in ten minutes and put it together ready to run in ten minutes more."

*Georgia:* And for the telephones it keeps saying how easy they are to install. Here's what they wrote:

> 'They are easy to put up and easy to keep in order after they are put up. They are easy to repair if by accident any part becomes damaged or broken. Anyone without the slightest electrical knowledge or telephone experience can put up a telephone line and install our telephones.'

*Ms. Progresso:* Well, I can see you are all doing some good work at thinking of reasons why long descriptions might be appropriate in this catalogue.

*Harold:* If my telephone or television broke, I wouldn't want to be the guy who would have to fix it, but it seems the people who wrote this catalogue expected you to be your own handy-man, even if your telephone quit on you. I'm glad I'm living now, instead of in 1908, so somebody can come to fix my phone.

*Julia:* But suppose you had lived on a farm in 1908, and your nearest neighbor was five miles away? There just weren't as many people then as now, so you might need to know how to fix your own cream separator and telephone.

*Ms. Progresso:* What do we know about population figures from the catalogue?

*Julia:* Well, we don't know exactly how many people there were, but they do keep saying how simple these machines are to operate and fix and they do have a lot of pictures and descriptions of things for farmers. It just seems like there must have been fewer people living in the United States then.

*Bill:* It does take a lot of space for big farms.

*Ms. Progresso:* I see what you mean. Harold's group has just given us a statement that the population was highly literate. Harold said he and his

## IT HAS A DOZEN NEW AND VALUABLE IMPROVEMENTS.

The new low down supply tank, just the right height and low enough that anyone, even a child, can fill it easily. High enough to be out of the way. At a convenient height to use for washing the tinware after you have finished skimming. The whole inside is visible from top to bottom. You can clean it without removing it from the machine if you want to. It is pressed from a single piece of heavy steel, with rounding corners, not a seam or joint anywhere, and is tinned and retinned so that there is no wear out to it. It has our improved flush key faucet and can be set on the table or anywhere when filled without the faucet key being driven up and leaking as the tanks of other makers all do.

### THE CRANK IS JUST THE RIGHT HEIGHT,

in the position recommended by medical authorities as the most natural and healthy. A position that makes the operation of a light running separator like the Economy Chief delightful and healthy exercise for man, woman, boy or girl. It is neither too high nor too low; at just the height where you would have it if you were to build a cream separator to suit yourself.

### IT RUNS SURPRISINGLY EASY.

The new Economy Chief is easily brought up to speed and after that almost runs itself. The simplest possible gearing, the fewest possible bearings or points of friction, perfect adjustment throughout, small, compact bowl and moderate speed all combine to make it an easy running wonder, just the separator for women and boys to operate.

### MANY OTHER IMPROVEMENTS

aid in making the new Economy Chief the most perfect separator ever produced. Our newly improved oil feed. The wonderful new self adjusting, easily removable upper bearing. The improved supply tank holder which prevents all noise and vibration. The new clean-easy tinware with rounding corners and no crevices where milk can collect and sour. The handy little drip cup which catches all the oil and dirt and keeps the inside of the separator clean and sanitary and prevents dripping on the floor. The new rigid frame, solid as a rock. No weaving or vibration as in four-legged machines. Improvements here and there and everywhere suggested by our own experience and that of hundreds of thousands of Economy Separator users put the new and perfect Economy Chief in a class by itself.

### THE MOST SIMPLE SEPARATOR

ever devised. With a screwdriver and wrench a boy can take the entire machine apart in ten minutes and put it together ready to run in ten minutes more. No chance to get out of adjustment, no tinkering, no places hard to get at. No special tools required. Every part true to pattern and interchangeable. No possibility of putting together wrong. Only one way and that is the right way. To take out and replace the upper bearing takes but a minute in the new Economy Chief. In all other machines it takes from one hour to a day. Every other part is just as simple.

### ONLY THE VERY BEST MATERIALS

and only the very highest class of skilled labor is employed in the construction of our telephones. They are mechanically and electrically perfect in every detail, correctly and scientifically designed. We spare no expense that will in any way improve the quality. Our object is to produce the most perfect, the most serviceable and the most satisfactory telephone that can be manufactured. Every part that enters into the make up of these telephones is as good as expert designers and skilled workmen can produce. There is not a loose joint in the entire instrument, every connection being soldered, making a solid circuit that cannot possibly get out of order. The workmen engaged in the construction of these telephones are men of the highest degree of skill—men of long and practical experience in actual telephone construction.

### SIMPLE AND EASY TO INSTALL.

Our telephones are made with the greatest possible simplicity, all complicated parts having been eliminated. They are easy to put up and easy to keep in order after they are put up. They are easy to repair if by accident any part becomes damaged or broken. Any one without the slightest electrical knowledge or telephone experience can put up a telephone line and install our telephones. There is nothing complicated about them—nothing hard to understand. The instruments are simple, they are right in every way, they reach you in perfect order, and they come to you with simple and easily understood directions, so that it is easy for anyone, without the slightest previous experience, to put up a line and install these instruments with perfect assurance that the line will give good service.

investigators were impressed by the lengthy descriptions of items. Can we say anything else, then, in regard to these very complete descriptions?

*Bill:* Well, we could say the population was very spread out because there were a lot of farms and people were expected to know how to fix machines on their own.

*Ms. Progresso:* Good! I'm glad we're considering this point. Can anyone think of a short way of saying people lived far apart?

*Margaret:* Maybe we could say the population was not densely settled. That's what we used to say when we were studying about people in the thirteen colonies.

*Ms. Progresso:* Thanks, Margaret. Let's write that on the board just as you said it.

*John:* If people lived far apart and had to know how to fix everything that broke down, that must mean they really did need to order things from a catalogue because they might not be able to go to many stores.

*Julia:* Yes, and they had to have some way of getting all these things from factories to people who might want to buy them, even if these people were spread out all over the country. They just used the mail to sell things instead of building a lot of stores!

*Ms. Progresso:* O.K.! Let's add that one to our list. How shall we word it? Maybe we can say that the catalogue mail-order business linked the manufacturer with his buyers. Is that all right with everybody?

*Harold:* The mail service sure must have been better then than it is now! (Mild laughter drifts through the room.)

*Ms. Progresso:* Margaret, what about your group?

*Margaret:* Well, we thought the main reason why this catalogue was so popular was because everybody would want to get things cheaper.

*Julia:* But that's what our group said. We've already talked about that.

*Ms. Progresso:* We did talk about cost, so maybe we have discussed this before. But perhaps Margaret has something a bit different in mind. Can you help us out, Margaret, by explaining more of what your group had in mind?

*Margaret:* The people who wrote this catalogue kept saying they were selling things cheaper than other stores.

*Ms. Progresso:* Do you mean cheaper than other businesses operating in 1908?

*Margaret:* Yes.

*Julia:* Oh, I remember that now. It says, "Don't forget that when you buy a separator from the Trust or from an agent you pay a long string of profits over the cost to build." I just didn't know what kind of business a trust was.

*Ms. Progresso:* You'll come across that name later in some of the other activities we'll do for this unit. A "trust" referred to a large business which often made and sold only one product. Usually a trust making cream separators, for instance, would try to drive out of business other factories that made cream separators. When small factories had been bought by the trust or driven out of business by not being able to sell as cheaply as the trust, then the trust might raise its prices and get more profits. In this case, the Sears Company is trying to sell cream separators cheaper than the trust is selling them.

Conley Camera Company

*Hereby guarantees that this Camera No 2 _____ is made of highest grade material throughout and is thoroughly inspected and adjusted and tested in operation. We guarantee it for twenty years and will replace any part that proves defective during that period of Time. Dated at Rochester this _____ day of _____ 190___*

Fred Conley

Conley Camera Company

Terry Conley

## WE ARE FIGHTING THE CAMERA TRUST

### WITH BETTER CAMERAS AT LOWER PRICES THAN THEY CAN OFFER.

**PRACTICALLY ALL CAMERAS** except ours are sold by the Trust or marketed by the Trust through their dealers, and these cameras are sold at prices from two to four times the prices which we ask for Conley cameras of corresponding styles and better quality. We have been threatened with all sorts of trouble by the Trust if we refuse to join this combination of camera manufacturers in an effort to compel you to pay two or three prices for your camera, but we refuse to be intimidated, and will continue to manufacture our own cameras, in our own factory and sell them at our own prices, prices which represent but the mere cost of materials and labor, with our one small percentage of profit added.

## OUR THIRTY DAYS' FREE TRIAL COMPARISON OFFER.

**SEND US AN ORDER** for any style of Conley camera, enclose our price as quoted in this catalogue, and we will forward the camera which you select, with the understanding and agreement that you can try it for thirty days, during which time you can put it to every test, you can compare it with other cameras of corresponding styles sold by the Trust at three and four times the prices which we ask you for the Conley cameras, and if you don't find it satisfactory in every way, far lower in price than any corresponding camera with which you may compare it, better in quality and entirely satisfactory to you in every detail, return it to us by express, at our expense, and we will refund to you, without question, the entire purchase price and also reimburse you for any transportation charges which you may have paid out.

*John:*   It also says, "No marks will appear on the inside or outside to show where you bought them." That sounds like some people might want their friends to think they paid higher prices for what they bought.

*Ms. Progresso:*   I see what you mean. In fact, they do say in the same section that sometimes people hesitate to buy at low prices because "of the antagonism of local companies or other interested parties." It does seem that they are asking people to buy from Sears at lower prices and no one will ever need to know you were shopping for a bargain. Some people do like to keep their bargain hunting a secret.

How can we write down what we've just been discussing?

*John:*   Why don't we just say they were in competition with other businesses?

*Margaret:*   But that doesn't tell us exactly how they were competing. They were selling things cheaper than the others.

*Ms. Progresso:* How about using the word "undersell" then? Doesn't that say what we want?

*Harold:* I think so, but I'd still rather see what I'm getting than to order from this catalogue. I think I'd feel that way even if I had been living in 1908.

*Ms. Progresso:* Why don't we take a quick look at all the things you have told me about industry in 1908 that you have learned from this catalogue? Here's the list of statements you gave me.

> (1) Things in a 1908 *Sears Catalogue* were priced lower than things in today's *Sears Catalogue.*
>
> (2) The U.S. population was highly literate in 1908.
>
> (3) The country was not densely populated.
>
> (4) The mail-order catalogue business linked a manufacturer with buyers.
>
> (5) The Sears Company tried to undersell its competitors.

Please keep in your notebooks a complete list of these points you've given me. I am really pleased with the things you brought up in discussion. Remember how long we talked about the first statement, and how we finally decided it would be better to change the words "less expensive" to "priced lower." Sometimes it's really hard when you know you have to be careful not to say more than the evidence you have will let you say.

Well, let's put these materials away for now. I'll bet, though, you could tell me a lot more things about industry which you can learn from studying this catalogue. I may even ask you to add to your list of statements tomorrow.

Recorders, please give me your notes on all the statements your groups discussed so I can see the points we didn't get to talk about in class.

## Role Model Analysis: Ms. Progresso and Ms. Chronicler Compared

Ms. Progresso took a good deal of pleasure in musing about the successes of her "catalogue" lesson. That lesson seems all the more effective as presented here, of course, because of the literary license we have taken in smoothing over its potential difficulties for the sake of brevity—just as we did for Ms. Chronicler in the last chapter. Ms. Progresso was genuinely surprised by the sophistication many of her students had displayed in their abilities to generalize and analyze and was quick to resolve that this lesson should be used again. She enjoyed it, particularly because her kids raised some issues which she had not assumed they would investigate. She knew several students had gotten the message about being careful not to say more in their generalizations than they could support by evidence at hand. She did resolve, however, that she would also reproduce some appropriate pages from a current catalogue so that students' comparative efforts would be more manageable. Having the two catalogues at hand would mean that her exercise could include additional printed material which would serve as concrete evidence. Thus, the kids would not be forced to use their memories or rely on personal assumptions when they were comparing the two catalogues.

But perhaps we are revealing too many of Ms. Progresso's private assumptions. So, let us examine the four components of our analytical tool, before we allow Ms. Progresso to give us stream-of-consciousness insights into her lesson planning habits and into her assumptions about the teaching/learning process.

Again, we must start with the question relating to behavior trends, since a teacher's behavior provides the only data for inferences about his or her answers to the first three questions in our analytical tool.

4. What behavior trend should one exhibit in order to carry out
   one's philosophical position?

Authoritarian World View        Non-authoritarian World View
(Convergent Thinking)          (Divergent Thinking)

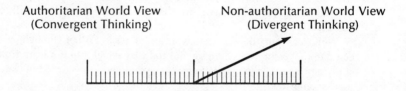

Remember that the phrase "authoritarian world view" connotes a teacher who typically attempts to sell students the expert's view of subject matter and who emphasizes convergent thinking. On the other hand, a teacher possessing a "non-authoritarian world view" strives to help youngsters make their own interpretations of subject matter by stressing divergent thinking. To determine whether convergent or divergent thinking has been emphasized here, we must ask ourselves what Ms. Progresso planned to be the ultimate outcome for her lesson. Did she encourage and accept alternate logical answers, or did she plan for everyone to leave the classroom with only one particular answer about industrialization and the 1908 *Sears, Roebuck Catalogue?*

There were many clues in this dialogue which indicate that Ms. Progresso rewarded alternate answers and planned that kids would have many different kinds of statements about industrialization which they could justify from the catalogue. In fact, she expressed surprise to Harold that his group had chosen to emphasize the length of descriptions in its statements. She had assumed, perhaps due to her introduction to the lesson which stressed the concept of industrialization, that students would immediately focus on manufacturing, rather than literacy in the general population. However, once Harold's group had presented its idea, she rewarded them by stating precisely that she was glad they had brought up the point about literacy. She also took care to let other class members, who for the moment found Harold's point humorous, know that the issue was quite significant although she had not anticipated that the class would think about the question concerning literacy.

Notice that her summary of the lesson reviewed the five generalizations which they had examined as a class, but she also indicated that she assumed kids "could tell a lot more things about industry which [they] could learn from studying the catalogue." She left the students with a promise to resume this activity soon in order to determine how much more they might be able to tell her about industrial development in 1908 just from perusing the catalogue. In other words, she apparently had defined her objective in terms of a process to be mastered—the process of formulating and supporting generalizations—rather than in terms of a set of facts to be learned. Such a focus on objectives stated in terms of processes and skills implies that any number of different sets of factual information might be equally acceptable for advancing the aim of skill development. Facts contained in each generalization, as well as the topic of each generalization, would vary from student to student and group to group. Clearly, then, with such variable answers having been expected and rewarded when they appeared, the mode of thinking emphasized in this lesson is divergent.

These qualities which we have just been examining in regard to divergent thinking are again reinforced when we study the question relating to contributions from learners. We have already determined, according to our chart in the first chapter, that a non-authoritarian behavior trend and an emphasis on divergent thinking place the role model within a broad philosophical category labeled "Experimentalist/Existentialist." Scrutiny of questions about learners and about subject matter will help us further refine our understanding and labeling of the role model.

1. What is the nature of the learner?

Lockean                                         Platonic

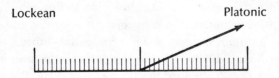

Learners certainly contributed many responses during Ms. Progresso's lesson; in fact, her approach could easily have degenerated into a sullen staring match, if students had been unwilling to make contributions. She expected, however, that kids would at least find the nostalgia of old catalogue pages appealing enough to want to begin a process of investigating and generalizing. She was correct about the students' state of motivation, of course, and had no difficulty in stimulating them to analyze and justify statements they had made. Since we already have determined that Ms. Progresso planned her lesson as an exercise in divergent thinking, we would expect the dialogue to evidence her approval of any and all attempts to formulate generalizations which could logically be justified by items from the catalogue pages.

Is this approval of kids' attempts to generalize actually displayed in Ms. Progresso's behavior toward learners? She expressed surprise and pleasure that Harold's group had thought to attend to the matter of literacy, despite the fact that several kids found Harold's manner of talking about the number of words on each page at least mildly amusing. She was supportive of Margaret's point about the catalogue's popularity being based on attempts to sell items cheaper, even though Julia wanted to dismiss the issue as already having been discussed. Ms. Progresso's remark that "maybe Margaret has something different in mind" encouraged youngsters to find what would be truly useful in Margaret's statement. Ms. Progresso and the kids were, in fact, rewarded by an analysis of elements involved in the competitive technique of underselling.

As the previous examples indicate, Ms. Progresso seemed truly intent on accepting and analyzing each generalization *at the time it was offered by students.* Her message was not, "Wait until the facts of your generalization happen to fit my plan"—the technique used by Ms. Chronicler, who readily reminded David that his point about the question of possible dates when the Kensington Stone might have been carved would be more appropriately considered at another time in the discussion. Ms. Progresso also recognized all students' attempts at generalization; thus, she asked group recorders at the end of the lesson to submit their notes, which would allow her to see statements the class had not had time to examine during the discussion. She even suggested that the activity deserved more time and that other worthwhile points about industrialization would be contributed as students formulated additional statements. Ms. Progresso, in fact, relied so heavily on original student contributions—not on answers rewarded in terms of their proximity to an expert's view of industrialization—that her lesson on generalizations from a 1908 catalogue should have the scale for this indicator's continuum pointing toward the "Platonic" position. We are assuming, of course, that this lesson is typical of Ms. Progresso's teaching style and that she has a "Platonic" view of learners in general.

The fact that Ms. Progresso welcomed all generalizations offered by students at the time they were offered and helped students analyze their statements implies that she was more interested in their skill at generalizing than in the specific facts and concepts contained in each statement. Let us apply this observation to our question about the nature of the subject matter.

2. What is the nature of the subject matter?

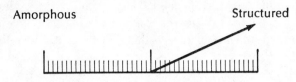

Amorphous                                 Structured

From the nature of Ms. Progresso's assignment students were required to deal with a structure because they had to relate specific items in the catalogue pages to statements which attempted to explain those items. In other words, youngsters were continuously dealing with relationships between "facts" and a "larger idea" (to use the phraseology we have employed in previous chapters). This characteristic of having youngsters sift through information to relate it to a larger idea is present in any problem-solving situation, whether in the Essentialist "discovery" model which Ms. Chronicler used or in the Experimentalist "inquiry" model which Ms. Progresso presented. Just as in Ms. Chronicler's case, Ms. Progresso definitely intended for her students to understand that history and the social sciences have a natural structure; therefore, the scale for this indicator should point toward the area which we have labeled "structured" on the continuum.

Please note, however, that the manner in which Ms. Progresso and Ms. Chronicler taught about structure differed according to the use of specific content and detailed information. Ms. Chronicler selected the specific information she wanted students to receive—the steps of historical methodology; thus, she used the Kensington Stone article as the vehicle for pulling her youngsters to an expert's view of the historical method. Ms. Progresso, on the contrary, emphasized skill development; therefore, a wide variety of sets of facts derived from the catalogue pages served equally well to help kids gain proficiency in analyzing and generalizing. In other words, for Ms. Progresso there were various content vehicles suitable to help her students reach the goal of skill development. Although she had planned that kids would generalize strictly about industrialization, when the discussion shifted to literacy and to population density she readily seized on these topics as acceptable content vehicles; consequently, she rewarded kids for thinking independently.

Ms. Progresso was also interested in helping increase students' awareness about information they were uncovering. She helped them with terminology about literacy and population density. She provided explanations about trusts when students were ready for such explanations: namely, when they realized the relevance of the concept "trust" to the concept "underselling." In other words, Ms. Progresso wanted her students to receive a great deal of information about industrialization, but she planned her lesson so that students would have some choice about the content. In fact, the details they received depended largely on "what happened to come up" in their own statements. Instead of administering only certain facts, Ms. Progresso advised students about facts that they thought were relevant to the statement under analysis.

Was Ms. Progresso's emphasis on cognitive or affective elements of subject matter? Just as in Ms. Chronicler's lesson on the Kensington Stone, Ms. Progresso hoped students would find it fascinating to investigate materials she had provided for them. However, although the curriculum materials may have been very appealing to youngsters, the skills of formulating generalizations about industrialization and then analyzing those generalizations for accuracy are notably cognitive.

3. How should one use the subject matter to guide students toward meaningful learning activities?

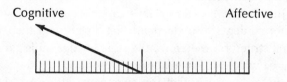

Cognitive                                                    Affective

Emphasizing the affective end of the continuum really concerns reminding each student in a personal way, either forcefully or subtly, of what Existentialists call the "death dread." This usually involves discussion of the fact that one day all of us will cease to exist in our present condition, but it may also include exposure to a personalized emotional encounter with potential injustice. Although we will have to wait until a chapter concerning the Existentialist Role Model to explore the "death dread" concept more fully, it may be helpful now if we consider what the lesson might have been like if this continuum's scale tipped toward the "affective" position.

For the sake of illustration regarding an affective emphasis, imagine the results if Ms. Progresso had structured her lesson differently. Suppose, for example, she had given directions similar to those which appear below.

I am going to give each of you copies of ten pages which have been taken from a 1908 edition of the *Sears, Roebuck Catalogue*, and I want you to try a brief writing exercise that I think you'll really like.

Pretend that you are in North America working for a team of archaeologists from the United States of Europe in the year 2600.

Copies of the *Sears, Roebuck Catalogue*, 1908 edition have been unearthed from the cornerstones of various business establishments on the sites of New York City, Chicago, Los Angeles, and Atlanta. You have become very interested in life on the North American continent at the beginning of the twentieth century, but so far the catalogues represent the only record which has come to light from the twentieth century. You have access to the ten pages of catalogue copy which I have given you.

Write a letter home in which you describe two things about the lifestyle in North America in 1908 which you really like but which, because of conditions in 2600, people can no longer enjoy.

Use your imaginations about conditions in 2600, but when you formulate two statements about life in 1908 be sure to say only what evidence in the catalogue pages will allow you to say. I am anxious to read the letters and will write comments to you personally about ideas you put in your letter. We will discuss next week some ideas which students decided to include.

Such a lesson would have helped Ms. Progresso assess a number of items, such as writing skills. She would also have gotten some insights into the way students like to spend their time and perhaps what they really cherish about their own lifestyles. Students would be confronted personally with problems which the "ravages of time" might bring for future generations and for themselves. Such affective elements, however, are absent from the lesson as Ms. Progresso actually presented it. Instead, youngsters attended to the intellectual skills of formulating generalizations about industrialization, and then determined if those generalizations could be supported from evidence contained in the catalogue pages.

Now that Ms. Progresso's lesson has been analyzed according to our four indicators, the significance of her role as an Experimentalist problem-solver becomes clearer. Experimentalist problem-solving is usually referred to as "inquiry," rather than "discovery," because kids are truly inquiring about subject matter in order to make their own interpretations of it. The teacher is not leading them to "discover" what experts in the discipline have known all along. In fact, Ms. Progresso saw her role as helping youngsters analyze, clarify, and justify the interpretations they had formulated. In other words, the specific subject matter content may vary for a lesson like Ms. Progresso's, without having the lesson's objectives adversely influenced. Statements about industrial development, about population density, or about literacy were all equally acceptable as vehicles for helping youngsters improve their analytical skills.

Since youngsters may contribute topics from a myriad of possibilities within any one aspect of the subject matter under study, lessons like Ms. Progresso's can be more difficult to plan, prepare for, and administer than lessons like Ms. Chronicler's. Because a teacher does not know exactly what details youngsters may decide to focus upon, the truly conscientious instructor may feel compelled to plan for as many of those myriad possibilities as possible. Such a thoroughly developed superego can drive a teacher to plan himself or herself into a stupor after a few short weeks. At least by the eighth month of any given academic year, the super-scrupulous Experimentalist problem-solver who never remembers being bothered previously by a kid smacking gum feels that every chomp goes straight to his bone marrow.

It is at this precipice of despair that those who wish to teach by inquiry methods usually learn either to balance their time and energy expenditures so that they can muster enough stamina to drive home at the end of the school day or decide that they do not ever again want to manage another class session in which the buzz of busy committee workers pierces the cerebellum. They are, instead, ready to make peace with their superegos by letting their kids learn about process through lessons like Ms. Chronicler's in which they have more control over selecting the product in terms of specific information to be analyzed. Teachers sometimes decide that too many traumas result from letting kids ask about whatever aspect of the subject they wish to investigate, while the teacher searches for that elusive and most stimulating primary source material about a topic that kids unexpectedly decide to take off on.

Moreover, every role model, as we have warned in previous chapters, does have its potential pitfalls. Despite its management and administrative difficulties, the Experimentalist problem-solving role model can be immensely satisfying because, when it is done expertly, it is based on a constant process of stimulating mutual feedback between teachers and students as they build their own courses of study. The psychic rewards to a teacher who has mastered this role model and enjoys it cannot be measured in the merely mundane terms of dollars and cents; this is really quite fortunate because, before anyone has spent two weeks in the classroom, it is obvious to him or her that taxpayers have planned carefully to have psychic rewards of the profession outweigh monetary ones.

When an Experimentalist "inquirer" nears "burn-out," however, and for one reason or another finds himself too tired even to change himself into the Essentialist "discoverer," disaster can result. Sometimes such a condition can cause a formerly competent teacher to become a leader in what some theorists have contemptuously labeled the "touchy-feely" movement in education. In other words, such teachers tend to play with motivating devices but never move beyond the devices into the difficult and challenging task of helping kids delve into and analyze information. They may use a commercially-produced simulation game involving foreign policy issues and notice after five days that the youngster who has not participated at all excuses his lack of involvement by telling the instructor he is a spy. Then the instructor forgets to have a debriefing session in which he could help kids analyze what they had learned. Or perhaps he uses Ms. Progresso's catalogue lesson, but never really bothers to question kids so that they are sifting through catalogue items, analyzing their relevance, and mastering concepts related to industrialization. At its very worst, the "touchy-feely" movement produces the instructor, similar to the one Max Rafferty observed, who teaches kids how to make igloos out of ice cubes as a lesson on Eskimo life. At its worst, it produces the kind of learning environment remembered so bitterly in the previous chapter and described so poignantly by Mara Wolynski as the "Sand and Sea" school. Sometimes this role model can also be handled so ineptly by a teacher that kids finally assume all learning is too "relativistic" and too difficult to substantiate by evidence and that a serious effort to investigate any new problem within a discipline yields insufficient rewards. Or, stated more directly, if one opinion is just as good as another, why bother?

All of the above rehearsal of pitfalls simply adds to the list of reasons why the Essentialist role model is dominant. To accentuate the differences between an Experimentalist and an Essentialist problem-solver, see page 76 for a comparison of the scales on each continuum.*

It is obvious from the diagram following that variations between Experimentalist and Essentialist problem-solvers involve different views of learners and the behavior trends exhibited. Nevertheless, let us examine a brief illustration to determine how these variations would translate themselves into specific classroom behaviors. Imagine that Ms. Chronicler, our Essentialist problem-solver from the previous chapter, had decided to teach a lesson using the *1908 Sears, Roebuck Catalogue.* Since she would wish to emphasize convergent thinking and the absorption of specific information by learners, her approach to the lesson would be quite different from Ms. Progresso's approach.

Ms. Chronicler would select the specific information kids should learn, as well as the process by which they should learn it. Students would not choose from a number of appropriate sets of facts and focus on the details they wished to investigate. Instead, perhaps Ms. Chronicler would decide to use the catalogue pages to teach youngsters only the generalization that mail-order catalogue businesses "bridged" the gap between one manufacturing complex and distant consumers during the early twentieth century.

---

*It is possible for teachers to display a more definite Lockean position than Ms. Chronicler and an amorphous emphasis, while still remaining Essentialists.

*Comparison of Experimentalist and Essentialist Problem-Solvers*

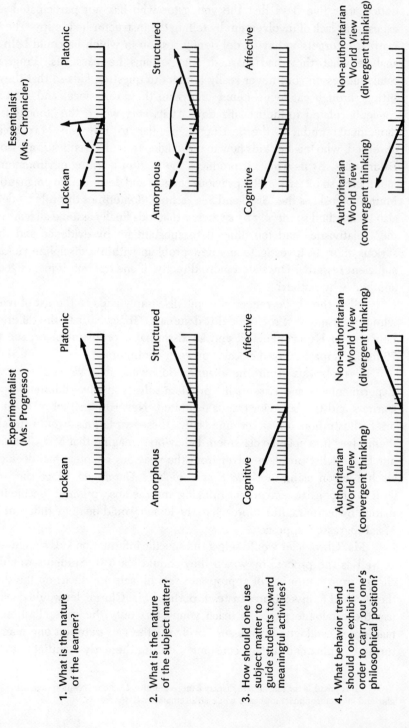

She would have youngsters gain insights into the process of formulating generalizations by structuring her lesson so that students would answer with specific items of evidence to support the generalization about a manufacturing complex and distant consumers. Answers leading to this generalization would be clearly rewarded, while those responses which did not fit the plan would be ignored or politely shelved. Consequently, her questions would lead students toward the one generalization she had originally planned for them to absorb. They would not receive reinforcement if they wanted to analyze items about literacy or population density.

Both models, whether based on "discovery" or "inquiry," have their advantages and disadvantages. Moreover, they do differ quite markedly, because one emphasizes convergent thinking, while the other stresses divergent thinking.

## PHILOSOPHIC PRINCIPLES SUPPORTING THE EXPERIMENTALIST ROLE MODEL

To gain additional insights into assumptions which help determine behaviors for teachers who have chosen a particular role model, let's analyze principles supporting the Experimentalist philosophy. Although our overview of scales underscored the "inquiry" problem-solver's use of divergent thinking, an adaptation of principles outlined by George Kneller in *Introduction to the Philosophy of Education* will help to contrast Experimentalism with the Essentialist position.

(1) *Education should be related directly to the interests of the child.* Perhaps this statement seems a bit puzzling, since Essentialists also want their lessons to interest youngsters. Nonetheless, when Experimentalists were first formulating their position and methodologies, the Essentialist role model was dominant. As we shall see later in this chapter, however, Essentialists at the beginning of this century were more prone to be charged with exemplifying an extreme position based on the "amorphous" view of subject matter than would be true today. Experimentalists, or "Progressives" as they were formerly called, wanted to build a coherent pedagogical position which would contrast sharply with what they saw as the most heinous results of rote memorization.

Progressives tended to associate the kind of learning which usually occurred in school with what we have called an "amorphous" view of subject matter. Allen Funt's interviews with five- and six-year-olds who were asked to explain the meaning of the *Pledge of Allegiance* to the United States' Flag would have confirmed the Progressives' worst fears.

I am sure we can all remember having similar difficulties when attempting to commit something to memory before we were skilled enough to visualize how that something would look in writing. I can remember an incident that occurred in first grade at the school where Mrs. Précis taught. At that time, there was a great deal of patriotic fervor among parents and students because this tiny school, which had functioned as a complete elementary and high school unit, was about to have its junior and senior high segments removed by a few "radical" members of the school board. Feeling ran so high over this proposed movement toward consolidation of secondary school students at two centers in what was basically a rural county that no one had problems identifying scapegoats. One day when the superintendent visited our school an overly zealous young man lifted the ignition key from the superintendent's car. A major article of faith in this consolidation battle was that everyone, even first graders, had to memorize the school song and sing it at every opportunity as a way of showing public devotion. Our alma mater was an extremely stirring piece, the words having been composed by our principal and skillfully attached by our music teacher to the tune of a patriotic song, "My Own America," which had appeared during World War II. I distinctly remember mastering the line, "Your 'taught-us' will be true; your sons will make a name," and wondering why the words were not something like "What you've taught us will be true." In grade two, or sometime soon thereafter, I realized the line was, "Your daughters will be true; your sons will make a name."

At any rate, as far as Progressives were concerned examples like those above showing pitfalls of rote memorization were characteristic of what generally happened in schools. They advocated what many people since that time have viewed as an extremely child-centered approach to learning. In fact, they felt that the traditional subject-oriented curriculum and the way that curriculum was exposed to children were twin factors most directly responsible for the tendency to rely too heavily on memorization. Making the child's interest the focal point of the curriculum and using a problem-solving approach would necessitate innovative ways of presenting subject matter. Therefore, child-centeredness and problem-solving were to be key elements in their pedagogical creed.

Ms. Progresso's teaching method reveals the Experimentalist concepts of child-centeredness and problem-solving. Kids in Ms. Progresso's class decided what the curriculum would be, because they decided what items from the catalogue to investigate and what questions to discuss. It is this kind of child-centeredness, which implies that students have a role in curriculum-making, that Progressives had in mind. Such a concept, which envisons curricula as evolving from the interactions of teachers and students with subject matter, differs widely from the Essentialist view of the teacher as expert curriculum-designer who selects specific content and chooses the teaching method by which that content is given.

Let us now examine the other key principle of Experimentalism—namely, problem-solving—and see what advocates of this philosophy mean by that term.

(2) *Learning through problem-solving should replace inculcation of subject matter.* At first glance, this statement may seem a bit puzzling. After all, have we not just looked at something called "Essentialist problem-solving" in the previous chapter? Nonetheless, when Progressives were first refining their position they wanted to present a credo which would contrast sharply with Essentialist practices. Therefore, their concept of problem-solving embraced what we have called "inquiry" and evidenced an emphasis on divergent thinking. For instance, Ms. Progresso accepted student contributions and helped kids analyze ideas at the time they were brought up. Progressives then believed, as Experimentalists believe today, that education should stress examination of alternative possibilities, particularly because a situation might ultimately require selecting one of those possibilities as a course of action. In fact, knowledge is seen by both groups as the quality which results when learners interact with their environment to analyze possibilities. To them, knowledge does not exist apart from an interaction between learners and the environment. Knowledge is seen as a tool for managing experience; and, in actuality, it must be useful in the management of experience to be significant.

Perhaps we should examine a "classic" Experimentalist example of problem-solving—one which includes interaction between learners and their environment, the analysis of alternative possibilities, and selection of one possibility as a course of action. Because Progressives, the forerunners of contemporary Experimentalists, tended to focus on the elementary school, we will do the same with this example. Notice also that it will involve an emphasis on the behavioral and social sciences, rather than on the physical sciences. This stress on social science disciplines was characteristic of Progressives, but is also characteristic of Experimentalists today.

Our example concerns a fifth grade class whose members decided at the beginning of the academic year that they wanted new curtains for their room. Their teacher had resolved on the first work day before youngsters returned from summer break that since the old curtains added little to the general appearance of the room, she would simply remove them; she assumed that kids might enjoy helping select the new ones. When she mentioned how deplorably unattractive the old curtains were, the students decided they wanted to make selecting new curtains a major project.

Wishing to capitalize on what Progressives used to call a "teachable moment," the instructor immediately began to discuss with her students some items they might want to consider before making a final selection. Together they concluded they would obviously need to know something about mathematics if they were going to make these curtains, since their limited funds made it necessary to buy carefully. They would have to consider more than just simple dimensions, however, because they knew they wanted to get material with a printed pattern depicting items that related to an era in United States history; hence, they would have to plan cautiously to match the print pattern when they sewed panels of the material together. They also wanted to be attentive to problems of glare and heat, since nearly the entire wall where the curtains would be placed consisted of glass.

The more students discussed the matter of selecting draperies, the more possibilities they began considering. Would it be better, for instance, to choose a natural fiber such as linen or cotton, or should they choose a man-made fiber like dacron? Which might last longer? How would color affect the problems of glare and heat? Should the curtains have a lining which would help to serve as insulation? As the project progressed, students reviewed and sharpened their mathematics skills; they investigated matters concerning the growth and harvesting of cotton and flax, as well as the manufacture of cotton and linen cloth; and they also learned a great deal about the geography and history of areas where flax and cotton are grown. In addition, they investigated the composition of several man-made fibers, studied economics relating to supply and demand, as well as the practice of competition through "underselling," and completed a unit on design for art.

It is obvious that this teacher and her students designed a curriculum for at least half the academic year which related to selecting new curtains. This embodies what Progressives meant by a child-centered problem-solving curriculum. The curriculum in this example was effectively oriented toward the children's interests and needs. Traditional exposure to time-honored subject matter categories gave way in this situation to an interdisciplinary and selective view of subject matter. Progressives saw educational approaches like the one in this example as especially effective, because kids obviously could determine the relevance of all subject matter they investigated to the problem they wanted to solve. One could, of course, have at least one or two youngsters so tired of relating everything to curtains that they might secretly wish to set fire to the new draperies when they were completed—that is, *if* the curtains ever were completed and hung.

(3) *Education should be life itself rather than a preparation for living*. Experimentalists and Progressives would see the curtain example above as embodying this third principle. Presumably the instructor did not have to give a sales pitch, such as, "Wouldn't it be great to learn about the manufacture of linen so that if you ever go to Ireland you'll be able to appreciate a major aspect of the Irish economy?" Essentialists had always been in the habit of selling subject matter by making it seem that, as an adult, one would desperately need the information. Progressives, on the other hand, were determined that the school environment could be effectively infused with real-life situations; thus students would understand immediately why they would need to know certain information while they investigated problems meaningful to them as people. And that's what the curtain example was designed to accomplish. Buying curtains was indubitably a real-life situation, one which could be used as a springboard to a comprehensive curriculum designed cooperatively by both teacher and students.

Detractors of this real-life stance, however, sometimes asked probing questions about the differences between life and school. Since the school was supposed to consist of real-life problems, why have a school? Why couldn't students just learn from real-life problems in real life? The ideal, of course, was mastery of what John Dewey called "critical thinking skills" while youngsters solved problems which they saw as meaningful. In other words, outside school problems are likely to be solved solely by trial-and-error means. For example, suppose a car refuses to start on an icy morning and the driver looks first at the battery. Since the driver discovers right away that not enough fire is coming from the battery, he borrows a neighbor's jumper cable to start the car. Then he rushes to work, knowing that he will soon have to buy a new battery. He has a battery installed that same day and, no doubt, fails to feel guilty that he did not take the extra time to list mentally five other possible hypotheses for his difficulty and analyze them thoroughly, while shivering in sub-zero temperatures. In other words, he solved this difficulty solely by trial-and-error. His first trial worked and, therefore, he saw no need to stand around intellectualizing about additional possibilities.

But school, according to John Dewey and to Progressives, is the place where this intellectualizing about real life should occur (and probably the only place where it might even be likely to occur). Thus, an educator begins with a real-life problem which kids find meaningful, and then proceeds to build the skills of critical thinking: i.e., formulating generalizations, analyzing those generalizations for accuracy, and making rational choices. For instance, one might begin with the simple problem of boiling an egg for a class which, during Dewey's time, would probably have been called "domestic science." One must not, however, stop intellectualizing once the egg had been boiled. In fact, this problem should be used to introduce students to an analysis of chemical changes which occur in the albumen and yolk during cooking. Youngsters should be stimulated to investigate alternate ways of preparing the egg and compare each method in terms of its effect on the nutritional value of the egg when served. William Heard Kilpatrick, an eminent popularizer of Dewey's thinking through what he termed the "project method" of directing classroom research, felt that such a strong emphasis on intellectualizing about every problem (the kind of emphasis typical of the curtain and the egg examples previously described) was a bit unnecessary.

(4) *The teacher's role is not to direct but to advise.* And what does it mean in practice to be effective as an adviser rather than as a director? William Heard Kilpatrick and other exponents of Dewey's position at Columbia University were quite successful as teacher-advisers. Ms. Progresso was ready with information about trusts when youngsters saw its relevance to their understanding of competition through "underselling." She kept up a steady flow of probing questions which stimulated analysis of generalizations once students had contributed their statements. As we have noted earlier, however, this kind of environmental management in which a teacher attempts to be prepared to field any questions students decide to investigate can be energy-draining. It brings to mind that old cartoon which was advanced as an unfortunate parody of the entire Progressive movement. In the cartoon an exhausted young teacher was shown surrounded by a number of wistful-looking students. One student mustered.enough courage to utter the immortal line: "Teacher, do we *have* to do what we want to do today?" But how could teacher preparation institutions instruct those about to enter the profession in appropriate techniques for being successful, non-directive teacher-advisers, while at the same time avoiding exhaustion, hypertension, or insanity?

Those teacher educators who were, and are, less talented than Kilpatrick have often been accused of divorcing method from content. It would be difficult indeed to explain what Ms. Progresso did in purely abstract terms, without any reference to the specific classroom dialogue based on those 1908 catalogue pages. But sometimes when other educators tried to convey information about the performance of an educational reformer like Kilpatrick, disastrous changes, due to misinterpretations, occurred in the reform message. Although Kilpatrick was an exceptionally potent reformer, inescapable constraints of time and space allowed him to serve as a model for only a select group of teachers. Those educators who tried to carry the reform message sometimes felt that their only alternative was to talk about the technique in the abstract, rather than attempt to exemplify it in a demonstration lesson built around stimulating curriculum materials. At worst, such educators have been accused of giving impassioned lectures on the evils of giving lectures. At any rate, Progressivism's message often suffered because talking about its pedagogical creed in the abstract led to considerable confusion.

That confusion was perhaps heightened by John Dewey's own style of writing and of presentation. That is, Dewey himself tended to divorce method and content. Some of his writing seems to cry out for examples that would make his position truly understandable to the world at large. The same point should be evident by this time in our own discussion, because we have had to qualify and enlarge upon what Dewey and his followers meant by the concepts of problem-solving, child-centeredness, and real-life situations. In fact, some of the definitions to which Progressives ascribed bordered on having a circular quality. Dewey's own definition of education may serve as a case in point: "Education is that reconstruction or reorganization of experience which adds to the meaning of experience and which increases the ability to direct the course of subsequent experience."

But Dewey was a brilliant theoretician who was concerned about the nature of thought processes. He was so concerned about thought processes that sometimes, while giving lectures at Columbia, he became so enamored by his own train of thought that he would simply forget to keep talking, or so the story goes! Many thought they were following Dewey's position, especially in the development of vocational educational programs; therefore, they were more than a little chagrined to find that Dewey himself would sometimes denounce their efforts soon after the reports of a particular innovation became widely known. It is, then, perhaps appropriate that Dewey's dictum, "With friends like these, who needs enemies?" has turned into such a famous line.

Nevertheless, despite the successes or failures of teacher preparation efforts among Progressives, the goal of teacher-adviser still holds its power. The goal still concerns skillful management of the learning environment, so that students will want to investigate and grow cooperatively with the teacher and with each other.

(5) *The school should encourage cooperation rather than competition.* In fact, competition is viewed as permissible only when it encourages growth. Progressives were convinced that traditional grading and promotion practices advocated by Essentialists were embodiments of crass Social Darwinist principles, because they were designed to weed out the academically and socially unfit from the educational establishment. In contrast to

what they saw as a Social Darwinist emphasis on unhealthy competition, Progressives stressed the cooperative sharing of information. In addition, Progressives often emphasized that grading practices should not be based solely on a student's ability to meet a predetermined standard, but should also consider the student's personal improvement relative to a standard or to a skill objective. Most of these differences hinged on the different connotations Progressives and Essentialists gave to the concept democracy. Essentialists of that day tended to emphasize the "struggle in the free marketplace of ideas" as the essence of democracy; therefore, they looked upon stiff competition as desirable. Progressives, on the other hand, when considering the concept democracy, emphasized what one receives immediately after a "struggle in the free marketplace of ideas." For Progressives, consensus represented the most desirable element of democracy—a consensus which comes cooperatively through the open discussion of alternatives, after which a workable course of action is chosen with sound insights about possible consequences.

(6)  *Only democracy permits—indeed, encourages—the free interplay of ideas and personalities which is a necessary condition for true growth.*  To Progressives, democracy was based on a shared experience, and that shared experience had to be made workable for classrooms if democracy were to be truly meaningful. That is, kids could not really learn to function effectively in a democracy, if all their classroom experiences had been lived under an autocracy, no matter how beneficent the autocrats. Their idea of democracy in classrooms goes back to child-centeredness and problem-solving and to a setting in which a teacher-adviser and a group of students interact to construct the most appropriate curriculum for themselves and for their needs. In fact, this ideal of the classroom as democracy was based on another key element of Progressivism—namely, pupil-teacher planning. The practice of pupil-teacher planning, however, caused such a storm of controversy that we need now to look briefly at the history of pupil-teacher planning efforts; we will also examine how Progressives' connotations for the concept democracy fared in the world at large. This discussion will reveal that Progressives ultimately splintered into two groups, due to different emphases on pupil-teacher planning and on democracy as consensus.

## HISTORICAL ANTECEDENTS

Throughout the previous section on philosophic principles we have been using two terms—Progressive and Experimentalist—which, for practical purposes, are almost interchangeable. However, the term "Progressive" usually implies a definite period in educational history, from the early translation of John Dewey's ideas into action in his laboratory school at University of Chicago through the Progressive Education Association's demise in 1957. We now need to examine factors which transformed Progressives into Experimentalists.

Although John Dewey (1859–1952) has been viewed as the veritable embodiment of Progressivism, his work has been even more influential, perhaps because it meshed with many other trends which ultimately helped to popularize his ideas. Joseph Mayer Rice, as Lawrence Cremin explained in *Transformation of the Schools,* has probably been too often overlooked as a source of preparation for the public's willingness to accept Dewey as the nation's educational soothsayer. A pediatrician by profession, Rice expressed his sophisticated lay interest in education by a series of articles for *The Forum* magazine during the 1890s (not the current *Forum* publication filled with risqué advice and photography, but a magazine highly respected for investigative reporting and creative journalism). Rice had been especially distressed with the uninspired curriculum of many schools in this country during his tour of establishment education which Walter Hines Page, the editor of *The Forum*, had sponsored. He was given explicit instructions to place "no reliance whatever" on reports by school officials in preparing his series of articles on the current state of schooling. (Rice had originally spent the years 1888 through 1890 studying pedagogy in Leipzig and Jena at his own expense; and a column he did for a small New York weekly led ultimately to a new career with *The Forum*). Rice's work built on feelings about educational reform which a number of industrialists had voiced ever since the success of a Russian vocational education exhibit at the Philadelphia Exposition of 1876. He was convinced that Americans wanted to profit by Russian efforts to give education a more practical flavor.

Rice knew he would find many sympathetic ears in his attempts to reacquaint Americans with the benefits of practical learning. As Daniel Boorstin has so succinctly reminded us in *The Americans: The Colonial Experience*, immigrants to these shores since the seventeenth century have been forced, partly because of the challenges of "talent-short" societies, to emphasize the pragmatic when it came to knowledge acquisition. Whereas Western Europeans by the seventeenth and eighteenth centuries had become accustomed to looking upon learning as the province of experts—as being locked up in a university and not directly accessible to those who were not experts—Americans saw no need to pay homage to a hierarchy of learned professionals. For most Americans, knowledge seemed totally accessible because it surrounded them completely. If one wanted to learn about the *flora* and *fauna* of North America, one simply went out and interacted with the environment of North America to gain the appropriate information. At any rate, there was no overwhelming tendency to feel one first had to study the *flora* and *fauna* of Europe to get the proper background before one could proceed to study biology as it applied to this continent. In fact, such an idea of acquiring the proper background would seem ludicrous to the colonist, whose major concern for knowing about the wilderness usually centered around elemental problems of survival; they had no time or inclination to study classifications of *flora* and *fauna* as presented in textbooks. Although many colonists did not want completely to forsake literary learnings for utilitarian information-gathering, even the emphasis on literary scholarship was often seen as serving some practical end; for instance, the attempt to cultivate and maintain religious sentiment through combining knowledge of theology and literature.

### James and "Games" in Philosophy?

William James (1842–1910) gave voice to this American fascination with the practical and utilitarian through his writings on Pragmatism, a philosophical position which Daniel Boorstin has insisted is unique to North America. James and his followers wished to apply the test of "workability" to whatever men chose to call "truth." Hence, the phrase "cash value" of an idea was frequently used to popularize the notion that "truth" should be "tested" to determine its appropriateness for particular conditions of time and place.

The major reason no truth was seen as an absolute commodity concerned the Pragmatist's concept of a fluid universe. In fact, to Pragmatists the universe was always in process and had none of the qualities of permanence usually associated with the concept of structure. Those items in the physical world which appeared to have a permanent structure (the Rocky Mountains, for instance) only looked that way because the process of change operating upon them was proceeding slowly. However, the Rocky Mountains are truly in the process of change by wind and water erosion, just as a river is in the process of change by the action of its currents, except that the changes in the Rockies are so subtle that they are scarcely noticed by humans.

This fluidity was not limited to entities in the physical world; in fact, a condition of flux was viewed as characteristic of the world of ideas. It was particularly due to this constant ebb and flow in the realm of ideas that any "truth" had to stand a test of "workability" by being translated into application. This procedure of testing an idea's "cash value" could, perhaps somewhat curiously and illogically, be applied even in the realm of spiritual realities. For instance, the idea of a personal Creator could be considered in terms of its "cash value." If there were no creative force in the universe, but one believed in a Creator, then the believer might be no better nor worse off after this existence. However, if one were to believe in a Creator and find after death that his belief had been warranted, then the "cash value" of his faith might be infinite. Therefore, belief in a creative force might be assumed to be worth the risk.

Despite this somewhat crude example of applying a test of "workability" to spiritual "truths," the Pragmatist's universal tendency to evaluate and re-evaluate knowledge, both in the physical and spiritual realms, cannot be overemphasized. Ideas had to be translated into application through interaction with the environment. This bond between the learner and his environment, a bond usually referred to as "experience," was viewed as responsible for the production of knowledge. Knowledge could never exist merely as an abstract entity, because knowledge was thought to be inseparable from its relevance to specific environmental conditions of time and place.

## Dewey and "Doing"

To all this thinking about knowledge wedded to experience, John Dewey added a new emphasis—the emphasis on consensus made possible through the shared validation of "truth." John Dewey's phenomenal rise as educational soothsayer happened to occur at a time when, as Rush Welter's *Popular Education and Democratic Thought in America* has reminded us, Americans were just beginning to see some of the pitfalls of using the English college model of higher education to impart learning and to perform *in loco parentis*. Thus, they were fastening their hopes on universities, in which the duty of scholarly research was regarded as perhaps even more sacred than the duty of teaching. First among the new models for higher education was Johns Hopkins in Baltimore, an institution fashioned on the ideals of research scholarship advocated by the leaders in German universities. It was to Johns Hopkins that Dewey went during the 1880s to complete the requirements for the degree of doctor of philosophy. It is, therefore, not surprising that Dewey was exposed at Johns Hopkins to German thinkers, and that he was ultimately strongly influenced by the philosophy of Georg Wilhelm Friedrich Hegel (1770–1831).

Most students are more familiar with an adaptation of Hegelian thinking, an adaptation made by Karl Marx which is usually referred to as "dialectical materialism," than with John Dewey's synthesis of Hegelian thought. But we will explore later in this chapter the peculiarly perverse connection some political leaders in this country from the 1930s through the 1950s were anxious to make between Marx and Dewey. It is, however, important at this point to remember that Hegel himself had been influenced by the Socratic and Platonic concept of the dialectic. That is, Hegel systematized the notions held by Plato and Socrates concerning ultimate agreement which any two people would reach through dialogue, if they had adequate time and skill to question each other and themselves about the nature of spiritual realities. The earlier use of the dialectic in Socratic dialogues envisioned ultimate agreement because spiritual truths were absolute and unchanging. If people talked about questions regarding spiritual reality long enough, they were bound to agree because spiritual truths were seen as absolutes and because before birth one's soul was in direct contact with those same unchanging spiritual truths.

Of course, Dewey was not interested in the quality of absolute truth in the spiritual realm. He was interested, instead, in how people might apply tests of "workability" to principles which could serve as "truths" in particular times and circumstances. Therefore, he chose to adopt Hegel's view of relationships among conflicting ideas. According to the Hegelian view, for every position (thesis) there is an opposite (antithesis). Promoting struggle between these two opposing positions regarding any issue would bring forth a new position (synthesis), which could be viewed as a "way station" on the approach to a consensus. That synthesis would become, in turn, a new thesis for an opposite position (antithesis). Promoting rational discussion would then lead to another synthesis, which would be a little closer to consensus.

Dewey took this model for conflicting ideas and stressed not the conflict, but the synthesis in terms of its usefulness in promoting consensus. In other words, his ultimate faith was that one could always resolve the conflicts in what appeared to be opposite positions, if one thought about the issues carefully and skillfully. A few of Dewey's titles take on new meaning when viewed in terms of the "thesis—antithesis—synthesis" model: *The School and Society* (1899); *The Child and the Curriculum* (1906); *Democracy and Education* (1916); *Experience and Nature* (1925); *Freedom and Culture* (1939). In each of these books Dewey proposed a new synthesis for apparent opposites.

The key to Dewey's influence was not just that he emphasized consensus after a struggle in the "marketplace of free ideas." Dewey also emphasized consensus in the context of the classroom as a living, working democracy and, thereby, enhanced the status of teachers, while promoting respect for the almost mystical art/science that is truly creative teaching.

## Eight Years to Decide?

What Dewey considered truly creative teaching has often been seen as embodied by pupil-teacher planning techniques contained in the Core Curriculum designs which were examined thoroughly in the Progressive

Education Association's mammoth Eight-Year Study. Core Curriculum designs provided the setting in which Dewey's followers envisioned an emphasis on consensus made possible by the shared validation of "truth."

It is a supreme irony that the voluminous and persuasive data on 1,475 matched pairs of students (each member from a school in the Eight-Year Study was paired with a member from a conventional school) has been largely ignored. This data clearly showed that the more closely schools participating in the study adhered to programs like the Core Curriculum, the greater was the success of their graduates in college, both for academic and extracurricular endeavors. Those not familiar with what was perhaps the best documented and most thoroughly studied of all experiments in education are often quite shocked that the five-volume report of the Progressive Education Association's Eight-Year Study had so little impact.[1]

And just what was the Eight-Year Study, and what was so magically effective about Core Curriculum designs? Between 1932 and 1939, the Progressive Education Association sponsored a massive study which included follow-up investigations on the college performance of graduates from thirty innovative high schools. These thirty schools had faculty members who worked with representatives from the PEA on many possible techniques for implementing John Dewey's ideas on the secondary school level. PEA officials also supported these spirited reform efforts by securing the promise of a number of prominent colleges and universities that graduates from these thirty high schools in the Eight-Year Study would be accepted into degree programs, without regard to traditional admission requirements. Out of these cooperative circumstances came the follow-up studies on 1,475 matched pairs of students—matched, that is, according to sex, socioeconomic level, interests, and several other variables, but differing in the type of high school preparation they had received. One member of each pair came from one of the thirty innovative schools with Core Curriculum designs; the other member of each pair came from a conventional high school, with the traditional system of required courses in which each course represented an academic discipline, as seen by experts in each subject matter field.

Perhaps our question about the nature of Core Curriculum designs can best be answered by the following "Proposal for an Updated Core Curriculum." Actually, this proposal is my own creation, but it follows closely the designs from the Eight-Year Study, as indicated in the footnotes. It involves my own attempt to avoid some potential disasters of pupil-teacher planning by teaching students and instructors the Great Books Foundation's systems of categorizing research questions and by employing certain values clarification techniques for dealing with controversial issues. Moreover, the proposal is true to the spirit of all Core Curriculum designs in the Eight-Year

Study, because they all emphasize pupil-teacher planning. Thus, this particular design is one I would like to see implemented and studied in depth.

## Proposal for an Updated Core Curriculum

I. Credo
   A. (stated positively) "The ideal curriculum makes functional use of the immediate and the contemporary, mobilizing the historical and the fundamental to help the student reach intelligent decisions about those things which concern him now."[2]
   B. (stated negatively) ". . . . [A] strong case can be made for the charge that anticipating needs may cause psychological scars which will hinder learning in the future when the need actually exists. . . . The pupil who dislikes history, the girl who hates science, the student who becomes physically ill over his mathematics problems—all may have been thus turned against fields of learning which they might otherwise have found exciting and valuable."[3]
II. Nature of the Proposal
   A. Establish "core" classes for students in grades 10, 11, and 12.
      1. Group students heterogeneously.
      2. "Core" students and teachers should use the question classification system advocated by the Great Books Foundation and values clarification techniques to plan a curriculum based on social demands and adolescent needs.[4] Units of study would be grouped under one or more of the following categories:
         a. protecting life and health
         b. making a home
         c. getting a living
         d. expressing religious impulses
         e. satisfying desires for beauty and recreation
         f. securing education
         g. cooperating in social and civic action
         h. improving material conditions[5]
      3. "Core" classes would last the length of two conventional class periods, and each team of "core" teachers would work with only two "core" classes.
      4. Students in a "core" class should have the same team of "core" teachers for grades 10, 11, and 12.
      5. "Core" courses should replace the state English and social studies requirements for high school graduation, and no other specific courses should be required in senior high school except for the prescription that students should take at least two, but not more than three, courses in addition to the "core" each academic year.

6. "Core" teachers should counsel students so that interests emerging in the "core," as well as skill shortcomings, can be dealt with in elective courses. All elective courses are to be taken when the student and "core" teacher agree that such electives would be appropriate to follow up interests manifested within "core" work.

7. After carefully explaining to students the purposes of "core" curriculum design and its usefulness, tenth graders should begin with a consideration of utopian societies.

   a. Suggested utopian works:
   Plato's *Republic*
   More's *Utopia*
   Bellamy's *Looking Backward*
   Skinner's *Walden II*

   b. Analyze utopian works according to methods each society used in dealing with the eight problem categories as outlined in #2 above.

   c. Have students compare suggestions for dealing with problem categories (as outlined above) in utopian societies, and what they would like to propose as solutions to those same problems today. (Or begin the process with student suggestions before considering the utopian works, if that is more appropriate for the group in question.)

   d. Use the comparison between contemporary problems and utopian solutions to investigate issues of concern—a process which should be continued in "core" classes until near the end of grade 12 (when the following unit should be considered).

8. Have twelfth graders complete their "core" work by considering the following volumes (or similar ones) and making predictions about how man might best solve contemporary problems under the eight categories as listed in #2 above.
   Orwell's *1984*
   Huxley's *Brave New World*
   Toffler's *Future Shock*

III. Nature of In-Service Education for "Core" Curriculum
   A. Qualifications for "core" teachers:
      1. A genuine fondness for students and optimism about their capabilities.
      2. A friendly, outgoing personality.
      3. Belief in Gestalt learning theories (reflective thinking), as stated in the Credo above.
      4. A major in English and/or social studies with a broad background in general liberal arts education.
   B. Summer workshop (for a six weeks' session prior to beginning the program in the fall).
      1. Review of Gestalt learning theories.

2. Training in approaches for pupil-teacher planning:
   a. use of an A-V aid on a content area to get students to formulate questions they would like to investigate.
   b. classification of questions as interpretive, factual, or evaluative (according to Great Books Foundation prescriptions).[6]
   c. cooperative effort by students and teachers of choosing questions and putting them into a unit framework for guiding research.
3. Training in values clarification techniques:[7]
   a. values clarifying responses
   b. value sheets concerning a wide variety of subject matter problems
   c. values clarification discussion
   d. thought sheets
   e. action projects
   f. simulation
4. Construction of resource units (as many as time will permit) for potential issues under each of the eight problem categories in II-2, so that "core" teachers will have adequate preparation to feel secure, but retain enough flexibility to engage in meaningful pupil-teacher planning.
5. Consideration of techniques for reporting (recording) the nature of the units studied, objectives set, activities engaged in, and evaluation processes used so that a resource center for "core" teachers can be available.[8]

Pupil-teacher planning, the key element of Core Curriculum designs, was to be the means whereby traditional subject matter categories were to be eliminated, as well as the process which allowed students a voice in making their own curriculum. In fact, the pupil-teacher planning procedure would assure relevance because it would automatically relate curriculum content to student experience. That is, the process would assure relevance if handled skillfully; if teachers were uncomfortable with pupil-teacher planning attempts, however, the technique could indubitably be disastrous.

What help did those Progressives associated with the Eight-Year Study offer to teachers who might want to feel confident in their use of pupil-teacher planning? They studiously avoided presenting formulas for pupil-teacher planning, because they feared formulas would destroy spontaneity.[9] In other words, the leading Progressives of the day were willing to leave to teachers the disconcerting management and administrative problems of trying to field any question students may decide to bring up; in addition, they were quite willing to have teachers bear this energy drain of completely constructing curriculum materials in the name of assuring spontaneity! Contemporary Experimentalists are quite familiar with the energy drain problem, but at least they are not constructing curriculum materials almost entirely from scratch, as were those Core Curriculum teachers during the 1930s.

At any rate, the Core Curriculum and pupil-teacher planning were to Dewey and his followers twin pillars of classroom democracy in action. But the fact that Dewey's concept of democracy stressed the possibility for consensus and cooperation as being more important than the elements of *laissez-faire* competition and struggle brought certain fears about social planning to the minds of many citizens. As evident in the "Proposal for an Updated Core Curriculum," the analyses of utopian societies would seem to be based on the assumption that perhaps large numbers of citizens might be able to plan a better society, especially a better economy. (Interestingly, the heyday of Progressivism coincided with the Great Depression.)

The following excerpt from a manual on conducting summer workshops for teachers who want to use Progressive techniques highlights a number of fears about social planning and about economic uncertainties:

> Another side of the practice of democracy is increased attention to the problems of our democracy as they exist outside of school. A large part of the work of these pupils is related in one way or another to the central problem which they face as citizens and workers: "How shall we provide for our common needs?" They are beginning to realize that the majority of our people have poor food, poor homes, poor family life, poor health, inadequate medical care, unwholesome recreation, and generally unsatisfactory lives. They realize that they, too, run the risks of unemployment, poverty, injustice, sickness, and war. They realize also that our people are wasting their resources and starving in the midst of potential plenty, and that their own generation could live abundantly if they only set about it with the degree of intelligence and social cohesion which they exhibit in planning their work in school.[10]

Obviously pupil-teacher planning had the potential for drawing students outside classrooms, while helping them focus on inequalities and injustices in the world at large.

## Progressing and Progressive

The fears, injustices, and inequalities of the 1930s bred investigation of many possible remedies—and not all those remedies were considered to be from the mainstream. Some, like Father Coughlin's "Share the Wealth" scheme, were based on a collection of ideas from Marxian Socialism. Our contemporaries sometimes tend to forget that the peculiar stresses of the Great Depression encouraged a number of intellectuals, as well as charlatans, to re-examine the doctrines of Karl Marx.

People were beginning to fear that Dewey's democracy in the classroom might not be many steps removed from social planning and Marxism. In the 1940s a mid-Atlantic State's Department of Education began producing a new curriculum guide for the social studies based on the latest Progressivist principles. The guide not only included a unit on telephone manners and communication, but also included some controversial phrases which underscored the plight of "citizens and workers." Within a short time after being issued, these curriculum guides were recalled and were ultimately burned. After all, such phrases about the "working classes" smacked of Marxism; so did the theme of "social injustice." Of course, Marx was a Hegelian, but so was John Dewey.

These fears about Marxism, coupled with the war effort which brought its own excesses when the Eight-Year Study was concluded, helped make it easy to overlook the five volumes of reports about benefits which could result from Core Curriculum designs. Perhaps many of our contemporaries have forgotten how economic anxieties in the 1930s prompted some, whose careers were just beginning to burgeon, to become members of organizations whose purposes and ideals were somewhat Marxist. Senator Joseph McCarthy didn't forget, however, and he succeeded in forging political clout from what many in the 1950s had assumed to be long-dead issues. However, McCarthy was making accusations about Communist ideological tendencies against those whose careers had begun in the turbulent 1930s.

These fears and anxieties about economics and about the tendency of classroom democracy to pull youngsters into the larger world of social injustice had its effect on the Progressive Movement. As early as the late 1930s, when the implications of pupil-teacher planning had been explored, and as late as 1957 with the Progressive Education Association's demise, two trends within the ranks of Progressivism were discernible. One trend emphasized the problems of pedagogy by stressing methodologies as ends in themselves and by focusing on the status of those who could practice skillfully the art/science of teaching. This is what John Dewey, William Heard Kilpatrick, and others did. They tended to talk about classroom democracy as "shared experience," with "shared experience" as a necessary condition of "true growth," although they did not explore fully the social overtones of their doctrines. In other words, they did not dwell on the question: growth toward what? They were not willing to push the implications of pupil-teacher planning outside classroom walls. Group members with similar tendencies are now called "Experimentalists."

But there was another group one could discern within Progressivism as early as the 1930s. This group sought to answer the question: growth toward what? In fact, they wanted to define the "good society" and move on to the business of using Progressivist teaching strategies with captive audiences in schools in their attempt to bring forth a more perfect world. Group members, originally led by George Counts and Harold Rugg and now represented by Theodore Brameld, are currently called "Reconstructionists."

## THE EXPERIMENTALIST ROLE MODEL AND THE TEACHER

Remember Ms. Progresso and the catalogue lesson? She seemed to enjoy having students decide which generalizations the class would analyze, or having students design the curriculum with her as the lesson proceeded. Perhaps the latter phrase is more accurate, because her willingness to follow students' desires in learning meant that she was allowing kids to help her design a portion of the curriculum.

### Natural Strengths and Weaknesses of Experimentalist Teaching

Remember Mrs. Précis from the preceding chapter—the sixth grade teacher whose extreme Essentialist position permitted her to use corporal punishment and to deliver frightening lectures on patriotism? Her behavior represented an immoderate, and somewhat irresponsible, adaptation of the Essentialist Role Model. Although we did not attach a specific personality to someone implementing a Core Curriculum design, the "Proposal for an Updated Core" represents something comparable to an extreme position for the Experimentalist Role Model. Many pre-service and in-service teachers could comfortably make a series of lessons similar to Ms. Progresso's catalogue exercise, to typify their teaching behaviors. Perhaps those same teachers, however, would decline to participate in any scheme which would have as its rather grandiose aim cooperative pupil-teacher planning for development of a complete curriculum. That might be seen as going too far with attempts to relate curriculum content to students' experiences; it might also bring up those anxieties about management problems that result when a teacher tries to follow students' interests, yet in the end burns out from too many minute plans.

### Who Wants to Manage Committees?

Whatever cluster of behaviors a teacher may adopt, the model must feel comfortable: that is, it must fit the teacher's personality. Suppose, for example, a teacher tries the Experimentalist Role Model. A teacher may begin by thinking he or she wants to allow students to help design the curriculum, and thus become the teacher-adviser for students' research projects. Then the teacher may discover that he or she does not like the strain of maintaining a number of activities simultaneously, or the noise generated by those activities, or the feeling that students are only learning that everything is so relativistic that one person's opinion is as good as another. Such a situation would mean that it is time to re-evaluate one's philosophy and role model; this re-evaluation may help the teacher to grow in new directions.

### Process and Product?

Those new directions may involve a solution of complex management difficulties by adopting the Essentialist problem-solver's stance. Remember our example described earlier in this chapter concerning how Ms. Chronicler might have taught Ms. Progresso's catalogue lesson? Ms. Chronicler chose to emphasize both the process by which information is learned and the specific information which served as the product. That is, she decided in advance that kids would learn how mail-order catalogue businesses bridged the gap between a factory and distant consumers. Then she rewarded student responses which closely approximated the information she planned to have the kids discover. At any rate, the Essentialist problem-solver's position has proven attractive to many who wish to emphasize process while, at the same time, maintaining control over the product which is taught. Some teachers may decide to choose this role model.

However, another teacher may find the Reconstructionist Role Model more to his or her liking, because it begins with Experimentalist techniques, but ultimately departs from those techniques to give students clear directions about necessary social reforms. At any rate, the real danger after adopting a philosophical stance is a teacher's refusal to re-evaluate his or her position and the role model adopted; another, perhaps worse, danger is that a teacher may be unaware that other role models exist.

In the next chapter we will discuss Reconstructionism. Reconstructionism gives the students a voice in curriculum design, while it simultaneously encourages teachers to give honest opinions about appropriate courses of action for reform.

### Notes

1. See the following:
   Wilford Aikin, *Adventure in American Education Vol. I: The Story of the Eight Year Study* (New York: Harper and Brothers, 1942).

H. H. Giles, S. P. McCutchen, and A. N. Zechiel, *Adventure in American Education Vol. II: Exploring the Curriculum* (New York: Harper and Brothers, 1942).

Eugene R. Smith and Ralph W. Tyler, *Adventure in American Education Vol. III: Appraising and Recording Student Progress* (New York: Harper and Brothers, 1942).

Dean Chamberlin, Enid Chamberlin, Neal E. Drought, and William E. Scott, *Adventure in American Education Vol. IV: Did They Succeed in College?* (New York: Harper and Brothers, 1942).

Progressive Education Association, *Adventure in American Education Vol. V: Thirty Schools Tell Their Story* (New York: Harper and Brothers, 1943).

2. H. H. Giles, S. P. McCutchen, and A. N. Zechiel, *Adventure in American Education Vol. II: Exploring the Curriculum* (New York: Harper and Brothers, 1942), p. 83.

3. *Ibid.*, pp. 84–85.

4. Great Books Foundation, *A Manual for Co-Leaders* (Chicago: The Great Books Foundation, 1968), pp. 14–27.

5. Giles, McCutchen, Zechiel, *op. cit.*, p. 74.

6. Great Books Foundation, *op. cit.*

7. Louis Raths, Merrill Harmin, and Sidney Simon, *Values and Teaching* (Columbus: Charles Merrill Publishing Co., 1966).

8. For a more complete treatment see Lloyd Duck, "Pupil-Teacher Planning in Open-Space Secondary Schools," *Education*, Spring, 1978, pp. 301–306.

9. Kenneth L. Heaton, William G. Camp, and Paul B. Diederich, *Professional Education for Experienced Teachers: The Program of the Summer Workshop* (Chicago: University Press, 1940), pp. 25–29. See also H. H. Giles, *Teacher-Pupil Planning* (New York: Harper and Brothers, 1941), p. 73.

10. Heaton, Camp, Diederich, *op. cit.*, p. 115.

# THE RECONSTRUCTIONIST TEACHER
## as "Experimentalist-Turned-Reformer"

# CHAPTER FOUR

*The Setting:*

## MR. REMONDE WORRIES ABOUT CLUB ROME'S PREDICTIONS FOR UTOPIA OR OBLIVION

Mr. Remonde had been recently disturbed by the glum prognoses of that group of scientists known as "Club Rome," and he found it impossible to banish from memory all those graphs with steeply inclining "demand" curves shown in conjunction with plummeting "resource" curves. Newspaper clippings about Club Rome always pained him with recollections of helpless anger and impotence he used to feel during the energy crisis when he would make himself drive out on bone-cold mornings to begin waiting in line for five gallons of gasoline.

Waiting in line had given him plenty of time to worry about the wisdom of his recent move from a fairly rural setting to the suburbs of a large city. He remembered being concerned enough to speculate about having perhaps placed the future happiness and well-being of his family in considerable jeopardy and to enumerate possible solutions. During one of these pre-dawn vigils he recalled having come up with the ultimate solution and began to feel quite smug about his cleverness in licking a cowardly dependence on machines. If worse came to worse, and all gasoline supplies were exhausted, he would bundle up his family in their warmest clothes, pack the barest necessities, and hike the hundred miles or so back to the farm—treating it all as a new adventure in camping, which he knew the kids would love. He would calmly explain that after the hike they would all be partners in growing their own food, making their own clothing, and so forth—in short, their very own "back to nature" enterprise. This scheme satisfied him, until he rather unwisely told a colleague about his plans. The colleague's rejoinder, "Yes, but do you have any seeds?" rudely woke him to the brutal fact that he not only had no seeds, but that he also had no know-how about farming. He consoled himself with the slender hope that there must be a more perfect solution, but that remained his only consolation because the more perfect solution kept eluding him.

It was this painful and personalized question, "Yes, but do you have any seeds?" that he continued to remember after reading about Club Rome. As an educator, he decided he had some measure of responsibility to help kids sort through their feelings about technology and declining energy resources, particularly since he kept remembering his own feelings of inadequacy which had haunted him since the days of acute gasoline shortage. In researching the history of Club Rome for his proposed unit of instruction, Mr. Remonde found an encouraging sentiment expressed in a *Saturday Re-*

*view* (August 24, 1974) editorial, titled "Prophecy and Pessimism." The writer's rather heartwarming thesis was that pessimism itself might be its own corrective against an impending doom. If everyone could become sufficiently aware of the certainty of crises stemming from overpopulation and from declining food and energy resources to become truly depressed and pessimistic, then perhaps something would be done to avoid doom. At any rate, Mr. Remonde determined that he might be able to turn his students' anxieties about population crises and food crises to more productive ends than the wastefulness of inactivity and feelings of impotence about unresolvable world problems. To him, the key to this increased productivity, which might be the by-product of pessimism, would be an awareness and acceptance of the proposition that world problems of unprecedented scope must be attacked with world solutions. Mr. Remonde decided that his mission would be to convince students, and perhaps even their parents, that only a powerful world government could effect solutions to crises of overpopulation, famine, and decreasing energy reserves.

To Mr. Remonde, helping to convince people that powerful world government offers the best hope for survival would be no small task. Crisis must be presented in terms personal enough to awaken in students the same kinds of feelings he had experienced due to the remark made by his colleague. But how can kids be helped to see that in many ways their own technology-dependent lifestyles may be as fragile as the existence of those who rely on uncertain and ineffective farming methods for barely enough food to subsist? He thought he had found the most appropriate vehicle for this lesson in the Wombat film, *Mila 23*.

*Mila 23* shows Simion, inhabitant of a small Rumanian fishing village whose houses are built on several tiny islands in swamps near the Danube's mouth, as he gives a tour to the film's narrator. The narrator, presumably a Western European city-dweller who is thoroughly enamored with technology, has trouble understanding how anyone could tolerate life in such a bleak and nondescript village as one whose name comes from the phrase "Settlement—23 kilometers from Danube mouth." The film's sparse dialogue results from conversations in which Simion and the narrator attempt to analyze the appeal of Mila 23's lifestyle. In this marshy setting reeds are almost everywhere, and they provide roofing for houses, fences for each island, and fuel for cooking and heating. The narrator wonders aloud to Simion why people do not desire to find alternatives to the reed. Simion affirms the villagers' satisfaction with their lot, and he remarks that they are better off now than previously and that it matters little whether a rich man provides a few necessities to supplement the reed, as was formerly the case, or whether the state provides those same necessities.

During a brief religious ceremony of the Eastern Orthodox Church the film's narrator poses the question, "Simion, why are you praying?" Implicit in Simion's remarks are many assumptions about the worth of relying on God and religion to foster continued prosperity, as opposed to depending on the machinations of technology to improve life. Simion talks about his fear of the city and technology, and he affirms his feelings of security about existence in Mila 23. He seems secure enough about the future to be mildly contemptuous of the narrator's lifestyle when he says, "Forgive me, but I believe it is only city people like yourself who have come to feel they 'have all the answers.'" As the screen darkens at the film's end, one statement appears and belies Simion's confidence: "Mila 23 no longer exists due to floods in the spring of 1970."

Let us see how Mr. Remonde's lesson fared, as we examine dialogue which occurred immediately after his students had viewed *Mila 23*. Just before showing the film Mr. Remonde asked that youngsters consider whether living in Mila would appeal to them and whether they might be concerned if there were no more communities like Mila 23.

## Classroom Dialogue for the Reconstructionist Role Model

*Mr. Remonde:*   How do you feel after watching *Mila 23*?
*Perry:*   I wouldn't want to go for a visit, and I'm sure I wouldn't live there!
*Rick:*   I don't know; it might not be so bad to live there. You'd be forced to learn to get by on just simple materials in the marsh. Lots of people wouldn't know how to use whatever is at hand from nature, and I really think it's great to be able to get by on whatever is just outside your front door. I know I'd like to be independent enough to do what Simion did.
*Mr. Remonde:*   Rick, suppose I told you Mila 23 had no survivors of those floods in 1970? Would that make a difference about how you feel?
*Rick:*   I'm not sure it would. We all take lots of chances—driving cars, flying, even just waiting to see if some guy's going to use the neutron bomb or other weapons. I think I'd just as soon take the chance of going in a natural disaster as getting killed in other ways.
*Pam:*   I just don't think I could be happy at Mila 23. Did you see that little girl—she couldn't have been more than three—hanging over the side of the boat when the kids were getting ready to be rowed to school? Lying on the side of the boat, she just dangled one foot in the water. And it must have been a cold day! She had on something that looked like a snow suit. And none of the adults seemed to notice her. It was just as if everybody expected to see three-year-olds hanging over the sides of boats like that! I don't think I'd want to bring up kids that way, with so few pleasures and so many dangers, I mean.
*Sandi:*   But maybe the kids really have a great time. Maybe they really do like the freedom of dangling over the sides of boats and living near the water.

> Just because we might not be happy there, that is no reason to think the kids in the film didn't have any pleasures.

*Mr. Remonde:*    I see. I must confess my own hangups, if you want to call them that, made me really anxious too about the little girl hanging over the side of the boat. I'm afraid I'd have all the anxieties of that city-dwelling narrator about what I might be doing to harm my children by moving to Mila 23.

*Gerald:*    As a kid I think I could have had enough fun living on the water so that I wouldn't even have missed TV very much! Mila doesn't seem bad to me at all.

*Mr. Remonde:*    Well, I expected you might have very different ideas about the prospects of living at Mila 23. But what about Mila 23 itself—are communities like that worth preserving as alternatives to the way we and that city-dwelling narrator live?

*Pam:*    Oh, sure. Just because I wouldn't want to live there doesn't mean I wouldn't care if there were no more places like it.

*Bob:*    I don't have any strong desire to go there now, but I might change my mind.

*Mr. Remonde:*    I see from your reactions, then, that most of you think communities like Mila 23 should continue to exist. How could we help them continue to exist?

*Bob:*    Build dams so you could control the floods!

*Pam:*    No, I think we just ought to let them alone. Building dams would take out some of the danger of living there that at least Rick and Gerald seem to like.

*Sandi:*    But why would you object if the government did something to make it safer to live there, like building dams, especially if the community is so fragile? It was wiped out by floods, and I thought we were talking about preserving a community that had a fragile kind of existence. Why shouldn't the government actively try to help preserve Mila and other places like it?

*Mr. Remonde:*    It's interesting that you should mention things the government might do. What advantages do you suppose people at Mila 23 had from being under the nation-state of Rumania? Might there be any disadvantages in being under the protection of a nation-state?

*Bob:*    I don't believe those people cared much one way or the other. Didn't Simion say it didn't make any difference to him whether the government or a rich man provided the few necessities they couldn't get from the environment?

*Pam:*    I know, but if the government built dams it would be changing the environment. That's the whole point, and I don't think Simion or any of them would want the government or anybody to to change their environment. They only want outsiders to provide things like cooking equipment and a few other supplies they can't make for themselves. They're certainly not asking the outside world for things that would change their environment—things like dams that might even keep the place from being a marsh, for instance.

*Sandi:*    You really are making the place sound fragile! Are you saying you can't do anything to help them at all? It seems that you just want the world to go away and leave them alone, except for providing a few items the people at Mila have already asked the outside world to give. Couldn't the government at least make some laws to help keep Mila the same; for instance, laws that might keep too many people from moving there?

*Pam:* No, I really do think that communities like this should be left alone. Anything the government tried to do would change the environment; even trying to keep too many people from moving there would be a bad idea because any regulation by the outside world would make things too artificial.

*Mr. Remonde:* We've certainly heard the gamut of suggestions about how to preserve communities like Mila—everything from building dams, to government regulations on population density, to leaving such communities alone. Is it possible to leave a community like Mila 23 alone?

*Perry:* It is for me, because I wouldn't want to go there!

*Pam:* I think it is. If people really want to preserve a place's charm and relationship with nature, then they decide it is better not to interfere.

*Mr. Remonde:* Do you think it might be possible for the government, or other interested parties, to wish to interfere because of other reasons than helping preserve Mila?

*Pam:* I'm not sure what you mean.

*Mr. Remonde:* Well, Mila is marshy and has all those reeds. Suppose some kinds of vegetation, which were ancestors of the present reeds, had remains which were converted into oil or coal thousands of years ago? Suppose the government decided they wished to use much more efficient techniques for harvesting fish from the Danube than methods practiced by Mila's fishermen, because of some impending crisis in the food supply.

*Pam:* So you're saying that under such circumstances Mila would have to go?

*Mr. Remonde:* I'd probably go so far as to say that the government might give no more than a passing thought to Mila's existence, if some crisis could be solved by using oil, coal, or food resources to be found on the site we saw in the film. Officials might, perhaps, help people of Mila relocate. In the long run, though, if you believe that Club Rome's predictions of overpopulation, worldwide famine, and declining resources are accurate, it is practically certain that the interests of Mila 23 and the nation-state would ultimately clash head-on.

*Rick:* But that would be a long time coming, wouldn't it?

*Mr. Remonde:* Not if you accept the projections of Club Rome! Such a state of affairs will almost certainly come before the end of this century, before, that is, any of you have settled comfortably into middle age. All you have to do is consult headlines about problems of famine in India, in Africa, in many third world nations. Even U.S. food surpluses are not so plentiful as before. You have from time to time mentioned the word "fragile" in our discussions of Mila. Do you think our society and life styles are less fragile in view of the Club Rome predictions? Will nation-states not resort to the use of nuclear weapons, when they know their stability is threatened because their people are starving and because they know they must secure adequate resources for survival, no matter what the cost?

We may not be as anxious about floods as those in Mila, but what about our anxieties over the atomic bomb, dwindling fuel supplies, soaring prices, the decline of the dollar, economic uncertainty in general? How panicky do we become, for instance, when we are deprived of electricity and must spend a few hours in darkness without it, especially in a large city? Is this situation what Simion was hinting at when he berated the narrator mildly because "city-dwellers think they have all the answers"? If we really do persist in following current lifestyles, until the supreme "back-to-nature" movement becomes a necessity because our energy resources have been totally consumed, who will be better equipped for survival—someone like Simion or someone like you?

My real point is that, in view of impending worldwide overpopulation and resource-availability crises, the present system of politics based on rivalries among struggling nation-states cannot adequately protect the existence of such divergent lifestyles as ours and Simion's. It is almost incredible to me that, in the face of worldwide population and food crises, people find it difficult to attempt a beginning of solutions that are worldwide in scope. We probably have little choice, that is, between working toward the utopian solution of world government or facing ultimately a holocaust bred by nation-states grappling to secure what is left of the world's resources.

It is because I am so convinced about this lack of any real choice between attempting worldwide solutions on the one hand and ultimate oblivion on the other hand, that I want you to examine a plan for world government proposed by Grenville Clark and Louis Sohn. Take about five minutes to examine this handout which is taken from Clark and Sohn's book, *World Peace Through World Law*, which was published by Harvard University Press in 1966. As you will see from the handout, this plan is similar to a "beefed up" United Nations and would involve disarmament, as well as emphasis on a Court of Justice, to help arbitrate international disputes. Its basic structure would be similar to the federal structure of the U.S. government and of the United Nations. There would be a General Assembly, in which member nations would be represented by one to thirty delegates in proportion to each country's population. The Executive Council is composed of seventeen representatives elected from the General Assembly. No nation can have more than one representative on the Executive Council, and eight of the larger, as well as four of the smaller, nations on the Council must agree before any police action can be taken. Well, I'll let you read for details.

*     *     *     *     *

*Mr. Remode:*   Now that you've had a few minutes to examine this plan, do you think it would help preserve both societies like our own and those like Mila 23 effectively?

*Sandi:*   Maybe it would, if you could get nations to join. But how would you convince leaders to follow the disarmament provisions? How would you be able to convince nations to join because any plan similar to this is bound to restrict a country's freedom to act or to set its own policy? You couldn't force them to join.

*Mr. Remonde:* Those are excellent points, and perhaps the only hope we have is to convince people that situations all governments will be facing over the next few years will be serious enough to call for drastic solutions. It seems, too, that your generation may have a greater tendency to think in global terms than mine did.

For instance, in the town where I used to teach, a neighbor, who was then in her sixties, had graciously loaned me some Canadian public school history textbooks so that my students could see how Canadian authors had written about relations between the United States and Canada during certain periods of history. Our class had been looking at the development of the concept *nationalism* during the War of 1812, and we really wanted to see how Canadian authors might treat this period as part of our examination of changes in attitudes about nationalism.

When I mentioned to this neighbor that the topic in class was nationalism, she hastened to tell me that a student from a nearby university had recently interviewed her at a local shopping center about problems of developing nations and had actually intimated to her that nationalism is wrong. She had apparently been quite upset about the interviewer's questions because she told me with some intensity that she could understand how de Gaulle must have felt when England had to "step in and save France" during World War II. She also mentioned, using that same example of de Gaulle's patriotism when talking to her student interviewer, who, she said, seemed unmoved by such nationalistic attitudes.

During a lull in the conversation, I ventured to mention that perhaps what the student might wish to see is a new kind of nationalism, one which would turn down slightly the emphasis on national glory and focus more on long-range interests and common benefits for groups of nations. My neighbor and I continued to talk, but we obviously were trying to communicate across a considerable attitudinal gap, something similar to the Grand Canyon.

At any rate, I have a feeling that those of your generation may be less inclined to extreme nationalism and war than those of previous generations, because of your willingness to see the seriousness of approaching crises and maybe because of our country's dissillusionment with conflict in Southeast Asia. Since the discussion in this class will often turn to international relations, I will be asking from time to time for your reactions about the possibility of moving toward some plan for world government.

## Role Model Analysis: Mr. Remonde, Ms. Progresso or Ms. Chronicler?

Mr. Remonde's faith in youthful wisdom and judgment is no doubt typical among some educators. Let us examine the effects of this faith as manifested in his behavior during the follow-up lesson for *Mila 23*.

**4.** What behavior trend should one exhibit in order to carry out one's philosophical position?

Authoritarian World View        Non-authoritarian World View
(Convergent Thinking)            (Divergent Thinking)

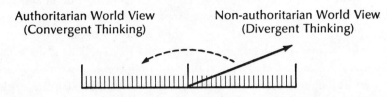

All one has to do is glance at the list of speakers during classroom dialogue to realize the change in Mr. Remonde's behavior and attitude from the first half to the second half of this lesson. At the most elemental level, it is readily apparent that Mr. Remonde talked more after the topic shifted to scarcity of resources; in fact, he talked almost continuously. He seemed to have become so dedicated to the goal of world government that he was willing to step up onto a soapbox in order to persuade his students. Yet, if one examines the earlier segments of dialogue, it becomes apparent that Mr. Remonde encouraged youngsters to contribute suggestions about means to help preserve Mila and its lifestyle. Bob, Pam, and Sandi received acknowledgment and positive feedback from him when they suggested building dams, regulating population density, or simply following a hands-off policy toward Mila. In fact, Mr. Remonde reviewed positively what he called the "gamut of suggestions about how to preserve communities like Mila," before moving to the issue of whether it was possible to leave such settlements entirely alone.

He might even have asked students to speculate on the power of publicity contained in the film *Mila 23* for changing the community and its lifestyle. Turning the spotlight of renown upon such technologically unspoiled enclaves at least carries with it the risk of inviting numerous sightseeing well-wishers. Students might have been surprised to realize that the mere fact of their discussion's occurrence increased the likelihood of Mila's disappearance. But such points were precisely what Mr. Remonde apparently wished kids to discuss, and he did accept and reward student contributions, even when it became clear from the second half of this lesson that their answers did not contain what he regarded as the best solution for Mila's dilemma.

It is this characteristic shift from acceptance of student contributions to an emphasis on the best solution—a shift from divergence to convergence—which gives Reconstructionism its special appeal to many teachers. Those who enter teaching with a crusader's zeal about a pet issue, but who wish to encourage youngsters to examine many facets of that issue before deciding on an appropriate course of action, may find Reconstructionist teaching styles especially suitable. What could be more honest than to have strong convictions and to wish to air them and to have a firm belief that kids should be permitted to examine alternatives freely before deciding to accept or reject the best solution? At least, these sentiments seem to be dominant among teachers who don't want to be seen as copping out by refusing to give personal opinions on controversial issues, while at the same time expecting kids to be willing to reveal their souls in willy-nilly fashion. This shift, from an emphasis at the outset on divergent thinking to the tendency for a teacher to focus on his/her solution as best, characterizes Reconstructionism, as demonstrated by the straight and curved arrows on this continuum's indicator.

Let us look more closely at the precise way in which this shift from divergence to convergence has been illustrated in the preceding diagram. Since Mr. Remonde's purpose was to persuade, not to force his students to accept the idea of world government, it would appear that he recognized and expected alternate reactions or answers to his proposal of world government. That is, even at the close of classroom dialogue there is an implicit understanding that divergence is possible and acceptable. However, it is evident that Mr. Remonde has strong feelings for a plan of world government and will reward with his approval those who support such a plan. Since he has, by this position, moved away from rewarding equally all student contributions based on logic, it seems appropriate to indicate this ultimate tendency toward convergence by an arrow indicating the switch in the scale's balance. Since total convergence is not mandated by the teacher, however, and since at least the alternatives of accepting or rejecting the best solutions are recognized, the scale properly extends toward divergence and the non-authoritarian world view. That is, Reconstructionism seems to belong appropriately to that camp of teaching styles and philosophies which emphasize divergence.

There is, undeniably, a tendency on the part of some Reconstructionists to de-emphasize divergence and emphasize convergence. To the degree that such teachers mount the soapbox, without rewarding students for their own potential solutions to the problem under discussion, they become extremists. In fact, if they become extreme enough not to emphasize divergence at all, they leave this camp of Experimentalist, Reconstructionist, and Existentialist styles entirely and become what we might call radical "Behaviorists." In other words, they become social reformers who would like to remake the world according to their own designs, but who do not wish to reveal those designs to others. They simply wish to establish a system of rewards and reinforcements which will, almost automatically, bring about the desired reforms as long as reinforcement mechanisms are employed carefully. *Brave New World* and *1984* describe such radical Behaviorist programs. (In subsequent chapters we will discuss further the relationships between these two camps of philosophies and their corresponding teaching styles; moreover, later in this chapter we will examine the risks and challenges of extreme Reconstructionism.)

For the moment, however, let us turn our attention to the effects of this tendency to shift from divergence to convergence on other indicators of our analytical tool. Remember that we have followed the practice of examining the indicator about behavior trends first, since the teacher's behavior is readily observable, and then we make inferences about that teacher's opinion regarding the other three questions. We shall continue to follow this practice as our analysis of teaching styles proceeds.

How does Mr. Remonde regard learners? Does a shift from divergent thinking to convergent thinking imply that a similar shift must be indicated for this scale's continuum?

1. What is the nature of the learner?

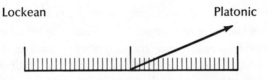

Lockean      Platonic

We have already seen that Mr. Remonde's purpose was to persuade, not to force, youngsters to believe in the feasibility of, and benefits to be derived from, a certain plan for world government. He asked for their own suggested remedies regarding a personalized dilemma before attempting to persuade. Therefore, it certainly seems that "Platonic" is the appropriate direction for this scale's dial, since students are expected to make original contributions. Even at the end of the exercise, and despite Mr. Remonde's hope of persuading all students, there is implicit recognition that two major outcomes will occur: some will support the plan and some will reject it. But forcing all to accept it would actually be self-defeating. Who would maintain the pressure for a forced consensus where social reform is concerned? Students must freely accept the validity of a reform program on its own merits after examining alternatives, or else they'll forget what the reform is worth, just as they often forget other school learnings based on attempts to have learners absorb or converge on consensus. Therefore, they must contribute some of their own insights about the reform in order for belief in its worth to take hold. They may even contribute something akin to the best solution in their discussion of remedies for whatever dilemma is under investigation.

To the Reconstructionist, learners must stumble upon a dilemma, be stimulated to investigate it for themselves, and contribute potential solutions before they can really understand its import and the need for reform action. Only then, when they have embraced a reform program for themselves, is the teaching effort worthwhile. They cannot simply be told about a problem, informed about a proper course of action, and be expected passively to absorb the reform spirit. Hence, the scale appropriately indicates "Platonic," although the teacher makes part of his lesson an attempt to persuade.

And what about Mr. Remonde's views regarding the nature of subject matter?

2. What is the nature of the subject matter?

Amorphous                                          Structured

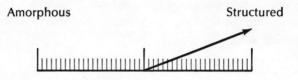

Mr. Remonde is indeed having his students attempt to solve a problem, one which has extremely special significance to him, because of a commitment to world government as the only agency capable of providing remedies of the proper scope for crises involving rapidly declining food and energy resources. He attempted to pose this problem graphically through use of the film, *Mila 23*. As he listened to students' solutions for preserving communities like Mila, he stimulated them to relate facts about one community to trends in international relations. Thus, he caused them to relate bits of information to generalizations in political science. As in any true problem-solving situation, then, he emphasized the structure of his subject matter.

And what about his use of that subject matter?

3. How should one use the subject matter to guide students toward meaningful learning activities?

Cognitive                                          Affective

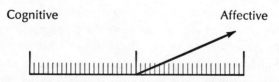

Why did he ask students to think about a circumstance in which technology might grind to a halt due to lack of energy resources and then ask, "Who will be better equipped for survival—someone like Simion or someone like you?" Before the classroom dialogue, we already had received some insights into Mr. Remonde's attempts to personalize his lesson for students. He had felt more than small amounts of anxiety during the energy crisis and a sense of impotence from not being skilled enough to provide his own family with

Comparison of Three Role Models: *Essentialist, Experimentalist, and Reconstructionist*

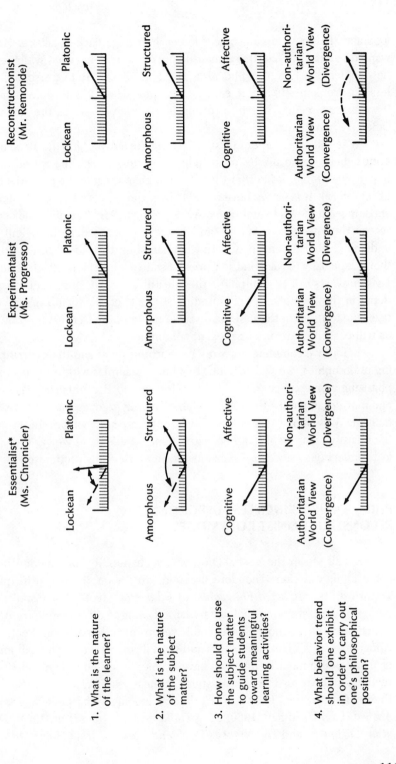

*Please note that as indicated in Chapter II, pp. 74–77, variations from Ms. Chronicler's style are possible within Essentialism.

food and shelter, if circumstances forced him to go back to nature. He also wanted students to feel this same dilemma in a personal way, which is why he decided to show the film *Mila 23*. Such an effort to personalize the lesson's problem—to ask, in essence, and how would *you* be able to survive if we were forced to live in a setting like Simion's?—gives the activity an "affective" emphasis.

It is this affective emphasis which is a major tool for the Reconstructionist, because he or she must help youngsters to see the seriousness of impending problems in order to spark enough interest in the potential benefits of reform. It is, as we have noted above, the means whereby the teacher encourages students to embrace the reform spirit. Mr. Remonde took care to accent the specters of famine and energy resource depletion, and then to demand that students deal with what hardships this would surely bring to them, especially to them in their present state of dependence on technology. Existentialists call this emphasis the "death dread," a concept discussed in detail in the next chapter. Reminding students of the "death dread" often takes the form, as in this case, of discussions about the fact that one day all of us will cease to exist in our present condition.

Before we complete our work on teaching styles and their corresponding philosophies, we will consider two more examples within the camp emphasizing convergence (namely, Behaviorism and Perennialism), as well as one more example for the camp emphasizing divergence (namely, Existentialism). We will now focus on the divergent camp and look briefly at some of the identifying principles of Reconstructionist thinking, as well as the historical connections between Experimentalism and Reconstructionism.

## PHILOSOPHIC PRINCIPLES SUPPORTING THE RECONSTRUCTIONIST ROLE MODEL

As we shall see in the next section of this chapter, Reconstructionism has come a long way since Theodore Brameld wrote about its basic principles in *Toward a Reconstructed Philosophy of Education* (1956). For instance, the philosophy has attracted such a popular following that contemporary Reconstructionists have enjoyed an enviable record of authorship and book sales. Apparently, righteous indignation and not a little anger over the malpractice of many educational institutions have accomplished almost miracles of directness and wit for the writing styles of those who have often been called the romantic critics. The vigor, freshness, and angry charm of *Growing Up Absurd* (Paul Goodman, 1960), *How Children Fail* (John Holt, 1964), *Death at an Early Age* and *The Night Is Dark and I am Far from Home* (Jonathan

Kozol, 1967 and 1975, respectively), *Teaching as a Subversive Activity* (Neil Postman and Charles Weingartner, 1969) and *Deschooling Society* (Ivan Illich, 1970) have unfailingly heightened speculation about using education to effect social reform. Although writing styles of the romantic critics may have greater power to shock and charm than the prose of *Toward a Reconstructed Philosophy of Education*, Brameld's principles of Reconstructionism are still quite applicable. It is those principles, and George Kneller's treatment of them, which we will examine. Basic to all these is the tenent that schools make a difference because they provide help in reconstructing society in order to meet the crises of our time.

(1)  *Education's main purpose is to promote a clearly thought-out program of social reform.* Although Reconstructionists approved heartily of the Progressives' emphasis on inquiry problem-solving, they felt Progressives placed too much emphasis on the condition of a society engaged in planning. They were not only willing but anxious to reject the goal of a society engaged in planning and, instead, to embrace the objective of a planned society; in other words, to focus more on the ends than the means, or to de-emphasize the process of planning in order to stress the product of social outcome. They wished to continue to use teaching methods of Progressivism, but they were equally determined to follow the full implications of a Core Curriculum, as discussed in the previous chapter, in order to work directly for a society which they saw as more fully democratic. In the late 1950s Reconstructionists had begun to be that element within Progressivism seeking to push kids outside a classroom infused with real-life situations into the phenomena of social and economic issues existing in the national community. Thus, Reconstructionists applauded when youngsters realized "that their own generation could live abundantly if they only set about it with the degree of intelligence and social cohesion which they exhibit in planning their work in school," to use the Heaton, Camp, and Diederich phrase from *Professional Education for Experienced Teachers: The Program of the Summer Workshop*. In fact, it is noteworthy that the "Updated Core Curriculum" outlined in Chapter Three can easily become Reconstructionist through a Core teacher's productive use of persuasion.

(2)  *Civilization now faces the possibility of self-annihilation, so educators without delay must create a new social order which will fulfill basic values of our culture.* Reconstructionists begin from a crisis mentality in order to convince the uncommitted that a certain program of reform is indispensable. Any reform ideal must draw from the social and behavioral sciences to develop means for harmonizing human needs with social and

economic forces. (Remember how Mr. Remonde was dealing with the same issue in his Mila 23 lesson?) In Mr. Remonde's view, social and economic forces evident through bitter rivalries among nation-states may not allow communities like Mila 23 to exist. World government might indeed provide the only atmosphere in which people can preserve what is of greatest worth in both industrialized and non-industrialized societies; and human needs may require that both alternatives continue to be available as a necessary condition for each person's individual development.

(3) *The new society must be a genuine democracy whose major institutions and resources are controlled by the people themselves.* Any issue affecting the public interest is to be the responsibility of elected representatives. Any proposed program of reform must be instituted by changes which are realized democratically—that is, through the processes of rational discussion, critical thinking, and persuasion. In Mr. Remonde's view, people will come to understand the necessity for world government through convincing, persuasive, rational dialogue and will bring about this change by expressing their will democratically through the selection of similar-minded representatives in their government.

(4) *People must be persuaded to reconstruct society, and this persuasion should begin in the school.* No matter how much romantic critics may rail against the perniciousness of traditionally organized formal education, schools contain a very useful ingredient for social reform—namely, captive audiences. Students are required to attend schools; thus, there they are, waiting to be persuaded. Whatever persuasion occurs, however, must be done democratically. Just as in Mr. Remonde's lesson, students are encouraged to present alternative solutions and to defend whatever positions they may take in regard to any number of solutions. Indoctrination about that best solution the teacher hopes kids will adopt may occur only if youngsters are willing to be indoctrinated.

If indoctrination seems an inappropriate term, think of the process as involving a strongly persuasive rationale for a particular course of action, after other logical alternatives have been examined. There is always the realization that there may well be those who remain unconvinced, but the power of this persuasive technique really derives from its openness. The uncommitted will hopefully at some later time think about how objective the teacher was in exposing all points of view and encouraging analysis of the merits and demerits of each position; and then, in the final analysis, be convinced that the teacher really was right after all. To those critics like Jonathan Kozol who wish to abandon formalized schooling as it now exists, such persuasive techniques represent the most subtle form of mind control in democratic societies which have taught their constituents to prize openness.

It is sometimes startling to contemplate just how much our society has come to honor openness and an almost compulsive honesty. Though it hardly seems fair or logical to suggest that the Watergate burglary and subsequent investigations in any way caused this pehenomenon, there is little doubt that Watergate has encouraged both whistle-blowing honesty and the assumption that, when whistles blow, they are blown for excellent reasons. One sees the most intimate details of individual lives probed on national television—not just in dramas but also on game shows, and not just on soap operas but also in talk show interviews where nationally known celebrities reveal everything about their personal lives.

One sometimes wonders where those individuals are who value privacy and who feel openness can go too far. Those doubts are encapsulated in the story of a somewhat reserved gentleman who expected his three-hour flight to reward him with time for private contemplation and reading. Instead, he found himself seated next to a gregarious passenger who proceeded to reveal the most intimate details of her current anxieties, fears, hopes, and all the vicissitudes of recent love affairs. It was almost as if this passenger felt uncomfortably dishonest about sitting quietly with all those secrets pent up inside. She had to share the details, to be open about her life.

At any rate, if the rather unscientific observations above actually do represent a growing trend toward prizing openness and toward an almost unexamined assumption that openness is always to be desired, Reconstructionist teaching methods are imminently well suited to exploit the trend.

(5) *The means and ends of education must be completely refashioned to meet the demands of the cultural crisis and to accord with findings of the behavioral sciences.* If constituents of our society are found to view techniques of debate and discussion, which emphasize openness, as highly appealing, and tend to support conclusions reached by such techniques, then the schools' curricula should be reorganized to harmonize with this verdict of behavioral scientists about openness. In any case, curricula must deal with both knowledge and emotion: that kowledge and those emotions directly related to the creation of a reformed society.

(6) *Reconstructionism stresses the extent to which the child, the school, and education itself are shaped by social and cultural forces.* According to Reconstructionists, the Progressives overstated their case for freedom and didn't emphasize enough how much we are all conditioned by social forces. Ideally, however, Reconstructionists wish to overcome the negative

effects of conditioning by teaching individuals that they are not powerless to effect change. They attempt to educate for "social self-realization," the skill of participating in organized groups seeking to change society. In other words, they try to overcome what Jonathan Kozol feels is the far too prevalent tendency of all formalized schooling to teach the fallacy of no connections between social ills, and those who perpetrate or benefit directly from those same social ills.

Kozol, in *The Night Is Dark and I Am Far from Home*, deals specifically with the feeling of impotence students get from the "write-a-letter-to-your-Congressman" syndrome of social activism. Kozol sums up what he feels kids actually learn: "Ask, and you may rest assured that you will be refused, but you will have done as much as you should, or as much as anybody has the right to ask, by the very fact of making the request." In that same chapter on "impotence" Kozol proceeds immediately to his own analysis of this syndrome's effect on curricula.

---

It is not the effort, not the wistful try and not the good idealism I wish to condemn. It is the will to lead ourselves to think that we are "doing something" *if we are not doing anything at all* except to carry out a ritual of effort-and-denial. "With earnestness we will petition if with compassion you will promise to refuse." This is, by now, a bedrock item in the course of classroom preparation: Ask, try, fail and be refused. Speculate somewhat (write a little essay) on the reasons for that failure. Now go on to a new subject.*

**\*Reprinted from Jonathan Kozol, *The Night Is Dark and I Am Far from Home* (New York: Bantam Books, 1977) p. 98.**

---

Reconstructionists are convinced kids can reach "social self-realization," not through the "write-a-letter-to-your-Congressman" brand of activism, but by learning enough about power politics to know how to organize to apply pressure legitimately. Teaching about power politics can be a dangerous business, however, as Jonathan Kozol knows, and as many Reconstructionist teachers discover. Although we will in a later section of this chapter take a direct look at special insecurities and anxieties that adherence to the Reconstructionist position can bring, it may be helpful to keep firmly in mind two general points about this philosophy. First, adherents of Reconstructionism tend to be zealous in their devotion to principles; however, emotionalism and devotion to principles do not, in and of themselves, indicate the Reconstructionist position. One can be emotional about, and highly devoted to, principles from other philosophies. Reconstructionism always concerns itself either implicitly or explicitly with a program of social reform.

Secondly, Reconstructionism, just as the term suggests, involves "making the world over." However, Reconstructionists seek to reform society *only* by adapting the inquiry problem-solving methods of the Progressives (or Experimentalists, the term which has been more appropriately used since the demise of the Progressive Education Association in 1957). Attempts to "make the world over" without building upon inquiry problem-solving techniques are likely to represent extreme Behaviorism.

## Historical Antecedents

In the preceding chapter, we discussed the transformation of Progressivism due to intricate historical and sociological forces at work during the twentieth century. That transformation largely involved a split, which became official only after the dissolution of the Progressive Education Association in 1957. It would certainly not be appropriate here to recount once more the complexities of Progressivism's evolution. However, the diagram below should serve as an adequate reminder that Progressivism's two strains, held in uneasy partnership largely because of Dewey's stature, eventually separated themselves into what we now usually call "Experimentalism" and "Reconstructionism." Our last chapter's treatment of contemporary Experimentalism will be left to stand or fall on its own without further elaboration. However, the Reconstructionist mode of thinking emphasized the determination to follow the Progressivist emphasis on growth, by posing the reformist question of: Growth toward what? Reconstructionists were sure they could adequately define the good society, and they were impatient to get on with the business of using Progressivist teaching strategies with captive audiences in schools in their attempts to bring forth a more perfect world.

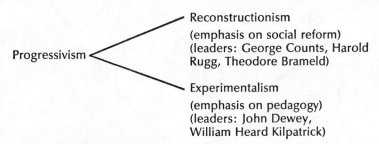

Progressivism

Reconstructionism
(emphasis on social reform)
(leaders: George Counts, Harold Rugg, Theodore Brameld)

Experimentalism
(emphasis on pedagogy)
(leaders: John Dewey, William Heard Kilpatrick)

## To Deschool or Not to Deschool?

Reconstructionists are still certain they can bring forth a more perfect world through democratic means. Although their battle slogans are as contemporary as microwave ovens in every kitchen, the techniques and persuasiveness of their more noteworthy adherents—for example, Jonathan Kozol in *The Night Is Dark and I Am Far from Home* and Pat Conroy in *The Water Is Wide*—are those of angry Progressives in only slightly more stylish dress.

This anger results mostly from the direct way in which Kozol, Conroy, Ivan Illich, and others deal with what we might call the "Reconstructionist" question: What are schools for? Put more precisely into Reconstructionist phraseology, the question goes something like this: Can we, or do we dare, use the schools to effect social reform? It is because Reconstructionists answer this question with a thundering "yes" that they are so change-oriented. Since those who are not change-oriented do not usually even think to ask the question about what schools are for, Reconstructionists tend to embrace reform fervor with a special sense of mission to awaken those who are status quo oriented to the inevitability of change and to the benefits of planning for change.

Let us review briefly, with the aid of the graph below, how the Reconstructionist question on schooling's functions has been addressed in the U.S. since the beginning of the public school movement. Although Reconstructionsim is basically a post-1957 phenomenon, spurred by Theodore Brameld's work, *Toward a Reconstructed Philosophy of Education*, insights about Kozol's, Conroy's, and Illich's understanding of contempory dilemmas facing institutionalized schooling can be gained by a search for antecedents.

### Reform Trends in the U.S. Educational System

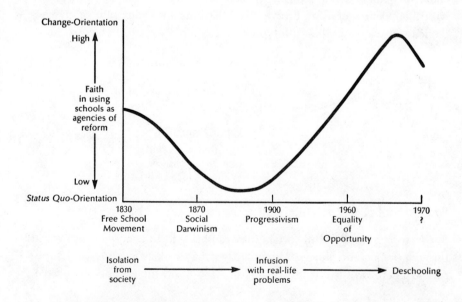

Let us make the mid-point of the "Reform Faith" axis on this graph represent the position of those who followed Horace Mann and Henry Barnard, as that position about universal free public schooling has been described by Michael Katz in *The Irony of Early School Reform*. In Katz's view, when Mann and Barnard advocated a universal system of public education in the 1830s, they were really advocating schooling which would isolate youngsters from society's ills, would place them in settings where intellectual skills could be developed using standardized textbooks and other graded materials, and where even the school architecture was supposed to be uplifting. Schools would also allow the "have-nots" to arm themselves with the means of successful competition in economic life without requiring the "haves" to give up advantages of material wealth. In other words, when Mann and Barnard asked the Reconstructionist question—Dare we use the schools to effect social reform?—their answer was a modified "yes," according to Katz. They were advocating gradual social change by helping youngsters of all socioeconomic groups attain skills for competition within an ever rapidly industrializing country. The kind of gradual social change they proposed, however, was not generally perceived as threatening by those already in positions of leadership, basically because it did nothing to alter the ground rules for economic competition. Sometimes this position of gradualism is called "anarchy with a schoolmaster," because there is no attempt to legislate social classes directly or to prevent a certain amount of social mobility, as long as the ground rules for competition are not altered and as long as people are taught that participation *within* the prevailing economic and governmental systems will be in everyone's best interest. If Katz's interpretation has any merit, then, it would seem that this kind of faith in gradual social reform belongs at the mid-point on our "Reform Faith" axis.

## Effective or Affective Reform?

If we continue to follow our graph's curve to the low point of the 1870s—the time when Andrew Carnegie was advising the wealthy not to bequeath their fortunes to their offspring because such a step would wrongfully rob them of the growth-producing benefits of economic struggle—the school tended to be seen as an institution which preserved the status quo by weeding out those ill-suited to make it in a burgeoning industrial society. Peter Schrag in "The End of the Impossible Dream" (*Saturday Review*, September 19, 1970) talked about the time when schools separated the unfit from the fit, as a period for which "every poor little boy who became a doctor represented a victory [but] poor little boys who became ditch diggers disappeared from the record." It was an era when "crass" Social Darwinist thinking made many fear that attempts to aid the unfortunate would hamper progress by perpetuating undesirable elements of society and the problems those undesirables presented to the body politic. It was a time when Herbert Spencer's essay entitled "What do Social Classes Owe Each Other?" provided an answer to its own query which in summary amounted to the one-word reply: "Nothing!" As George Frederickson noted in *The Inner Civil War*, that conflict in the 1860s hastened the spread of Social Darwinist ideas and helped reformers to adopt a rather stern self-help attitude toward all reform efforts—if, indeed, any leaders would be found who had managed to convince themselves that reform efforts of any kind had merit. Andrew Carnegie, who felt it was potentially destructive to bequeath money to one's children, approved only of self-help varieties of charity, such as donating money for libraries and for higher education. Nevertheless, higher education, and schooling in general, was still seen as preserving the status quo by screening out the unfit.

### Breaking the Goose-Step?

Those Progressive Era journalists we often call "muckrakers" were largely responsible for moving popular modes of thinking about reform away from adherence to stern self-help charities. Upton Sinclair, a truly prolific "muckraking" journalist, achieved acclaim for his attacks on "crass" Social Darwinist thought in his novel about Chicago meatpackers, *The Jungle*. He is, however, perhaps less well known for his emphasis on the Reconstructionist question in two works on education: *The Goose-Step* (1923) and *The Goslings* (1924). His ideas, along with those of John Dewey, William Heard Kilpatrick, Harold Rugg, and many others, helped account for the upswing in the graph's curve after the beginning of the twentieth century. Sinclair fell into the Progressivist educator's expanding desire to remove schools from an isolationist position regarding the social mainstream into a position where real-life situations and problems would become the mainstay of curricula. He advocated using higher education to reform society through what he called an "Open Forum" approach to dialogue about public issues.

Sinclair used Barnard College as a case study in awareness of social issues among college students, and as an exemplary setting for higher education's role in social reform. Sinclair wrote despairingly of President Nicholas Murray Butler of Columbia University, calling him "Nicholas Miraculous" in the passage quoted below, largely because of his "betrayal" of academe through too great a zeal for "money-grubbing" among conservative businessmen. (It may also be helpful to remember, while reading the following passage from *The Goose-Step*, that Dr. Margaret Mead graduated from Barnard with a Phi Beta Kappa key in 1923—the year Sinclair published this work.)

---

More significant yet, the students of Barnard have got busy, right under the nose of Nicholas Miraculous! They organized a committee on their own initiative, and have constructed an "ideal" curriculum. Listen to what these progressive young ladies propose requiring of freshmen: a course of the history of mankind, counting ten points, "a synthetic survey course designed to bring out the chief aspects of man's relation to his environment by tracing present conditions and tendencies to historic processes; the physical nature of the universe . . . man as a product of evolution . . . the early history of man . . . the concept of culture . . . the historical processes leading to present cultural conditions . . . modern problems, political, economic and social." Next they want a course, counting six points, in human biology and psychology, "giving an outline of human development and distribution on earth, man in relation to his nearest kin, a survey of human powers and functions, an introduction to general biology, the structure of the human body, outlines of embryology, functions of the body and their interrelationships"—and laboratory work on all these problems. Also—imagine young ladies actually putting such things on paper!—they asked for:

"Specific human development and the sex-reproductive-child bearing function.
a. "The facts of structure, functions, development and hygiene of the sex and reproductive apparatus of the male and female.
b. "The outstanding facts of maternity and paternity.
c. "Effects of sex on individual human development from fertilization to maturity.
d. "The nature and power of the sex impulse.
e. "The gradually developed sex controls imposed on the individual by society.
f. "The pathological effects of perverse and unsocial uses of sex in society.
g. "The facts underlying a satisfactory adjustment in marriage and homemaking."

Also they want a course in "general mathematical analysis," counting six points; "the technique of expression," counting two points; and "English literature," counting six points, with the aim "to present literature as an aspect of life; the emphasis throughout is therefore on subject matter rather than on technical or historical problems."

Yes; and also these young ladies of Barnard have taken up the problem of having Nicholas Miraculous tell them whom they may listen to. It was declared to them that the good repute of the college must be preserved, and after an argument they submitted to that imposition; but one thing they laid down very emphatically—they want the college authorities to give up the idea of protecting their tender young minds!*

*Reprinted from Upton Sinclair, *The Goose-Step*. Published by the author at Pasadena, California, 1923, p. 476.

---

As a remedy for the too watchful eye of Nicholas Miraculous, as well as the eyes of other faculty members and administrators in higher education, Sinclair proposed in his next chapter to make higher education a dialogue about social issues. He wished to insist that all important controversial social issues become subjects of debate among college faculties and students so that the most workable, pertinent, and significant ideas regarding such issues would emerge. But this explanation seems all too prosaic when compared to Sinclair's own words:

---

We deported Emma Goldman, and thought we had thereby prevented the spread of anarchism; which shows that whatever else our colleges and universities have done, they have not taught us the psychology of martyrdom. I agree with the university trustee in thinking that anarchism is wrong—at least for a hundred years or so; but my way of handling Emma Goldman would have been to run her on a lecture tour in every American college and university, in a debate with some thoroughly trained expert in the history of social evolution. I would have let all the students hear her, and keep her until midnight answering questions; so, if there was truth in her views it would have spread, and if there was error the students would have been inoculated against it for life.*

*Reprinted from Upton Sinclair, *The Goose-Step*. Published by the author at Pasadena, California, 1923, p. 476.

---

Sinclair, along with many others in the Progressive tradition, saw attractive possibilities for using schools as agencies of reform; therefore, the curve on the graph proceeds upward. We already have examined, in the preceding chapter, reformist thinking inherent in Core Curriculum designs of the 1930s. Even though the 1940s and 1950s brought reactions against Dewey and the Progressives—reactions that we have analyzed through our look at Essentialism in Chapter Two—there continued to be, until recently, an almost boundless faith that more and better education administered through institutions of schooling would benefit all. This faith was not in the "crass" Social Darwinist sense of benefitting society by screening the unfit, but faith that upward social mobility and economic status might be promoted effectively for each individual through schooling. As a result, the curve on the graph still proceeds upward.

This faith in schooling was refueled by the National Defense Education Act (1958) and by the Elementary and Secondary Education Act (1965). Civil rights issues caused widespread support for "Head Start" and "Upward Bound" programs and the assumption that somehow equal opportunity for schooling of uniform excellence would help end some ethnic and economic discontent in this country, by moving us closer toward equality of condition—an equality of condition which would help banish poverty by opening up the professions and all forms of meaningful employment to every category of race, ethnicity, and sex. Consequently, the curve continues to proceed upward until the late 1960s.

In 1966 James Coleman's report on the "Equality of Educational Opportunity" amassed impressive data which revealed surprisingly little difference between achievement level for students in predominantly white and in predominantly black schools, despite what many had expected to be the results in an era of expanding compensatory education programs like "Head Start" and "Upward Bound." Many re-examined their faith in compensatory education generally. Some came to believe what Elizabeth Leonie Simpson said in *Democracy's Stepchildren* (1970): namely, that school came too late to help the poverty-stricken and the culturally deprived. Arthur Jensen and others began to look again for ethnic and genetic explanations regarding differences in achievement and I.Q. levels among students. As a result, the curve has plummeted into uncertainty, and a number of romantic critics have begun to deal with the Reconstructionist question differently by calling for alternatives to traditional formal schooling: these alternatives range from "free" schooling to "deschooling." Others who have given up on the idea of school as a reform agency insist that educators should concentrate on the "basics," forget social activism, and worry more about grammar, composition, and mathematics. Those in the mainstream of "back-to-basics" seem again to be toying with the old screening function for schooling, under the guise of awarding different kinds of diplomas as determined by performance on statewide competency tests. While faith in the school's power to reform continues to plummet, a few Reconstructionists like Kozol persist.

Michael Katz, in the *Irony of Early School Reform*, advanced a theory to explain the changes noted on the graph. According to his theory, when popular thought places more emphasis on environment than heredity as the major determinant of success, faith in using the school as an agency of social reform will be high. I can remember not being too surprised upon first beginning graduate school to hear an educational psychologist exclaim, "Intelligence is *all* learned." A stimulating environment may indeed be all that is necessary to overcome early deprivation, at least that seemed to be the assumption bolstering most efforts in compensatory education.

When popular thought places more emphasis on heredity than on environment as the major determinant of success, however, faith in using the school as an agency of reform will decline. Is that an appropriate explanation for viewing the school as an institution which screened the unfit, an attitude dominant in the late nineteenth century? If Social Darwinists viewed humans as having descended from lower life forms and if some humans had developed or inherited a few characteristics which would allow them to cope more effectively with environmental problems, was not acceptance of these evolutionary processes the most appropriate response of institutions? Should institutions not aid evolutionary processes based on heredity, rather than trying to subvert them by attempting social reform? Is I.Q. a more valid and powerful indicator of success, since schooling often seems to come too late to help the culturally deprived? Is heredity currently being viewed as important a determinant of success as environment, or is heredity being viewed as more important than environment?

Perhaps Katz's theory sounds too much like an uninspiring rehash of the nature/nurture controversy. Whether it is a tool powerful enough to explain the shifts in thinking just reviewed concerning the school as a possible agent of reform is less significant than the existence and detectability of such shifts among the populace. The most important item for anyone who is teaching or preparing to teach, however, is not how most people feel about using the school to maintain the status quo or to effect reform, but how he or she answers the Reconstructionist question.

## THE RECONSTRUCTIONIST ROLE MODEL AND THE TEACHER

In essence, kids try to find out why their teachers decided to become teachers; in other words, students try to determine how their teachers have answered the Reconstructionist question. In elementary school this process of students studying teachers usually begins with an exhilarating attempt to find out personal tidbits about a teacher's lifestyle and out-of-school behavior: sometimes this involves a fervent investigative process full of good-natured fun, but sometimes it involves a more serious attempt to understand a teacher's personal joys and sorrows. By the time youngsters reach secondary school they have generally become quite adept at reading teacher behaviors. My first experience with this phenomenon made me quite certain after two days that all my classes of "slow learners" (a very inappropriate label indeed) consisted of Ph.D's in psychology who had been mysteriously transported to a high school setting, just to try out their expertise in behavioral engineering for my benefit.

### Teaching and Social Conscience

What high school kids often attempt to analyze quite purposefully is the teacher's motivation for becoming a teacher. They are, in short, trying to determine how each teacher has dealt with the Reconstructionist question:

i.e., whether this person is teaching to change the world or to preserve the status quo. The students' honesty about their search can be electrifying. On his first day in a classroom one of our recent student teachers was asked, "Who are you?" When he explained he would soon be student teaching there, the student's rejoinder was, "Are you any good at it?" That caught him a bit off guard. Students often ask forthrightly about the way a teacher voted in local and national elections, about recreational activities, about special interests, about involvement in causes kids may find attractive. In any case, they will generally expect any teacher to live up to whatever ideals he or she professes because they tend to be skeptical of any ambiguity they detect in one's lifestyle. I remember once being a little surprised and amused at this probing of personal tastes when, somehow, during a class discussion the Carol Burnett show was mentioned. One young man remarked, "Oh, *you* watch *that*; I think it's the dirtiest show on television!" I spent two days wondering what made Carol Burnett's show the "dirtiest" on television, until I remembered some of the veiled sexual humor she often used in skits with one of her co-stars. At any rate, that was all I could come up with, although it didn't seem to fit my own assessment of what constituted pornography.

This process of probing went on so regularly and so intensely in the school where I taught that some black students insisted they could read prejudicial thoughts simply by glancing into a teacher's eyes.

## How Revolutionary Do Teachers Want to Be?

We have been talking about assuming a professional role which makes one the object of intense study by youngsters who may have had more than a decade of consistent opportunities to refine their skills of scrutinizing the personalities of all teachers. We have also been examining in this volume a number of teaching styles and the philosophical assumptions underlying those styles so that prospective teachers and in-service teachers can assess themselves and choose a repertoire of teaching behaviors which will fit their personalities. Such self-assessment and rational choice of teaching behaviors can provide the key to effectiveness—or the inspirational quality which observers may term "charisma" and which kids may simply call being a "together" person.

One of the best ways to stimulate this charisma-building process is to begin with an honest analysis of why one decides to enter teaching or to continue teaching. Is one motivated basically by a desire to help kids fit into society as it now is or by something akin to the crusader's desire to change the world? For pre-service teachers I am convinced it is absolutely essential for them to analyze their motives for becoming teachers, before they are surprised by a barrage of insistent questions amounting to, "Who are you, what are you about, and why should we listen to *you*?" When a pre-service teacher has decided what his or her motivation is, verbalizing it to friends and acquaintances until the phrases no longer sound uncomfortable, may be excellent preparation. One will soon verbalize the same reasons and feelings in front of thirty pairs of intensely searching eyes.

If a teacher's verbalization of his or her motives involves a commitment to "make waves" and to change the world, then that teacher may wish to remember the difficulties Jonathan Kozol faced in the Boston School System, which he described in *Death at an Early Age*. Kozol's were the same difficulties faced by Pat Conroy when he decided the children on Yamacraw Island had to have better instruction and at least adequate facilities before they could ever hope to break out of the intellectual bondage he portrayed in *The Water Is Wide*. Both of these Reconstructionist teachers lost their jobs. Institutions have their own methods of convincing constituents not to make waves, but then making waves, taking stands, and blowing whistles may have higher rewards. I remember a truly noble academic advisor of mine who was fond of repeating that no teacher was really worth anything until he had lost one job, or at least until he had been threatened once or twice with the loss of his job.

I remember in my own teaching experience when tensions became so intense concerning an incident which occurred at a Black Culture assembly, that we decided to close school for a cooling-off period. Small groups of parents, students, and faculty members were scheduled to meet and talk through problems in an attempt to prepare for resuming classes. In one of our planning sessions for those community meetings, I recall mentioning that we had been discussing in some of my classes the role of students as social revolutionaries. Although many students and their parents had decided to boycott classes, we managed to try to sort through various assessments of what was happening around us by carefully examining responsibilities which political leaders had placed on students. Since the days of Reconstruction, we decided, political leaders had been attempting to forge a society with equality of opportunity for all ethnic groups; moreover, those adult leaders had, for the most part, failed in their endeavors. They had, in fact, failed so miserably that in more than one hundred years of trying they had not produced one harmonious racially integrated neighborhood or one harmonious racially integrated school to serve as models for youngsters.

I tried to convince kids that, in effect, political leaders had admitted their failures but had persisted in their beliefs that youngsters could—if placed in schools where close proximity of all ethnic groups was mandated— create a harmonious, pluralistic, multi-ethnic society. They had said to youngsters, in essence, "You can do it; you will be the social revolutionaries who will create for us a new society which comes as the by-product of the formal education you're being given." We talked at some length about the roles of students as social revolutionaries, about whether they felt comfortable in such roles, and about whether this interpretation of their responsibilities helped them cope more easily with conflicts that are inevitable when a new society is being created.

Not every faculty member in that meeting approved of using the phrase "social revolutionaries." The following day our daily newspaper, which was quite a conservative publication, featured an editorial using the same concept of students as "social revolutionaries" and capitalized on the phrase. Somehow my comments of the previous day apparently seemed less revolutionary and less surprising to most colleagues.

My use of the phrase "social revolutionaries" was almost tame when compared to the example of one instructor at a private school who reported attempts to teach the concept of revolution by offering workshops in simulated guerrilla warfare techniques. (That anecdote was related in Chapter One as an example of an extremely affective use of subject matter in which students were participating in a survival experience.) However, both teaching behaviors can be considered Reconstructionist and, as such, open one to many potential consequences of making waves.

Suppose a teacher doesn't wish to make that many waves? Suppose the teacher would prefer to use subject matter affectively, without the attempt at permissive indoctrination of students regarding a certain reform activity? Existentialism, then, may offer this teacher the appropriate blend of affective subject matter with almost no tendency on the part of the teacher to propagandize, proselytize, or persuade.

# THE EXISTENTIALIST TEACHER
## as Inquirer into Human Nature

## CHAPTER FIVE

*The Setting:*

## MR. SARTORIUS IN THE CASBAH WITH A STRANGER

For some years Mr. Sartorius had viewed his main mission as an educator to help youngsters understand the complexities of the human temperament and to relate issues in the subject matter to their own personality development. He had at first been borne along in this conviction by a number of writers whose careers spoke rather loosely about "humanistic education"; thus, he became fond of freely using that same phrase. One might suspect that Mr. Sartorius's conviction, which had been so long and deliberate in its development, would have led him to be a psychology teacher. On the contrary, however, he was certified in a few traditional areas: English literature, sociology, and history.

Mr. Sartorius took his convictions about humanistic education seriously enough to explore them more deeply, and he ultimately fastened himself to the theories and techniques usually known as "values clarification." Let us examine briefly a lesson in Mr. Sartorius's world literature class for high school seniors, a lesson which had been sparked by the mass murder and the mass suicide tragedies in Guyana among the Jim Jones/People's Temple cult in November of 1978. All his students were wondering aloud why more than nine hundred people could follow so blindly into a "suicide pact," why they were persuaded to go to Guyana in the first place, and why the cult's leaders were so intolerant of anyone's interpretation of reality except their own. In fact, the students' stark curiosity about this incident seemed limitless in its power to generate questions regarding the psychology of leadership, the strength of peer pressure, the unquestioning attitudes many people display in the face of generally accepted customs.

Mr. Sartorius decided to have youngsters explore their own attitudes about customs, and their efforts to establish an identity strong enough to question customs, by using a situation which he thought might seem less bizarre to his students than the People's Temple tragedies. The situation he chose was deliberately intended to help kids understand how a custom which is pervasive and has a long history may be one which people simply do not think to question; such pervasiveness could make a custom more powerful in its ability to influence an individual's behavior than the startling procedure of "mass suicide drills" instituted by Jones in Guyana. He also meant to use his lesson as introduction to Camus's novel *L'Étranger*, a striking record of the individual's battle with custom.

At the lesson's outset Mr. Sartorius asked youngsters to respond briefly in writing to four questions: Who am I, where am I, what am I, and what is the worst thing one human being can do to another? After reminding kids that he did not want their responses to be signed, he collected their papers. He promised to make personal comments about the responses on each paper. When papers were returned, students could then identify their work by their handwriting styles. Mr. Sartorius was convinced that one might gain some insights into how keenly aware youngsters are about problems of identity through their answers to this exercise. After all, there would seem to be a vast difference in mood, at least, between the student who writes, "I am sitting in the desk closest to the door of Room 335 in Central High," and the one who writes, "I am a mere speck of dust in the enormity of the cosmos." (At any rate, that is how Mr. Sartorius's thinking had progressed while he was planning this lesson.)

Next he asked the students to watch a film, *Heritage of Slavery* (CBS News, 1968), and think about any new ideas they might have regarding the four questions they had just answered. *Heritage of Slavery*, from the *Of Black America* series, depicts several joltingly controversial, yet matter-of-fact, confrontations between a very dark-skinned black interviewer and four people representing various viewpoints about customs in the black and white communities near Charleston, South Carolina. The filmmaker's major point is blatantly announced at the outset: too many descendants of former slaves work for descendants of former slaveowners; or, in essence, too many blacks still act like slaves, and too many white still act like masters. In one particularly arresting interview a well-to-do white planter is asked if he feels slavery was a necessary institution in the early history of this country. The planter's remarks quickly move over points about the absence of a common language or religion and stereotypes regarding the childlike quality of slaves, as he supports his answer that slavery was indeed necessary. When the interviewer follows with a question about how the planter regarded blacks before they were seen as ready to participate fully in society, the planter responds with, "I'd say we regarded you almost as a 'superior pet.'" Thus, the discussion proceeds quite calmly, following lines that participants seem to accept as totally rational.

A wealthy white female resident of Charleston is interviewed about her childhood in the 1920s, when her parents would take her to the plantation on weekends. After describing the scene as encompassing a "lovely happy time" in which all the animals and all the people "had to be thoroughbred," she remembered "'Fortune, the old cook whom we adored'" with the phrase, "'and all he had to do was love us and skim the cream'" off huge bowls of clabber at the dairy.

After the interviewer talks with a retired black female school teacher and a young black male who is attempting to mobilize voting power among blacks, one gets a sense of the widening chasm between two worlds and two totally different concepts of reality. Scenes from a church service, in which a black minister preaches about Denmark Vesey's attempted slave revolt, skillfully display the emotional crescendo blacks were approaching in the 1960s.

Mr. Sartorius knew that on the following day kids would be more than willing to talk about the influence of pervasive customs and long traditions.

## Classroom Dialogue for the Existentialist Role Model

*Mr. Sartorius:*  Remember yesterday I asked you to answer briefly the following questions: Who am I, where am I, what am I, and what is the worst thing one human being can do to another? I appreciated the opportunity to read your responses last night. I've made brief comments on each one of your papers. Some of my comments are really questions. If you decide you'd like to make a response to my questions and comments, please do so by writing me a note or by talking to me when just the two of us are present. Why don't you take a moment or two to find your own paper in this folder by identifying your handwriting? Then read the comments I wrote.

*     *     *     *     *

Although I consider the first three questions—Who am I, where am I, and what am I?—much too personal to discuss in a group, I do want us to talk for a few minutes about the last question—What is the worst thing one human being can do to another? Perhaps you've even thought of some new ideas regarding that question after watching *Heritage of Slavery*. What is the worst thing one human being can do to another?

*Nathan:*  I'd say it would be to kill another person.

*Mr. Sartorius:*  O.K. What is so bad about that?

*Toni:*  I don't think I understand why you're saying, "What is so bad about that?" After all, isn't the protection of human life one of the main reasons we have government and law?

*Mr. Sartorius:*  I agree, Toni, but what about the circumstances of death? Might the person being killed find it less horrible to die under some circumstances than other circumstances? I am asking you for the very worst thing one person can do to another.

*Barbara:*  Are you asking if it would be better to be killed fighting for something you believe in during a war as opposed to being murdered?

*Holt:*  What about torture? What if you were tortured, say, in a prison camp like the Jews in *Holocaust*, and you thought you were going to die but didn't?

*Mr. Sartorius:*  Are you asking whether torture is worse than death? Do you think survivors of some Nazi concentration camps, for instance, might feel they underwent experiences worse than death?

*Cindy:*  I wasn't thinking of anything as morbid as what we've been talking about, when I answered this question yesterday. I was thinking about ignoring someone completely, making that person feel totally unwanted, as being the worst thing you could do to somebody.

*Mr. Sartorius:* That's an interesting point, Cindy. Why is what you've mentioned so bad?

*Cindy:* Well, if someone completely ignores a person and makes him or her feel totally isolated, it's very sad. I'm thinking mostly of children who are abused or neglected but of other people too, like old people who have no families and must live alone, or maybe they do have families who don't want to care for them.

*Jim:* Yes, but is that really worse than death?

*Cindy:* Well, it might mean, if you're an old person, that you know you have to face death alone and uncared for. That could make it worse than just death itself, I'd think.

*Holt:* I wrote about denying someone's humanity when I answered this question yesterday.

*Mr. Sartorius:* What do you mean by a "denial of humanity"?

*Barbara:* It certainly seems like killing somebody would be denying that person's humanity.

*Holt:* Yes, but I was thinking more in terms of making a person feel worthless, really good for nothing. It's really, I guess, the same kind of thing the film was saying about slavery—making people feel less than human.

*Mr. Sartorius:* Well, we've certainly had a number of suggestions about the worst thing you could do to another person, including items from murder, death, torture, and denial of humanity to ignoring another person totally. I've brought along two examples of "worst things" that I want you to consider.

   The first example was written by a student who a few years ago answered the same question you were asked yesterday. Let me make it clear before you read his answer that he is basically a happy person and was only answering the question as an intellectual exercise. Here's what he wrote:

> The worst thing one human being can do to another is to let him know that he is going to be killed—especially slowly and painfully—at a specific time in the not-too-distant future (a matter of hours to a week) with absolutely no hope of escaping his fate. Also let him know that he will be killed because of no particular dislike for him personally or for any real reason, but just through the caprice of circumstances. Make it clear that he won't be missed or really even noticed during his prolonged death; in fact, there's a ball planned for the time of his execution—just circumstantially.*

*Holt:* Wow! I'd say that's a "bummer" all right.

*Mr. Sartorius:* Why is it so terrible?

*Holt:* Just knowing you're going to be executed and nobody cares! People seem to be ignoring this guy, but maybe it's even more than that because they seem to be almost mocking him.

*Mr. Sartorius:* That's an interesting point. Isn't what I just read, though, pretty close to a description of the ultimate fate for all of us? In fact, that was my comment on this student's paper: Isn't this really what we all face?

---

*Used with permission.

*Holt:*   But how can you say that?

*Mr. Sartorius:*   It's not so much that I say it but that many people who study human nature emphasize the fact that man is aware of his own death and can brood about it. Not that we all are likely to be executed, as the student's response indicated. However, we do know that death is coming and that we stand a good chance of being forgotten after death, but maybe even before death, because people are sometimes so afraid of their own deaths that they quite effectively, if unintentionally, isolate the individual who is dying.

*Cindy:*   I guess I see your point about this situation representing the worst thing that could happen, but I'm not so sure I buy the point about all of us having to face a similar situation.

*Mr. Sartorius:*   Well, the next novel we study, *The Stranger* by Albert Camus, will be dealing with the same points we've just discussed. It's a story about someone whose battle to define himself gets him so caught up in the prevailing prejudices and customs of his society that he commits a crime for which he must pay with his life. The last part of the novel puts its main character in the same situation as the one we just read about— that is, he is waiting to be executed. However, Camus's skill as a writer helps us realize that our own fates are not really very different from this man who must pay with his life as a consequence for one impulsive act.

I did say, though, that I had brought another example for consideration in our "worst thing" category. Some would say it indeed represents the worst thing one human being can do to another, even though it is more subtle than the description of an execution which I just read. Let's see if you agree.

Pretend you have to take a bus trip alone—one you have taken at least fifty times before, so that every landmark along the route is totally familiar to you. You have forgotten to buy a copy of today's paper, have no other reading material, and know no one who is traveling with you. You settle down for a thoroughly boring ride, until you spy a vivacious-looking lady who is at least twenty-five years your senior, but who seems to have an amazing capacity to look as if she is immensely enjoying this trip. Since you want to know "what makes her personality tick," you decide to analyze her expressions and gestures. It's really very easy and entertaining, because you know she can't see you staring at her. Suddenly, her continuing glance at a landmark the bus is passing causes her to look directly at you.

What might be your reaction when her eyes meet yours, and she realizes you have been staring at her?

*Toni:*   I'd probably look away from her in a hurry.

*Mr. Sartorius:*   Good point! What are some other options?

*Andy:*   I suppose you could just smile. You might even use this opportunity to begin a conversation, if she's not sitting too far away from you.

*Nathan:*   I don't know. If you're a male, a smile might be misinterpreted.

*Mr. Sartorius:*   Well, we've got several options anyway. Why do they seem appropriate? Why, for instance, would several of you look away in a hurry?

*Jim:*   Maybe it's just because my mom taught me that it is impolite to stare.

*Mr. Sartorius:*   O.K. Is there anything in addition to being initiated into the customs and etiquette that prevail? Well, what might be your motivation, for instance, if you decided to smile and begin a conversation?

*Cindy:*   Maybe I wouldn't want her to think I had just been sitting there staring a long time.

*Mr. Sartorius:*   Why not? What would be so bad about staring at her?

*Holt:*   Maybe it's something like denial of humanity. Anyway, that's the phrase I used in my answer yesterday.

*Mr. Sartorius:*   There are certainly some people who would say, Holt, that staring at someone in the situation we've outlined is a denial of humanity—that is, it is the equivalent of studying a person as an object under a microscope. The act of studying someone that way might cause no guilt pangs in the observer, until the object of such study realizes he or she is being stared at. At the moment of that realization the observer is likely either to look away quickly, or to attempt to begin a conversation, or to smile. All of these actions, however, could be interpreted as attempts to say, "You see, I wasn't really studying you as an object; I wasn't really denying your humanity." This may seem a bit farfetched to you, but those reasons are why some students of human nature would insist that this example belongs in our "worst thing" category. In fact, their position is that any denial of human worthiness—whether by look, word, or deed—is the ultimate taboo, if you are trying to relate meaningfully to others.

We're going to be reading a novel in which several people will seem to have forgotten these points about human relationships we've just been studying. The same thing might be said about characters in the film, *Heritage of Slavery*, because they existed in a society where prevailing customs often operated to undermine meaningful human relationships.

As extra preparation for the novel *L'Étranger*, I have a brief assignment to help you think seriously about the implications of our discussion today about human nature. I want you to choose one person from the film *Heritage of Slavery* and write, in no more than one page, advice for that person about two or three important choices he/she should make. Please feel free to choose the interviewer, the planter, the lady who remembered her past in rather romantic terms, the retired teacher, the young man who was working on voter registration, or anyone else in the film. I want to read your advice and make comments to you. Then after we're through discussing *L'Étranger*, we'll go back to what you've written to see if following your advice might have been a help to *L'Étranger's* main character.

## Role Model Analysis: Mr. Sartorius, Mr. Remonde, Ms. Progresso, and Ms. Chronicler in the Dissecting Pan

Is it surprising that Mr. Sartorius talked so directly about death? Would many teachers use such a teaching style? Although we already know something about Mr. Sartorius's motivation and his faith in values clarification techniques as aids for accomplishing his mission as an educator, we need to examine his teacher behaviors according to our analytical tool before we attempt to answer the foregoing questions.

**4.** What behavior trend should one exhibit in order to carry out one's philosophical position?

Authoritarian World View   Non-authoritarian World View
(Convergent Thinking)     (Divergent Thinking)

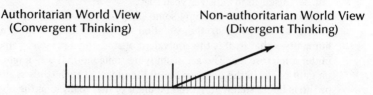

Notice that Mr. Sartorius was careful to avoid artificial consensus among class members. Before the discussion began they wrote answers to his questions about identity and injustice. He encouraged student responses to his comments on their papers by personal notes or in private conversations. Advice students might have chosen to give to any character in the film was to be collected, held, and used in a discussion, only after the novel *L'Étranger* had been read. Even during the course of the discussion recounted above, one sees such phrases as, "some students of human nature would insist," and, "what are other options for." Divergence was expected and deliberately encouraged, even to the point of preventing discussion until youngsters had had the opportunity to put their own thoughts into writing. Such a practice of delaying discussion in this manner is typical of values clarification and is meant to avoid giving one or two vocal students the opportunity to pull more reticent youngsters toward someone else's position.

**1.** What is the nature of the learner?

Lockean           Platonic

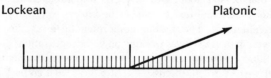

As one might expect from a teacher who is so attentive to fostering divergence, Mr. Sartorius viewed his students in a "Platonic" manner. He made their contributions—whether concerning identity, injustice, or the appropriate advice for a character in *Heritage of Slavery*—central to the lesson. He was indeed unsure before the lesson began what the form and substance of the students' contributions might be, but he consciously built on this student input whether or not it happened to match the preconceived notions of experts. When he mentioned the "bus trip" example, he was careful to say that "some students of human nature" would say its point would qualify under the "worst thing" category, but he did not insist that students adopt such a view. In fact, Mr. Sartorius did not say he himself held this same viewpoint about the seriousness of the bus example regarding a denial of human worth. In short, the emphasis was always on the originality of student input and on safeguarding students' spontaneity against the teacher, against the expert who may not be present in class, and against each other. The Existentialist role model places perhaps a higher premium on the desirability of original contributions from students than for any other role model, even to the point of delaying the voicing of any personal opinions until students have had ample opportunity to explore for themselves issues and problems under study.

2. What is the nature of the subject matter?

Amorphous              ·         Structured

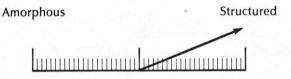

We have said many times previously that any attempt at solving problems requires students to emphasize the structure of subject matter, because they must relate bits and pieces of information to larger ideas implied by the issue or problem at hand. Certainly, as youngsters gave advice to characters in the film, they had to relate their points to aspects of human nature they had just studied and also to historical facts highlighted by the filmmakers. In this sense they were emphasizing structure, testing items for usefulness regarding the task at hand, and drawing on facets of psychology, sociology, and history. We have, in fact, so thoroughly discussed this question and the others in our analytical tool that little else needs to be said, except for one caveat about the nature of problem-solving as viewed by Existentialists in general.

Although many Existentialists may talk about bringing the intellect to bear on solving problems after the students' emotions have been truly piqued, they usually do not think of problem-solving in such formal terms as Essentialists and Experimentalists think of it. Their emphasis, rather than being on the discreet steps of problem-solving and of the thinking processes involved, focuses more on how a problem relates to an individual's personality development and how that problem may really be attacked in haphazard ways by "fits and starts." In fact, Existentialists are perfectly comfortable with assuming that one may receive, probably through some sort of emotionally charged peak experience, a solution in a flash of insight, before one even identifies a problem to be solved. For our purposes, however, the term *problem-solving* is still quite appropriate to cover this possibility. After all, if one receives a flash of insight which is deeply satisfying to the individual precisely because it is a flash of insight, then it may be supposed to satisfy some need or problem whose outlines can be reconstructed after the fact, although the problem itself had not been delineated by the individual before reaching the insight.

3. How should one use the subject matter to guide students toward meaningful learning activities?

Cognitive                                            Affective

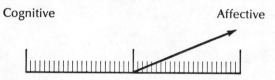

With this last question, we return once again to the emotionalism inherent in Existential approaches to teaching. Existentialists are careful to remind students of the "death dread"—that is, one day all of us will cease to exist in our present conditions, and perhaps no one will miss us. Existentialists use the term "death dread" in an attempt to help people understand the overwhelming importance of making thoughtful choices and living according to those choices in order to create a meaningful and psychologically satisfying existence. Much of Mr. Sartorius's dialogue with students concerned death directly, but that is not the only means of stressing the "death dread." As revealed in the bus example, it is possible by subtle looks or words, as well as by blatant deeds, to remind people of the ultimate denial of their human worth: in essence, to remind them that one day they may cease to exist, and perhaps no one will care that their remains are only skin and bones, devoid of personality. Such lessons can focus on real or potential injustices, such as shown in the film *Heritage of Slavery*, as a vehicle for reminding students of the "death dread." Or they can focus on the passage of time and the finite imperfections of any attempt to live according to an ideal within a limited span of time. Any of these examples serve as direct or indirect reminders of what Existentialists call the "death dread," and give lessons what we have called an "affective quality."

## PHILOSOPHIC PRINCIPLES SUPPORTING THE EXISTENTIALIST ROLE MODEL

As we begin to examine common themes among Existentialist thinkers, it may be helpful to offset what appears to be an undue emphasis on the macabre. As George Kneller and Van Cleve Morris continuously remind us,

*Comparison of Four Role Models: Essentialist, Experimentalist, Reconstructionalist, and Existentialist*

|  | Essentialist* (Ms. Chronicler) | Experimentalist (Ms. Progresso) | Reconstructionist (Mr. Remonde) | Existentialist (Mr. Sartorius) |
|---|---|---|---|---|
| **1. What is the nature of the learner?** | Lockean — Platonic | Lockean — Platonic | Lockean — Platonic | Lockean — Platonic |
| **2. What is the nature of the subject matter?** | Amorphous — Structured | Amorphous — Structured | Amorphous — Structured | Amorphous — Structured |
| **3. How should one use the subject matter to guide students toward meaningful learning activities?** | Cognitive — Affective | Cognitive — Affective | Cognitive — Affective | Cognitive — Affective |
| **4. What behavior trend should one exhibit in order to carry out one's philosophical position?** | Authoritarian World View (Convergence) — Non-authoritarian World View (Divergence) | Authoritarian World View (Convergence) — Non-authoritarian World View (Divergence) | Authoritarian World View (Convergence) — Non-authoritarian World View (Divergence) | Authoritarian World View (Convergence) — Non-authoritarian World View (Divergence) |

*Please note that as indicated in Chapter II, pp. 74–77, variations from Ms. Chronicler's style are possible within Essentialism.

139

Existentialist educators do not use the "death dread" in an attempt to be morbid. They wish to encourage individuality and a zestful determination to live life to its fullest, because life is finite and is filled with choices by which we establish psychologically satisfying identities. Remember, however, that the emphasis is not on the "death dread" as an end in itself, but rather on the "death dread's" power to stimulate self-assessment and growth.

(1) *Philosophy should become a passionate encounter with the perennial problems of life and with the inevitability of death.* In more direct terms, Existentialists see it as supreme duty to bring the "death dread," the *Angst,* to full consciousness in themselves and in others. They wish to force the recollection that death does not come in the abstract; rather, it comes physically for each person. It is not someone else's death that Existentialists ask to be contemplated, but one's own personal end that must be considered.

This contemplation of one's own demise is productive, because it creates the potential situation of despair in which constructive thought about the meaning of life can begin. Or, as some Existentialists are fond of saying, philosophy should begin "just this side of despair." This condition of virtual despair forces one to realize the personal quality of death and the ultimate absurdity of conditions in which humans are asked to give some meaning to an existence certain to be terminated by death. This mood of despair (for no philosophy and no knowledge can, or should, be separated from human emotion) sets the stage for thinking about life and its choices.

(2) *Existence precedes essence.* This phrase from Jean-Paul Sartre can appropriately be used in a beginning attempt to construct an Existentialist's view of reality, after the previously mentioned mood of despair has provided its proper stimulation for thought. Indeed, Existentialists point out that objects exist before man puts meaning onto those objects, and the fact that objects exist is more basic, or more real, than any meaning a person may add to them. Any essence or meaning humans abstract from the world is less real than the data from which it is abstracted.

From the two basic positions just outlined, Existentialists separate themselves into groups that are basically atheistic or theistic in orientation. We must first look at the atheistic orientation in order to understand the theistic emphasis more clearly.

(3) *The universe is without meaning or purpose.* A person is not part of a single cosmic design, because what we call "design" only represents a

person's attempt to project order onto this chaotic world. Humans are cast into this alien and chaotic universe knowing that they must die. In fact, humans alone of all animals are aware of their own thought processes and of their own anxiety about impending death. This awareness of the "death dread" is what makes life in an alien and chaotic world so burdensome. However, real heroism comes with taking hold of this absurdity of having to make meaning from a meaningless world and living life as if there were a true meaning in existence.

Although the foregoing principle may seem close to defeatism and nihilism, Existentialists do not focus on its negative aspects, but instead use the point to emphasize the importance of individual decision-making and action. I was recently working with a student teacher whose literature class had been considering personal qualities which our culture has labeled as heroic. During a discussion several youngsters expressed great difficulty in choosing a contemporary figure whom they considered heroic. Finally one young man attempted to solve the difficulties by exclaiming, "You know, we're really all heroes just to get through the day!" Although his statement represented an Existential awareness of any individual's problem of defining himself or herself in a technological society and making oneself really count for something in the maze of organizations, bureaucracies, and institutions we experience daily, his position did not seem to go much beyond the condition of despair with which Existentialists begin. Putting meaning into one's life is the quality that Existentialists call "heroic," not the individual's attitude of hopelessness in the midst of difficulty.

(4) *Human beings have absolute freedom because they do not form part of any universal system.* This emphasis on absolute freedom is what allows one to become truly heroic. Freedom is not seen as liberating in the popular sense of the term because it is omnipresent and totally burdensome. The completeness of this freedom, however, does allow each individual to take responsibility for his/her own welfare and development; moreover, this sense of responsibility in the use of freedom is what elevates man and woman to the highest pinnacle of worthiness. Freedom is seen as burdensome because it is so complete that no one can blame anyone else—not mother, father, siblings, or social conditions—for any choices one may make or for the outcome of any choices.

(5) *Human beings make themselves.* If humans have absolute freedom, then they truly define themselves by the actions they take. By consciously analyzing and sifting among choices and options, one makes oneself

through actions upon options as perceived. Or, as Existentialists like Sartre
have said, "Freedom being pure potentiality until it actualizes itself in
deeds, man is 'nothing' until he acts."

These three principles, regarding meaninglessness, absolute freedom,
and humans as self-defining organisms, are held with varying degrees of
tenacity among Existentialists, depending upon whether their outlook is
atheistic or theistic. Atheists within Existentialism subscribe to the "universe devoid of meaning" principle and insist that humans not only "make
themselves," but also make their own belief systems, cultures, and view of
God because these items "help them get through the day and night." Or, in
more direct terms, people heroically create whatever it takes for them to
"make it through the night" of despair. This creation of meaning in a universe devoid of meaning is the essence of heroic living.

While theorists obviously do not subscribe to the "universe devoid of
meaning principle, they do view humans as possessing absolute freedom
which can be used to define oneself in any way one chooses. That is, one may
choose to "make oneself" into a being pleasing to God and to the Forces of
Meaning which pervade the universe, or one may choose other options
freely. For theistic Existentialists the following phrase provides a succinct
summary of human development: What you are is God's gift to you; what you
make of yourself is your gift to God.

(6) *The philosopher has an obligation to expose tendencies which dehumanize people.* Regardless of how differently Existentialists may view the
three principles previously mentioned, they unite wholeheartedly about increasing sensitivity to forces and processes which tend to dehumanize. The
ultimate taboo inherent in all dehumanizing processes is a negativistic focusing on the "death dread." That is, dehumanizing processes in themselves tend to remind people of that final denial of humanity when we will
each cease to exist in our present conditions and when we perhaps may not
be missed. Unless philosophers and educators skillfully call attention to
this danger of dehumanizing trends, it is not possible for them to use creatively the "death dread's" healthy stimulus for decision-making and growth.
For Existentialist philosophers and educators the major goal is highlighting
injustices to remind people of the "death dread," and hoping that the
sensitivity and indignation they thus awaken in hearers will spur their
audiences to thoughtful decision-making and action. Nevertheless, they do
not hope to spur their hearers to adopt any one reform program, as a Reconstructionist might do, but they seek instead to create an intellectual and an
emotional climate that stimulates each individual to make his or her own
meaning and implement his or her own plan of action.

Existentialist tendencies infuse Mr. Sartorius's motivation for focusing on injustice, whether in the People's Temple cult or in more subtle forms among Charlestonians in the late 1960s. He talked directly about the "death dread" and required students to analyze the concept in some depth by posing a question about the worst thing one human being can do to another. Although his example about staring at a passenger during a boring bus trip exposed many Existentialist viewpoints, he apparently saw no need to use the term Existentialism or deal formally with its tenets in order for students to make their own judgments about injustice. In fact, he said almost nothing about injustices recounted in the film *Heritage of Slavery*, since he knew quite well that youngsters would be stimulated to make their own judgments and compose their own letters of advice to characters in the film. This expectation of extreme divergence and individualistic creation of meaning is the hallmark of an Existentialist educator. Consider the usefulness of such divergence and lack of direct teacher input in a situation, for instance, where the school setting has been noted for extremely polarized attitudes about race relations. A lesson like Mr. Sartorius's might be even more productive in such a setting, because the injustice inherent in the "death dread" can be examined in the abstract, without running the risk of having a discussion about racial injustices degenerate into name-calling or trading of recriminations. Students are perfectly capable of making their own judgments about injustice after a general discussion like Mr. Sartorius's and then applying those judgments to concrete settings in which emotionalism has long since reached a crescendo and continues to remain at a high level of intensity.

These issues which Mr. Sartorius faced have a contemporary sound, and so it is with Existentialism itself. As a mode of thinking, it is really so recent as to lack a great deal of coherence and is still considered by some to be more of a tendency or manner of approaching philosophical problems than a philosophy itself. Therefore, what we will say about antecedents will be brief, but what we need to say about Existentialism and your own decisions about choice of teacher behaviors requires some in-depth treatment. The decision to use Existentialist techniques, especially strategies normally referred to under the heading of values clarification, deserves much attention because such a decision would in many geographic areas be hardly less controversial than adopting a strong Reconstructionist stance.

## A Short History Troubled with Many Obstacles to Understanding

Although its antecedents go farther back in time, what is generally thought of as Existentialism is really a philosophy born of despair over economic and military uncertainties in twentieth century Europe. After World War I the most notable leaders of the movement were Martin Heidegger in Germany and Jean-Paul Sartre in France. However, the Existentialist emphasis on man as meaning-maker may be seen as a re-emergence of the Sophists' dictum from fifth century B.C. Greece: "Man is the measure of all things." Existentialists also trace their antecedents to the nineteenth century Danish philosopher Sören Kierkegaard, whose stress on subjectivity and individuality represented a revolt against the systematic philosophy of Hegel. Hegel's ideas about forces and trends in history was discussed briefly during our analysis of Experimentalism in Chapter Three.

Kierkegaard began a tradition of philosophical writing which has remained characteristic of Existentialism and which sometimes presents a special barrier to understanding. Instead of couching his thought in organized and systematic expositions typical of most philosophers, he often wrote in imaginative, quasi-fictional formats. Perhaps because that style of writing is quite suitable for the subjectivism inherent in Existentialist thinking, the trend of expression through novels and other forms of fiction has remained prominent. We already have talked about *The Stranger*, by Camus, through Mr. Sartorius's lesson. But Camus also wrote *The Plague*, *The Myth of Sisyphus*, and a number of plays. The reader, in this case, interprets philosophical points by inference from novels and plays. A similar situation is found in Victor Frankl's work, *Man's Search for Meaning*. Although this is an intense and inspiring Existentialist statement about personal experiences as Frankl struggled to derive meaning from his existence in a Nazi concentration camp, the same difficulties of inference and interpretation are evident. Though statements of philosophical points may be appealingly embodied in plays, novels, and other highly personal modes of expression, problems of interpretation abound when the philosopher does not talk directly and systematically about his thought.

Another difficulty of interpretation closely related to the problem of inference from fictionalized writing is the point that mere words sometimes seem inadequate for conveying the depth of feeling inherent in Existentialism. When Martin Buber spoke of the beauties of human interaction based on mutual respect, of the destructive quality inherent in talking *past* someone rather than talking *to* someone, and of the exhilaration of "I-Thou" relationships, mere words seemed inadequate indeed. Perhaps such semantic problems are inevitable within a philosophy whose adherents insist that only subjectivity and alignment with Existentialist principles can produce understanding of those same principles.

Coupled with the stylistic difficulties and the subjectivity which we have just mentioned are the many divisions among thinkers who call themselves Existentialists. Major divisions are the theistic and atheistic viewpoints discussed in the preceding section of this chapter. Although commonalities among atheistic adherents like Sartre and Camus and among theistic proponents like Martin Buber and Paul Tillich do exist, there are many divergent strains within Existentialism which defy organization and systemization, perhaps because the Existentialist tradition is still quite young. At least this diversity adds considerable richness. For our purposes, however, Van Cleve Morris's application of Existentialist thought to teaching has to be considered as central to any decision-making about building a comfortable style of teaching that is uniquely one's own.

## THE EXISTENTIALIST ROLE MODEL IN THE CLASSROOM

In *Existentialism in Education* Morris has presented several basic concerns about the Existentialist in a classroom setting. Those concerns and their implications need to be examined closely before one makes a decision about building a teaching style based on Existentialist thought.

### The "Death Dread" as Stimulus and Depressant?

First of all, there is the dilemma of how a teacher can stress creatively the principle that death is the most important event in a person's life. We are not speaking of death as an abstract condition; instead, we are focusing on ways to encourage youngsters to consider the meaning of death as a personal event. How does one reassure youngsters that contemplating the "death dread" is productive in that it heightens a sense of responsibility for choices and stimulates examination of one's values? How does one avoid the attitude of morbidity expressed by a remark I overheard while working with a student teacher who was using John Gunther's *Death Be Not Proud* as part of her unit on death in literature: "I'm so tired of coming to this class every day and having to get ready to cry!"

One can often focus on the finiteness of life without risking morbidity. In effect, the finiteness of life and of many objects (a rose, for instance) is the quality which makes that object or condition so special. A rose is just that much more precious because we know its beauty will soon wane.

This quality of finiteness as viewed by Existentialists has been capsulized potently in the story "King Solomon's Ring" as told by Judith Ish-Kishor in *Tales from the Wise Men of Israel* (J. P. Lippincott Company, 1962). It seems that King Solomon, half in jest and half seriously, wanted to test one of his most faithful captains of the guard, who had often boasted that he had never failed his king in any task. Solomon asked this captain to procure for him a certain wonderful ring six months in advance of the celebration at which Solomon wished to wear this jewel. The king described the desired ring's magical powers succinctly: "If a happy man looks at it, he at once becomes downcast and gloomy; but if a person in misery or mourning beholds it, hope rises in his heart, and he is comforted."

After pledging to Solomon his undying determination to procure this special ring, the captain interviewed all the tradesmen and merchants in the city to urge them to search for the ring as their caravans moved to distant parts of the earth. In subsequent visits the captain was always told that, not only had they not been able to find such a ring, the traders had not even met someone who had heard of a ring with those wondrous qualities. In sleepless despair the captain walked the streets alone on the night before he was to present his prize to Solomon. As he approached a poor trader on a street corner, he decided to ask one last time the question which had now become almost meaningless to him. When the trader replied that he had not heard of such a ring, but felt he might be able to make one, the captain was truly astounded. The trader engraved on a simple gold band the phrase, "This, too, shall pass," and immediately the captain knew he had the proper ring and went away rejoicing that he had again not failed the king in any task.

When Solomon asked his captain at the celebration on the following day to produce this magical ring, he expected to meet the downcast face of his loyal servant, because Solomon knew no such ring existed. Other courtiers waited in mischievous expectation to witness the consternation of this man who had too often boasted that he would never fail his king. When Solomon, in astonishment, received the ring and read its inscription, he was reminded that all his glory must one day fade. He also understood that someone in deep misery would be given hope by reading the phrase, "This, too, shall pass." Solomon praised his faithful servant and repented for having misjudged the captain's sincerity and intelligence by charging him with this apparently impossible task.

The Existentialist educator's view of finiteness is similar to that presented in the foregoing story. Reminding one of the finite should serve as a creative stimulus for self-assessment, not as a recounting of doom's approach. Whether one focuses directly on death, or on injustice, or on the failure to live up to an ideal within a limited time span, the emphasis should always be on having the individual decide on positive choices, on a course of action designed as a creative response to the dilemma at hand. That is certainly what Mr. Sartorius had in mind when he asked youngsters to advise characters in the film, *Heritage of Slavery*. Each individual can respond creatively and positively to the dilemma of injustice because none of us is impotent; we just have to make our own meaning through thoughtful response.

## Existential Relationships with Students

A second concern for Existentialists in the classroom follows an implication of presenting issues which remind students of the "death dread"—namely, the concern about how humans interact, especially when an emotionally charged issue is being considered. To Existentialists all social relationships, every human interaction, is doomed to frustration, because the logical tendency is for one or some members of a group to dominate while others submit. However, group participation must ideally be based on the interplay of free personalities as equals, not on forced conformity or artificial consensus. Helping students to interact and think as equals is far from easy, yet it can occur. When such interaction does occur, it is particularly special because it is likely to be short-lived. This is why values clarification theorists like Sid Simon insist on withholding the teacher's opinion about an issue until kids have had time to think, rather than just react, and on delaying classroom discussion until youngsters have pondered the issue at hand as individuals.

This special quality of human interaction—the quality which makes human relationships truly meaningful—applies not only to students but also to teachers. Such an existentially ideal relationship between teachers and students can be an attractive goal to work towards. Of course, a classroom atmosphere lacking the typical artificial restraints of classroom governance, such as grades, hall passes, and detention for lack of cooperation, may not survive for any length of time.

In essence, such an atmosphere of mutual respect is a goal to be sought after, reached, sometimes retreated from, and then perhaps reached again as teachers and students come to know, respect, and cherish each other more fully. Teachers should let students know that they care about their progress by helping students to see that there are many avenues to success—more avenues, in fact, than the traditional performance on written tests. Allow students to have a part in planning issues to be studied. Teach them to write successful essay tests, if those are the types of written tests the teacher prefers, by constructing "model" essay answers during classroom discussions. (I use the essay questions as an example because they generally encourage students to express their knowledge, rather than artificially restricting their responses as true/false and multiple choice items usually do. So-called objective questions, which can be scored by tallying little blackened spaces on answer sheets, usually discriminate reversely, because the more information and insight one has, the more likely one is to think of more subtle aspects of the question and, therefore, the more likely one is to answer incorrectly.)

Make essay questions challenging, but not obscure: that is, be sure that the test matches what has been taught in terms of both skills and knowledge. For instance, if students were given at the beginning of an instructional unit a set of questions to guide research and analysis for that unit, then teachers should use some aspects of questions on the unit sheet as part of the test. They should also help students understand that the longer they work with the teacher and come to know the objectives the teacher wishes to reach, the higher their grades are likely to become, as long as they continue to strive.

Teachers should also make it clear to students that they know there are other items in the students' lives besides school and the subject matter being taught. Therefore, the teacher may need to hold conferences with each student so that the student is aware of factors which compose the final grade, and so that he or she can plan realistically with the teacher the amount of time and effort which can reasonably be invested in order to secure a satisfying grade.

Teachers should also allow students to talk about various methods which might be used in studying succeeding topics, and then permit them to have some input for deciding which method they would like most to emphasize. Although a teacher may have built a teaching style composed of methods which stress either convergence or divergence, there should still be sufficient options to present kids with several different choices without violating the teacher's style. Attention to those choices can give the teacher an opportunity to educate students regarding the merits and drawbacks of any one method. Such discussions should go far in helping them gain insights into the skills and knowledge both teacher and students hope to develop.

Attention to all the foregoing items regarding what is usually called classroom management should help a teacher strive toward that "free interplay of personalities" as equals which is the special Existentialist ideal of meaningful human relationships. Hopefully, at the end of an instructional unit the teacher should be able to talk openly and honestly about the progress students have made. Conversely, students should be able to talk openly about activities they found either helpful or tedious. Teachers can ask students if they feel they have learned anything they would be better off not knowing; moreover, this might be a helpful way to begin a process of mutually evaluating the effectiveness of a unit of study.

However, precisely because this ideal of mutual respect in interaction is so difficult to achieve, but at the same time so attractive because it is idealistic, one must be prepared to retreat from it, if necessary, and rely on more traditional approaches to classroom management which involve rewards and punishments. After a time of renewed striving for the ideal, it may again be reached and, thus, prove increasingly satisfying to all. One should expect these fits and starts in building meaningful human relationships, which are all the more precious because they tend to be short-lived. Just as Existentialists see a truly meaningful love relationship in marriage as a logical impossibility because of the tendency for one partner to dominate and the other to submit, the counterpart of this love relationship in a classroom between students and a teacher is exceedingly special when it does occur.

Although the suggestions made for achieving this ideal relationship between students and teachers most appropriately support the Existential role model, it is entirely possible and indeed desirable to move toward this ideal whatever teaching style one constructs. Although elements of pupil-teacher planning and extreme divergence which belong to the Experimentalist and Existentialist role models would be inappropriate for an Essentialist educator, emphasis on mutual respect is appropriate in every teaching/learning situation for any teaching behavior to be effective. For any teaching style we have examined there must be sufficient cooperation between teachers and students for learning to occur, whether the teaching style employed emphasizes convergence or divergence. Moreover, if a teacher decides to use Existentialist techniques, he or she must move carefully toward the ideal of truly meaningful relationships, since the ideal condition tends to be delicately short-lived. It may, therefore, be unwise for beginners to consider entirely eliminating traditional means of classroom management, such as letter grades and detention.

## How Well Do Teachers Like Controversy?

A third concern for Existentialists in the classroom involves the degree to which knowledge must engage the emotions in order to stimulate thoughtful choices and promote the development of one's values. To Existentialists knowledge cannot occur apart from emotional involvement. In fact, the detachment and emphasis on purely intellectual skills advocated by Essentialists and Experimentalists may lead to information transfer, but not to true knowledge. Both the intellect and the emotions must be involved before any learning can occur. But then arises the practical question of how much emotion. How controversial should an issue be which spurs analysis of choices and the process of clarifying values? Since values must be freely chosen by each individual to be meaningful, does an overemphasis on emotional and controversial issues automatically contaminate the process by making it less than free? How affective can a lesson be before it becomes counter productive?

Let us look briefly at some of the assumptions underlying values clarification as set forth by Louis Raths, Merrill Harmin, and Sidney Simon in *Values and Teaching*, first published in 1966 by the Charles Merrill Company. Their approaches and assumptions contain practical advice on how much emotionalism a lesson should involve, or how Existential in orientation a lesson should be. They insist that no course of action can be associated with the term "value" unless the action has been selected after thoughtful consideration of alternatives, unless there is definite translation of this decision into action, and unless the individual publicly affirms his support for the course of action; therefore, their emphasis is on reflective thinking which involves both the intellect and the emotions. Any course of action adopted without reflective thinking about alternatives, such as behavior selected merely because one's peers approve or because it represents the prevailing sentiment of one's family and community, cannot be seen to represent one's system of values; on the contrary, such behavior would mean an individual is simply adhering to custom and habit.

## Clarifying Values

Instead of slavish attention to convention and custom, actions consciously selected according to one's system of values indicate an awareness of anxiety resulting from the chasm between the ideals one cherishes and the realities of one's typical behavior pattern. This awareness of the frustrating gap between ideal and reality is an excellent vehicle for reminding youngsters of the "death dread" and of the responsibilities they have for making thoughtful choices. Existentialists believe that one's feeling of self worth, or lack of it, is closely associated with living according to one's ideals, according to the meaning one has made for oneself. Therefore, the freedom of choosing is to be welcomed because this burdensome freedom stems from the inherent forsakenness of the human condition and provides the opportunity for an individual's growth through actions that are self-defining.

Stimuli for thoughtful choosing can come in a variety of guises. Value clarifiers have suggested many techniques and numerous topics—such as money, friendship, love and sex, religion and morals, leisure, politics and social organization, work, family, maturity, and character traits—to be used in promoting growth toward an organized system of values. Whatever the technique or topic, however, the goal is the individual who actually takes charge of his own existence and lives as he wishes to live, according to values he has actively and reflectively constructed. Raths, Harmin, and Simon have envisioned people as existing on a continuum from "values unclear" to "values clarified" as endpoints. As technological and social changes occur at increasingly rapid rates, those near the "values unclear" end of the continuum experience rising difficulties in coping, in making their lives satisfying because they lack an internal guide (whether one calls it a system of clarified values or a philosophy of life) which would allow them to make their own meaning out of existence. As the stress of change becomes greater, such people are apt to experience feelings of listlessness, impotence, and a general sense of being adrift. This condition, according to the authors, can and does lead to emotional disturbance and mental illness. Indeed, these states of mind will probably be increasingly evident as leisure time increases and as more people must be their own philosophers to give themselves direction in a society characterized by pluralism. Whereas in former times the masses may have been too busy with subsistence-level activity to worry about philosophical questions, so busy with efforts to survive that they could accept someone else's system of thought or some outside form of organized religion, today the confusion wrought by rapid change and by pluralism makes it impossible for rational people to avoid philosophical musings about the nature of reality and their places in that reality.

Near the other end of this continuum are those who have analyzed what they believe and have brought most of their behavior patterns in line with personal ideals. These are the people who have had the satisfaction of defining themselves through choice, of having given meaning to existence, of knowing that they are actively attempting to accomplish goals they set for themselves. Those near the "values clarified" portion of the continuum have reached what Abraham Maslow called "self-actualization" and what Carl Rogers has termed the "fully functioning" personality. Such individuals are actively and creatively coping with their environment, learning, and growing, not because they are merely struggling to meet physiological needs for food, shelter, and sex, or psychological needs for belonging and esteem. They are able to cope with difficulties precisely because they have managed to satisfy the physiological and more basic psychological needs and can now attend to the joys of "becoming," of striving to reach one's highest potential in a field or vocation consciously chosen and sought after. This end product—the fully functioning person, the self-actualized individual whose system of values has been clarified—is what the techniques recommended by Raths, Harmin, and Simon are planned to accomplish.

Techniques designed to spur youngsters toward self-actualization range from informal conversations which highlight chance occurrences, to discussions concerning emotional issues which are bound up with traditional subject matter and which glide into personalized strategies for individual and group counseling sessions. For instance, suppose a student remarked to his teacher between classes and with an obvious crescendo of excitement, "I'm going to D.C. this weekend!" This chance encounter can be used quite effectively, if the teacher responds in an unexpected manner in order to highlight the dilemma of passing time and how it is used. Instead of the teacher responding with a predictable, "Wonderful! I hope you have a great time!" suppose he said, "Oh, how do you feel about that?" The student might think, "What does he mean 'how do I feel about that?' Of course I want to go because it's going to be a great weekend, *I think.*" This example represents the essence of an informal values clarification situation which Raths, Harmin, and Simon have called a "one-legged conference," because it usually involves a brief encounter in the hallway.

Recently I was working with a student teacher who decided to use a technique Raths, Harmin, and Simon have named the "value sheet." She had developed a unit on the Cold War and used an original "value sheet" idea to introduce the lessons. Her value sheet exercise concerned an American male sitting comfortably in his easy chair reading the newspaper. As he glanced over the headlines, he was drawn to a story recounting famine, disease, and recent earthquakes experienced by the People's Republic of China. He began to feel a certain exultant satisfaction that all those Communists were having it so rough. Then he decided perhaps he didn't like the way he was feeling. Indeed, why should so much suffering experienced by those who happened to be living under a different ideology make him happy? The student teacher then followed this article with a few questions about students' understandings of the term *Cold War* and about their feelings when potential enemies experience hardship and disaster. Group discussion was delayed until each youngster had had ample opportunity to write answers to all the questions; the teacher then waited until students had voiced their own views before revealing her opinions, which, as she emphasized, were purely her opinions and not facts.

## Impotence and Injustice

It is pointless to continue here with values clarification examples when so many exist, especially in the two editions of *Values and Teaching* by Raths, Harmin, and Simon (Charles Merrill Company, 1966 and 1978) and in *Values Clarification—A Handbook of Practial Strategies* by Simon, Howe, and Kirschenbaum (Hart Publishing Company, 1973). However, the strategies all involve a deliberate heightening of anxiety, and sometimes indignation, about the pull between ideal and reality. This heightening of what Robert Coles has called "moral sensitivity" is meant to spur youngsters to act out values which they have chosen and to act upon them in their own ways; it is not done to convince an audience to adopt any one course of action as Reconstructionists attempt to do. In Volume II of his *Children of Crisis* series Coles recounted the story of a privileged youngster whose father used migrant labor extremely profitably. When this privileged child became empathic after playing regularly with a child from his father's migrant camp, and after he told parents and teachers about his feelings of empathy in no uncertain terms, the "establishment" became quite alarmed. Teachers and principals couldn't understand how the youngster could have developed such bizarre notions of morality. Parents were dismayed that their son evidenced feelings of guilt about the disparity between his own life style and the manner in which his playmates at the migrant camp had to live. After many counseling sessions with teachers and psychiatrists this youngster was desensitized and talked out of his guilt feelings. As an adult he became a socialized member of the establishment, ready to take over the family's agricultural business upon his father's retirement.

Perhaps because of the Civil Rights struggles which grew white hot in the 1960s, there has arisen a heightened awareness of moral sensitivity and the need for values clarification. Lawrence Kohlberg's writings on moral development, along with the works of Robert Coles and the values clarification theorists we have just mentioned, have done much to formalize these concerns and give them a place inside public school curricula. This attention to moral issues, controversial topics, and values clarification as a part of the public school purview has also been bolstered by Existential psychologists like Abraham Maslow and Carl Rogers. This movement approximately fifteen years ago was called "third force" psychology; this "force" belonged neither to the Behaviorist orientation of B. F. Skinner nor to the psychoanalytic orientation of Sigmund Freud. While Freudian and Skinnerian approaches had defined good behavior in terms of how most people actually behaved, this "third force" was quite different. It has provided a model of excellence which views desirable behavior as "something to shoot for," because most people have not yet succeeded in clarifying values and becoming "self-actualizing"; it definitely does not define good behavior in terms of "norms." Whereas a psychologist in the Freudian or Skinnerian tradition would be likely to condition a person out of unpleasant feelings of guilt, an Existential psychologist would perhaps deliberately attempt to heighten guilt feelings in order for the person to formulate a value system on which one might act as one chose to act.

Such an approach, whether we call it values clarification or Existential psychology, tends to make waves, just as with the results of Reconstructionist approaches to teaching. However, the Existentialist educator encourages youngsters to formulate their own values based on thoughtful examination of choices and their consequences; he or she does not try to pull students into one social reform activity. This brings us to a special consideration of the pitfalls and dangers one may incur in adopting the Existentialist Role Model.

## Raths and Wrath

Similar to the construction of a teaching style based on any of the philosophies we have studied, a decision to be an Existentialist teacher is a highly
personal choice. The teacher is entirely on his or her own in making such a
choice because no body of research exists, nor is it ever likely to exist, to
support the efficacy of any set of teaching methods or techniques as always
successful. Therefore, a teacher must develop his or her own rationale for
teaching behaviors and be able to explain the rationale to any student, parent, administrator, or interested citizen who may ask.

Being able to explain one's rationale clearly and coolly is especially
important in this instance, however, because many people become quite
upset that controversial issues are analyzed in public schools. Critics seem
sometimes to assume that any attempt at values clarification, or just hearing
the phrase itself, indicates an evil predisposition on the part of educators to
tamper with the values of youth. It is entirely possible that what critics call
"values" are really nothing more than students' slavish adherence to custom
and habit. It is entirely possible that once students analyze custom and habit
within their families and communities, the behavior patterns represented
will not be changed at all. In fact, such behaviors which parents have dili-
gently tried to enforce may end up as values and be held all the more dearly
by youth, because they have been examined and have been seen to possess
considerable merit. The point is, however, that the educator cannot be sure
of an outcome in this case, if ever he can, because divergence is so clearly
expected. Divergence opens up a world of possibilities; a radical departure
from local custom is certainly one of those possibilities.

One example may help to illustrate clearly that teachers cannot predict
the outcomes of values clarification and cannot assess in any formal way the
readiness of students to tackle a specific controversial issue. Within a unit
concerning industrialization in the United States during the nineteenth
century, I decided to stress with my eleventh graders the relationships between Darwinism, Social Darwinism, and *laissez-faire* economics. I had
them read an article on "Bigfoot" and on sightings of the creature, and then
we discussed possibilities for its existence. Students were excited about
hypotheses about Bigfoot, but at first they were silent when I asked whether
they might feel differently about themselves as human beings, if they knew
for certain that Bigfoot actually lived. After a few moments of silence, I explained that someone who believed in Darwin's ideas might insist Bigfoot
represents the missing link between man and the lower animals and might
cite his existence as proof that we do not have souls. I definitely wanted
youngsters to see in a personal way how Darwin's ideas were applied so
readily to society.

We followed this conversation by looking at various aspects of the conflict between "science" and "fundamentalist religion" through the 1920s by culminating with the Scope's "Monkey" Trial, which tested a Tennessee statute prohibiting the teaching of evolution. To conclude our study of the conflict and to prevent fundamentalist Protestantism from being shown in so unfavorable a light, I asked youngsters to bring in religious materials they might have seen about evolution. A number of sophisticated items came to me, among them Hal Lindsey's *The Late Great Planet Earth* (Zondervan Publishers, 1970).

Feeling bound to use these materials because I had asked kids to do the research, yet suffering trepidation about any presentation based on Lindsey's analysis of Biblical prophecy and contemporary events, I decided to make our discussion of current trends in fundamentalist Protestantism optional. Although I explained to youngsters that they did not have to participate in the discussion, but could instead work in the media center on several other options, no one left. The discussion was lively; to me, the entire unit seemed quite successful, and the kids affirmed this in their evaluations. No students, parents, or administrators complained about the topics or their controversial nature. In addition, two years later, one student wrote to explain that she had just seen a short movie on Bigfoot and that she still "didn't believe any of those things Darwin had to say." Although I may not agree with the students' beliefs, I still think teachers should decide responsibly whether the youngsters are ready to deal with controversial issues and to employ values clarification strategies.

Not everyone, however, would honor the teacher's professional role and decision-making power. While teaching a recent unit on values clarification for one of my undergraduate methodology classes, I was surprised by an evening newscaster's report that one of the supplementary texts I was using had been banned from the professional library of a neighboring school division. Citizens of Kanawah County in West Virginia demanded to rid the schools of certain texts dealing with controversial issues. The furor over sex education courses is not dead either, but many school divisions skirt the issue by refusing to sanction any discussions about responsibility and sex, or values and sex, or choice and sex; this solution is bizarre, since youngsters rarely need to know only about biology, but often need to talk with adults about morality and values.

Another consideration teachers will face, in addition to the complaints about controversial issues openly discussed, is the feeling of many critics that "basic skills" are not emphasized in methods employed by Existentialists, Experimentalists, or Reconstructionists. My own feeling is that all responsible teaching must help youngsters grow in their use of written and oral communication. Sometimes critics assume that controversial issues and values clarification techniques are used as shocking attention-getters, as a means of helping tired and harassed teachers compete against the young person's tendency to turn off the teacher the way one turns off the television dial. Some controversial issues are, no doubt, misused. However, educators should go beyond motivating devices and work with students on developing skills of oral and written communication and of critical thinking.

Each teacher must make his or her own decision concerning a teaching style to develop. In fact, building one's own teaching style, planning units of instruction, and writing educational objectives are gigantic exercises in values clarification for any teacher. Those tasks are designed to provide insights into one's own nature. Moreover, the Existential Role Model is designed to promote the understanding of human nature. But perhaps a teacher would prefer to emphasize inquiry into human nature within a framework that does not encourage so much divergence. Let us look, then, at Perennialism, a teaching style which uses open-ended questions with the faith that convergence about all matters which are truly important will ultimately emerge.

# THE PERENNIALIST
# TEACHER
## as Inquirer into Human Nature

# CHAPTER SIX

### *The Setting in Microcosm:*

## MR. LONGMAN ANALYZES NAT TURNER AFTER THE LATE INSURRECTION, 1831

Mr. Longman's assistant superintendent had decreed that all secondary English and social studies teachers in the school division must complete the Great Books Foundation's course in discussion leadership. Elaborate preparations were made. Substitutes were hired for all English and social studies classes. Excitement, and some trepidation, mounted when word got out that the instructor would be flown in from Chicago (a distance of about twelve hundred miles) for a series of eight Thursday afternoon sessions. But, when the packets of course materials arrived, they contained only selections of literary works, except for one brief excerpt from the writings of the ancient historian Xenophon and a portion of *The Declaration of Independence*. Mr. Longman, a social studies teacher, felt his anxiety rise and silently agreed when he heard a colleague remark, "Those history teachers had better jump in and show what they know while we're discussing *The Declaration of Independence* and before we all get bogged down in literary criticism."

Determined to squelch any latent feelings of insecurity, Mr. Longman resolved to profit by this in-service experience. After all, he could be doing less noble things with his leisure time than improving discussion leadership skills. And skill improvement might have substantial payoff. For instance, it might help avoid recurrence of those disconcerting times when he had felt he was tossing out to students creative and stimulating questions, only to have kids stare blankly as the questions fell to the floor with a forlorn thud at the rear of the classroom. In addition, he had heard the assistant superintendent remark that she herself had taken the discussion leadership course and that it had been a profound intellectual experience which had completely overhauled her mode of thinking and of attacking problems. Dr. Besting was indeed convinced that everybody should share in such a high-powered experience; moreover, she felt that the English and social studies teachers could use extra insights into ways of conducting discussions because of tensions and human relations problems evident in the secondary schools.

At the first class session several teachers talked openly with the instructor about their hopes for adapting what they would be learning for use in secondary classrooms and asked for her suggestions. The instructor simply confirmed her beliefs that discussion leadership skills she would teach would be appropriate for junior high and senior high kids. In fact, she took this opportunity to play her organization's promotional tape of third graders discussing stories from *Winnie-the-Pooh*, according to the Great Books methods. However, she said she was determined to teach the skills "straight" for the informal discussion group setting and leave it up to her hearers to decide for themselves exactly how to proceed in classroom discussions. She pointed out the almost universal applicability of Great Books procedures by calling attention to the title for the packets of materials participants had been given. The Foundation, after completing its *Junior Training Course for Discussion Leaders*, had decided there was no need for a "Senior" training course packet because of the method's adaptability. Therefore, materials were purposely being distributed with the old title *Junior Training Course* although no "Senior" course or "Senior" materials existed. Using such materials with the original title simply provided an opportunity to emphasize how applicable the method is to varieties of groups and age levels.

Mr. Longman swallowed all those bits of information and convinced himself that the instructor was too sincere to be copping out when teachers asked her for special help with their own class discussions. The key to successful discussion leadership, Mr. Longman was told, involved asking questions for which he, as leader, had no answers. Although there was some resistance to a suggestion that teachers should ask kids questions they didn't have answers for, Mr. Longman decided it did make sense after all. If he didn't know the answer, then he wouldn't listen for one student to repeat that magic phrase he might have in mind. Result: more thinking and listening because kids and teachers are actually dealing with real questions, instead of mind-reading exercises designed to see if factual information can be regurgitated. In other words, Mr. Longman decided it would be a healthier development if this technique could help him reward kids for honest attempts to find answers, rather than praising them for reading his mind.

Mr. Longman entered fully into the practice sessions, since everyone was required to organize interpretive questions (the kind without definite answers) into clusters which could be asked of participants in any order to match the direction of discussion. The main topic of investigation was to be encapsulated in a basic interpretive question, and then included in a cluster of at least eight follow-up questions about the same topic. It all seemed to work quite smoothly, except for that rule about not bringing in "outside information" during the discussion.. Participants were told to deal only with ideas presented in the document to be discussed. During the first session's discussion one anxious history teacher had mentioned that *The Declaration of Independence* embodied John Locke's political philosophy, whereupon the instructor cried "Stop!" That ended work with the *Declaration*, and the opportunities for social studies teachers to "display" what they knew about it. Instead, participants were treated to an explanation of the rule about "no outside information." It had something to do, Mr. Longman surmised, with the belief that the author of a great work of literature can communicate directly to the reader without interpretive aids or "outside information" of any kind.

Mr. Longman decided, however, that to use this technique in his own classes, "outside information" would be precisely what he would want his kids to bring in, because he would want them to relate their discussion of any document to other topics they had studied. He talked with his students excitedly about the benefits of the Great Books discussion method and prepared them for a first attempt at the method by having them become thoroughly familiar with participants' rules. He decided that since he wished to introduce a unit on life in the United States before the Civil War with a case study on Nat Turner's insurrection, he would have kids discuss according to the Great Books design. He asked youngsters to read *Confessions of Nat Turner*, published by Thomas Gray shortly after his interview of Nat in 1831, to prepare for the next day's discussion.

The following describes participants' rules and contains excerpts from *Confessions of Nat Turner*, which Mr. Longman distributed to his class.

---

## Rules of Discussion*

1. Read in advance. You must complete the reading before the class in order to participate well in the discussion.

2. Read carefully. You will not get much out of the discussion unless you remember accurately what you have read. List in your notebooks as you read questions which occur to you and which are *not fully answered* by the text references. These may be useful points to bring up in discussion.

3. Back up your statements. Don't judge a statement by who makes it or how many participants agree with it, but by how well it is supported. Statements are supported in discussion by: 1) Reading from the book. 2) Giving an accurate summary of what the book says. 3) Offering reasons or examples you think of yourself. If you repeat an opinion, definition, or idea you have heard or read elsewhere, you will be expected to back it up as if it were your own.

4. Stick to the subject under discussion. You and your fellow participants should work together to explore each question fully. Try to find new ideas about what is being discussed. Don't make a comment that no longer fits into the discussion; perhaps it will fit into the discussion at some later point.

5. Speak up freely. Say what you think, and be ready to give your reasons. You may agree or disagree with anything said by your fellow participants. Make your statements or ask your questions to fellow participants, not to the leader.

6. Listen carefully. When others speak, do not pay so much attention to your own thoughts that you fail to hear what is said. Question them about any remark that you do not understand before you contribute your own ideas.

7. Be courteous. Be sure to speak clearly so that your remarks may be heard
by everyone in the room. Don't interrupt when someone else is speaking.
Be willing to withhold your comments if you start to speak at the same
time as others. Don't engage in private conversations.

## The Confessions of Nat Turner*

Agreeable to his own appointment, on the evening he was committed to
prison, with permission of the jailer, I visited Nat on Tuesday the 1st
November, when, without being questioned at all, he commenced his narrative in the following words:

Sir,—You have asked me to give a history of the motives which induced me
to undertake the late insurrection, as you call it—To do so I must go back to
the days of my infancy, and even before I was born. I was thirty-one years of
age the 2nd of October last, and born the property of Benj. Turner, of this
county. In my childhood a circumstance occurred which made an indelible
impression on my mind, and laid the ground work of that enthusiasm, which
has terminated so fatally to many, both white and black, and for which I am
about to atone at the gallows. It is here necessary to relate this circumstance—
trifling as it may seem, it was the commencement of the belief which has
grown with time, and even now, sir, in this dungeon, helpless and forsaken as I
am, I cannot divest myself of. Being at play with other children, when three or
four years old, I was telling them something, which my mother overhearing,
said it had happened before I was born—I stuck to my story, however, and
related some things which went, in her opinion, to confirm it—others being
called on were greatly astonished, knowing that these things had happened,
and caused them to say in my hearing, I surely would be a prophet, as the Lord
had shown me things that had happened before my birth. And my father and
mother strengthened me in this my first impression, saying in my presence, I
was intended for some great purpose, which they had always thought from
certain marks on my head and breast—(a parcel of excrescences which I believe are not at all uncommon, particularly among Negroes, as I have seen
several with the same. In this case he has either cut them off or they have
nearly disappeared)—My grandmother, who was very religious, and to whom
I was much attached—my master, who belonged to the church, and other
religious persons who visited the house, and whom I often saw at prayers,
noticing the singularity of my manners, I suppose, and my uncommon intelligence for a child, remarked I had too much sense to be raised, and if I was,
I would never be of any service to any one as a slave—To a mind like mine,
restless, inquisitive and observant of everything that was passing, it is easy to
suppose that religion was the subject to which it would be directed, and although this subject principally occupied my thoughts—there was nothing that
I saw or heard of to which my attention was not directed—The manner in
which I learned to read and write, not only had great influence on my own
mind, as I acquired it with the most perfect ease, so much so, that I have no
recollection whatever of learning the alphabet—but to the astonishment of the

family, one day, when a book was shown me to keep me from crying, I began spelling the names of different objects—this was a source of wonder to all the neighborhood, particularly the blacks—and this learning was constantly improved at all opportunities—when I got large enough to go to work, while employed, I was reflecting on many things that would present themselves to my imagination, and whenever an opportunity occurred of looking at a book, when the school children were getting their lessons, I would find many things that the fertility of my own imagination had depicted to me before; all my time, not devoted to my master's service, was spent either in prayer, or in making experiments in casting different things in molds made of earth, in attempting to make paper, gunpowder, and many other experiments, that although I could not perfect, yet convinced me of its practicability if I had the means. I was not addicted to stealing in my youth, nor have ever been—Yet such was the confidence of the Negroes in the neighborhood, even at this early period of my life, in my superior judgment, that they would often carry me with them when they were going on any roguery, to plan for them. Growing up among them, with this confidence in my superior judgment, and when this, in their opinions, was perfected by Divine inspiration, from the circumstances already alluded to in my infancy, and which belief was ever afterwards zealously inculcated by the austerity of my life and manners, which became the subject of remark by white and black.—Having soon discovered to be great, I must appear so, and therefore studiously avoided mixing in society, and wrapped myself in mystery, devoting my time to fasting and prayer—By this time, having arrived to man's estate, and hearing the scriptures commented on at meetings, I was struck with that particular passage which says: "Seek ye the kingdom of Heaven and all things shall be added unto you." I reflected much on this passage, and prayed daily for light on this subject—As I was praying one day at my plough, the spirit spoke to me, saying "Seek ye the kingdom of Heaven and all things shall be added unto you." *Question*—What do you mean by the Spirit. *Answer.* The Spirit that spoke to the prophets in former days—and I was greatly astonished, and for two years prayed continually, whenever my duty would permit,—and then again I had the same revelation, which fully confirmed me the impression that I was ordained for some great purpose in the hands of the Almighty. Several years rolled round, in which many events occurred to strengthen me in this my belief. At this time I reverted in my mind to the remarks made of me in my childhood, and the things that had been shown me—and as it had been said of me in my childhood by those by whom I had been taught to pray, both white and black, and in whom I had the greatest confidence, that I had too much sense to be raised, and if I was I would never be of any use to any one as a slave. Now finding I had arrived to man's estate, and was a slave, and these revelations being made known to me, I began to direct my attention to this great object, to fulfil the purpose for which, by this time, I felt assured I was intended. Knowing the influence I had obtained over the minds of my fellow servants, (not by the means of conjuring and such like tricks—for to them I always spoke of such things with contempt) but by the communion of the Spirit whose revelations I often communicated to them and they believed and said my wisdom came from God. I now began to prepare them for my purpose, by telling them something was about to happen that would terminate in fulfilling the great promise that had been made to me—about this time I was placed under an overseer, from whom I ran away—and after remaining in the woods thirty days, I returned to the astonishment of the Negroes on the plantation, who thought I had made my escape to some other part of the country, as my father had done before. But the reason of my return was, that the Spirit appeared to me and said I had my wishes directed to the things of this world, and not to the kingdom of Heaven, and that I should return to the service of my earthly master—"For he who knoweth his Master's will, and doeth it not, shall be beaten with many stripes, and thus have I chastened you." And the Negroes found fault, and murmured against me, saying that if they had my sense they would not serve any master in the world. And about this time I had a vision—and I saw white spirits engaged in battle, and the sun was darkened—the thunder rolled in the Heavens, and blood flowed in streams—and I heard a voice saying, "Such is your luck, such you are called to see, and let it come rough or smooth, you must surely bear it." I now withdrew myself as much as my situation would permit, from the intercourse of my fellow servants, for the avowed purpose of serving the Spirit more fully—and it appeared to me, and reminded me of the things it had already shown me, and that it would then reveal to me the knowledge of the elements, the revolution of the planets, the operation of tides, and changes of the seasons. After this revelation in the year 1825, and the knowledge of the elements being made known to me, I sought more than ever to obtain true holiness before the great day of judgment should appear, and then I began to receive the true knowledge of faith. And from the first steps of righteousness until the last, was I made perfect; and the Holy Ghost was with me, and said, "Behold me as I stand in the Heavens"—and I looked and saw . . . the lights of the Saviour's hands, stretched forth from east to west, even as they were extended on the cross on Calvary for the redemption of sinners. And I wondered greatly at these miracles, and prayed to be informed of a certainty of the meaning thereof—and shortly afterwards, while laboring in the field, I discovered drops of blood on the corn as though it were dew from heaven—and I communicated it to many, both white and black, in the neighborhood—and I then found on the leaves in the woods hieroglyphic characters, and numbers, with the forms of men in different attitudes, portrayed in blood, and representing the figures I had seen before in the heavens. And now the Holy Ghost had revealed itself to me, and made plain the miracles it had shown me—For as the blood of Christ had been shed on this earth, and had ascended to heaven for the salvation of sinners, and was now returning to earth again in the form of dew—and as the leaves on the trees bore the impression of the figures I had seen in the heavens, it was plain to me that the Saviour was about to lay down the yoke he had borne for the sins of men, and the great day of judgment was at hand. About this time I told these things to a white man, (Etheldred T. Brantley) on whom it had a wonderful effect—and he ceased from his wickedness, and was attacked immediately with a cutaneous eruption, and blood oozed from the pores of his skin, and after praying and fasting nine days, he was healed; and the Spirit appeared to me again, and said, as the Saviour had been baptized so should we be also—and when the white people would not let us be baptized by the church, we went down into the water together, in the sight of many who reviled us, and were baptized by the Spirit—After this I re-joiced greatly, and gave thanks to God. And on the 12th of May, 1828, I heard a loud noise in the heavens, and the Spirit instantly appeared to me and said the Serpent was loosened, and Christ had laid down the yoke he had borne for the sins of men, and that I should take it on and fight against the Serpent, for the time was fast approaching when the first should be last and last should be first. *Question*—Do you not find yourself mistaken now? *Answer*—Was not Christ crucified? And by signs in the heavens that it would make known to me when I should commence the great work—and until the first sign appeared, I should conceal it from the knowledge of men—And on the appearance of the sign, (the eclipse of the sun last February) I should arise and prepare myself, and slay my enemies with their own weapons. And immediately on the sign appearing in the heavens, the seal was removed from my lips, and I communicated the great work laid out for me to do, to four in whom I had the greatest confidence, (Henry, Hark, Nelson, and Sam)—It was intended by us to have begun the work of death on the 4th July last—Many were the plans formed and rejected by us, and it affected my mind to such a degree that I fell sick, and the time passed without our coming to any determination how to commence—still forming new schemes and rejecting them, when the sign appeared again, which determined me not to wait longer.

Since the commencement of 1830, I had been living with Mr. Joseph Travis, who was to me a kind master, and placed the greatest confidence in me; in fact, I had no excuse to complain of his treatment to me. On Saturday evening the 20th of August, it was agreed between Henry, Hark, and myself, to prepare a dinner the next day for the men we expected, and then to concert a plan, as we had not determined on any. Hark, on the following morning, brought a pig, and Henry brandy and being joined by Sam, Nelson, Will, and Jack, they prepared in the woods a dinner, where about three o'clock, I joined them.

Q. Why were you so backward in joining them?

A. The same reason that had caused me not to mix with them for years before.

I saluted them on coming up, and asked Will how came he there, he answered, his life was worth no more than others, and his liberty as dear to him. I asked him if he thought to obtain it? He said he would, or lose his life. This was enough to put him in full confidence. Jack, I knew, was only a tool in the hands of Hark, it was quickly agreed we should commence at home (Mr. J. Travis) on that night, and until we had armed and equipped ourselves, and gathered sufficient force, neither age nor sex was to be spared, (which was invariably adhered to.) We remained at the feast, until about two hours in the night, when we went to the house and found Austin; they all went to the cider press and drank, except myself. On returning to the house Hark went to the door with an axe, for the purpose of breaking it open, as we knew we were strong enough to murder the family, if they were awaked by the noise; but reflecting that it might create an alarm in the neighborhood, we determined to enter the house secretly, and murder them whilst sleeping. Hark got a ladder and set it against the chimney, on which I ascended, and hoisting a window, entered and came down stairs, unbarred the door, and removed the guns from their places. It was then observed that I must spill the first blood. On which, armed with a hatchet, and accompanied by Will, I entered my master's chamber, it being dark, I could not give a death blow, the hatchet glanced from his head, he sprang from the bed and called his wife, it was his last word, Will laid him dead, with a blow of his axe and Mrs. Travis shared the same fate, as she lay in bed. The murder of this family, five in number, was the work of a moment, not one of them awoke; there was a little infant sleeping in a cradle, that was forgotten, until we had left the house and gone some distance, when Henry and Will returned and killed it; we got here, four guns that would shoot, and several old muskets, with a pound or two of powder. We remained some time at the barn, where we paraded; I formed them in a line as soldiers, and after carrying them through all the manoeuvres I was master of, marched them off to Mr. Salthul Francis', about six hundred yards distant. Sam and Will went to the door and knocked. Mr. Francis asked who was there, Sam replied it was him, and he had a letter for him, on which he got up and came to the door; they immediately seized him, and dragging him out a little from the door, he was dispatched by repeated blows on the head; there was no other white person in the family. We started from there for Mrs. Reese's, maintaining the most perfect silence on our march, where finding the door unlocked, we entered, and murdered Mrs. Reese in her bed, while sleeping; her son awoke, but it was only to sleep the sleep of death, he had only time to say who is that, and he was no more. From Mrs. Reese's we went to Mrs. Turner's a mile distant, which we reached about sunrise on Monday morning. Henry, Austin, and Sam, went to the still, where, finding Mr. Peebles, Austin shot him, and the rest of us went to the house; as we approached, the family discovered us, and shut the door. Vain hope! Will, with one stroke of his axe, opened it, and we entered and found Mrs. Turner and Mrs. Newsome in the middle of a room, almost frightened to death. Will immediately killed Mrs. Turner, with one blow of his axe. I took Mrs. Newsome by the hand, and with the sword I had when I was apprehended, I struck her several blows over the head, but not being able to kill her as the sword was dull. Will turning around and discovering it, dispatched her also. A general destruction of property and search for money and ammunition, always succeeded the murders. By this time my company amounted to fifteen, and nine men mounted, who started for Mrs. Whitehead's, (the other six were to go through a by way to Mr. Bryant's, and rejoin us at Mrs. Whitehead's), as we approached the house we discovered Mr. Richard Whitehead standing in the cotton patch, near the lane fence; we called him over into the lane, and Will, the executioner, was near at hand, with his fatal axe, to send him to an untimely grave. As we pushed on to the house, I discovered some one run round the garden, and thinking it was some of the white family, I pursued them, but finding it was a servant girl belonging to the house, I returned to commence the work of death, but they whom I left, had not been idle; all the family were already murdered, but Mrs. Whitehead and her daughter Margaret, when I discovered her, had concealed herself in the corner, formed by the projection of the cellar . . . from the house; on my approach she fled, but was soon overtaken, and after repeated blows with a sword, I killed her by a blow on the head, with a fence rail. By this time, the six who had gone by Mr. Bryant's, rejoined us, and informed me they had done the work of death assigned them. We again divided, part going to Mr. Richard

Porter's, and from thence to Nathaniel Francis', the others to Mr. Howell Harris', and Mr. T. Doyles'. On my reaching Mr. Porter's he had escaped with his family. I understood there that the alarm had already spread. . . .

I here proceeded to make some inquiries of him, after assuring him of the certain death that awaited him, and that concealment would only bring destruction on the innocent as well as the guilty, of his own color, if he knew of any extensive or concerted plan. His answer was, I do not. When I questioned him as to the insurrection in North Carolina happening about the same time, he denied any knowledge of it; and when I looked him in the face as though I would search his inmost thoughts, he replied, "I see sir, you doubt my word; but can you not think the same ideas, and strange appearances about this time in the heavens might prompt others, as well as myself, to this undertaking." I now had much conversation with and asked him many questions, having forborne to do so previously, except in the cases noted in parenthesis; but during his statement, I had, unnoticed by him, taken notes as to some particular circumstances, and having the advantage of his statement before me in writing, on the evening of the third day that I had been with him, I began a cross examination, and found his statement corroborated by every circumstance coming within my own knowledge or the confessions of others whom had been either killed or executed, and whom he had not seen nor had any knowledge since 22d of August last, he expressed himself fully satisfied as to the impracticability of his attempt. It has been said he was ignorant and cowardly, and that his object was to murder and rob for the purpose of obtaining money to make his escape. It is notorious, that he was never known to have a dollar in his life; to swear an oath, or drink a drop of spirits. As to his ignorance, he certainly never had the advantages of education, but he can read and write, (it was taught him by his parents), and for natural intelligence and quickness of apprehension, is surpassed by few men I have ever seen. As to his being a coward, his reason as given for not resisting Mr. Phipps, shows the decision of his character. When he saw Mr. Phipps present his gun, he said he knew it was impossible for him to escape as the woods were full of men; he therefore thought it was better to surrender, and trust to fortune for his escape. He is a complete fanatic, or plays his part most admirably. On other subjects he possesses an uncommon share of intelligence, with a mind capable of attaining anything; but warped and perverted by the influence of early impressions. He is below the ordinary stature, though strong and active, having the true Negro face, every feature of which is strongly marked. I shall not attempt to describe the effect of his narrative, as told and commented on by himself, in the condemned hole of the prison. The calm, deliberate composure with which he spoke of his late deeds and intentions, the expression of his fiend-like face when excited by enthusiasm, still bearing the stains of the blood of helpless innocence about him; clothed with rags and covered with chains; not daring to raise his manacled hands to heaven, with a spirit soaring above the attributes of man; I looked on him and my blood curdled in my veins.

I will not shock the feelings of humanity, nor wound afresh the bosoms of the disconsolate sufferers in this unparalleled and inhuman massacre, by detailing the deeds of their fiend-like barbarity. There were two or three who were in the power of these wretches, had they known it, and who escaped in the most providential manner. There were two whom they thought they left dead on the field at Mr. Parker's, but who were only stunned by the blows of their guns, as they did not take time to re-load when they charged on them. The escape of a little girl who went to school at Mr. Waller's, and where the children were collecting for that purpose excited general sympathy. As their teacher had not arrived, they were at play in the yard, and seeing the Negroes approach, she ran up on a dirt chimney, (such as are common to log houses), and remained there unnoticed during the massacre of the eleven that were killed at this place. She remained on her hiding place till just before the arrival of a party, who were in pursuit of the murderers, when she came down and fled to a swamp, where, a mere child as she was, with the horrors of the late scene before her, she lay concealed until the next day, when seeing a party go up to the house, she came up, and on being asked how she escaped, replied with the utmost simplicity, "The Lord helped her." She was taken up behind a gentleman of the party, and returned to the arms of her weeping mother. Miss Whitehead concealed herself between the bed and the mat that supported it, while they murdered her sister in the same room, without discovering her. She was afterwards carried off, and concealed for protection by a slave of the family, who gave evidence against several of them on their trial. Mrs. Nathaniel Francis, while concealed in a closet heard their blows, and the shrieks of the victims of these ruthless savages; they then entered the closet where she was concealed, and went out without discovering her. While in this hiding place, she heard two of her women in a quarrel about the division of her clothes. Mr. John T. Baron, discovering them approaching his house told his wife to make her escape, and scorning to fly, fell fighting on his own threshold. After firing his rifle, he discharged his gun at them, and then broke it over the villain who first approached him, but he was overpowered, and slain. His bravery, however, saved from the hands of these monsters, his lovely and amiable wife, who will long lament a husband so deserving of her love. As directed by him, she attempted to escape through the garden, when she was caught and held by one of her servant girls, but another coming to her rescue, she fled to the woods, and concealed herself. Few indeed, were those who escaped their work of death. But fortunate for society, the hand of retributive justice has overtaken them; and not one that was known to be concerned has escaped.

*From Thomas R. Gray, *The Confessions of Nat Turner* (Baltimore, Lucas and Deaver, 1831), pp. 7–20.

---

## Classroom Dialogue for the Perennialist Role Model

*Mr. Longman:*  I'm going to assume you've all finished reading *Confessions of Nat Turner* by Thomas Gray because I've already heard a number of good questions from you about Nat's personality. Today we're going to be discussing just that topic—Nat's personality. Now that we're all in a circle I want to remind you about our rules for discussion. Remember that I will be serving as leader in questioning and will not be providing any answers during discussion. Let's see how it goes! Why did Nat lead a rebellion? (pause) Meg, can you help us with that?

*Meg:*  This reading was just unbelievable! I can't understand why anyone would think ghosts would appear and say, "Go out and murder a few people!"

*Mr. Longman:*  Does anyone else have something to add to Meg's comments?

*Meg:*  He seemed to think the whole thing was religious, but I can't see how it was religious to murder people!

*Mr. Longman:*  It's interesting that you've brought up the point about religion. Why did religion seem to occupy so much of Nat's thinking?

*Chris:*  I don't know. It just seems that almost everything he talked about in the interview was mixed up with religion and with visions of spirits. It all seems so crazy!

*Mark:*  Didn't he see himself as a holy person? When the fellow interviewed him, he was talking about a vision of "when the first should be last and the last should be first." Then the guy who was interviewing said, "Don't you find you're mistaken now?" But Nat answered, "Wasn't Christ crucified?" How can you deal with that? If you see yourself as a holy person, then you can convince yourself that anything you want to do is right.

*Judith:*  But what about all those things he had known about religion even before he decided to rebel? Did he really at first intend to be a minister? Maybe he thought his duty would be to preach to other slaves, since he learned to read so fast and understanding the Bible was so easy for him, I mean.

*Allen:*  It might be too that he knew white people wouldn't consider him dangerous if he was a preacher. They did have laws sometimes to keep slaves from learning how to read and write. But if you were a slave and would preach to other slaves about how good it is for servants to obey their masters, then what harm would whites see in that?

*Aileen:*  Are you saying that he always wanted to kill slaveowners and was just using the image of "preacher" to look peaceful?

*Allen:*  No, it might be that he really was peaceful until he started having all those visions about spirits fighting. By then maybe people trusted him so much that he could do all that planning for the murders without looking suspicious.

*Mr. Longman:*  Well, that's an interesting point. Is that why he said, "Having soon discovered to be great, I must appear so, and therefore studiously avoided mixing in society?"

*Judith:*  But I got the feeling that he avoided people a lot just to seem more mysterious so he could have more blacks look up to him as a leader. Wasn't that the big reason?

*Mr. Longman:*  I'm not sure. Can anyone else help us here?

*Mark:*  Well, do we really know for sure that Nat said, "Having soon discovered to be great, I must appear so. . ."? This whole thing was written up by someone else—by a white man who must have been pretty scared by all those ax murders; and maybe he was just making Nat look like someone who always tried to trick people into thinking he was special. I mean, we don't really know he talked like this, do we? The story just has so many big words in it all strung together.

*Mr. Longman:* So you think we may be getting so much of Thomas Gray's interpretation that we can't know what Nat Turner was really like?

*Mark:* Yeah, I think maybe that's it. I just don't believe he talked like that, even if Gray does say "he commenced his narrative in the following words."

*Aileen:* I think Mark's right. Gray seems really bent out of shape because he is talking with Nat. He does call Nat a "complete fanatic" and then he says, "I looked on him and my blood curdled in my veins."

*Mr. Longman:* Even though it may be hard to separate what Nat must have been like from what Gray thought he was like, can you give us some ideas about what he might have hoped to accomplish by leading the rebellion?

*Aileen:* First of all, I don't think Nat was just trying to fool people into thinking he was special. I think he really believed that he was special and that he was going to "strike a blow" for freedom—freedom for himself and for other slaves. I think Gray realized this and, as scared as he might have been by these murders, he might even have admired Nat for the guts he showed by doing something so extreme. Unless Nat was totally convinced he was special and could accomplish something for blacks, I don't think he would have started off on a series of ax murders.

*Chris:* But if you really look at what happened, Nat didn't commit many murders. It was always Will, with his "handy" ax! And look how long it took him to make up his mind about a plan! Why didn't he just rely on the spirits to tell him how to do this when the time was right?

*Mr. Longman:* That's a good question. I think we should consider whether Nat believed more in supernatural direction for helping him complete his mission or in his own ability to plan for rebellion.

*Meg:* Going back to what Chris said, maybe he did rely on the spirits in the end. He had taken so long to plan. He got a sign in 1828, and then planned until 1831! He finally got a second sign while the planning was still going on and decided not to wait any more. It says, "still forming new schemes and rejecting them, when the sign appeared again, which determined me not to wait longer." Maybe he really didn't have much confidence in his ability to plan for this thing and actually ended up going ahead without a finalized plan, just trusting instead in supernatural direction.

*Mr. Longman:* I see what you're saying. Could there be other reasons for his taking so long to make up his mind besides lack of confidence?

*Judith:* I don't care how much you believe in a cause, it seems that planning this many murders would be extreme enough to make anybody want to wait awhile. And that's what he did; he kept on planning and waiting. He also must have liked the Travises, at least a little. He says, "Since the commencement of 1830, I had been living with Mr. Joseph Travis, who was to me a kind master, and placed the greatest confidence in me; in fact, I had no excuse to complain of his treatment to me." If somebody's been reasonably kind to you, it must be hard to think of murdering that person with an ax.

*Allen:* It might not make any difference that the Travises were kind to him. Sure, maybe they gave him food and clothes and didn't beat him, but how "kind" is that if the Travises own you and you can't even leave their plantation without permission? Even if they don't beat you, you know they could. He could say the Travises were kind to him, but only in some ways that are not really important. If they honestly wanted to be kind, they would have given him his freedom and helped him get a new start. I don't think they were "kind" to him at all, and I understand why he might have wanted to rebel. If I were Nat Turner, I might have done just what he did!

*Mr. Longman:* I'm glad you've brought up these issues! Does it strike anyone as surprising that Nat is the one who led the most publicized of slave revolts and that it occurred in Southampton County, Virginia, in 1831?

*Meg:* It does seem surprising that he was treated so well. But I can't understand about Allen saying he might do the same thing. We're talking about all this killing. Do you *approve* of *that*?

*Allen:* No, I'm not saying I approve of the killing. I'm just saying I can understand why he did it. If I were in his position it wouldn't make that much difference to me that someone gave me food, clothes, and didn't beat me. I just wouldn't be able to stand being a slave. It would bother me so much not to have any personal freedom and to know that this family had life-and-death control over me! That's what I wouldn't be able to accept; and maybe Nat couldn't either.

*Mark:* I think I see what Allen means. In one way it is surprising that Nat would lead a rebellion because his owners showed him some kindness, and in other ways it doesn't seem surprising because he was probably aware of how bad it is to be called a "slave" under the law. Maybe other slaves who couldn't read and didn't think as much as Nat would have been happy because the Travises gave them clothing and food.

*Judith:* I remember that Southampton County is not too far from the coast, so that would mean the land there would have been worn out by 1831, and people didn't know that much about using fertilizers then. That's also the time when people really needed slaves in Mississippi and Alabama and the "deep" South—not in Virginia. Maybe Nat was in an area where slaves were not needed so much and didn't have to work so hard. Maybe he just had more time to think about all these things and decided he just couldn't stand being unfree, being a slave under the law, no matter how many kindnesses the Travises showed him. Maybe that's why he did what he did.

*Mark:* Maybe so, but how can we know for sure what reasons he had? We've already said we don't know how much of this story really is Nat and how much of it is what Thomas Gray thought of Nat.

*Mr. Longman:* That's right. We can't know for certain, but you've done a good job today investigating a lot of possible reasons in your discussion. I'm impressed with what you've accomplished. You've brought up many topics that we ought to examine as we study lifestyles in this country just prior to the Civil War.

Mr. Longman was impressed by the students' discussion. He had applied the Great Books approach to discussion leadership and he had discovered that students could respond amazingly well when teachers ask questions for which they have no definite answers in mind. Although he had begun with the two question clusters outlined below, he had not been able to ask all of them.

Cluster #1: Why did Nat Turner lead a rebellion? ("Follow-up" questions below to be asked in any order appropriate to discussion.)

1. Why did religion occupy so much of Nat's thinking?
2. Did Nat believe the wisdom for managing this undertaking came from God? Why or why not?
3. Did Nat believe in his own wisdom? Why or why not?
4. Why did he say, "Having soon discovered to be great, I must appear so, and therefore studiously avoided mixing in society?"
5. Why did he withdraw for the "avowed purpose of serving the Spirit"?
6. Did Nat believe more in God-given wisdom for leading a rebellion or in his own "sense"? Why or why not?
7. Why didn't the Spirit tell him what plan of rebellion to follow?
8. Why did Nat appear to believe in the justice of his cause to the end?
9. In leading the rebellion did Nat seek death? Why or why not?
10. If he believed so much in the justice of his rebellion, why did he give himself up so readily to Mr. Phipps?
11. Why did the revolt occur in Southampton County, Virginia, in 1831?

Cluster #2: Did Thomas Gray admire Nat Turner? Why or why not? ("Follow-up" questions below to be asked in any order appropriate to discussion.)

1. Why did Gray include a paragraph which gives his assessment of Nat's character?
2. What did Gray mean by a "complete fanatic"?
3. Why did Gray say, "I looked on him and my blood curdled in my veins"?
4. Why did Gray say he would not describe the effect of Nat's narrative?
5. Why did Gray say he would not "give details of their fiend-like barbarity," when he had done just that?
6. Why did Gray include the story of the little school girl's escape and give so much emphasis to it?
7. What is the significance of the remark, "The Lord had helped her"?
8. What change in Gray's attitude do you notice in the last two paragraphs?

Mr. Longman obviously did not need to ask all these questions because youngsters brought up many of the same points on their own. He also adeptly changed the phrasing and shifted the order of several questions to suit more precisely comments that students had just made. Moreover, as the Great Books instructor had so carefully explained, once a discussion takes hold the leader will have to do little to keep participants involved. He had even followed the precept not to summarize what participants had said. Summarizing, according to the instructor from Chicago, would only make students rely on the leader to do all their thinking for them. At any rate, Mr. Longman decided that students had become aware on their own of the subtle historiographical problems one always meets in trying to sort out causation and motivation. He could at least afford to wait until the day after his discussion to help students see by a summary just how much awareness they had gained.

Although Mr. Longman was very pleased with his success, we need to delay our analysis of his dialogue with students briefly. Because of the changes he saw fit to make in adapting Great Books techniques—changes that are quite typical for public school classrooms—he actually pulled methodology out of its larger philosophical context. In short, he used the method, without buying its philosophical support. Therefore, we need to examine the Perennialist curriculum at St. John's College before we can establish the appropriate context for using our analytical tool.

## The Setting in Macrocosm: Perennialism at St. John's

St. John's College in Annapolis, Maryland, is a special bastion of Perennialism. According to an article by Kenneth Turner in *The* Washington *Post's Potomac* magazine ("Civilization and St. John's," May 4, 1975), the college is so special that one of its graduates was able to affirm, "In case the world were ever destroyed, a St. John's person could rebuild civilization from its roots." Although the graduate's claim may sound like an astounding hyperbole, this community of about four hundred students focuses on 130 great works of literature in such an intense discussion format that they undoubtedly leave St. John's with profound insights into ideas central to Western civilization.

Their intense probing accustoms them to posing sometimes unorthodox questions, a trait in which they take special pride. It also encourages them sometimes to offer startling answers. The same article from *Potomac* recounts the story of a Black Panther group who in the mid-1960s ended up in the office of Dean John Kieffer. After speaking at length about the malaise in the United States which they felt resulted directly from exploitation built into the capitalist system, Dean Kieffer broke the long silence. "I don't think that's really the cause," said the Dean. When the Panthers wanted to know exactly what he did consider the cause, he politely replied, "Original sin." The Panthers were a bit stunned and decided to leave quietly.

This intense questioning and sometimes unusual dialogue so central to the St. John's curriculum occurs mostly in the Great Books seminars. These seminar sessions meet twice weekly (including the time between semesters), contain fifteen to twenty students who are responsible for approximately one hundred pages of reading per session, and are conducted by two group leaders. The Great Books are considered chronologically by classes as indicated in the list on pages 174–175, taken from a recent catalogue.

The Great Books Foundation used to "push" these same volumes through major magazines by ads carrying the caption, "These are the books Hitler burned!" Such ads usually contained a small black-and-white photograph of people gleefully burning books in one corner and, in another corner, a large full-color picture of handsome, leather-bound volumes in a well-polished solid wood bookcase. The Foundation's ads also underscored a major tenet of St. John's, as well as other Great Books seminars, through emphasis on the *Syntopicon*, a key volume in the set.

The *Syntopicon* contains cross-references to other books in the series, references arranged to help one find at a glance what all the great authors have had to say about topics of general interest and about components of the human personality, such as love, hate, and envy. If the human personality has not substantially changed during the last several thousand years, then great authors of the ancient world can and do have insights which are as powerful and pertinent for today as authors who have written more recently. That is what seminar participants are supposed to discover, along with insights into human personality and into the traditions of Western thought systems. In addition, the emphasis is on insights which come from working directly with the Great Books; insights must come this way because the great author communicates best when "speaking" directly to the seminar participant. A host of interpreters, experts, and secondary sources which attempt to tell what the great author has said are superfluous, if not downright pernicious, because they can usurp one's right to do one's own thinking.

What about the rest of the curriculm which supports the seminar's ambitious and all but overwhelming attempt to analyze the greatest works of literature in four years? That supporting portion of the curriculum consists of tutorials—one each in languages, in mathematics, in music, as well as a laboratory tutorial dealing with the physical sciences. The general purpose of all tutorials is to help students cultivate habits of careful and methodical study. Tutorial sessions consist of eight to fifteen students who follow a modified discussion format which is much less intense than that of the Great Books

## FRESHMAN YEAR

Homer: *Illiad, Oddyssey*
Herodotus: *History**
Aeschylus: *Agamemnon, Choephoroe, Euminides, Prometheus Bound*
Sophocles: *Oedipus Rex, Oedipus at Colonus, Antigone*
Euripedes: *Hippolytus, Medea*
Aristophanes: *Clouds, Birds*
Plato: *Ion, Gorgias, Meno, Republic, Apology, Crito, Phaedo,*
     *Symposium, Parmenides,** *Theaetetus, Sophist, Timaeus, Phaedrus*
Thucydides: *The Peloponnesian War*
Aristotle: *On the Soul,** *Physics,** *Metaphysics,** *Nicomachean Ethics**,
     *Politics,** *Organon,** *Poetics*
Euclid: *Elements**
Lucretius: *On the Nature of Things*
Lavoisier: *Elements of Chemistry**
Nicomachus: *Arithmetic**

## SOPHOMORE YEAR

Epictetus: *Discourses,** *Manual*
Apollonius: *Conics, I– III*
Virgil: *Aeneid*
*The Bible**
Tacitus: *Annals**
Plutarch: *Lives**
Gibbon: *The Decline and Fall of the Roman Empire*
Ptolomy: *Almagest**
Galen: *On the Natural Faculties*
Plotinus: *Fifth Ennead*
Augustine: *Confessions*
*Song of Roland*
Anselm: *Proslogium*
Thomas Aquinas: *Summa Theologica,** *Summa Contra Gentiles**
Dante: *The Divine Comedy*
Chaucer: *The Canterbury Tales**
Rabelais: *Gargantua and Pantagruel**
Machiavelli: *The Prince, Discourses**
Luther: *A Treatise on Christian Liberty, Secular Authority*
Calvin: *Institutes**
Copernicus: *On the Revolution of the Spheres**
Montaigne: *Essays**
Bacon: *Novum Organum*
Kepler: *Epitome of Copernican Astronomy, IV, V*
Donne: *Poems**
Shakespeare: *Richard II, Henry IV - Part 1 and Part 2, As You Like It,*
     *Twelfth Night, Othello, Hamlet, Macbeth, King Lear, The Tempest,*
     *Coriolanus*
Harvey: *On the Motion of the Heart and Blood*
Darwin: *Origin of Species**

## JUNIOR YEAR

Cervantes: *Don Quixote*

Galileo:  *Two New Sciences\**
Descartes:  *Rules for the Direction of the Mind,\* Discourse on Method,*
  *Geometry,\* Meditations*
Hobbes:  *Leviathan\**
Spinoza:  *Theologico-Political Treatise*
Milton:  *Paradise Lost,\* Samson Agonistes*
Pascal:  *Pensées\**
Racine:  *Phèdre*
Newton:  *Principia,\* Optics\**
Huygens:  *Treatise on Light\**
Locke:  *Essay Concerning Human Understanding,\**
  *Second Treatise on Government*
Berkeley:  *Principles of Human Knowledge*
Leibniz:  *Discourse on Metaphysics, Monadology*
Swift:  *Gulliver's Travels*
Fielding:  *Tom Jones*
Hume:  *Enquiry Concerning Human Understanding,*
  *Dialogues Concerning Natural Religion*
Rosseau:  *The Social Contract*
Adam Smith:  *The Wealth of Nations\**
Kant:  *Critique of Pure Reason,\* Critique of Practical Reason,\**
  *Fundamental Principle of the Metaphysics of Morals*
*The Declaration of Independence, Articles of Confederation,*
  *United States Constitution*
Madison, Hamilton:  *The Federalist\**
Melville:  *Billy Budd, Benito Cereno*

## SENIOR YEAR

La Fontaine:  *Fables\**
Goethe:  *Faust\**
Hegel:  *Philosophy of History,\* Preface to the Phenomenology of Spirit,*
  *Logic,\* Philosophy of Right\**
Kierkegaard:  *Fear and Trembling, Philosophical Fragments*
Lobachevski:  *Theory of Parallels\**
Marx:  *Capital,\* Communist Manifesto, Preface to Critique of*
  *Political Economy,\* Economic and Philosophic Manuscripts\**
Tolstoi:  *War and Peace*
Nietzsche:  *Birth of Tragedy, Beyond Good and Evil*
Austen:  *Pride and Prejudice*
Dostoevski:  *The Possessed, Crime and Punishment,*
  *The Brothers Karamazov, The Idiot*
Baudelaire:  *Poems\**
Wagner:  *Tristan and Isolda*
Freud:  *A General Introduction to Psychoanalysis*
De Tocqueville:  *Democracy in America, Documents from American*
  *Political History*
Pierce:  *Philosophical Papers\**
Valéry:  *Poems\**
Einstein:  *On the Electrodynamics of Moving Bodies*

\*Studied in the tutorials or laboratory

seminars and which is punctuated by information-giving on the part of the tutorial leader.

Language tutorials aim at training in the means of precise communication and at restoring the studies of grammar, rhetoric, and logic to what those at St. John's think is their proper place in the curriculm. The emphasis is on understanding relationships between language and thought; *not*, for example, on studying French so that one might eventually be able to converse smoothly with a Parisian waiter. The first two years concern obtaining a reading mastery of ancient Greek, while in the last two years students are expected to master the reading of French. This plan supports the Great Books seminar directly because students must read some Greek and French works in the original languages.

St. John's emphasis on mathematics may be surmised from the following statement in a recent catalogue: "Next to their mother tongue the language of number and figure is the most important symbolic possession of men." Students begin with Euclid's *Elements*, progress eventually to the study of Ptolemy's astronomy as background for reading Dante, investigate Copernicus' views of the universe, and by the time they are seniors will be found studying calculus and non-Euclidian geometries. Another statement from the catalogue provides many insights about rationale for what tend to become astounding requirements: "Insofar as the modern world is the creation of the Age of Reason, the St. John's handling of mathematics and science is an excellent and almost indispensable experience for anyone who wishes to know what modernity means."

St. John's music tutorials attempt to restore music to the curriculum as a liberal art. Their study of music approaches what Plato might have approved because emphasis is on the sense of ratio and proportion one can derive from examining principles of harmony and general relationships among tones, as well as from attending to form and analysis for various styles of musical composition. This formal study of music is bolstered by a requirement to sing in a chorus during the sophomore year—the only year in which music is a mandated part of the curriculum.

Laboratory tutorials follow the same general pattern as for mathematics tutorials: in essence, major works in the field are considered chronologically so that one approaches each set of disciplines through an historical framework. Freshmen study theories of measurement and of chemical atomism concerning the development of the periodic chart of elements. Sophomores read seminal works in biology. Juniors investigate mechanics, optics, and force fields. By the senior year students take a look at electromagnetism, thermonuclear dynamics, and quantum physics. Such astounding comprehensiveness at least helps one understand why the St.

John's catalogue implies that graduates are prepared well for professional education in any field, though there could be a few specific courses they lack here and there for fulfilling some entrance requirements to particular professional schools.

All this comprehensiveness in the formal curriculum is supplemented by a round of lectures and concerts, many of which are mandatory. Even though the St. John's man or woman is viewed as fully prepared for any type of professional education, the St. John's experience "is not pre-professional or pre-anything but a thing in itself," according to a former dean's remark reported in *Potomac*. Students find this comprehensiveness packaged in a curriculum consisting of the same four basic courses each year: Great Books seminars and tutorials in languages, mathematics, and physical sciences. And these courses can only be begun as a freshman student in either September or January, no matter what one's previous undergraduate collegiate experience may have been.

Their faculty members, called "tutors" because the actual faculty consists of authors of the great books to be studied, must promise eventually to teach all classes. The reeducation this requires of graduates from most Ph.D. programs might be astounding in itself, but is usually seen as well worth the effort because it preserves the status of the scholarly amateur whose vitality comes mostly from one's capacity to view learning as a whole entity that has too often been artificially subdivided. Beginning faculty members attend special study groups where they learn new disciplines and the skills necessary for managing discussions and for toning down one's desire to follow lecture modes of instruction. Faculty members who teach successfully for two years at St. John's may apply for a special master's degree. Despite obvious pressures for St. John's tutors, the *Potomac* article reported about five hundred applicants for each vacancy, perhaps because the college has no "publish or perish" doctrine and because prospective tutors find the "Great Books" brand of Socratic questioning attractively stimulating.

Students seem to leave the college with inordinate pride in St. John's itself, in their tutors, and in this approach to learning which is still being called the "New Program," although it was introduced in 1937. In that year Stringfellow Barr and Scott Buchanan, who had been close friends as Rhodes Scholars at Oxford, pushed the nation's third oldest college, founded as King William's School in 1696, off into what Barr has continued to call an "extraordinary adventure." That adventure is best described in Barr's own words, as reported in *Potomac*:

> Most people, Barr is aware, equate education with the amassing of facts, the collection of up-to-the-minute data, something he scornfully refers to as "feeding little birds with spoons, cramming it down their

little throats. People feel if you have enough information, what more can you ask unless you're God Almighty." That something more, the thing St. John's revolves around, is "the handling of ideas. You can get information in a library. The thing we were interested in doing was getting the mind to work again."*

And getting the mind to work again involves reading those who were handling ideas on a grand scale, the authors of great books, and avoiding the use of secondary sources to help one understand their insights. Taking the Great Books seriously, really questioning according to the methods of discussion we saw Mr. Longman use, provides a high-powered adventure in learning. It was the kind of experience which inspired philanthropist Paul Mellon to say, "It makes you think, very much more certainly than I had to at Yale." Mellon spent a year at St. John's, although he already had three college degrees, and liked it enough to give one million dollars of his personal fortune, while inducing the Old Dominion Foundation to give eight million more.

St. John's is a special place, with a special dropout rate. According to the same *Potomac* article, approximately half of each class leave between freshman year and graduation. The stringent requirements and the far from leisurely pace provide telling commentaries for that statistic. There is a private interview before admission. Freshmen, sophomores, and juniors present major essays on some topic suggested by the seminar readings—essays which serve as central themes for final oral examinations each spring. Oral examinations are also administered at the end of each semester by each student's Great Books seminar leaders.

This strenuous examination schedule is also sprinkled with special "enabling" examinations. For instance, the sophomore essay is part of this "enabling" process and must meet the approval of an Instruction Committee before one is admitted to the junior class. Students must also pass an examination to demonstrate a reading knowledge of French before they may become seniors. A special seminar "enabling" oral examination during the fall of one's senior year is based on about a dozen Great Books which the student has selected from seminar assignments for concentrated re-reading during the previous summer. In the spring seniors have approximately four weeks for writing their final essays, which must be successfully defended before the entire faculty and student body before they can graduate.

Despite what one might think from a description of this seemingly mind-boggling examination schedule, evaluation is supposed to be informal

*From Kenneth Turner, "Civilization and St. John's," *Potomac* magazine, May 4, 1975.

and based on total personality and performance. Grades are sent to the dean but not to the student unless he or she requests them, and it is considered "bad form" to make such a request. Students are counseled informally in "don rag" sessions and are encouraged to leave by tutors who know them well, if their level of performance seems inadequate.

All this intense intellectual activity is set in a milieu designed to get students to talk with each other and with their tutors. Overspecialization, which is viewed as pernicious because it tends to subdivide knowledge into artificial compartments, is definitely frowned upon. Even the library is not permitted to house specialized volumes—only the Great Books and general supplementary literature. Because the student body showed signs of increasing to more than four hundred, in 1964 a new campus at Santa Fe, New Mexico, was opened. As one student put it, "St. John's is a community of learning, not a city." Or as Stringfellow Barr remarked, "It has to be small so you can converse; you can't converse with the whole of Manhattan." So the second campus idea was tried in order to keep conversation in the community to a maximum, even though many objected from fear that the new facility would cause too great a drain on the faculty and resources at Annapolis.

At any rate, St. John's is a special place of conversation and learning. A recent catalogue put it this way: "Perhaps the most distinctive mark of St. John's College is the fact that all the students of the same year are reading the same books at the same time with the same immediate preparation." The ideal, which might cause consternation in many who are unaccustomed to Perennialist ways of thinking, is spelled out more carefully in the following passage:

> At the head of the class is the author-teacher, at the foot of the class the poorest student in relation to the subject matter. All the others are both teachers and pupils, each learning from those above and teaching those below. The aim in all the classes is to exploit the differences in knowledge, character, and skill as they are distributed among students and tutors.*

Perhaps one former student quoted in the *Potomac* article put it most eloquently: "St. John's is a place where you can find students talking about the Good like it was their cousin."

We should keep both these settings—the microcosm of Mr. Longman's class and the macrocosm of St. John's—in mind as we analyze the Perennialist role model.

*From *St. John's Catalogue*, 1972–1973.

## Role Model Analysis: Adding Mr. Longman to the Dissecting Pan

This analysis will be slightly different from those for the other four role models, because we must go deeper than what is merely observable in the context of a Great Books discussion or Socratic dialogue. Such a statement is merely another way of saying that one cannot simply observe a teacher's behavior and on that basis alone reach a decision that a Perennialist label is appropriate. One must also examine the special assumptions underlying a particular teacher's use of Great Books discussion techniques or Socratic dialogue before knowing whether that person is actually a Perennialist or is at least approaching the Perennialist position. Nowhere is this concern of possible difference between "appearance"—what is observable—and philosophical assumptions more crucial than in our question about behavior trends.

4. What behavior trend should one exhibit in order to carry out one's philosophical position?

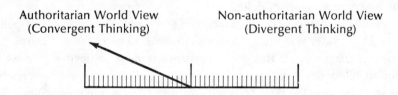

Authoritarian World View        Non-authoritarian World View
(Convergent Thinking)            (Divergent Thinking)

At the outset it may seem quite incongruous that this scale's dial is pointing toward convergence. After all, what could be more "open-ended," more calculated to encourage divergence, than asking a question for which one does not have answers and for which there indeed might not be any one definite and exact answer. The kinds of questions just described are exactly the types Mr. Longman set out to ask, as one can see by referring again to his question "clusters" previously listed in this chapter. How, then, could it be appropriate to apply the term "convergent" to any outcome of a lesson begun with Mr. Longman's questions and managed according to his "hands-off" approach?

One must remember Mr. Longman's efforts and, at the same time, remember certain assumptions underlying Great Books seminars at St. John's before we can answer this troublesome question about convergence. The real benefit of studying Great Books is supposed to be that the human personality has not changed; in essence, that human nature is the same as it was thousands of years ago. Consequently, an ancient author's insights into human nature and into moral principles governing human relationships are viewed as still pertinent for today's audiences. Such a position implies that there will ultimately be convergence about questions dealing with the human spirit and about moral truths; in fact, why else would they be called "truths"? Yet, there is no automatic expectation that convergence will or should occur when examining questions about the ever-changing environment in which one happens to be living. This implies that knowledge about the physical environment is not nearly so important as insights into human personality and moral truths which govern conduct.

Remember that Mr. Longman, in the true Perennialist tradition, was focusing on personality in his study of Nat Turner. Remember also how the dialogue progressed under his typically "hands-off" Great Books approach to discussion leadership. He did not guide students toward an insight into how offensive the term "slave" might be to one who was fully aware of the legal status and the psychological stigma inherent in the term. Such a person might indeed find being a slave unbearably offensive, even if he or she possessed every physical comfort or convenience one could possibly imagine. In one sense, students discovered for themselves—through the process of discussion and by reacting to Allen's remarks about the stigma inherently associated with the term "slave"—something that is quite universal about anyone's desire for personal freedom. To a Perennialist this universal quality of human nature, this desire for personal freedom, is as applicable to Socrates as it is to Mr. Longman, and is as applicable to Nat Turner as it is to Allen. In fact, this is what makes the quality universal. Moreover, kids discovered this fact on their own, without any attempt on Mr. Longman's part to guide them or even to summarize what they had "converged" on.

## Synthesis and *Syntopicon*

In spite of the fact that Mr. Longman's discussion happened to arrive at convergence, such an outcome usually is not the result when kids are present in a discussion group. The same eventuality is equally true of Great Books seminars at St. John's. While convergence might be presumed and expected to occur in language tutorials and in information-giving exchanges during other kinds of tutorials, convergence might rarely occur while students are grouped together for a Great Books seminar. In fact, it is of little importance whether convergence is reached while the group is together in a formal session.

Since the seminars focus on personality and on moral questions, however, convergence may be presumed to occur eventually on issues affecting the human spirit, if students have enough time to engage in dialogue. That is, any dialectic can be presumed eventually to lead to convergence about issues that really matter, because they are related to universal truths. That is why the young man's remark about St. John's as the place where one finds students "talking about the Good like it was their cousin" was not only eloquent but also useful to our analysis.

Let us focus on these issues of goodness and truth by examining our question about the nature of learners. This indicator also accentuates an interesting and crucial relationship between the observable, on the one hand, and an underlying philosophical assumption on the other hand.

1. What is the nature of the learner?

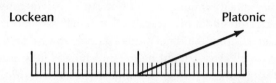

Lockean                                                          Platonic

At the outset there seems to be an obvious kind of illogic which would couple a "convergence" reading on one indicator with a "Platonic" reading on another. But let us look again at the possible difference between appearance and the reality of underlying assumptions. If one is merely observing a discussion based on the Great Books approach, an approach touted by the Foundation as a faithful modern rendering of Socratic dialogue, one is able to see what appears to be an open-ended, divergent-oriented situation in which students contribute original ideas. That certainly fits our previous use of the term "Platonic" in our analytical tool, a usage referring to active learners who contribute original knowledge which is created in the very act of dialogue. This use of "Platonic" we have contrasted with the "Lockean" view of a passive learner who deals with knowledge as *received* through perception. But, in actuality, it is only this surface quality—the appearance—that we have been discussing when we used the term "Platonic."

Now it is time for us to probe more deeply into Platonic views of the nature of knowledge and into Perennialists' special faith in the process of the dialetic; this faith probably matches Socrates's view of the dialectic's power more precisely than Plato's view. The general Platonic world view, however, turns the scale for our question about the nature of learners into a "bowed" continuum when we probe beneath the appearance of active learners contributing original knowledge down into the reality of philosophical assumptions. Perhaps this enlargement of the "Platonic" position for Perennialism will be clearer if one visualizes our indicator as shown below:

1. What is the nature of the learner?

Lockean                                                          Platonic

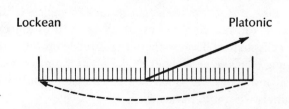

In the first chapter of this volume we emphasized that both Socrates and Plato saw learning as a process of remembering or "reminiscing" about knowledge which one's soul had possessed directly before the soul had been tied to a body. Plato envisioned birth as a trauma so great that it caused the soul to "forget" its pure knowledge. To Plato, then, all subsequent learning was a lifelong struggle to "remember" that direct and pure knowledge, a process which was aided by interaction with others or with one's own inner nature by a style of questioning known as the dialectic.

In Plato's philosophy the dialectic provided the means by which men could travel back to the "world of forms" or "world of universals" which held the exact concepts of Truth, Beauty, and Goodness. Since these concepts were seen as more real than the tangible world in which men existed, everyone would eventually agree about principles of Truth, Beauty, and Goodness after use of the dialectic, because these concepts were eternal— true for all men in any time period. The dialectic was viewed as ultimately effective in bringing men from their imperfect ideas about the "world of forms" back into direct knowledge of that world, because an idea (thesis) and its opposite (antithesis) could be analyzed until a more nearly perfect idea (synthesis) was attained. Use of this process, the dialectic, would weave a chain of analysis by which increasingly pure syntheses would be reached, until those most skilled in dialectic would again attain direct communication with the "world of forms."

In the initial discussions of the dialectic in this volume, we referred to the *Meno*, in which Socrates has a conversation with a slave boy about the Pythagorean theorem. Although the youngster insists he has never heard of the Pythagorean theorem, he discovers, or teaches himself, the formula $c^2 = a^2 + b^2$, where right triangles are concerned and where $c$ is the triangle's hypotenuse. Although the answers the slave boy contributed looked quite open-ended, mathematics is a discipline in which one would expect convergence. Since in the course of this volume we have grown to expect convergent types of thinking to predominate among teachers in mathematics and the physical sciences, we might find it difficult to say this example from the *Meno* represented a "Platonic" position on our indicator. Unless, of course, we could know that the questioner had so much faith in the dialectic's power to push his pupil to truth that he did not plan to tell his student when the goal was reached; thus, the youngster would automatically know when he had arrived at Truth, because he would still retain a dim "remembrance" of the "world of forms" to guide his quest for perfect knowledge.

What would be the result, however, if the example concerned definitions? There is a dialogue in which Socrates converses with a young student of geometry about the differences between wisdom and knowledge. Socrates skillfully brings his pupil to an *elenchus*, the point of perplexity where he realizes his "yes" and "no" responses have led him to an illogical position in which he has affirmed wisdom and knowledge to be identical qualities. At this point of *elenchus*, according to Plato, thinking actually begins. If one were to converse with Socrates or with one's inner self long enough, one would reach a synthesis regarding the qualities of wisdom and knowledge; this synthesis would incorporate some connotations of both and would represent a purer understanding because it would be slightly closer to Truth. Socrates would not have to say, "Here is Truth!" when the pupil reached his goal, because the pupil himself would recognize Truth automatically, since he was formerly a "citizen" of the "world of forms."

Such an overwhelming faith in the dialectic is basically what motivates the Perennialist. Why should he not ask students open-ended questions, or questions for which potential answers cause widespread popular disagreement and discord? If those questions are about issues that really matter, such as Goodness, Truth, Beauty, human nature, moral conduct, and so forth, then everyone skilled in the dialectic's use will ultimately agree. It matters not whether they agree while the formal discussion proceeds. The dialectic is really all-powerful, nonetheless. Students may agree as they talk informally about points which emerged in a previous formal discussion, or they may arrive at Truth while continuing a private dialogue with their own inner natures. What does it matter? If they are skilled in the dialectic, they will each ultimately arrive at Truth, even if by circuitous routes, because Truth is eternal. It has its own existence separate from that of "tangible reality." Therefore, what has the appearance of open-ended questioning, with student contributions that look like original insights created on the spot through dialogue, may only *appear* to be that way.

To a Perennialist this is merely appearance. The teacher does not have to guide students consciously to the Truth; such a procedure, in fact, would indicate a bizarre lack of faith in the power of dialectic, as well as in the allure of Truth. This is why our scale for this indicator must look "bowed." For Perennialists, convergence comes naturally and automatically through no conscious effort on the part of the teacher or learner, but only through the appeal of Truth and the strength of the dialectic.

When we first talked about the "Platonic" position on our indicator, there was some deliberate oversimplification which now needs to be refined. We were, at that point, dealing with the surface—the appearance—of dialogue which we termed "Platonic." Going back to Plato's concept of the doctrine of reminiscence in its original form, however, serves to bring the concept into that special focus which is appropriate only for the Perennialist role model. What looks like original knowledge, because it is created in dialogue, is to the Perennialist not original at all because it is subtly guided at every step by the dialectic and by the seeker's inner nature.

Yet it is entirely appropriate for us to use the term "Platonic," although it is coupled with "convergence" on another indicator, because the learner is most actively pursuing his own search for knowledge. Ultimately, this search should get him to Truth. Socrates, at least, seemed to think everyone was capable of such skillful use of the dialectic. Plato was apparently less convinced that everyone could make it back to direct communication with the "world of forms"; accordingly, he talked about people of "brass," "silver," and "gold," in the *Republic*. Only the "golden" philosopher-kings were capable of getting all the way back to Truth.

How does one interpret this supreme problem-solving activity of a search for Truth in regard to our question about the nature of subject matter?

2. What is the nature of the subject matter?

Amorphous                                          Structured

Since the search for eternally fixed truths about human nature and about morality can be considered the paramount problem-solving exercise, we merely need to remind ourselves that solving a problem means emphasizing the structure of whatever subject matter is under study. Students must sift through data and ideas for the appropriate relationships which provide a solution. Nevertheless, the Perennialist sees this structure as embodied in dialectic as shown below.

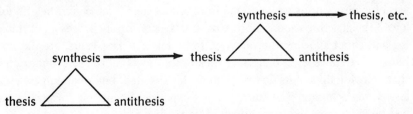

Through this emphasis on structure students are viewed as building their own ladders back to Truth.

How does this search for Truth influence the question concerning use of the subject matter? Just how emotional, or how affective, is this search to be?

3. How should one use the subject matter to guide students
toward meaningful learning activities?

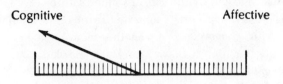

Cognitive                                                                Affective

It might seem illogical that our indicator reads "cognitive." One may
wonder how this is possible, when we saw Mr. Longman dealing with a
passage about some ax murderers! However, it is the instructor's plan of
emphasis which this indicator records, not the emotional or affective "connections" which students may make individually and on their own. Notice
Mr. Longman's introduction of the lesson and his handling of the dialogue.
He certainly did not focus on the ax murderers themselves, but rather on
Nat's personality. He introduced the lesson's materials in a matter-of-fact
manner and began right away with the question, "Why did Nat lead a rebellion?" When Meg answered with an emotional comment about how "unbelievable" the reading had been, he accepted this remark in the same simple,
matter-of-fact manner, and that remained his tenor throughout the discussion.

Mr. Longman's attitude was indeed an embodiment of the Great Books
Foundation's advice to emphasize rational, orderly thought processes, and to
stress what we have called the "cognitive." A great work of literature is perfectly capable of "standing on its own without fanfare or hoopla," and, as a
result, must be considered only in light of the facts the great author chose to
use. To a Great Books person, "facts" mean the words of the selection—
words used deliberately to fulfill a special purpose. Although Mr. Longman
was obviously not using a passage from one of the Great Books, he still followed the strictures about emphasizing rational, orderly processes of thinking and about allowing the selection to be taken at face value. He did not,
however, require that youngsters stick to the "facts" of the selection, rather
than drawing upon outside information. He decided, before attempting this
lesson, to encourage students to relate the passage about Nat Turner to what
had been studied and to what would be studied.

This emphasis on the cognitive (in essence, on the rational and on the
intellectual) is a cornerstone of the Great Books approach. Althought Robert
Maynard Hutchins, Mortimer Adler, and other founders of this contemporary brand of Perennialism—or Classical Humanism, as it is sometimes
known—insist that they have faithfully followed Plato's prescriptions for
education at the Academy in fifth century B.C. Athens, it is noteworthy that

Plato's emphasis on the rational was perhaps quite different from theirs. Plato, as we will see when we talk about historical antecedents for this role model, felt that the youth of Athens should follow more closely the old aristocratic ideals for education—ideals which mandated that education emphasize physical training most heavily, at least through the time of puberty. Even in young adulthood the dialectic was hardly emphasized; moreover, his plan probably did not include such a study of questioning until the student reached the age of about thirty or thirty-five. If one remembers anything about our description of life at St. John's, it should be more than obvious that intellectual, cognitive, verbal skills are emphasized above all else, although there is some minor attention given to physical prowess through an intramural program.

Although Mr. Longman's attitude and demeanor emphasized the cognitive domain throughout his lesson, the Nat Turner passage itself was certainly fraught with affective overtones which youngsters could respond to individually. Nevertheless, using material with highly affective qualities is in this case quite useful to us for two reasons. First, the material used and the manner in which the lesson was managed remind us that it is the instructor's plan and his behavior, not something inherent within the learning materials employed, which determine the role model and the teaching style. Secondly, we cannot know for certain that Mr. Longman's teaching style is Perennialist simply by observing lessons similar to the Nat Turner discussion. Remember that we need to know something about the assumptions underlying his use of Great Books discussion techniques before using any label to indicate dominant tendencies within his teaching behaviors.

Let us look at a few indications which make it likely that Mr. Longman is moving in a Perennialist direction. One of the most obvious indications might be his willingness to follow most of the Great Books Foundation's discussion guidelines. A second indication is his attention to Nat's personality as the major focus of his lesson. A third piece of evidence was his willingness to end the lesson when Allen and the others taught themselves fundamental points about the human personality's need for integrity and individual freedom. But we would have to know more before using the Perennialist label. We would have to know that Mr. Longman, in the act of asking open-ended questions, retained faith that the dialectic's power would ultimately bring convergence about the truths of human nature and human relationships. If a teacher has such a faith, then he or she adheres to Perennialism, a teaching style placed in the "camp" with Essentialism and Behaviorism because it honors convergence.

Nonetheless, many who have no such faith in the dialectic use the Great Books techniques of discussion leadership solely as a means for asking open-ended questions and encouraging divergence. For instance, a typical way to witness Great Books discussion strategies is to observe a teacher who is Existentialist or Experimentalist and who finds it helpful to organize discussions around "clusters" of interpretive questions. Such strategies can be used effectively to emphasize the affective, as an Existentialist would do, or to begin an emotionally-charged problem-solving lesson which culminates in Reconstructionism. The techniques are equally valid and potent for the Experimentalist, who emphasizes divergence through problem-solving based on the cognitive domain. When what is observable with these techniques of discussion is all the teacher has in mind, then he or she is operating within the "camp" of teaching styles which honor divergence. Yet, when there is more than meets the eye of the observer, when there is an underlying faith in the dialectic's power to guide students to Truth, then the teacher is considered to be a Perennialist.

Although Perennialism is perhaps the rarest of the role models, it does offer many possibilities for charismatic teaching in parochial schools or for educating youngsters in settings with strongly religious overtones. Moreover, there are probably many tutors even at St. John's who use Great Books strategies merely as techniques of instruction and who care perhaps not at all for any underlying assumptions about the dialectic and Truth.

## PHILOSOPHIC PRINCIPLES SUPPORTING THE PERENNIALIST ROLE MODEL

The philosophic underpinning for the role model called Perennialist is also known by various other names, including Idealism and Classical Humanism. Each name is appropriate because it implies something basic about the philosophy we are examining. "Idealism" gives tacit testimony that ideas are viewed as more powerful, and somehow more real, than tangible items in the world around us. "Classical Humanism" refers to this position's origin with the Greek philosophers who were interested in preserving and nurturing those qualities which make men and women more fully human, which allow them to reach that degree of human excellence that the ancients called "paideia." In addition, our term, Perennialism, intimates that Truth is perennial—in other words, that it is changeless, just as human nature and moral principles governing human relationships are changeless. Leading spokesmen for Perennialist education during this century have usually used their position to attack what they considered an unhealthy strain of anti-intellectualism within public education in this country—a point which should be quite clear from Kneller's analysis of Perennialist assumptions and from our comments about Kneller's observations.

(1) *Human nature remains the same everywhere; hence, education should be the same for everyone.* This is a fundamental assertion of Perennialists despite obvious diversities among cultures and blatant differences in skill levels among individuals. It simply takes more time and effort to give slow learners the same kind of education as that given to gifted children.

Knowledge is also basically the same everywhere because knowledge is produced when people (should we say learned people?) reach agreement as to their opinions. It is, therefore, quite inefficient for youngsters to discover everything for themselves, since many insights can be imparted quickly by receiving them secondhand from those who know. We already have seen how this process of imparting tradition operates at St. John's in the tutorials and, to a certain extent, within Great Books seminars. Perennialists, however, do not rule out gaining many insights firsthand; and this is, of course, a major function of Great Books seminars. Since the purpose of education is to improve human beings through an emphasis on rational qualities which make us all most fully human, the discoveries sparked by seminar discussion, and the new convergences which ultimately will come, represent the capstone for Perennialist examination of tradition.

(2) *Since rationality is humanity's highest attribute, we must use it to direct the instinctual nature in accordance with deliberately chosen ends.* A person's rational qualities must be emphasized and highly developed because he or she is free and, therefore, responsible for his or her own actions. Rationality is, then, one's only guide through an astounding maze of choices and alternate courses of action. Self-control, the use of one's rational powers to make choices, is achieved through discipline that is first imposed from external sources. Although the disciplined thought patterns are supposed to be imbibed from using the dialectic, it takes an external source like a Socrates, a Plato, or a skillful tutor at St. John's to initiate one into the mysteries and benefits of the dialectic for all seekers of Truth.

(3) *Education's task is to adjust human beings to the truth, which is eternal, rather than to the contemporary world, which is not.* Perennialists reject a curriculum geared mostly to contemporary problems. Such problems are, after all, transitory; moreover, they will be attended to naturally within a democratic society because people have been educated to think for themselves, not because they were forced to deal with specific social problems while they were in schools. According to Perennialists, it is entirely outside the scope of the school's duties to encourage a desire for social reform. Just how far away from a Reconstructionist position they are is best encapsulated in Kneller's restatement of a basic tenet: "Democracy will

progress because people are educated and not because they have been taught to agitate for certain reforms."

(4) *Education is not an imitation of life, but a preparation for life.* If the preceding principle removed Perennialists from any direct link with Reconstructionists, this principle performs the same function with regard to Experimentalism and Existentialism. Those holding this principle should forget any attempt to infuse the school with real-life problem situations, whether those are based in the cognitive or affective domains. The school must create a deliberately artificial environment in which development of the intellect, rather than children's interests, is the first concern. Only in such a setting can the benefits of a culture's heritage be transmitted adequately.

(5) *The child should be taught certain basic subjects that will acquaint him or her with the world's permanencies.* Subjects which deal with the world's impermanencies, auto mechanics for instance, have no place in a school's curriculum. In fact, the special appeal of any subject to a certain age group should surely not be a primary reason for offering a class in that topic. What one usually thinks of as the traditional academic liberal arts courses, such as those offered at St. John's, produce educated, "well-rounded" people. Vocational or professional "training" (the term is intentional) should definitely not be considered part of one's education. All training that is purely occupational should simply be given at the job site.

(6) *Education should introduce the pupil to the universal concerns of humanity through the study of the great works of literature, philosophy, history, and science.* Following this principle allows one to learn truths far more important than those he or she would acquire by pursuing personal interests or by studying the contemporary scene. Indeed, individualizing instruction to allow children to develop at their own pace is a pernicious cop-out. And this cop-out, with all its perils, can be avoided by following the Great Books curriculum and being rewarded with increased verbal skills and with the dialectic.

## HISTORICAL ANTECEDENTS

### Hutchins and Synthesis

Those responsible for the two St. John's communities have remained convinced their settings offer a faithful rendering of the kind of education Plato sanctioned for the youth of fifth century B.C., Athens. Robert Maynard

Hutchins, at the time he became President of the University of Chicago in 1929, was imbued with admiration for Plato's academic community. When *Time* magazine reported his new position, their writers emphasized the special dedication this country's youngest university president exuded for all things intellectual. *Time* said that Hutchins was fond of quoting Mark Twain's epigram about the pitfalls of a sedentary life: "Sometimes I feel the need for exercise, but if I lie down that feeling goes away." Hutchins continued to admire Socratic and Platonic intellectual styles as the Great Books idea took form under his tutelage. For a number of years, particularly during the 1930s, students receiving graduate degrees in humanities disciplines from the University of Chicago were strongly urged to complete theses or dissertations which would advance the cross-referencing efforts for the *Syntopicon*. This volume "keys" the Great Books set by showing at a glance citations from works of great authors about certain topics, especially topics related to human personality development.

When St. John's experienced economic troubles in the 1930s and began seeking an attractive means of reorganization which would make the institution financially successful, would transform it into a special learning community, and, at the same time, would keep it a small college, exciting days were ahead for Hutchins's Great Books concept. Here was the perfect opportunity for Hutchins, Adler, Barr, Buchanan, and other devotees to set up a working model of Plato's Academy. As we have already seen, this model is quite meticulous in the way it translates Plato's ideas about the dialectic into a contemporary educational setting. As a modern rendering of exactly what went on at the Academy, however, St. John's is probably not an accurate analog.

## Plato and Synthesis

Plato's Athens was a city-state which had already evolved to the condition of "direct" democracy—that is, a condition in which all free male citizens served as lawmakers. Thus, Plato was uncomfortable about this situation. Perhaps calling the Athens of that day a "mobocracy" would give a clearer indication of Plato's misgivings. He resented those who said they taught "practical" wisdom and the skills of speaking well so that students would be able to "carry the day" in their discussions as members of the legislative body for the city. These purveyors of "practical" wisdom, usually known as Sophists, were men whom, for the most part, Plato regarded as little better than charlatans successfully blurring Truth for the mere sake of winning an argument. Even though the Sophistic brand of learning—in essance, the tendency to emphasize verbal skills, knowledge of history and practical politics, and information about one's own environment—is the type of education that survived in the ancient world and in succeeding years fostered the tradition we now call "Essentialism," it was far from what Plato envisioned.

Plato had stepped out of the mainstream of Greek tradition, which the Sophists quite accurately represented, because he was convinced that there was an Eternal Truth which men should seek. This truth provided far more inspiring bases for morality than slavish adherence to anthropomorphic deities—gods, inhabiting human forms, who had grown big in their capacity to love as well as hate and who might just as easily zap an unsuspecting human with thunderbolts of vengeance, as he or she might help a poor mortal out of difficulty.

Plato's search for Truth, Goodness, and Beauty through the process of the dialectic has already been examined at length elsewhere in this chapter. Little needs to be said about it here, except to point out that this aspect of Plato's philosophy—the facet which involves devotion to a higher morality—represents an area of his thinking which is furthest away from typical Greek views of the world in the fifth century B.C. It was also a very convenient mechanism whereby the Church Fathers could integrate concepts of Judaic-Christian morality with knowledge inherited from ancient times. It is, after all, not far from Plato's "doctrine of reminiscence" to the Judaic-Christian search for Goodness, Truth, and Beauty as manifested through the one personal God. This connection has enabled Perennialism to function as a powerfully attractive role model in religious education through the centuries. In fact, this role model is usually not seen in public education today, but it may be evident in some parochial school settings.

In another aspect of Plato's thinking, a facet not so closely connected with higher morality, this leader of the Greek "School of Philosophers" wanted strict adherence to time-honored educational tradition. He felt the Sophists had pulled men too far away from aristocratic ideas of learning which emphasized physical education before intellectual education. In a sense, he wanted his newer emphasis on a search for Truth to occur within the framework of older ideas about Greek aristocratic education. It is Plato's stress on that framework of older concepts of aristocratic learning which causes me to view St. John's as a less than faithful rendering of education at the Academy.

According to James Bowen in *History of Western Education* (New York: St. Martin's Press, 1972), the Academy doubtlessly had students who were required to attend to physical education before intellectual education. Youngsters there also probably spent little, if any, time with formal studies of the dialectic because we know from *The Republic* how carefully Plato reserved such learning for those in adulthood. If the Academy functioned as a place where the dialectic was practiced, it probably did so on an informal level as leaders of Athens, who were beyond the age of enrollment as students, met to converse with Plato at their leisure. Consequently, students at the Academy probably spent most of their time studying mathematics.

To Plato, mathematics was the ideal discipline for "readiness exercises" leading eventually to work in the process of dialectic. The key to the dialectic's power is, of course, its capacity to pull people back to the highest level of what Plato called the "world of forms," where concepts of pure Truth, Goodness, and Beauty exist. Mathematics was perfectly suited to push students' minds into the lower regions of the "world of forms." For example, if a student is working on a simple exercise in which he or she calculates the area of a table top, the pupil is encouraged to think of the table's surface as a plane. Since the surface of any table top is bound to be pockmarked and at least slightly askew, any effort on the student's part to imagine a perfectly smooth surface with only two dimensions (i.e., a plane) will push him or her immediately into the "world of forms."

No plane can exist in the tangible world, or Plato's "world of becoming." Thus, we are left to visualize only in our minds what the perfect two-dimensional figure would be like. To Plato, of course, that perfect figure has more reality attached to it than any imperfect table top one could possibly touch. An attempt to imagine the perfect shape of a geometrical object, whether plane or solid, immediately carries one into the "world of forms."

St. John's does make mathematics an integral part of the curriculum. It is also probably quite an accurate translation into reality of most of Plato's ideas about learning, except for his thoughts about physical education. In all likelihood, however, it probably represents little of what actually occurred at the Academy.

## Louisa May Alcott's Father at the Temple School

Usually Plato and his Academy are the only major points of focus when historical perspectives on Perennialism are given. However, we need to examine one other exemplar of the Perennialist role model who is almost always overlooked—Amos Bronson Alcott, the New England Transcendentalist and father of Louisa May Alcott.* His work at the Temple School in Boston during the mid-1830s is especially useful to our purposes, because it shows so clearly the relationship between true Perennialism and the use of teaching strategies associated with the Perennialist philosophy as a means of bolstering Experimentalist, Existentialist, or Reconstructionist styles of teaching.

*For a more complete treatment see Lloyd Duck, "Bronson Alcott, Abraham Maslow, and 'Third Force' Psychology." *Education*, Winter 1977, pp. 210–220.

In other words, comparing his work with contemporary values clarification theories points up clearly what we have previously examined as the relationship between the surface, observable teacher behaviors and the underlying reality of philosophical assumptions.

The excerpts reproduced below are from an 1836 edition of *Record of a School* by Elizabeth Peabody. Miss Peabody served as Alcott's associate for the first three years of Temple School's existence and attempted to publicize his efforts through two works: *Record of a School*, which first appeared in 1835, and *Record of Conversations with Children on the Gospels*, which appeared in 1836. It will be obvious, as you read these excerpts from the chapter called "Analysis of a Human Being," why many in Boston during the 1830s would find Alcott's methods surprising and controversial.

Even Elizabeth Peabody, who later studied in Germany with Friedrich Froebel and observed his pioneering work with kindergarten children firsthand, was somewhat critical of Alcott's work in her preface to the 1874 edition of *Record of a School*. The book was reissued largely because readers who had enjoyed Louisa May Alcott's *Little Men* kept asking where she got her ideas for the Plumfield School, which she had so carefully protrayed in her novel. When she gave credit to her father and his insights about teaching, there was enough interest for the publishers to do a reprint of *Record of a School*. Elizabeth Peabody apparently decided that Alcott's ideas were still quite radical and mildly refuted some of her earlier work with him in order to give more credit to Froebel's educational practices.

While reading and considering the controversial nature of Alcott's techniques, one should remember that he did not live and work in the milieu of Puritan Boston. The fervent Bostonian visions of a Puritan Commonwealth had been gone since the end of the seventeenth century. What had replaced those older, formalized, gloomier ideas about men and women finding themselves "predestined" to Heaven or Hell, with little or no recourse, was a notion that men can effect their own salvation by studying the beauty of the natural world and the operations of their own inner natures. They viewed themselves, in actuality, as being capable of transcending the natural in order to find comfort and fulfillment in the supernatural. Knowing that two of Alcott's closest friends were Henry David Thoreau and Ralph Waldo Emerson might help one understand the cultural setting in which Alcott wrote. Van Wyck Brooks's *The Flowering of New England,* which first appeared in 1936, offers superb insights into how different the Boston of Alcott's time was from the same city during Puritan control.

In addition, these written excerpts are the only information we have of Alcott's performance in a classroom. We have no videotapes or audiotapes, and no record of voice inflection to guide us in assessing informally the kind of learning environment Alcott might have created. We, therefore, have no direct indication of the ways he might have used nonverbal communication to establish psychologically supportive relationships with his students. It has been one of our major contentions in this volume, in fact, that any instructor may sincerely and responsibly adopt or lean toward any one of the role models we have considered and, thereby, accomplish beneficial outcomes for himself and his students. On the other hand, one could adopt any one of the role models and non-verbally project negative feelings about youngsters with disastrous results for both oneself and one's students. (I personally suspect Alcott had such a special personality that he could ask what seemed to be threatening questions in an extremely supportive and non-threatening manner. General descriptions of student responses to Alcott, as well as accounts of how Alcott related to children and colleagues when he was superintendent of schools for Concord in the 1860s, have convinced me that his manner was quite supportive and non-punitive. Not everyone agrees with this interpretation, however, as will be discussed in a later section.)

Moreover, in Alcott's day it was not unusual for children of five to twelve years old to converse about moral abstractions in the manner which Elizabeth Peabody described for pupils at the Temple School. Many of these youngsters were children of New England literati and were, therefore, quite economically privileged. Their families would have the time, the wherewithal, and the inclination to talk with offspring about many subjects which we might consider far beyond the maturity level of youngsters in this age group today.

## CHAP. III.

### ANALYSIS OF A HUMAN BEING.

I have now given about five weeks of the Journal. But before quite dismissing it, I will give some farther extracts, comprising a weekly exercise, which was suggested by the following conversation, on the 9th of February.

The word *bless* came up among the words of the spelling lesson. It was defined as wishing well to others; wishing God's blessing; making happy. Mr. Alcott asked, if any one felt he comprehended all its meaning? No hands were raised, and a small boy said: Mr. Alcott, I do not believe you comprehend all its meaning yourself. Mr. Alcott asked what blessings God gives? They answered severally, food; sun; air; clothing; dwellings; flowers; wisdom; our souls; parents. Do we have blessings whether we deserve them or not? Some said yes; some said no. But there is one blessing greater than all you have mentioned. They severally answered, after some consideration, Spirit; God's Spirit; the Bible.

The Bible, said Mr. Alcott, is God in words. But the Bible is not the only Revelation of God. There are many Bibles, to those who think. Nature, the outward world, is a Bible. Its objects typify God's thoughts. The soul is a Bible. What do we read in the passions? I will tell you: God's punishments, for the passions are the over-mastering effects of indulgence. What tremendous pains they involve, by necessity!

But what blessings have you had? He addressed a boy, who thinks little, but who catches the habit of answering. He replied, the Bible. How is that a blessing? said Mr.

Alcott. The Lord blesses us with it, said he. In what way? He makes us happy. With the Bible? He makes us good. Your answers do not sound as if they were your own reflections; but like parrotry. Tell me what blessings you have been blessed with to-day. With a mind. Are you thoughtless? said I, (referring to a confession or excuse he always makes, when he has done wrong.) Yes. But does not thoughtless mean without thoughts? Yes. Can there be a mind without thoughts? No. Then how can you say your mind is a blessing to you? I have been baptized, said he. How is that a blessing? It purified me. Are you pure, purified? I was for a little while after I was baptized. Was your soul or your body baptized? My body. Does not purity belong to the mind? Yes. Do truth and love keep the mind pure? Do you understand what I mean, when I say, the soul is baptized with truth and love? Yes. Was your soul ever baptized so? Yes. How often? Every day. How long does it last? A little while.

All these answers seemed given without thought; and Mr. Alcott pursued it still farther, his object being to show this fancifully worded boy, that he had no self-knowledge; and that his ideas were not representations of his own thoughts and feelings, but mere verbal associations, and meaningless images. This boy's memory of words and images, which has been over-cultivated, is great; and he seems to have been led into a shallow activity of mind and tongue, that deceives himself. I thought he was enlightened a little to-day; and the rest of the scholars, who were very attentive, and occasionally joined in the conversation with much intelligence, evidently understood his mind very well, and were guarded against the same fallacy.

Mr. Alcott here opened the Bible, and read the beatitudes in paraphrase, thus:

Blessed, inconceivably happy, are those who feel as if they were without any thing; for such are prepared to receive Heaven.

Blessed are they that mourn; for comfort comes to the mourner that others cannot understand.

Blessed are they that desire goodness more than any thing else; for they shall be filled with it.

Blessed are they that are kind and merciful; for they will not be in danger of being cruelly treated.

Blessed are those who are pure, and have no wrong affections or false thoughts; for they see God, his goodness, excellence, love and truth.

Blessed are they who suffer in order to do right; for they already have heaven.

We began with our own definitions of bless, said he; and now you have heard Jesus Christ's definitions : do you understand, now, what bless, blessed means? They all held up their hands.

When they returned to the school-room after recess, Mr Alcott said : such of you, as gained some clearer ideas than you had before, of one boy's mind this morning, hold up your hands. The older ones all did. Mr. Alcott here explained the difference between fancy and imagination, and asked which principle was in greatest activity in the mind of that boy? They replied, fancy. What boy has an opposite kind of mind? Several were named. One of them, Mr. Alcott said, was literal. Two of them, he also said, had a very high degree of imagination. One had fancy and imagination also. Some farther questions were asked, which proved how truly children analyze each others minds, when brought to attend to them; and it occurred to Mr. Alcott that there might be a regular lesson, the object of which would be, to analyze individual characters, by means of certain testing questions : and this he carried into effect, although, practically, it became, instead of an analysis of individual character, an analysis of human nature in its more general point of view.

In pursuance of this plan, the next day Mr. Alcott arranged all the children, in two semicircles, around his black-board, which was divided into compartments, thus :

| Spirit. | Soul. | Mind. |
|---|---|---|
| Love. \| Faith. \| Conscience. | Appetite. \| Affection. \| Aspiration. | Imagination. \| Judgment. \| Insight. |
| Good. | Happiness. | Truth. |

Having explained the operations of Spirit, Soul, and Mind, after their respective objects, he asked the children what they thought he was going to do? They did not know. He asked who among them would be willing to be analyzed, and tell all their faults and virtues, for the bene- fit of themselves and the rest in self-knowledge? All held up their hands but one.

He then selected a little girl, who is remarkably simple and truth loving, and asked if she was willing to answer all his questions truly, whether they laid open her faults or her virtues? She replied, yes; and all the rest expressed satisfaction.

### LOVE.

Having drawn them into two concentric arcs of circles round his table, over which the blackboard hangs, Mr. Al- cott began to speak of Love: Do you think you love? Yes. Whom? My mother. What do you love in your mother? She was silent. Her voice, her manners, her appearance, her spirit? Yes, all. Suppose she should lose her voice; and her appearance should change; should you still love her? Yes. You think that, independently of all that pleases your eye and mind, and of the good she does you; even if she were to die, and you should see, hear, be taken care of by her no longer, you should still love her? Yes. What do the rest think? (These questions are not as many as were asked, however; the answers were very deliberate.) They all said; Yes, she does love, it is real love.

Mr. Alcott then said: if your mother were going to die, and the physicians said, if you would die, your mother's life could be saved; would you die for your mother? She was silent. Mr. Alcott then went on to speak of the im- portance of her mother's life, to her father, her brothers, and sisters. She was still silent. How would it be with the rest? said he. One boy said, I should not hesitate one moment. Mr. Alcott enquired into this, and he said: Be- cause his mother's life was more valuable to her friends than his was; because she was important to his younger brother; and because he should not be very happy in life if his mother were dead. There was some conversation with some other boys; and one said, that he was sure he could not die for his mother, though he cared more for

her than for any one else.  Mr. Alcott said, and what do
you think you should lose, if you died?  He replied, I do
not know.  You would lose your body, said Mr. Alcott;
and then turning to the little girl, he asked her if she had yet
concluded whether she could die for her mother?  Yes,
said she, very quietly, and after this long deliberation; in
which it had been evident, she endeavoured not to deceive
herself.  Do the rest think she could?  said Mr. Alcott.
Yes, said several; I do not doubt she could.  Well, said
Mr. Alcott, do you think, if by suffering a great deal of
pain, you could make your father and mother happy all
their lives, you would be willing to suffer?  She was silent.
Others cried out : Oh yes!  I know she could; and pro-
fessed that they could.  Mr. Alcott turned to the cast of
Christ, and spoke of his life; his sacrifice of enjoyment;
his acceptance of suffering ; his objects; his love.  Questions were asked whose answers brought out a strong view
of his spiritual, unselfish love of the spirits of men : and
she was asked if she thought her love had any of this deep
character.  She was silent; and even the rest were here
awed into some self-distrust.  But few thought their love
had any of the characteristics of Christ's love.

Mr. Alcott then asked her if she could bear the faults of
others, and love them still?  Sometimes.  Can you bear
with the impatience of your sisters and brothers at home?
She smiled and said, she never had any occasion.  Have
you ever had occasion for forbearance and patience any
where else?  She did not remember, she said.  Never in
any instance ; not in this school nor any where?  Yes, she
recollected once ; but not in this school.  Well, did you
forbear?  Yes.  Does any one else think this little girl has
had occasion to forbear in this school?  Several said, yes.
How many think she acted with forbearance?  All held up
their hands.  Who think they have required her forbearance?  Two held up their hands ; and Mr. Alcott congrat-
ulated them on their acquisition of a better spirit, than they
had shown formerly.

Do you still think, said Mr. Alcott, that you really love,
— love enough to sacrifice and forbear?  Yes, said she.
Nothing you have heard, has led you to doubt this?  No.
What do the rest think?  That she loves, she sacrifices,

she forbears, that hers is real Love. Well, look at the scale. You see the first division is Spirit. The Spirit comes from God; it loves, believes, obeys. We obey what we have faith in; we have faith in what we love; love is pure spiritual action. The Spirit loves. The Spirit, with its Love, Faith and Obedience, sanctifies or makes holy the Soul, in its Appetites, Affections and Aspirations, so that it gets Happiness. And it clears and purifies the Mind, in its faculties of Insight, Judgment and Imagination, so that it discovers Truth.

### FAITH.

Mr. Alcott began : we discovered, last Wednesday, that Love sacrifices and forbears. We might say a great deal more about Love, but now we will go on to Faith. What is Faith ? Soon, all the hands went up.

He began with the youngest, who said, faith is spirit. Did you ever have any ? Yes. The next said faith is not to doubt goodness in the spirits of people. Another said, faith is a thought and feeling. When did you have faith ? Yesterday. What was it about ? I thought school kept yesterday afternoon,—mother thought it did not,—I was sure it did. Another said, faith is only a feeling. Another said, faith is love. There is faith in love, said Mr. Alcott. Another said, faith is liking people from their looks. Who have you faith in from her looks ? I have faith in my mother. Why ? Because I like her looks, and love her soul. All the children who had answered thus far, were under six years old. One of seven years old, said, faith is confidence in another. In another's what ? In another's spirit ; that people will do what they promise. A boy who is continually doing wrong, and failing in duty, said, faith was obedience. Have you much faith ? No. You have come pretty near losing your faith ? Yes. Have you more now, than you had some time ago ? Yes. How will you get more faith ; By doing as I am told. He looked serious, and somewhat distressed ; and Mr. Alcott said : Well, go on and be obedient, and you will find faith. Another boy said, faith is confidence. Who have you confidence in ? In you. Why ? I don't know. A little girl

Goods; Knowledge—Intellectual Goods; and Spiritual
Goods—Faith, Hope, Charity, &c.  Is knowledge a good,
when it is used for our own, rather than others' sake, and we
are proud of it?  They severally said, we should use it for
others; for ourselves;—for ourselves, but some also for
other people.  Is it Aspiration to seek knowledge for our
own good alone?  No.  Does a lawyer, who is using his
knowledge to make himself admired and powerful, aspire?
No.  Does a school teacher, who teaches in order to get
money, aspire; even though he does help his scholars?
No.  Does it seem to you that the people you see, are trying after Spiritual Good, generally?  No.  After Intellectual Good?  Some of them.  Do many people seem to be
striving after money, houses, carriages, reputation?  Yes.
Do many seem to try to get money to do good with?  A
few.  Who think people seem to be striving for money for
themselves only?  Several; and Mr. Alcott said, when did
you find that out?  To-day, said a boy of ten.  When I
was five years old; said a reflective and conscientious boy
of eight.

A gentleman present, here asked a series of questions,
calculated to bring out their opinion of Mr. Alcott's disin-
terestedness; and they signified their undoubting confidence in it, not only by holding up their hands, but by
jumping into their chairs, and stretching out both hands.
So you think, was his last question, that some people aspire
after something higher than physical good?  Yes.  Such
of you as think Mr. Alcott would make as good use of his
mind, as he does now, if he kept his thoughts to himself,
signify it.  They jumped down from their chairs, and said,
No.  The gentleman remarked to me, Mr. Alcott has his
reward.

Where do you think Truth and Beauty are?  resumed
Mr. Alcott.  In God.  And there is some in our souls; said
a little boy of five, after a pause.  How do we get it in our
souls?  We ask God for it, and he puts it in.  If we do
not want it much, does he put it in?  Oh no; we must
want it very much.  Did you ever hear these words, said
Mr. Alcott; Ask, and ye shall receive; seek, and ye shall
find; knock, and it shall be opened unto you?  Yes, Jesus
Christ said them.

Who think that Spiritual Good is the best?  All.  Who

think that in aspiring after Spiritual, we get all other good?
All. Who said, seek first the kingdom of heaven, Spiritual
Good; and its Righteousness, or act accordingly; and all
these things shall be added unto you, for then they can do
you no harm? Jesus Christ, said all.

Little girl, after all that has been said about aspiring, do
you think you aspire after Spiritual Good more than any
other? I think I do, said she. And next to that for the
Intellectual Good, which helps the soul, as the hand helps
the body? Yes.

Who among you think that a school which does not aim
at Spiritual Good, has the right aim? None. Who have
received some new thoughts to-day, which they think they
shall remember always? Many. Who know themselves
so well, that they fear they shall forget? Several.

Who now think that they shall aspire to be the strongest
and most cunning in their plays? None. Do you know
what ambition is? Striving to get more than you have,
said one. What is your ambition? I don't know. To
be admired? No; but to have the best things. Who else
says so? A younger one said, the best Spiritual things;
and many joined with him. Who has not much ambition?
Several. Who will let things go on in their own way?
One, (who is very indolent.) Who feel within, Power or
Will to do everything? Almost all.

When they were dismissed, the visiter called a little
boy of five to him, and said, Do you know what Jesus
Christ meant by these words, "If you had faith, like a
grain of mustard-seed, you could say to this mountain," &c.
I have read it, said the child; but I do not remember what
it represents. What does the mountain mean? said I. It
is a mountain in the mind, said he, without hesitation. And
the mustard-seed? A little faith, that will grow larger;
and he bounded away to go home with his companions.

#### IMAGINATION.

Mr. Alcott began thus: Who enjoy this exercise? Several. Who have brought fresh minds this morning, ready
to attend? Many. Who have dull minds this morning?
None. One boy said, his mind was fresh from the Well!

Some boys in this school have Insight, and some Outsight; and it would be very easy to show who have insight, and who have outsight, in the greatest degree, by thinking on what subjects each answers most readily. But all have both classes of thoughts, in a degree, said he; the power of seeing shapes without, and seeing the feelings and ideas in their own souls also.

I am going to read what St. Paul says about these two classes of thought, said he. And he read in paraphrase the last part of the fourth chapter of 2nd Corinthians and the first part of the fifth chapter.

He then addressed the little girl analysed, by name. What is there in the outward world that you like best; that you think most beautiful? After a while she said Nature. What objects in particular? No answer. Do you like flowers? Yes. Do you like running brooks? Yes. Do you like the ocean? Yes. Do you like the pebbles on the shore? Yes. Can you describe the feelings that you have, when you see the ocean? imagine yourself there, how should you feel? The power, said she.

A series of questions were now asked as to the comparative effect of different scenes on the feelings of the several children; and some preferred ocean; some mountains; some rivers: some caverns in the earth; some cataracts; some shells; some stars, &c. He went on to ask questions which might show into what departments of natural history their tastes would lead them. He found some zoologists; some geologists; some botanists; some astronomers, &c. One at last remarked that he liked machines, engines, &c. Many other boys agreed with him. Mr. Alcott said things were interesting to us, just in proportion as they seemed to be alive, or manifested Spirit.

The next series of questions was calculated to bring out what was their taste for the Arts; and there was considerble variety of taste; some were architects; some painters; some sculptors.

Who think dollars and eagles are very beautiful, and take great delight in seeing them? One boy said he took great delight in having them.

Who like carriages and splendid equipage? One said I like sleighs. Another said, I like to be inside of them.

Who like beautiful clothes, dresses? None. Those may stand up, who would not play with beggar boys, even if they were good, because of their looks? Several rose; and Mr. Alcott said that many of those who were standing up, would make the beggar boys worse probably; so it was very well. Who would play with beggar boys, if they were good? Several rose with great emphasis. Who would not play with colored boys, if they were ever so good and well instructed? The same boys rose as did at first. I am afraid your minds are colored with prejudices, said Mr. Alcott; and that you would darken their minds with your faults. So it is very well. The rest laughed, and when those sat down, rose up, and said they would play with black boys, if they had cultivated minds.

What if you were blind, and could not look out upon things at all; would there be any thing left to make you happy? He said this to the little girl analysed. Yes, inward things, said the little girl. What inward things? Thoughts; feelings; a good conscience, &c. were named. Who are most truly blind, those who cannot see inward things, or those who cannot see outward things? Those who cannot see inward things. You know when we talked a while ago, we said something about a net. Outward things, perhaps, form a net which catches our minds sometimes. Perhaps some of you are caught! I should like to see one person caught, said a little boy. Should you, said Mr. Alcott, like to see a boy, whose eyes and ears are so caught by outward things, that his mind is all taken up, and never looks inward? Yes. Well, there he is; said Mr. Alcott, holding a looking glass before him.

He then turned again to the little girl. Which power had you better use, the power of outsight or of insight? Insight. Why? Because it sees the real things. What are those things which the Outsight sees? Shadows of real things. Now each one think, said Mr. Alcott, what idea have you gained from this conversation? One said Insight is better than outsight. Another said inward things are better than outward things. Is that an idea in your head, or a feeling in your heart? I don't know, said she.

Suppose you saw a man born into this beautiful world, and all his life long he was running round to catch bubbles,

every one of which broke in his hand ?    They all laughed.
Or a man running after his shadow ; and he went on with
several similar analogies which made them laugh.    Such
are the persons, he said, who live for outward things, instead of inward things.

Who says play is a bubble ?    Some held up their hands.
But play is a very proper exercise in its place.    Who says
pleasure is a bubble ?    All held up their hands.    Yet it is
a bubble that it is innocent to look at a little.    Is Love a
bubble ?    No.    Is Happiness ?    No.    Is the Soul ?    No.
Is Heaven ?    No.    Is Immortality ?    No.    Who says
they have no doubt about inward things, but about outward things there is an uncertainty ?    Several did.

Mr. Alcott then said, we will close with some words of
Jesus, words which he uttered when he lived in a body like
ours.    Lay not up for yourselves treasures on earth, where
moth and rust do corrupt, and thieves break through and
steal ; but lay up for yourselves treasures in heaven—in the
inward world—where moth and rust do not corrupt, nor
thieves break through and steal.

### GENERAL SURVEY OF THE ANALYSIS.

Mr. Alcott called the class to analysis, for the last time.
He said we had now gone through the scale ; but it had
often been changed since we began, for almost every week
had improved it.    He then drew their attention to the one
which was now on the black board ; and said that the arrangement only was altered ; for the same subjects were
brought up by both scales.

We began with Love ; and then went to Faith ; and then
to Conscience, speaking of Obedience, Temptation and
Will ; and then to the Appetites, Affections, and Aspirations of the Soul ; and then we went to the Mind, and
spoke of Imagination, Judgment, and Insight.    To-day I
intend to talk a little more about Insight ; and I shall read
what Jesus Christ says about it.    He says we should not
strive to get outward things which may be stolen and cor-
rupted ; but we should strive to get things within, which
cannot be taken away, because they are God's ; for what
we love will take up all our exertions.

He here stopped and said that one of the boys in this

school had said that he did not know before he came to this
school, that he had inward eyes; but now he felt that
they were open.   They began to guess who it was, but they
did not guess the right one.   Mr. Alcott said that many of
them, when they came. were blind, were in midnight.   And
then he went on reading different passages of the Gospels.
He ended with, the light of the body is the eye; what eye?
This eye, said a little boy of five.   That is the body's eye;
what is the spirit's eye?   That eye which can see every
thing that it wants to see, and which can see God; the
body's eye cannot see what it wants to, but the spirits's eye
can; and Mr. Alcott, I think that when we are asleep, the
spirit goes out of the body, and leaves the body dead; and
bye and bye it goes back again, and makes the body alive
again.   But is the body entirely dead, in sleep? said Mr.
Alcott.   Why, perhaps a little spirit stays in the body to
keep it alive.   But almost all the spirit goes out, and sees
and hears with its inward eyes and ears, and that is dreaming.
   Now let us take a survey of the whole, said Mr. Alcott.
Such of you as think that the spirit acts in Instinct, may
hold up their hands.   No answer.   As soon as a baby is
born, it cries; it seems to be astonished to find itself in the
world, amidst so many things it does not know, and which
are so unlike itself; not one thing it sees, or one word that
it hears, does it understand; it cries——By Instinct, interrupted one of the children.   Yes, said Mr. Alcott, and it
moves its hand to take hold of the sun, or fire, or whatever
it sees; for it does not know how far off things are, or
what will hurt, and what will not.   Is there not instinct in
a baby's first motions?   Yes.   Does Spirit act in Instinct?   Yes.   Does Spirit act in a baby when it loves its
mother?   Yes, a good deal; said one.   Does Spirit act
in Appetite?   Yes.   Does Spirit act when it sees and
feels something beautiful?   Yes.   What is that action?
Aspiring.   Does Spirit act in Thought?   Yes, for the
body cannot think.   Thought, said Mr. Alcott, is the
ladder by which Spirit climbs up to heaven, i. e. into
itself.   Instinct, Love, and Faith, go out from the soul.
Thought goes back to the soul.   By Insight we go into the
soul and see what is in ourselves.   By Judgment we compare thoughts.   How many have Insight?   But a few

thought they had.  One of the most thoughtful said, a very little.  Who do not go in, for whole days?  Two boys, one a lazy boy of eight, another a new scholar of five, held up their hands.  Who cannot live a week without being taken captive and carried into the inward or spiritual world? No answer.

Who, every night, before they go to sleep, go inward and think of what is within?  Many.  Who think of this over again, in the morning?  Several.  You know that Jesus said, there was a fountain in there of living water, which springs up into everlasting life.  What is this fountain? The Spirit.

We talked about dreaming a good while ago; who among you, dream?  Several.  Most of you dream when you are awake, you see things vaguely, and dimly; not as if they all belonged together, but as if they were in disjointed pieces.

How many of you think God can be discovered with the eyes?  None.  Such as think you can see his works only with your body's eyes; and that He himself is to be found by looking within, with inward eyes, hold up your hands. All did.  How many of you look within enough to know a good deal about God?  None.  How many do not?  All. How many think it is hard?  One indolent boy held up his hand.  How many think an idle person can see God? Some.  It was here found that some confounded idleness with repose; when all comprehended it, they all said no idle person could see God; and made the same answer to the questions, How many think an intemperate person can see God?  An obstinate-willed person?  An angry, passionate person?  A person living for the outward?  A liar, deceiver?  There was some talk about the difference of liking truth in others, because it is convenient to ourselves; and loving it, so as to speak and act it.  Who think that those who love truth will probably know most of God? All.  Who think that those who deny themselves; who try to control their feelings, even their love, will know most of God?  All.  Such as think they cannot love God fully without being willing to die and lose their body, may hold up their hands.  All did.  Such as think that to find God, we must keep all our nature in its right place; that no part should be asleep; that we should be like the child aspiring, (he pointed to the cast;) may hold up their hands. All. He then went on, making remarks on each of the scholars, and saying what parts of the nature of each were asleep. This took a good while; but it was not lost, as it brought the subject home.

He then spoke of the effect of the passions: how, in the drunkard, appetite swallows up the nature; how, in the avaricious, the love of riches swallows up the nature; but when the Spirit swallows up the nature, nothing is destroyed, but every part is strengthened and purified, and put in the right place.

Who think that we must know ourselves, in order to know God? All. Who thinks he cannot know God, till he knows himself a great deal? All. Who think that they can know God by studying outward things? None. What are outward things? Shadows of inward things, said the little girl, who was generally the subject of analysis. The Representation of Mind, said a boy of nine. Who was called the Image of God? Jesus Christ, said the whole school. Yes, the outward world is the image of the perfect Mind; and Jesus Christ was the Image of God; or his nature was all Spirit, as he said. Who think that until we study ourselves, we cannot study outward things to much advantage? Many.

Mr. Alcott then remarked that many naturalists who never studied themselves, but studied outward things, did not believe in any spirit; and some who believed in spirit, yet did not think it was the most important, and did not therefore believe in Christianity, or what Jesus Christ taught about spirit. Others have gone out into the outward world, thinking it a shadow of the inward, and followed on until they found the Spirit that was in themselves, and God. One boy said, if I study botany, can I go on from it and find God? Mr. Alcott explained, but I could not hear him, as he walked to a place, where he stood with his back to me. Some remarks were made on the Free Enquirers, calculated to produce charitable feelings towards the honest among them.

What have these analysis lessons taught you? To know ourselves. Yes, your inward selves, your spirit.

Perhaps, some time next winter, I shall get some one who
knows such things better than I do, to come and teach
you about the human body—your outward selves—how
your eyes are formed and adapted for sight; and your ears
for hearing; and your stomach for digestion;—who will
like to hear this? All held up their hands. Which do you
think you should like best, to hear about the construction of
your bodies, or about your Spirits? Spirits. You prefer to
talk of inward things rather than outward things? Yes.
Who think the analysis has taught you a good deal about
yourselves? All. Who think it has taught you a good deal
about the meaning of words? All. I intend you shall
learn outward things too: I shall get people to come and
tell you about many outward things, which I do not know
much about myself. I can teach better about the inward
things. Next quarter I am going to teach you about inward things, not in yourselves, but in another—a Perfect
Being. In Jesus Christ? asked some. Yes; we will study
Jesus Christ; how many will be glad to do this? They
all held up their hands. How many have learned something from the analysis—they are very sure; they know it?
Almost all held up their hands. How many are sorry these
lessons are over. Several. Some said they were glad the
next subject was coming. Who would like to hear the
Record of the Analysis read? All.

Mr. Alcott then recurred to the blackboard, and said he
would read the scale. This diagram had been altered,
many times, during the quarter. It was intended merely
to systematize the conversations in a degree; and never
was presented to the children as a complete map of the
mind. Some have objected to these diagrams, as if they
would be fetters on the minds of the children. But their
constant renewal and changes preclude the possibility of
their being regarded as any thing but what they are. After
having read the scale through, he began at the end asking
the meaning of each word, and as they were defined, he
obliterated them, until all were gone.

Mr. Alcott opened his Temple School, pictured here on the first page of *Record of Conversations on the Gospels*, in 1834.

He derived his school's name from the fact that he had rented the space on the second floor of Boston's Masonic Temple. He had by this time reached a mature philosophical position, and he expected this school to be a special model. In contrast to his earlier experimentation in Connecticut village schools, "this time he would begin with the Idea and a school should be created to exemplify it," according to Dorothy McCuskey in her prizewinning biography, *Bronson Alcott, Teacher* (New York: Macmillan, 1940). Alcott's "Idea" contained a set of assumptions about education and human perfectibility which may seem the product of a distant place and time, but which are nonetheless Perennialist in nature.

These Perennialist assumptions were founded in a strong belief that true education is based on self-discovery, brought about through the interaction of teacher and pupils. Alcott saw education as a way of life, a continuing process through which individuals learn to obey the laws of their own natures and, in so doing, discover the laws of the "good" society. A "good" society would ultimately be possible because examination of one's conscience brings true knowledge, since one's conscience is a part of the Oversoul or God. The perfected society would come naturally as individuals examined their inner natures in search of true knowledge. This individual pursuit of truth would open the possibility for human concordance with God's Eternal

Truth, as more and more individuals influenced each other and bolstered each other's efforts at truth-seeking. The whole process would occur naturally as one individual influenced another; there would be no need for organization by the government or by any external force. Sometimes this concept has been known as "Emersonian reform," but it may seem quite strange to us because it has its roots in a dynamic faith in man's perfectibility which has not been in the mainstream of this country's intellectual history for more than a century.

This view of perfectibility is supposedly based on supreme faith in human nature. Some people who called themselves "Transcendentalists," as well as others who were merely influenced by Transcendentalism, were sure that human beings on their own could create a perfect society. Alice Felt Tyler's volume, *Freedom's Ferment* (New York: Harper & Row, 1962), provides many insights concerning the early nineteenth century's dreams of utopian socialist communities. Robert Owen, the British industrialist and founder of the New Harmony community, and Joseph Smith, originator of Mormonism, are only two of the utopian visionaries. There were many others who felt that man could formulate a community so perfect, so blissful, that the whole world would be transformed as individuals were gradually caught up in its appeal. Even Bronson Alcott, shortly after the demise of his Temple School, journeyed to England to meet reformers in preparation for his own attempt at a utopian community. It was called "Fruitlands" and managed to survive only a few years, despite Alcott's idealism, financial backing from Emerson, and the goodwill of many friends.

This faith in human perfectibility can be seen most clearly perhaps, if we contrast the dominant views of religious revivalism in this country during the early nineteenth century and today. Though many Transcendentalists were not part of organized Christianity, it is noteworthy that religious revivalism in the early nineteenth century fed on the same general notions of perfectibility that Transcendentalism embraced. In theological terms early nineteenth century revivalists subscribed to the post-millenial interpretation of scriptural prophecy. In essence, they believed the Millenium—the thousand years of perfection foretold by the Book of Revelation as occurring just before all true believers are immortalized and separated forever from non-believers and the strife they foment—would occur solely through man's efforts. No supernatural force would need to intervene in history to bring about this Millenium because human society was viewed as constantly improving. This position is usually called post-millenialism because Christ is viewed as returning to intervene personally in history after the Millenium has ended.

The pre-millenialist position, which is more common today, is that Christ will intervene personally in order to establish the Millenium. Man will not be able to bring about the thousand years of perfection unaided by supernatural forces, because problems of famine and resource scarcity are looming in overwhelming proportions while man's ability to cope with such staggering difficulties is obviously declining. The idea of man's perfectibility, strongly shared by many in the early nineteenth century, seems odd to most of us today; consequently, it is hard to comprehend the post-millenialist position's power in Alcott's day.

If we can bring all those theoretical precepts of Alcott and his Transcendentalist colleagues back into focus for the classroom, we will see that they translated into three quite manageable practices. First, Alcott was convinced of the value his pupils would derive from keeping journals. When youngsters arrived at school, those who already knew the skill of handwriting would spend an hour working with their journals, while younger pupils would practice handwriting. The handwriting lessons were always handled in the most supportive manner in order to encourage all honest efforts, "knowing [as Alcott said] that practice would at once mend the eye and hand, but that criticism would check the desirable courage and self confidence."[1]

Through journal writing Alcott sought to encourage the beginnings of probing one's inner nature by being just as supportive as he was in the case of handwriting instruction. Part of the effectiveness of journal keeping for self-analysis came no doubt from perseverance in the technique, for, as Alcott noted, it was some time before journals "became any record of the inward life."[2] Students who were "unused to composition . . . at first . . . set down only the most dry and uninteresting circumstances."[3] Such documents, when they did become records of thought and emotion, provided more than excellent instruction in the art of composition. When examined in retrospect, as Alcott was to do with his fifty volumes of journals in the last years of his life, they can become material for a stinging evaluation of how well one's cherished principles have been reflected in one's behavior.[4]

Secondly, Alcott believed in appealing to the group conscience for determining disciplinary policies. On the first day of instruction at Temple School he held a rather lengthy conversation in which he asked youngsters for their ideas as to the purpose of coming to school. In addition to their belief that various traditional branches of knowledge should be learned, students also agreed they should learn to behave well. The standard for behavior was determined cooperatively by an appeal to the group conscience of pupils as a higher authority than any individual conscience.[5] According to Peabody, "there was some correction; but still, in every individual instance, it was granted as necessary, not only by the whole school, but it was never given without the assent of the individual himself, and never given in the room."[6]

Thirdly, Alcott couched much of his teaching in the form of Socratic dialogue—a technique which he called "conversation." His use of the dialectic is modeled after Plato's writing of the dialogues; employing the *elenchus* to clarify definitions is especially evident in the preceding selection. The dialectic is again used as a tool whereby youngsters work their way back to truths about human nature and moral conduct.

In short, Alcott's use of the dialectic, his requirement for journal writing to serve as a record of the inner nature's development, and his appeal to the group conscience for standards of conduct make it seem appropriate to use the scales for Perennialism as shown below. Alcott, it should be noted, seemed to agree more with Socrates than with Plato in implying that everyone, not just a few fortunates, could use the dialectic to examine inner nature and thereby work themselves back to Truth. But we need to allow Alcott to describe his behaviors and philosophy in his own words because his comments are so eloquent.

### *Perennialist Role Model (Bronson Alcott)*

1. What is the nature of the learner?

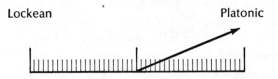

2. What is the nature of the subject matter?

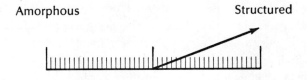

3. How should one use the subject matter to guide students toward meaningful learning activities?

**4.** What behavior trend should one exhibit in order to carry out
one's philosophical position?

Authoritarian World View       Non-authoritarian World View
(Convergent Thinking)          (Divergent Thinking)

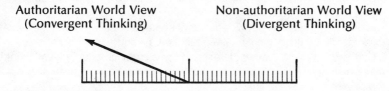

Comments by Alcott and Elizabeth Peabody highlight their beliefs
about the nature of the learner and about convergence. Indeed, Plato's doctrine of reminiscence is implied in the following statements.

---

There is in man a star of whose rising he retains a dim remembrance. . . .

Bronson Alcott, *Journals*, 1834

Go thou and look into an infant's face, and say if thou hast that yet within
thee which there beholdest . . . .

Bronson Alcott, *Journals*, 1835

For in childhood the sense of Justice, and the sentiment of the Good and
Beautiful, have not yet lost the holiness and divine balance of Innocence, or
the glow and impulse first received from the Divine Being, who projected the
individual soul into time and space, there to clothe itself with garments, by
which it may see itself, and be seen by its fellow beings.

Elizabeth Peabody, *Record of a School*, 1836

He who kindles the fire of genius on the altar of the young heart unites his
own prayers for humanity with every ascending flame that is emitted from it
through succeeding time. He prays with the Universal Heart, and his prayers
bring down blessings on the race below.

Bronson Alcott, *Journals*, 1835

Gradually, self-knowledge becomes psychology; knowledge of language,
grammar; and the practice of composition leads to the principles of true
rhetoric. Even if by removal from the school, these results are not attained
under his [Alcott's] immediate observation, he cannot doubt that they will
surely come out from the principles which he sets into operation.

Elizabeth Peabody, *Record of a School*, 1836

To go inward, and become fully conscious of what goes on there, and to
verify it in action, is therefore the Alpha and the Omega of a true life. Yet no
sect of religion has asserted with sufficient distinctness the great truth which
makes all this practical; namely, that all other souls are [potentially] what Jesus
was actually; that every soul is an incarnation of the infinite; that it never will
think clearly till it has mentally transcended time and space; that it never will
feel in harmony with itself until its sensibility is commensurate with all beings;
that it never will be fully alive, till, having finished the work given it to do, it
has passed through the grave.

Elizabeth Peabody, *Record of a School*, 1836

It is indeed an interesting parallel to Plato, and a telling statement of
faith in the dialectic's power to effect convergence after the group influence
is absent, that Peabody says of Alcott as quoted above, "he cannot doubt that
they [the desired objectives] will surely come out from the principles which
he sets into operation." Yet one may read excerpts from "Analysis of a
Human Being" and wonder if Alcott really had enough faith in the dialectic
to ask open-ended questions and to wait patiently for the dialectic to work its
magic. Was he actually just repressing these children and forcing them to
give the answers he wanted by appearing as a stern and rather threatening
father figure? I have tried to include excerpts from that chapter which have
given rise to positive, as well as negative, interpretations of Alcott's relationship with his students.

Not everyone agrees with me that Alcott asked open-ended questions
and actually expected a number of divergent responses, before the dialectic
would ultimately bring students toward convergence about human nature
and morality. The passage below from *Conversations with Children on the
Gospels* is a good example of many exchanges that can be cited which seem
to bear out Alcott's patience with alternate responses to open-ended questions. The reference concerns Zacharias, who was temporarily struck dumb
because he refused to believe a promise God was making directly to him
could possibly be fulfilled.

*George K.*   Now, Mr. Alcott! Do you think it was right for God to make
    Zacharias dumb?
*Mr. Alcott.*   Why do you think it was wrong?
*George K.*   I don't think Zacharias was wrong in not believing in the angel on
    the angel's own word. . . .

Notice that Alcott did not say, or even imply, anything close to "You
blasphemous little imp! How could you indicate that God was wrong?" That
kind of response might indeed have been expected from a Puritan. Alcott, on

the other hand, asked in a matter-of-fact way why George thought God was wrong. Certainly that should also qualify as one example in which Alcott is using a cognitive emphasis.

Throughout the series of dialogues about human nature the diagram showing relationships among facets of personality was periodically re-arranged. This fact is tantamount to an admission that both Alcott and his pupils were learning together and were willing to change the diagram as they uncovered insights which became progressively closer to the Truth. The tendency to work with the diagram, to solve specific questions about human conduct, and then to alter the diagram also shows that Alcott was stressing the structure of the discipline by using what we might call "action research in psychology" to help youngsters begin their probing for Truth.

My own interpretation is that Alcott could create such a supportive learning atmosphere that even those situations which seem harsh and puni-tive were handled humorously or in such a way as to be less threatening. Reading Alcott's school reports when he was Concord's superintendent dur-ing the 1860s, examining his journals, and scrutinizing descriptions of the way his students responded to him confirm my belief in his gentleness.

Even Charles Strickland, who painted a slightly harsher picture of Al-cott in "A Transcendentalist Father: The Child-Rearing Practices of Bronson Alcott" (*History of Childhood Quarterly*, Summer, 1973), stressed the gen-tle, almost indulgent, nature of his relationship to Louisa and Elizabeth. He tried to awaken in them the search for Truth by altering the environment to get them to explore their own consciences for guidance: for example, he once left an apple in the nursery and said he hoped they would save it for him if they could. Most important, he was usually willing to wait patiently for the dialectic's outcome. When he did not wait, for instance, when he resorted to spanking, it seems more of an aberration from his typical behavior. Those times when patience is exhausted come for every parent, and they may come even more quickly for one's own youngsters because of the intensity of emo-tional involvement. It is, after all, harder to wait and be professional in the home with one's own children than in the classroom. It is remarkable, how-ever, how closely Alcott's techniques for developing conscience parallel a number of recent studies on conscience development among children. Dur-ing those studies of the late 1950s and early 1960s, however, children usually had candies left to tempt them rather than apples.

There is another question about Alcott's behavior which may or may not represent an aberration. Although in many conversations he seemed to retain a matter-of-fact, cognitive emphasis, there are also times when he put students into affective situations. Is it surprising that he would interview a little girl before other students and ask her publicly if she would die for her mother? Was it also out of character for Alcott to ask a youngster if he would like to see a boy who "never looks inward" and then show that same youngster his reflection in a mirror? Perhaps one might say the second incident was handled humorously, but it is difficult to imagine that Alcott could have meant for the first situation to be anything but stressful. Was the mirror incident a time when Alcott's "impatience was showing"—when he simply grew tired of waiting for long-term effects of the dialectic? Alcott is no longer available to be asked, and neither are his associates, so we will never really know.

Nevertheless, this tendency toward the affective, not usually typical of Perennialists, is especially useful to our purpose here because it underscores how open-ended questioning and other techniques associated with this role model can be used with Existentialism and Reconstructionism. It is especially striking to note how closely Alcott's questions to the little girl parallel a values clarification technique which Raths, Harmin, and Simon in *Values and Teaching* have called the "public interview." And Alcott's use of journal writing is quite similar to the same volume's advocacy of "thought sheets" and "time diaries," except that Alcott's is a more comprehensive approach and is, therefore, perhaps a more effective clarifier of values. When Alcott helped his pupils clarify their values, however, he had faith that the dialectic would ultimately bring them to the convergence of Truth. Contemporary values clarifiers, on the other hand, expect and reward divergence.

The key to differences between contemporary Existentialists and Alcott—especially between Existential psychologists, such as Abraham Maslow, Earl Kelley, and Carl Rogers, when compared to our nineteenth century Perennialist—lies in the separate connotations they applied to the concept "inner nature." That phrase appears with great frequency in Alcott's writings and in the writings of Existential psychologists. Alcott used the phrase interchangeably with the word "soul," however, a practice which Existential psychologists are certainly not in the habit of doing. Alcott and the Transcendentalists saw "inner nature" as coming from forces outside men, from a higher Ideal within the Universe. To the Existential psychologist "inner nature" is almost certain to be viewed as originating with human beings as physiological organisms. Again, the techniques may look the same, but the underlying philosophical assumptions can be poles apart. But Alcott said it best.

---

[in reference to a note from Emerson]
... the first sympathy that has stolen on my ear from the desolate and doubting present. Only Emerson, of this age, knows me, of all that I have

found. Well; one man, *one very man through and through!* Many are they who live and die alone, known only to the survivors of an after-century.

*Journals*

I have lived in myself . . . so that I am unfitted for the general mind, intent as this is upon the outward and phenomenal rather than the inward and permanent. But I do not despair. Time will make me intelligible, and I shall not wholly misrepresent myself.

*Journals*

---

Alcott is perhaps better understood by "survivors in an after-century." But a chain of events begun by horrified reactions to references regarding human birth in *Conversations with Children on the Gospels* ultimately wiped his Transcendentalist school from Boston's mentality.[7]

## THE PERENNIALIST ROLE MODEL AND THE TEACHER

### Examining One's Inner Nature

As discussed previously, there are two basic styles of teaching which seek to explore the human personality—Existentialism and Perennialism. In both styles the techniques may appear similar, but their philosophical bases are quite different. In one sense, Perennialism is the more conservative approach to exploring human relationships because it presumes ultimate convergence. Nonetheless, to the extent that Perennialist techniques look like values clarification, those techniques are subject to the same kinds of controversy associated with Existentialist teaching styles.

Suppose teachers want to encourage students to explore the nature of human relationships and views of moral conduct. Will their attempts at values clarification expect and reward divergence in the manner of Existentialists, or will they presume that students will ultimately converge on Truth, in the Perennialists' manner? My own tendency has been to ask open-ended questions and expect divergence, perhaps because my teaching experience occurred in public school settings. However, something similar to Perennialist brands of convergence do have a way of emerging.

One example of this emergence occurred quite surprisingly during a discussion session in one of my English history classes. I had talked with students about the Great Books approach, and we all decided to organize much of our work in the next instructional unit around the same rules of discussion which appear at the beginning of this chapter. In one of our discussions about medieval society a student asked me, "Which came first—the crossbow or the longbow?" I was at first somewhat astounded that anyone would be concerned about that question; it certainly was not central to our discussion, but had just emerged in the course of conversation. I explained that, according to the rules of discussion, I would not supply the answer directly, since they had already uncovered enough information to be able to develop answers for themselves.

I sat silently for nearly thirty minutes watching in amazement as the question took hold and students reasoned through a number of points on their way to convergence. Then one student left the circle to consult a few sources, just to see if his colleagues were correct. Here is a case where students insisted on considering a question which the teacher had not thought to ask and followed the issue circuitously to convergence. I was amazed that the question had sparked enough interest to sustain a discussion for thirty minutes. (The answer is "longbow," by the way!)

### Platonic or Rogerian?

The preceding example does not concern an issue which Perennialists usually consider, although the topic originally emanated from discussion about human relationships and concepts of morality in medieval England. Nonetheless, it does illustrate how a "Platonic" view of learners can combine, somewhat surprisingly and perhaps even illogically, with convergence.

It is still the teacher's choice whether to stress convergence or divergence when and if one uses open-ended questions about human nature. Or will the teacher prefer to avoid moral questions and values clarification exercises altogether as a planned portion of his or her curriculum? How does one make such a decision? To aid this decision-making process, we will examine in the next chapter an overview of all the role models we have considered. We will encourage teachers to make a self-assessment about where they are in their growth toward teaching with charisma.

### Notes

1. Elizabeth Peabody, *Record of a School*, 3rd ed. rev. (Boston: Roberts Brothers, 1874), p. 20.
2. Elizabeth Peabody, *Record of a School*, 2nd ed. rev. (Boston: Russell, Shattuck, and Co., 1836), p. xxxviii.
3. Ibid.
4. Odell Shepard, *Pedlar's Progress: The Life of Bronson Alcott* (Boston: Little, Brown, & Co., 1937), pp. 516–517.

5. Elizabeth Peabody, *Record of a School*, 2nd ed. rev. (Boston: Russell, Shattuck, and Co., 1836), p. xiv.

6. Elizabeth Peabody, *Record of a School*, 3rd ed. rev. (Boston: Roberts Brothers, 1874), pp. 20–21.

7. For a more complete treatment see Lloyd Duck, "Bronson Alcott, Abraham Maslow, and 'Third Force' Psychology," *Education* 98 (1977): 210–220.

# TOWARD TEACHING WITH CHARISMA:
## Role Models, Philosophy, and Individual Preference

# CHAPTER SEVEN

## *The Role Models in Perspective:*
# ONE LAST LOOK—EVERYBODY IN THE DISSECTING PAN

Where are we now in terms of our explanations of role models, the philosophical assumptions supporting those role models, and the styles of behavior which cluster around each model? Ideally we are closer to helping one decide how to behave as a teacher, closer to helping one build a repertoire of behaviors, which we have called "establishing a style," that complements one's personality. If the style and personality fit, then students are likely to see the teacher as a "together" person who can teach with charisma because he or she knows how to function well in the learning environment.

Let us take one final look at our array of role models. We will continue to call each role model by its philosophical name, because that name has come to stand for a meaningful tradition in education and serves to remind us how each model has evolved through a long and distinguished history. There are many who insist that these names are no longer relevent; current trends, as well as creativity, demand newly coined terms to take their places. I insist, however, that these terms help us relate to our educational past, force us to see how the best ideas about teaching and learning emerge, change, re-emerge, and develop.

Perhaps the greatest insistence on new terminology has come from those who have objected to seeing these philosophical terms used to indicate teaching behaviors which are viewed as separated neatly into mutually exclusive categories. Here we are *not* referring to role models and their accompanying philosophical assumptions as existing in separate and distinct compartments. Since those of us who teach, and a great many who only watch practicing professionals in their classrooms, are all too aware that life belies "glib" categories and trips us at every turn when we try to make reality fit into tiny boxes, it is most important to remember that we have used labels here to imply only *preferences and dominant behavior tendencies.*

We all know that, from time to time, any teacher will borrow from behaviors which cluster naturally in sets around different role models. It is only those behaviors which are most dominant in a teacher's style, however, that determine the use of any one of our "labels." In that sense any label for a role model is applied loosely—loose enough to leave room for growth and loose enough for the understanding that one whose behavior is mostly Experimentalist, for instance, does not violate the natural order of things or upset student sensibilities by occasionally giving an "Essentialist" quiz or even by asking convergent questions—as long as the teacher lets students know his or her rationale and shows clearly how this activity or assignment relates to the teacher's true style. That style, of course, is evidenced by behaviors which are dominant.

## A Question of Camps: To Converge or Diverge

While examining the role models and scales, remember that they have consistently been applied loosely to indicate only behavior preferences. They have been used, in fact, to indicate a direction in which one may be moving professionally, rather than implying slavish adherence to a single category. We have divided the models into camps honoring convergence and divergence. In addition, we have added the name of a new role model.

Let us examine more closely the way our chart of role models and scales has been organized. We have divided them basically into "camps": one camp honors convergence, and the other camp honors divergence. That organization follows Marie Wirsing's categorization of philosophies in her seminal work, *Teaching and Philosophy: A Synthesis* (Houghton Mifflin Company, 1972). Such a division is particularly useful to one who is beginning to study how teacher behaviors cluster around philosophical assumptions and manifest themselves as style. Suppose, for instance, a student observes one teacher for ten hours and is careful to follow the field experience guidelines enumerated below. As one examines those guidelines it becomes obvious that they relate as follows to our analytical tool.

## Guidelines for Classroom Observation and Personal Assessment

### Field Experience Guidelines*

The following suggested field experience activities are designed to help one prepare for writing a paper that analyzes teaching styles and clusters of techniques which complement the various teacher role models we have studied.

1.   Observe a discussion session for the kinds of student participation that occur. How often are students asked to participate in divergent thinking? How often are students asked to participate in convergent thinking? (*See the analytical tool for questions about behavior trend and the nature of the learner.*)

* NOTE: If you use these guidelines for personal assessment, observe your own behaviors, answer the questions as indicated, and discuss with yourself the ways you prefer to teach.

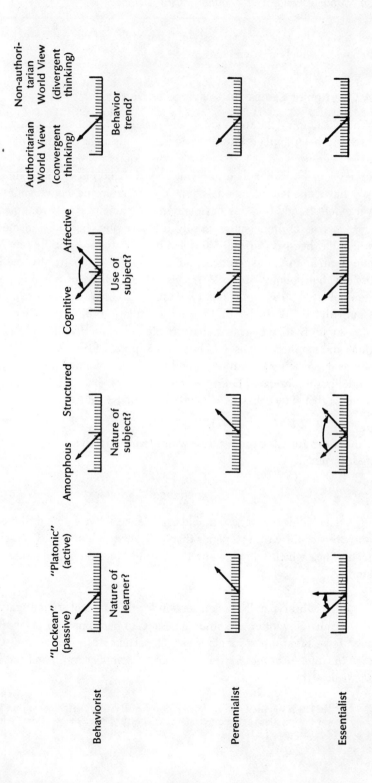

Overview of Role Models and Dials

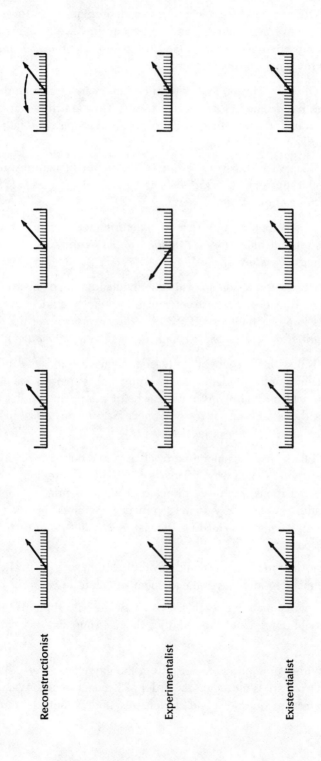

Reconstructionist

Experimentalist

Existentialist

2.  Observe teaching techniques to determine which ones involve students in convergent thinking and which ones involve students in divergent thinking activities. (*See the analytical tool for questions about behavior trend and the nature of the learner.*)

3.  Observe a lesson and determine how many academic disciplines the teacher has decided to use in that lesson. How are these various disciplines integrated? (*See the analytical tool for the question about nature of the subject matter.*)

4.  Observe a "discovery" lesson to determine the nature of the investigation and its outcome. (*See the analytical tool for questions about behavior trend and the nature of the learner.*)

5.  Observe an "inquiry" lesson to determine the nature of the investigation and its outcomes. (*See the analytical tool for questions about behavior trend and the nature of the learner.*)

6.  Observe a lesson in which individualization of instruction is a major focus. How does the instructor plan for helping students at different skill levels improve their expertise? (*See the analytical tool for questions about nature of the subject matter and use of the subject matter.*)

7.  Talk with the cooperating teacher about the kinds of controversial issues which his or her students may be studying. Ask permission to observe a session in which a controversial issue is being examined in order to determine what the issue is and its resolution(s). (*See the analytical tool for the question about use of subject matter.*)

8.  Talk with the cooperating teacher to find out which method(s) he or she prefers to use and why: "discovery," "inquiry," problem-solving discussions, simulations, lectures, directed reading of primary sources, directed reading of secondary sources, practice exercises, learning centers, individual research, and so forth. (*A summary activity for all questions in the analytical tool.*)

*Note:* All proper names should be omitted from your paper. References should be made to methods and classroom situations *in general.*

Ask your cooperating teacher if you may talk with students briefly and at appropriate times about the activities they are pursuing.

A number of implications arise from the guidelines. For instance, if a discussion's pattern is mostly on the order of "teacher questions and student responds; teacher questions and student responds," then the emphasis is probably on convergence. However, if the pattern shows one teacher's question is followed by a number of student responses before the teacher poses another question, then the emphasis is quite probably on divergence. A student would also not expect to observe all items indicated by the guidelines; this in itself might help to determine a teacher's style because it would automatically indicate preferences.

The last item, of course, is meant to persuade the teacher to give insights into his or her philosophy, without actually having to mention a philosophical label. At the mere mention of terms like Experimentalism or Essentialism some teachers will begin to think judgmentally, as if Experimentalism is inherently "good" and Essentialism is inherently "bad," or *vice versa,* depending on the teacher's perspective. Such terms have often been used judgmentally in the past. How, therefore, would a teacher know our position is that each of the role models, when assumed responsibly, offers a superbly valid and effective way for teachers to teach? One might also find a teacher who verbally espouses one philosophy, although his or her behaviors actually match another philosophy. Thus, it is perhaps better to avoid the names of traditional philosophical positions, when one tries to understand the nature of style, role model, and philosophy through studying an experienced teacher's behavior. If, however, ten hours of observing and following guidelines are not long enough, what does one do then?

That situation points up the usefulness of our division of role models by "camps." If one cannot decide precisely what seems to be a logical choice of role model, one can almost certainly determine whether a teacher's assignments, discussions, and learning activities in general emphasize convergence or divergence. If the stress is on convergence, one might say that this teacher is a "Perennialist/Essentialist." If the emphasis is on divergence, however, one might use the category "Experimentalist/Existentialist."

If one cannot determine a preference for either convergence or divergence, it would perhaps be acceptable to apply the sometimes overused term, "eclectic." When overused, that term indicates one who borrows from a number of different philosophies and role models to establish his or her own teaching style, but we all do that to some degree. Here we will use the term in a more exact and, I think, more meaningful sense to indicate the person who borrows so successfully that there is no clear indication regarding convergence or divergence in his or her behavior trend. Either one uses both effectively—as in the phrase, "he really likes teaching better than eating"—or one has not clearly examined what one's teaching behaviors imply and may not understand the differences between convergence and divergence. At least, those are two logical possibilities.

In the preceding paragraphs, we have assumed that one would observe a teacher, collect data, and make decisions about that teacher's behavior. Note, however, the statement about personal assessment which is attached to the list of guidelines. If one is currently teaching, as well as observing and analyzing one's own behaviors, then the process is equally valid and appropriate. In fact, one has an added advantage when using the guidelines for self-assessment because we have direct access to our own thought processes. One is not watching someone else's behaviors or attempting to infer what that person's thought patterns may be. Asking one's self the following questions can spark a productive dialogue with one's inner nature.

1. How often do I emphasize convergence in discussions? How often do I emphasize divergence?
2. In my teaching strategies generally, do I tend to emphasize convergence or divergence?
3. How many different disciplines do I tend to incorporate within each lesson or activity?
4. Do I use "discovery" lessons? What is the nature of the investigation and the outcome for one of my typical "discovery" lessons?
5. Do I use "inquiry" lessons? What is the nature of investigations and outcomes for one of my typical "inquiry" lessons?
6. How do I attempt to individualize instruction? How do I help students at different skill levels to improve their expertise?
7. How do I deal with controversial issues in the classroom? What kinds of resolutions are typically reached for a lesson dealing with a controversial issue?
8. What methods and activities do I prefer to use: "discovery," "inquiry," problem-solving discussions, simulations, lectures, directed reading of secondary sources, practice exercises, learning centers, individual research, and so forth?

These eight straightforward questions should easily start one on his or her way to self-assessment about behavior preferences and role model "camps." And one has the superb advantage of having all the materials for study readily accessible.

## Completing the Picture with Behaviorism

But this explanation about our division into "camps" has only involved four role models. What about Reconstructionism and Behaviorism? Those two role models refer to educators who would really like to make the world over, or at least a society or a classroom, according to their respective "camps." In other words, Reconstructionists seek social reform while honoring divergence. As we have seen earlier, Kozol, as well as others, believes Reconstructionist techniques of persuasion are the most subtle forms of mind control because they appear, on the surface at least, to honor divergence by being extremely open about alternatives. And Behaviorists seek reform by honoring convergence; often they advocate extreme convergence administered through an almost "air-tight" system of rewards and punishments.

Our chart then, in order to be complete, has to include a Behaviorist role model. Two famous Behaviorist schemes based on "air-tight" systems of rewards and punishment are presented in the societies of Aldous Huxley's *Brave New World* (New York: Bantam, 1962) and B. F. Skinner's *Walden II* (New York: Macmillan, 1965).

*Brave New World's* social structure is certainly based on a frightening system of rewards and punishments. If one has a recording playing under the pillow at night to program one's behavior and thoughts, if one is conditioned to respond in predictable ways to the most superficial and most sensual of pleasures, then one conforms. Usually the reward system which ushered in this conformity seemed innocuous enough, but sometimes it was shatteringly emotional and affective. For instance, the scene in which crawling infants were encouraged by the nursery's staff to move toward a glass wall bordering a garden profuse and alive with colors and sunlight, emphasizes the affective element used by the same staff. The staff sent an electric shock through the floor just before these infants reached their destination. The technique, of course, sent the babies back howling with pain. A few sessions like this, and *voilá*, one had a budding factory technician who would love to toil in rooms away from sunlight and who might be expected to behave docilely in such circumstances almost indefinitely.

This example of crawling babies helps to explain why, in our chart of role models, the scale for a Behaviorist's use of subject matter is shown as either cognitive or affective. It also should help to remind one that the Behaviorist's efforts to influence behavior are diffuse. In short, they represent a truly amorphous position regarding subject matter, because their very success depends upon the victim's (or should I say "learner's"?) inability to look beneath the surface aspects of the system and understand its elements. Of course, the potency of all Behaviorism depends on the learner's passive willingness to absorb a predetermined bit of information or way of acting (what we have called a "Lockean" perspective). In addition, Behaviorism depends on the power of a system to pull its members to convergence.

But let's look at *Walden II*, a Behaviorist scheme with more subtlety and freedom than the scheme portrayed in *Brave New World*. In *Walden II* people feel free, so free in fact that they choose to return to Walden and live according to its precepts. This is a more sophisticated system, because most adults in the society seem to understand quite fully the principles of behavioral engineering which operate, and they are perfectly willing to submit themselves to these principles. In brief, this is quite different from the level of behavioral shaping that was done with pigeons in Skinnerian boxes. The community is organized around a system of labor-credits which gives greatest rewards to those who do work generally regarded as distasteful; this ensures a great deal of meaningful leisure for everyone. Education is largely informal and notoriously unfettered by bureaucratic and administrative paraphernalia, such as grades and the traditional elementary-secondary-college hierarchical scheme. Children are depicted as learning so well on their own the principles of thinking and inquiring, because the community purposely seeks to nurture and develop each youngster's natural desire to succeed or to be competent. As Frazier explained in Chapter 15,

> We made a survey of the motives of the unhampered child and found more than we could use. Our engineering job was to *preserve* them by fortifying the child against discouragement. We introduce discouragement as carefully as we introduce any other emotional situation, beginning at about six months. Some of the toys in our air-conditioned cubicles are designed to build perseverance. A bit of a tune from a music box, or a pattern of flashing lights, is arranged to follow an appropriate response—say, pulling on a ring. Later the ring must be pulled twice, later still three or five or ten times. It's possible to build up fantastically perseverative behavior without encountering frustration or rage. It may not surprise you to learn that some of our experiments miscarried; the resistance to discouragement became almost stupid or pathological. One takes some risks in work of this sort, of course. Fortunately, we were able to reverse the process and restore the children to a satisfactory level.*

And there you have it. According to Frazier, the techniques of behavioral engineering, applied to infants and youngsters in order to program into them appropriate responses, will shape their actions effectively far into the future. Thus they will not need direct control later; they will have been conditioned into the right responses and will feel free and natural as they continue those prescribed behaviors. As Castle, another character being treated to a tour of Frazier's community, lamented, "I can't believe you can really get spontaneity and freedom through a system of tyrannical control. . . .What is freedom, anyway, under such a plan?"

For Frazier, and perhaps for Skinner, it is quite acceptable that people feel free enough to submit themselves willingly to the system. And this is the desired outcome of most teachers who practice behavioral engineering in their classrooms. They are certainly not concerned about working with the

---

*From B. F. Skinner, *Walden II* (New York: Macmillan, 1965), pp. 123–124.

large populations of a *Brave New World* or a *Walden II*, but would often be quite grateful to be able to modify students' behaviors effectively to get learning tasks completed. For example, I once worked with a student teacher whose class just before lunch presented a special challenge. Several students preferred to walk into the room and throw desks out the window rather than to sit down at a table and make themselves ready for the day's activity. The student teacher immediately set up a "token economy" for that class and gave "points" for coming in quietly, sitting in a desk instead of hurling it out the window, speaking politely to classmates instead of showering them with four-letter epithets, and so forth. One day per week, usually on Friday, students got to trade in their tokens for a number of desirable items—everything from chocolate cakes to ski socks. Consequently, the spirit of cooperation in that class improved markedly. The student teacher moved quickly to skew this system so that youngsters would repeatedly have the choice of either buying immediately a less expensive, and perhaps less desirable, item or saving for a more expensive article that was auctioned off approximately every two weeks.

This particular student teacher, however, was not an advocate of behavior modification and he did not usually embrace the philosophy of Behaviorism. Nevertheless, in this situation he saw a "token economy" as his only solution. He knew he couldn't be humanistic or emphasize divergence, until students no longer had to fear bodily harm from each other.

As the previous three examples indicate, Behaviorist approaches honor extreme convergence. Indeed, those who advocate convergence may be so sold on its efficacy that they wish to make the world over, or at least a tiny portion of the world, so that people will be forced into some favorite brand of convergence. Many such schemes depend largely on keeping people in the dark about the rationale behind a system of rewards and punishments. Usually, however, those in control wish to have their followers understand enough of the system's operation to choose willingly to submit themselves to the system; this approach was evident in *Walden II* and in the student teacher's token economy. In brief, the Behaviorist position represents an extreme which may be considered an outgrowth of Essentialist teaching styles.

## Role Model Choices and Administrative Settings

This view of Behaviorism, however, depends entirely on one's perspective. For instance, Reconstructionists have often insisted quite loudly that institutionalized schooling in this country has always been based on Behaviorist principles of rewards and punishments. In short, either one accepts and conforms to the reward system of grades and diplomas, or one gets "weeded out" as an academically unskilled and unsuccessful person. This "weeding-out" function was seen as one major task of schooling in this country, especially during the last half of the nineteenth century; moreover, this function is still ascribed to by some people today, as discussed in the chapter on Reconstructionism. In that chapter we spent a great deal of time examining the rise and fall in faith among Americans that formal schooling could be an agency to effect social reform. As our discussion in that chapter implied, both Behaviorism and Reconstructionism have tended to be viewed as philosophical positions which operate on large numbers of youngsters in institutions. These positions, whether in a traditional school organization for Behaviorism or some type of alternative schooling for Reconstructionism, have often been seen as institution-wide solutions, rather than as philosophies which provide teachers with role models to be used at the individual classroom level. Viewed on the broad institutional level, of course, Behaviorism tends to support Essentialist/Perennialist styles for classroom teachers, and Reconstructionism tends to support Experimentalist/ Existentialist styles. One would still, however, have the freedom to develop a teaching style honoring divergence within an institution operating according to Behaviorist assumptions, or *vice versa*; however, one would need to be quite aware of the potential problems and pitfalls of "going against the grain" which an institution has established.

Let's look briefly at examples of two institutional support systems: one system could be considered Behaviorist in its general orientation, and the other, Reconstructionist in orientation. They illustrate quite well that either philosophy can be successful (in this case, for eliminating school violence), if one uses the approach with a responsible attitude, with conviction, and with a sincere interest in helping youngsters.

The Behaviorist orientation is apparent in the following excerpt from "Crackdown" by Joseph Wint*:

---

Three years ago Wyandanch High School was filled with violence. Today it is one of the most peaceful and highly organized schools in the nation. The miracle man behind this remarkable change is Ernest Kight. Kight has established several principles and strategies which I consider to be very important in the organization and administration of schools in a world torn by violence, vulgarity, and a conglomeration of lifestyles. . . .

Now, *how is discipline handled?* Here are the guiding principles:

1. Kight spells out the rules in the students' handbook. No student can plead ignorance of school rules.
2. Kight supports his teachers at all times.

3. Punishment is swift. Cases are usually dealt with on the same day an infraction occurs.
4. Punishment is consistent for all students. There are no favorites. It doesn't matter whether the student is black, white, or the son of a board member; he gets the same treatment.
5. Accurate records are kept. There is a file for every student. If students use foul language, teachers are asked to record the exact words the students used. Parents are often shocked when their children admit to such usage.
6. Parents are brought into the picture. When a student is sent home, he may not return without his parent. Parent involvement is extremely important in solving discipline problems.
7. Students who are chronic disciplinary cases are removed from the regular school setting to an afternoon adjustment program.
8. Court cases are pursued to the end. Many principals fail to do this because it is time consuming. Kight takes time to see them through.

As these operating principles make clear, Wyandanch High is no place to fool around in. The word has gone forth. Students know that they are there to get a certain kind of education. Strangers no longer hang around the school grounds. They know that they will be arrested—often by a plainclothes police summoned by the principal.

*Reprinted with permission from Jospeh H. G. Wint and Dennis Van Avery, "Contrasting Solutions to School Violence," *Phi Delta Kappan,* November, 1975.

---

The Reconstructionist orientation is revealed in the following excerpt from "The Humanitarian Approach" by Dennis Van Avery:

---

In Wint's closing remarks, he states that "if violence in our schools is to end, we must have strong principals." Violence also may cease if we have even stronger *principles*. Principles and strategies that nurture humaneness and foster respect for individual differences are possible solutions to the strife in our schools. These principles may best be examined by asking the same significant questions that Wint chose to explore. . . .

The third question is: How is discipline handled? This question has become the main concern of almost all people involved with schools. Our society thinks that "more discipline" will make a better world and certainly better schools. But doesn't the cry for discipline really translate to, "Let's try to help people act in a responsible manner"? This society desperately needs people who accept responsibility, not simply accept discipline. Schools can teach responsibility. Young people need to grow up with the idea that other people are trustworthy. Young people learn responsibility by having it given, not withheld. Human rights are rights that individuals have because they are human, but schools so often say, "You must earn them." Responsibility can be expected to exist and be fostered in an environment which is positive, where people are respected and liked; which is open, where choices can be made;

which is caring, where concern is modeled by others; and which is supportive, where people are helped in gathering information.

School rules are important. For inherent in teaching responsibility is the opportunity to make choices. Rules set limits; they define choices. Once the choices are made clear, the choosing must be left for the individual. It becomes the teachers' and principals' role to help clarify the choices. The process of learning responsibility can best take place between people who can really get to know each other. We need continually to be concerned about allowing small groups of young people to interact with responsible adults. Such things as classroom meetings in elementary schools, homebase sessions in middle schools, and rap sessions in high schools are essential. Adults need training to be helpers, clarifiers, listeners. This modeling behavior is a positive answer in learning responsibility, of which discipline becomes only a small part.

**\*Reprinted with permission from Joseph H. G. Wint and Dennis Van Avery, "Contrasting Solutions to School Violence,"** *Phi Delta Kappan,* **November, 1975.**

---

It should be clear, after brief reflection on these two approaches, that one seeks to "make the school society over" in Behaviorist terms which emphasize convergence; and the other attempts to change the school society in Reconstructionist ways that honor divergence. And just as with any role model defined by individual teachers, each of these approaches can be assumed responsibly and effectively.

Despite the fact that what we have termed Behaviorist and Reconstructionist role models have often been applied on a broad institution-wide basis, there are those, such as Jonathan Kozol and Ivan Illich for instance, who have great misgivings about any and all institutionalized schooling. As Kozol affirmed, even Reconstructionism is negative because it is the most subtle form of mind control in that it appears to be so open. He sees all institutionalized schooling as a trick to make people accept the "diploma-mill" and "weeding-out" views of education as valid. In this sense, he looks at all education in formal schools in nearly the same light as many educators view the extreme Behaviorism of a *Brave New World* or a *Walden II.* Those who like this deschooling position would, in general, tend to use Existential styles but would probably not eschew Essentialism, Perennialism, or Experimentalism as long as those styles were managed informally, and teachers and learners were to decide rationally on their appropriateness. Then, again, it depends on one's perspective.

We began this section with efforts to put our six role models into perspective. So far we have only dealt with the flexible application of terminology and with rationales for including in our chart Behaviorism and Reconstructionism—two approaches which have often been cast into institutional settings and used in attempts to reconstruct the world. Before we take a final look at the horizontal nature of this chart, notice that vertically all role models are organized generally with the most structured curricula and the most teacher-directedness at the top. Positions associated with the least structured curricula and least teacher-directedness have purposely been placed at the bottom.

The horizontal organization of our chart reflects the continuum idea. Each question we have asked in our analytical tool, as well as each scale we have used, implies indications on a continuum. It is possible to be more or less affective, more or less "Lockean," more or less "Platonic." The same implication is true for the role models themselves. It is possible to be more or less authoritarian in one's world view, and to exercise more or less teacher-directedness. Thinking of all these as continua helps to account for the marvelous complexity inherent in growth toward teaching with charisma. Indeed, a number of indicators must be looked at in concert to clarify the complexities that creative and charismatic teaching styles exhibit.

How does one refute, however, the charge of oversimplification? How does one dispel the myth that attempts to categorize and analyze role models or their accompanying philosophies and behavior styles are futile because teaching behaviors are too complex to be looked at in clusters? In the previous chapter we examined one aspect of this issue of oversimplification in regard to our question about the nature of the learner. We had been using the term "Platonic" to indicate a teacher's opinion that learners are active and can *create* knowledge through the dialogue. Our use of "Lockean" had referred to a learner seen as passive, as one who must *receive* knowledge through his or her individual perception. Although our study of Perennialism required modification in our original use of the indicator, the terms were still quite useful, if for no other reason than to show that contemporary understandings about divergence, convergence, and the nature of learners can be related to historical and philosophical roots.

How does one get to know about these roots? In essence, one looks at the history of role models and their philosophical underpinnings, then discovers how elements of teacher behaviors cluster together naturally and rationally into what we have called styles. Although sometimes such endeavors might provoke the charge of oversimplification, who would benefit by the admission that creative and charismatic teaching behaviors are so complex that one can study them only on an individual, technique-by-technique basis? Would such a position help pre-service and in-service educators analyze their own teaching styles, reconstruct a repertoire of behaviors, or grow professionally? I seriously doubt that it would. Those in teacher preparation institutions have often graduated with a vague notion that teaching successfully means being as proficient as possible at as many techniques as possible from an overstuffed grabbag of the profession's tricks. I would, quite frankly, like to see this vague notion of teaching—fed perhaps by the idea that teaching behaviors are so complex and individualistic—buried as quickly as possible, so we can get on with the business of helping educators construct teaching styles that are meaningful to themselves because they consist of behaviors which fit their own personalities and which appear to be rationally and philosophically sound.

In short, there is no one right way to teach; there aren't even two correct ways. Teaching with charisma comes from self-assessment, wise choices for one's own repertoire of behaviors, and the philosophical knowledge to manage one's own professional growth. Moreover, the phrase "philosophical knowledge" does not imply that one must use traditional terms in philosophy. Our names for the six role models we have identified come directly from educational philosophy, but we have not used words like "metaphysics" (the nature of reality), "epistemology" (the nature of knowledge), and "axiology" (the nature of goodness). Instead, we cast those concepts in down-to-earth terms. If the major reality for teachers will be learners in a classroom, why not simply ask how teachers regard the nature of learners? If teachers must deal directly with specific disciplines, why not ask directly how they view the nature of the disciplines they teach? If teachers have a clear option about dealing with controversial moral issues, why not ask them directly whether they wish to emphasize cognitive or affective approaches, rather than dwelling on a general question about axiology?

## HOW TO ANALYZE ROLE MODEL DEVELOPMENT AND PROFESSIONAL GROWTH

In the preceding section of this chapter we compared a list of field experience guidelines to questions in our analytical tool as a way to put our role models and chart into perspective. Suppose we now imagine using those same guidelines in specific school settings and attempt to envision some difficulties inherent in recognizing role models and teaching styles among others. We already know it is probably advisable not to mention any of our labels from philosophy, because we do not want a teacher to feel defensive or to feel we will be making judgments about inherent values for any given role model. Perhaps it is more appropriate to say that we would like to study teaching styles by observing how certain methods and techniques fit together naturally and complement each other. We also will be alert, however, to remember details which can be written down later. Few things can be more disconcerting to some teachers than an active note-taker in the classroom, especially one who smiles at inappropriate times during the lesson.

We have discussed previously at least eight items from the guidelines to observe for or to participate in. We analyzed how to identify divergence or convergence in discussions, as well as in other activities. What, however, would we expect to encounter as evidence for using labels, even flexible labels? We need to examine general issues regarding subject matter, such as elementary *versus* secondary level of instruction, open-space *versus* self-contained floor plans, and testing.

## For Various Subject Areas in Secondary School Settings

First of all, if one is analyzing role models for secondary teachers, the task is usually more manageable than for other levels, because each teacher is often dealing with subject matter areas which are closely related. In addition, a decision to receive endorsement for teaching specific subject matter in a secondary school usually implies that the prospective educator has reflected carefully about a range of choices in order to select a major discipline in a degree program. Such a process also indicates that certain students gravitate toward physical sciences and mathematics, as these are usually taught, because they like stressing convergence. The same process of decision-making also indicates a tendency for students who like divergence to gravitate toward social sciences and humanities, particularly since disciplines in these areas are often taught in ways that emphasize divergent thinking.

At any rate, when observing for role model analysis, one should always check the ultimate outcome of a lesson first to see if divergence or convergence has been stressed. Then one can proceed to increased specificity about a role model and the behaviors which compose the teacher's style. One does expect, however, to find Essentialist teaching styles predominating in mathematics and science classrooms. In social science and humanities subjects, though, one would expect to see the full gamut of role models: Essentialism, Experimentalism, Existentialism, Perennialism, Reconstructionism, and Behaviorism. It is certainly possible to see something other than Essentialism in mathematics and physical science classrooms, especially if one emphasizes an environmental or ecological approach or deals with moral issues like cloning, for instance; nevertheless, some aspect of the Essentialist model is most often observed.

Similarly, in music education classes involving performance one would almost always expect Essentialism because the director or instructor wishes to pull students toward convergence, toward the "proper interpretation" of music being performed. One would imagine that for advanced instruction a teacher might discuss with the student in a studio class how the student feels the music should be interpreted; thus, we would perhaps have divergence. On the other hand, if one were to observe music appreciation or music history courses, one might expect to see the same range of role models as in classes for the humanities and social sciences, although Essentialist styles would probably predominate.

Instruction in physical education offers a striking parallel to music courses in terms of expected role models. On the secondary level physical education activity courses usually emphasize correct participation skills and rules of the game, especially where team sports are concerned, so the expected role model is Essentialist. If, however, we were to observe health education, sex education, and driver education courses, a wide variety of role models might be noted. It is quite possible, for instance, to teach any of these courses from a self-exploration, values clarification, Existential perspective. Nonetheless, Essentialism of either the problem-solving or information-giving variety will probably predominate, as it would in all courses whatever the subject matter, because of the relative ease with which this type of instruction can be planned, administered, and managed. We talked at length in chapter three about difficulties of management which accompany teaching styles that honor divergence.

One might expect, in contrast, to find a great deal of attention to divergence in physical education activity courses taught at the elementary school level, especially if the instructor is an adherent of "movement education." In such classrooms children may be asked to move in any way they wish which seems appropriate to a selection of recorded music, or they may be given a parachute and asked to see if they can move so that the silk will be perfectly round and without wrinkles. Children may even be given pieces of equipment and asked to design their own games. Such attention to divergence is Experimentalist in its thrust.

How would foreign languages be taught? This situation is analogous to the one in physical education, except that the expectation of role models is reversed according to the students' skill levels. Whereas in physical education activity courses one might be quite likely to observe Experimentalism at elementary levels, in foreign language instruction for beginners one would almost certainly see Essentialism. That is not surprising since proficiency in language is based on repetition and imitation. Nonetheless, there is a choice between information-giving and problem-solving. Compared with present teaching methods, it was formerly more common to see the "audio-lingual" approach, in which students were expected to discover the grammar and appropriate speech patterns by being barraged at first with sounds, rather than with the written language. Such Essentialist problem-solving in foreign language instruction is no longer quite so prevalent; one would now expect to see more direct information-giving and attention to mimicry of sounds while keeping the written language in mind.

A relatively new variant of this type of information-giving in foreign language instruction concerns various schemes to enlist the brain's right hemisphere and techniques of metaphoric thinking. Emphasis for instruction is on complete informality and relaxation, while soothing background music plays as students listen rather halfheartedly to dialogues in the language under study. It would appear that while the pressure for performance is off, the right hemisphere is stimulated to make metaphoric connections with snatches of melody, and students actually remember dialogues more efficiently and can repeat the sounds quite effectively under these circumstances.*

For the more advanced levels of foreign language instruction one can expect the possibility of as wide a variety of role models as with the humanities and social sciences in general. Students could be asked to practice divergent thinking by verbalizing in the target language about cognitive learnings or about affective issues. Such honoring of divergence may be an excellent means of giving more than lip service to the frequently touted objective of understanding another culture by penetrating its thought processes as they are embodied in language. Though it is possible to honor divergence on beginning levels of instruction—by getting rid of prepared, prepackaged dialogues and using, for instance, a controversial article (or perhaps a rewrite of that article) from *Paris Match*—such techniques are usually not tried.

Before we leave general considerations about subject matter as it relates to role models at the secondary school level, it might be helpful to remind ourselves about important indicators: namely, the issue of an interdisciplinary emphasis and the question of individualized instruction. Generally speaking, the more disciplines a teacher integrates into each lesson the farther away that teacher's role model will be from Essentialism, according to our chart explained at the beginning of this chapter. A cardinal principle of Essentialists is to keep the disciplines separated, primarily because this is a more manageable approach to learning. Generally speaking, the more attention a teacher gives to individualization of instruction, the more likely he or she will be to honor divergence. The one major circumstance in which this

---

*See "The Power of Suggestion" by Philip Miele in *Parade*, March 12, 1978, and "Mind Cycles and Learning" by Bob Samples in *Phi Delta Kappan*, May 1977.

suggestion is not accurate concerns teaching basic skills to a number of different students who are being allowed to proceed at their own rate. Under such a circumstance programmed materials may be used which are extremely convergent in nature, and the situation would be similar to an elementary school setting in which children are being taught basic skills, such as reading and computation. One should examine the nature of the materials carefully to make an accurate assessment.

## For Elementary School Settings

How are basic skills taught in elementary school? How does one analyze role model tendencies in elementary teachers who generally must deal with a host of subject matter areas in the course of each day? The task is not as simple as observing a teacher who instructs all day either in the same subject matter area, or in closely related disciplines. Although the task may be more difficult, it is still quite possible if one observes instruction in subject areas, such as language arts and social studies, where the range of role model options is largest.

If one analyzes teacher behaviors for subject areas where the range of options is greatest, then data concerning those behaviors should indicate an instructor's true preference. Under such a circumstance, all previous suggestions about subject matter and its use apply. For instance, in language arts instruction does a teacher use the option to teach creative writing, rather than emphasizing prepackaged practice sentences to teach principles of grammar? Does the instructor use the children's own compositions to teach grammar and spelling? Any effort to teach creative writing is sure to emphasize divergence and almost always stresses the cognitive skill of vocabulary building; hence, it is quite Experimentalist in nature. Does the instructor teach social studies by emphasizing major events on a time line? Or is the effort similar to the following instructions: Look at these pictures of colonists and Indians, and then tell me what you learn from them about life on the frontier in the 1740s?

It is vitally important to see how a teacher behaves when his or her range of role model choices is expected to be greatest. Though a teacher may feel locked to Essentialism and convergence in mathematics, he or she may take the option of emphasizing divergence where the subject matter easily permits such a course of action. The fact that such options are taken would probably indicate the teacher's preference for a role model which honors divergence, but the eighth activity in our guidelines—asking a teacher directly what methods he or she prefers—should go far in helping to clarify the issue.

## For Open-Space and Self-Contained Settings

How does one deal with the issue of role model analysis for educators who teach in settings with open-space floor plans? I am using the phrases "open-space" and "self-contained floor plans" here for a specific purpose. I consider "open" education to be comprised of the kinds of learning activities which honor divergence; moreover, honoring divergence can occur in small, self-contained classrooms about the size of closets, but it can also occur in spaces with so few walls that they seem to be about the size of warehouses. Placement and number of walls are merely coincidentals. Although open-space floor plans may have originally been designed to promote flexibility of scheduling and an array of free choices among learning activities, and to encourage Experimentalist/Existentialist teaching styles to abound, such styles are not necessarily seen there. Sometimes (perhaps I should say most of the time?) teachers do not ask to team in an open-space setting because they have made careful assessments of their own teaching styles and have found them to be compatible, since they all honor divergence for instance. On the contrary, they may be assigned by administrators to be a team in an open-space setting because they all are "good" teachers; perhaps the person making this assignment has not stopped to consider that there are a number of ways to teach well, although all of those ways may not be complementary to each other. In other words, some styles may honor convergence, while others emphasize divergence. But, *voilá*, a team exists, and its mere existence is sometimes considered inherently good.

It is because such teams are often assigned for a variety of reasons other than compatibility of teaching styles that one may observe in open-space settings the same variety of role models one may observe in self-contained settings. Although open-space settings tend naturally to support Experimentalist/Existentialist role models, some teachers who work in such environments are not accustomed to, do not feel comfortable with, and, hence, do not choose to honor divergence. Such teachers may feel overwhelmed by the enormity of the space, the accompanying distractions of free movement and commotion, as well as the problems of flexible scheduling. To compensate for all these anxieties they may set up barriers of bookcases and desks to make the space more manageable. In addition, they may resort to almost extreme forms of Essentialism as a defense mechanism. Although originally expected to "team" teach for a large number of students, they may resort to "turn" teaching, with each teacher taking a group of twenty youngsters for a short period and then changing groups when the clock says it's time to change. Flexibility of scheduling, then, has largely been structured out because cooperative planning has made it impossible for a teacher to stay with one group which is particularly involved in an activity while the mood is right. Perhaps a teacher cannot change to another group when interest in an activity has waned if the clock says it's too early for the change.

Because of the foregoing considerations, it is not surprising to find a large number of Essentialists in open-space settings. There are some very valid reasons for the existence of considerable team planning, but little team teaching. Sheer numbers make it administratively feasible in many cases to do only "turn" teaching. And student/teacher ratios often work against using Experimentalist approaches which incorporate pupil-teacher planning: for example, approaches like the Core Curriculum design which we considered in the third chapter. Pupil-teacher planning strategies are naturally complementary to open-space settings, and they might go far to remove the sometimes stultifying feeling students have of always being on the responding and reacting end of a pre-determined curriculum with every activity planned for them by a team.

## For Evaluation and Testing

Let us now take a brief look at the aspect of the curriculum where the student is most likely to view himself or herself as responding and reacting without taking any initiative—the aspect involving testing and evaluation. How does testing relate to role model selection and to teaching style? How does a prospective or in-service teacher make sure his or her classroom behaviors match the kinds of testing given? How does one integrate techniques of evaluation into one's teaching style so that there is a logical fit, and to avoid sending out verbal messages that conflict with nonverbal messages? Sentiments like those expressed in the following dialogue, overheard at a local pizza parlor on the night before a test, are probably all too familiar:

"Hey, what are you guys going to do about that test tomorrow in Mr. Bixby's class? I don't know what to study."

"I don't know what to study either, and I never do! He sure does teach better than he tests. Maybe I'll just put the whole thing out of my mind until he hands out the exam tomorrow. How about you?"

One can also, without too much difficulty, imagine a potential conversion between Mr. Bixby and his wife:

"Oh, good grief! [or some other appropriate expletive] I just remembered I have to make out a test for fourth period tomorrow, and it really needs to be an essay test."

"Look, since you're pressed for time again, why don't you let me help you? Just mark twenty-five of the most important statements in the text. I'll type them and leave some of them "true" and make some of them "false." Then I can help you grade them, and we can still have time to go on that camping trip."

If there is an area of instruction where teachers seem often to be working at cross-purposes, the testing versus classroom behavior match must be it. If one teaches to honor convergence, then most of his or her testing should also honor convergence. If one teaches to honor divergence, then a substantial proportion of the testing should also honor divergence. Testing and teaching often do not seem to match logically because convergent test items are popularly viewed as notoriously easy to measure and evaluate, while divergent test items are viewed as being notoriously difficult to measure. Therefore, it is quite typical to find someone, who teaches with emphasis on divergence, testing with items that are all convergent; some items may even depend totally on recall, requiring no analysis. It is even possible for students to sense this confusion when one teaches as an Essentialist problem-solver, but tests to emphasize only recall. In short, those who write "behavioral objectives" to state exactly what a student must perform, and at what level of proficiency it must be performed to be considered successful, are those who would be expected to teach as Essentialists and to test for convergence.* Those same teachers would be expected to grade tests according to a right-answer orientation in which so many points are given every time a question produces the correct specific response. By the same token, those who write what Marie Wirsing calls "cognitive/affective" objectives dealing with levels of understanding and awareness are those who would generally be expected to teach as Experimentalists, Existentialists, or Reconstructionists and to test for divergence. These teachers would be expected to grade tests according to how thoroughly one deals with the task required by each question, how well an answer is expressed, how logically consistent the answer is internally, and how well supported the writer's opinion is—but not on the specific answer as it relates to a predetermined, correct response.

Let us look at examples of both kinds of test questions:

*Convergent:*

1.   The corporation has an advantage over the partnership because it has (a) limited liability, (b) "perpetual life," (c) access to capital through sale of stock, (d) all of these.†

*See Robert Mager, *Preparing Instructional Objectives* (Palo Alto: Fearon Publishers, 1962).
   †From *Rise of the American Nation—Tests* (New York: Harcourt, Brace and World, 1966).

2.  What made Jurgis's aunt in Upton Sinclair's *The Jungle* want to withdraw her savings from a bank in a hurry? What federal agency makes it unlikely that a situation similar to that faced by Jurgis's aunt will occur today?

*Divergent:*

1.  Do you feel that most major American industrialists of the late nineteenth century were "robber barons" or "industrial statesmen"? Why or why not?

(Hints on how to construct the essay:

(a)  Make sure your essay includes a definition of "robber baron" or "industrial statesman."

(b)  Choose any two of the industrialists we have studied—George Westinghouse, George Pullman, Cornelius Vanderbilt, Andrew Carnegie, John D. Rockefeller, James Buchanan Duke, Madame C. J. Walker, Charles C. Spaulding—and use facts from their lives to support your opinion.)

2.  Read the following article. Then assume that Mr. and Mrs. Paretti and the author are Social Darwinists who believe in strict *laissez-faire* economics. In one page or less rewrite the article to reflect this belief in social Darwinism and *laissez-faire* economics. (Note: The accompanying article is a *Life* magazine report of the demise of the Bon Vivant Soup Company after some of its products had reputedly contained the microorganisms of botulism.)

The problems, pitfalls, and delights of these types of test questions are probably as familiar as the characters from Schultz's *Peanuts* series in the following segments.

As you read the cartoons, notice that Sally is aware of right-answer-oriented questions which expect a person to read the teacher's mind. We talked about this right-answer syndrome as one of the potential weaknesses for Essentialist teaching styles. Peppermint Patty and Charlie Brown have decided that taking a true-false test is easy, almost like "having the wind at your back." They seem not to have noticed, however, that if a person is restricted to one of two or four symbols for a response, he or she may be more likely to get the item wrong depending on the subtleties one understands about the issue. It is as if one has too much data on which to base an answer, and how can one make the test grader aware of all that knowledge, if one can only answer "A" or "B" or "T" or "F"? Peppermint Patty also seems to have fallen for the popular notion that essay tests are harder: they can be written so that students can use the knowledge they possess to their own

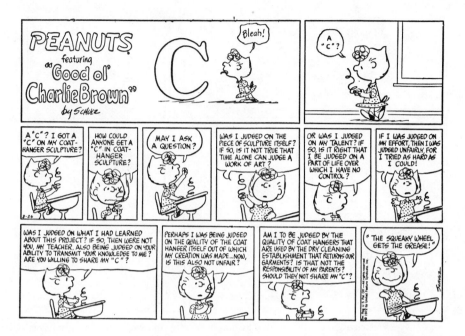

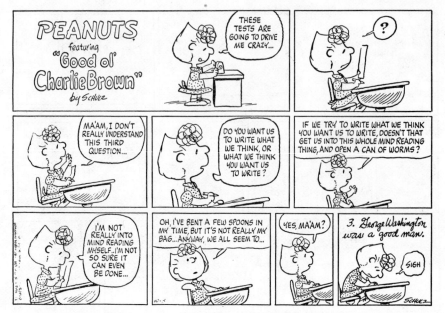

best advantage, but they can also be written to make it appear that any opinion is as good as the next—a relativist pitfall typical of many Experimentalist/Existentialist strategies in general.

At any rate, the whole process of grading is quite subjective, whether it is based on convergence or divergence, and Sally seems fully aware of this point as she attacks her "C." But how can teachers get over such anxieties about subjectivity? Perhaps teachers should make students aware that subjectivity exists, even with convergent items because the testmaker decided which of those items to include; and teachers should decide whether to give full or partial credit for certain answers. It is also beneficial to teach children how to cope with various kinds of test items: for example, teachers could explain how to organize essays, how to reason through multiple choice items using a process of elimination, and how to minimize errors that result from test anxiety.

Because of the anxiety surrounding tests many teachers plan to be scrupulously fair about the whole process by including a variety of types of questions on each test—some "true-false," a few "matching," several "fill-in-the-blanks," and perhaps an essay or two. That is certainly an appropriate strategy, if one explains the rationale to students. If one teaches to honor divergence, however, there must be some questions on tests which also stress divergence in order for the teacher to be looked upon as credible and honest.

Nevertheless, an occasionally convergent, Essentialist-oriented quiz to find out if youngsters really are comprehending concepts will not do violence to one's teaching style or one's efforts for charisma, as long as one explains the rationale to students before the quiz is given. Consistently teaching for divergence and testing for convergence, or vice versa, would do serious harm to one's efforts to build a logical teaching style; more important, it would be perceived as a source of frustration and confusion by the students.

Suppose, however, one observes a teacher—keeping in mind the expected role models for each subject matter area, the level at which instruction is occurring, and the match between teaching and testing—but one still cannot determine a preference for a particular role model? Perhaps this teacher seems to use activities emphasizing convergence in about the same proportion as activities which call for divergence. If one's use of suggestion number 8 on our guidelines—asking this teacher which methods he or she prefers to use—is no more helpful than one's lengthy and conscientious observation has been in pointing out preferences and dominant behavior trends, then perhaps this teacher is an eclectic. A true eclectic is someone who seems to have no preference for a particular style or role model, but who adopts all equally well, or equally badly, as the case may be. In short, one may be a true eclectic because one is so skilled at handling instructional strategies from all role models that one is recognizable in any crowd as a "superteacher." Such a circumstance could arise because one is so aware of role model nuances, so thoroughly familiar with teaching styles that one can take up any role model at will and be viewed by students as a sincere, effective, stimulating instructor. Or one might have natural talent and be so enthusiastic about teaching and relating to youngsters, as to be guided by an almost incredible sixth sense, which involves little conscious awareness of role models, philosophies, or styles. Either of these circumstances might produce what we could call healthy eclecticism.

But some people are eclectics by default. They have almost no awareness of role models, philosophies, or styles and are perceived by students as totally lacking in direction, since they try one technique after another from a grabbag of tricks. These are the eclectics who send out confusing and contradictory messages because their verbal and nonverbal cues do not match.

Most teachers are probably not true eclectics. They do evidence some preferences in their teaching behaviors, which fit into the flexible process of labeling which we have used in this book. It is appropriate that this labeling process has been flexible, especially because preferences can and do change. One who begins student teaching with a stated philosophy which emphasizes divergence may move very quickly into a role model emphasizing convergence. A teacher, who uses Essentialist problem-solving and refuses to move to an open-space setting this year, might later decide that her own professional growth toward Experimentalism during the course of a subsequent three-year period will make an open-space building suitable for her teaching style.

## ZEN, MOTORCYCLE MAINTENANCE, AND A JOURNEY THROUGH ROLE MODELS

Let us examine this refreshing human propensity to grow and change, to move from one role model to another, by referring to Robert Pirsig's *Zen and the Art of Motorcycle Maintenance*. Although this novel crams almost too many exciting ideas into the space of one book, and although Pirsig did not write primarily, or even consciously, to illustrate educational role models, the book will serve our purposes quite well. The main character begins his professional career as a teacher of rhetoric at a small college in Montana. As an Essentialist, he is convinced that he knows how to teach rhetoric properly, by stressing good models of writing and by making sure his students adhere to those models through an emphasis on correct grammar, as well as on appropriate principles of form and organization demanded by the specific type of composition. At the outset the main character is thrust into a situation which leads to a sweeping transformation of style and role model. He clearly thinks of himself as an Essentialist, although most of his work involves teaching creative writing: these two conditions in themselves are almost logical impossibilities, due to the convergence/divergence split.

The main character seems quite comfortable with this split—or ambiguity, until one afternoon a colleague, who is almost ready for retirement, makes an "innocent" remark as she walks around his desk on the way to water her plants in the window baskets. (It was one of those communal offices where everybody hears everything.) The colleague says, "I do hope you're teaching your students *quality* this semester!"

The teacher blurts out, "Of course!" But his unspoken reaction was really, "I *think* I'm teaching them quality." In fact, the more he thought about this question, the more uncomfortable he became. He finally realized, however, he didn't know how to define quality; he just couldn't put it into words. But how does one admit that to one's self, or to anyone else, especially if one is teaching rhetoric and lacks job security because one hasn't completed work on his Ph.D.?

He "forgot" to go home for dinner on that momentous day of his colleague's question about quality; in fact, he almost forgot to go home at all, despite one or two prodding telephone calls from his wife. At the next class session he asked his students to write papers defining and explaining quality. They were perturbed. They couldn't finish. He gave them more time. When papers were turned in and students discovered that their instructor couldn't define quality either, they were angry because they saw him "changing the rules." Professors weren't supposed to operate this way; they were supposed to ask questions, know when the answers were right, and dispense grade rewards accordingly. There was such a commotion during the discussion when these essay papers were returned that a colleague peered in to see if there was some special difficulty. The character remarked rather offhandedly to his associate, "We have all just discovered a real question and the shock is almost too much." And that marked the end of his days as an Essentialist.

What if there were no grades, no models of acceptable writing, and no attempts by an instructor to impose or even suggest topics for papers? He had by this time decided that each person knew quality when he or she saw it, whether in writing or in some other field, but that it actually could not adequately be defined by mere words. He knew that quality could definitely be recognized; it could be seen almost intuitively. He wanted students to help him select topics, help him organize the experiences they needed from his course, and help him evaluate their own performance. In brief, he moved into the Experimentalist position. Students at first found it hard to respond to his new role model. There were always those who "couldn't think of anything to write about." One student, after going through every traditional topic she had heard mentioned, such as topics in U.S. history and civics, finally gave up and admitted her perplexity. After being advised to select a building on Main Street and write about its façade, the student still came back empty-handed and dejected. The teacher at last asked her to go down to the old Opera House, count up from the right corner of the building a certain number of bricks, and write about that brick. She returned with an astonishingly "high quality" composition.

Similar to the student who "couldn't think of a thing" because she had never been taught to generate her own projects, there were a number of other students who couldn't respond meaningfully to the teacher's new role model. Specifically, they couldn't quite believe he would not be using traditional grades. They had been trained so long to consider academic progress in terms of "grade point averages" and to fear the stricture about "having at least a C standing" before one can graduate that the grading innovation was making anxiety skyrocket instead of abate.

The teacher's ideas about grading, and his satisfaction at seeing performances improve once students overcame their anxiety, made him want to apply grade reforms to the university system in general. Thus, he became a

Reconstructionist. He delivered impassioned speeches to his students about the university as the "Church of Reason." He became disgusted with the concept of higher education being fettered with a "degree and diploma-mill mentality" in which administrators, who were managers and not teachers, played with politicians over issues of funding, buildings, and athletics. The true university—the spirit of open inquiry which existed in the minds of scholars and students—was often left to "fend for itself," and when it actually prospered, this prosperity often came despite what the managers did. Due to difficulties with the administration concerning grades, the direction of growth for his own university, and the outmoded reward system for professors, he finally decided it was time to quit before being "forced out." That was the end of his days as a Reconstructionist.

He still didn't have his doctorate. He had worried about quality for so long. That topic, quality, would be ideal for a dissertation study, of course. But where in the world could one write a dissertation and receive the Ph.D. about a topic so abstract and elusive, a topic so void of the trappings of respect from academia, as quality? After all, one couldn't measure or define it. After investigating several potential programs, however, he finally decided that the only logical setting where he could pursue his study would be in the humanities division of University of Chicago's graduate school, under the guise of the Great Books Foundations' leaders. What he wanted to accomplish was certainly similar to the dialectic. He wanted nothing less than a sort of grand synthesis of ideas relating to the idea of quality. His desires embodied concepts shared by Plato and Perennialism. Quality's quest was bound to advance him more than a few steps closer to the Truth of Socrates. Therefore, he taught rhetoric at another college to maintain his family, while he dug his heels in to studying quality.

Unfortunately, at Chicago he happened to be a seminar student in a course run by the last Aristotelian holdout in a colony of Platonists. He and his instructor were at such odds philosophically that the situation rapidly degenerated to one of intense psychological warfare and general "one-upmanship." After a searing battle of wits in which he won and the professor failed to show up for subsequent seminar sessions, the character's own mental stability deteriorated rapidly. When he and his son Chris went for a drive to buy a Christmas tree, he lost contact with reality so completely that he had no idea where he was driving, and Chris had to ask passersby for directions. Chris finally ended up leading his father home. This marked the end of his Perennialist period, as well as the end of his former personality, that part of his personality called "Phaedrus."

Phaedrus was hospitalized and zapped by a series of electric shock treatments; he was zapped so completely that he has only glimmering snatches of memory left from his former personality. Thus, Phaedrus becomes the ghost of his old self, and this is the way he speaks of his previous life throughout the motorcycle trip which constitutes the main allegory for the novel. The story so far, however, must be pieced together through flashbacks and recollections as the cross-country motorcycle journey with Chris unfolds. The main character and Chris are Existentialists now in search of the Phaedrus self. Chris never believed his father was insane and, in fact, liked him better as Phaedrus. (The name, Phaedrus, is derived from the philosopher in Socratic dialogues who liked the countryside as much as Socrates liked the cities where he could discourse with men about Truth.) The main character uses the countryside and Chris to re-establish his own Truth and to put his two selves back together again in a grand synthesis, one which parallels his synthesis about quality.

In its broad outlines this volume is a *tour de force* within philosophy and psychology, trends deeply embedded in Western and Eastern thought. In prosaic terms it is the story of an educator whose personality structure became berserk because he worried so conscientiously about grading and what many have called the hidden curriculum in our country's schools. And on another level of analysis, the novel offers a richly rewarding opportunity to follow a conscientious educator through all five role models that we have examined in this book.

## SELECTING A ROLE MODEL AND BUILDING ONE'S OWN STYLE

How does one select a particular teaching style? For most people who wish to teach, thoughtful reflection about the role models and observation of experienced teachers' preferences will together provide enough stimuli for establishing one's own preferences in constructing a style. Watching others can be useful in helping one understand how teaching behaviors tend to cluster, and in helping one decide how one wants to teach. Again, there is no one way to teach successfully, nor even two or three successful ways. Effective styles of teaching emerge from the types of self-assessment and exposure methods we have been attempting throughout this volume.

If one has not yet decided on an initial role model guide, however, there may be two more items which will help one formulate tentative answers. All these answers are tentative, however, because our preferences change as we grow professionally. In addition, a clear statement of role model preference adopted before one begins student teaching may change drastically after three days with pupils, just as an experienced teacher's behavioral trends might evolve slowly during an extended time period. One of these two extra aids for finalizing one's current self-assessment is taken from our chapter on Reconstructionism, while the other one adapts Morris Spier's "S-C Teaching Inventory."

The basic Reconstructionist question reduces itself to a query about the purpose of schooling: What are schools for? As we looked at ways in which Americans have answered that question, we used in our fourth chapter a diagram showing the rise and fall in attitudes about the school's power to effect social reform.

As we look again at that diagram, we now need to add another, more personal element. In effect, we need to make the question about the role and function of schooling more immediate. It needs to be asked on an intimate level so that it no longer remains in the abstract realm: What are schools for? By asking one's self directly, there is no possibility for avoiding the question: Why am I teaching? Is it to help improve social conditions, or is it to help youngsters fit into the *status quo*? Children, as we have already said in our chapter on Reconstructionism, have their own effective ways of deciding how they think each teacher would answer that question. Thinking about it before one starts teaching, and before students have a chance to do their own probing into the teacher's motivation, should increase one's awareness; moreover, it will probably push one farther along the road to charismatic teaching by helping one to build a viable teaching style.

Let us now add this personal element to our diagram. Consider the power of schooling to effect social reform. Decide whether you would prefer to teach with a change-orientation or with a *status quo*-orientation.

*Reform Trends in the U.S. Educational System*

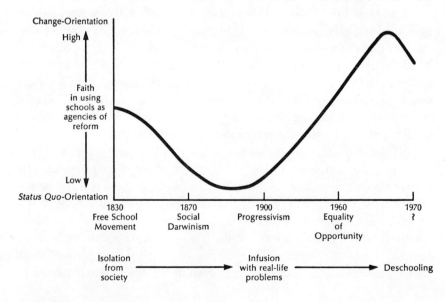

Many ideas embodied in this diagram came originally from Michael Katz's work, *The Irony of Early School Reform.* Katz advanced a direct theory about attitudes regarding schooling's power to effect reform. He insisted that the more emphasis there is on environment as a major determinant of success, the greater the faith in school as a reform agency; or, vice versa, the more emphasis one finds resting on heredity as a major determinant of success, the less faith there will be evidenced in school as a reform agency. Although Katz was referring to attitudes in society as a whole, we are examining the personal element. Does one teach to help improve social conditions or to help youngsters fit into the *status quo?* Once a teacher answers that question honestly, he or she is on the way to choosing a role model and building a style, because the answer can be related directly to what we have been doing in this volume. *Status quo*-oriented teachers are usually Essentialist/Perennialist in their thinking. Change-oriented teachers tend to be Experimentalist/Existentialist, whenever they encourage youngsters to chart the course of change for themselves. On the other hand, such teachers may be Reconstructionist or even Behaviorist, whenever they decide to take a conspicuous role in influencing the direction of change.

A second aid in determining behavioral preferences for teaching and one's potential role model choice is Morris S. Spier's "S-C Teaching Inventory"—an instrument which appeared in W. Pfeiffer and J. Jones, *The 1974 Annual Handbook for Group Facilitators.* The Inventory is reprinted below. For suggestions about how to interpret one's responses, see *Appendix A.*

---

### S-C Teaching Inventory*

#### Morris S. Spier

The following inventory concerns your feelings about some teaching practices. Its purpose is to provide you with meaningful information about yourself as a teacher.

There are no right or wrong answers. The best answer is the one most descriptive of your feelings and opinions. Therefore, answer honestly, because only realistic answers will provide you with useful information.

Each of the forty items consists of two statements, either about what a teacher can do or ways he can act. Circle the letter (A or B) in front of the statement that *you* think is the more important way for a teacher to act. In the case of some items you may think that both alternatives are important, but you still should choose the statement you feel is *more* important. Sometimes you may think that both alternatives are unimportant; still you should choose the statement you think is *more* important.

It is more important for a teacher:

1. (A) To organize his course around the needs and skills of every type of student.
   (B) To maintain definite standards of classroom performance.
2. (A) To let students have a say in course content and objectives.
   (B) To set definite standards of classroom performance.
3. (A) To emphasize completion of the term's course syllabus.
   (B) To let students help set course goals and content.
4. (A) To give examinations to evaluate student progress.
   (B) To allow students a voice in setting course objectives and content.
5. (A) To reward good students.
   (B) To allow students to evaluate the performance of their instructor.
6. (A) To allow students to make their own mistakes and to learn by experience.
   (B) To work to cover the term's subject matter adequately.
7. (A) To make it clear that he is the authority in the classroom.
   (B) To allow students to make their own mistakes and to learn by experience.
8. (A) To be available to confer with students on an "as needed" basis.
   (B) To have scheduled office hours.
9. (A) To give examinations to evaluate student progress.
   (B) To tailor the course content to the needs and skills of each class.
10. (A) To draw a line between himself and the students.
    (B) To let students plan their own course of study according to their interests.
11. (A) To take an interest in the student as a person.
    (B) To make it clear that the teacher is the authority in the classroom.
12. (A) To draw a line between himself and the students.
    (B) To be available for conferences with students on an "as needed" basis.
13. (A) To modify his position if one of his students shows him where he was wrong.
    (B) To maintain definite standards of classroom performance.
14. (A) To allow students to have a say in evaluating teacher performance.
    (B) To draw a line between himself and the students.
15. (A) To see that the class covers the prescribed subject matter for the course.
    (B) To be concerned about the student as a person.
16. (A) To let students learn by experience.
    (B) To maintain definite standards of classroom performance.
17. (A) To allow students a voice in setting course objectives and content.
    (B) To make it clear that he is the authority in the classroom.
18. (A) To discourage talking among students during class time.
    (B) To establish an informal classroom atmosphere.
19. (A) To allow student evaluation of faculty.
    (B) To make it clear that the teacher is the authority in the classroom.
20. (A) To draw a line between himself and the students.
    (B) To let students make mistakes and learn by experience.
21. (A) To be an authority on the class materials covered.
    (B) To keep up to date in the field.

22. (A) To be respected as a person of high technical skill in the field.
    (B) To up-date class and lecture materials constantly.
23. (A) To attend to his own professional growth.
    (B) To be an authority on the class materials covered.
24. (A) To attend to his own professional growth.
    (B) To set an example for his students.
25. (A) To see that each student is working at his full capacity.
    (B) To plan, in considerable detail, all class activities.
26. (A) To construct fair and comprehensive examinations.
    (B) To set an example for his students.
27. (A) To be known as an effective teacher.
    (B) To see that each student is working at his full capacity.
28. (A) To construct fair and comprehensive examinations.
    (B) To see that each student is working at his full capacity.
29. (A) To be an authority on the class materials covered.
    (B) To plan and organize his coursework carefully.
30. (A) To be a model for his students to emulate.
    (B) To try out new ideas and approaches on the class.
31. (A) To see that each student is working at his full capacity.
    (B) To plan and organize course content carefully.
32. (A) To have scheduled office hours to meet with students.
    (B) To be an expert on the course subject matter.
33. (A) To set an example for his students.
    (B) To try out new ideas and approaches on the class.
34. (A) To teach basic courses as well as more advanced courses.
    (B) To be a model for his students to emulate.
35. (A) To plan and organize the class activities carefully.
    (B) To be interested in and concerned with student understanding.
36. (A) To be an authority on the course content.
    (B) To be known as an effective teacher.
37. (A) To give examinations to evaluate student progress.
    (B) To be an authority on the class materials covered.
38. (A) To attend professional meetings.
    (B) To be respected as a person of high technical skill in the field.
39. (A) To be respected for his knowledge of the course subject matter.
    (B) To try out new ideas and approaches on the class.
40. (A) To be an authority on the course content.
    (B) To construct fair and comprehensive examinations.

*Reprinted from Pfeiffer, J. W. and Jones, J. E. (Eds.) **The 1974 Annual Handbook for Group Facilitators**. La Jolla, CA.: University Associates, 1974. Used with permission.*

## Teaching Effectively

After one has completed considerable reflecting and self-assessing, what happens next? After a person knows himself or herself well enough to select a role model with some understanding of its philosophy and to build a personal style of teaching, then one is just that much closer to charismatic teaching. But so far we have really looked at only one side of the coin, the side involving personal assessment and development. The other side involves performing effectively in the school setting by translating decisions into charismatic teaching with some students at a specific time and place in a particular setting. But what anxieties will arise to test one's coping power and decision-making skills when this other side of the coin turns up?

Although teaching youngsters at any stage of development and at any age level may from time to time trigger memories of one's own childhood and produce some anxieties, re-acquainting one's self with school settings through the types of field experiences we have talked about in this chapter will usually obliterate unproductive concerns and fears. One's skills of coping and decision making, however, can be expected to improve with increased awareness of possibilities for role model selection and with added exposure to school settings in which one can practice deciding which behaviors are most effective.

Although positive outcomes can especially be expected to result from exposure to elementary school settings, will the same results occur in high school settings? Awareness of adolescent identity crises and violence in many school systems may increase anxiety in some prospective teachers placed in secondary school settings. Ralph Keyes's work, *Is There Life after High School?* (New York: Warner Books, Inc., 1977.) offers indispensable insights into why anxieties tend to rise in prospective teachers when they are exposed to high school environments. This tendency to become almost paralyzed with paranoia is explained by Keyes as testimony to the truly pervasive power of the high school's tribal sociology.

Keyes sees the high school's communal experience as peculiarly characteristic of adolescence in this country; moreover, he insists that those unaccustomed to our culture have difficulty understanding the potency of the high school for shaping one's self-image. This potency, in Keyes's view, comes from a tight (and often cruelly sexist) reward system which makes success equal to status, and which bestows status on the basis of superficial external characteristics like owning a sports car, possessing an athletic physique for males, or knowing how to make the most of a beautiful figure and striking personality for females—rather than on the basis of accomplishments. Those who reap the adulation (and sometimes resentment) which goes with status—the "innies"—learn to emphasize superficial aspects of their personalities and bask in a limelight which is not based on struggling to accomplish goals. They become, in effect, self-satisfied and find it difficult to do anything for an encore after high school, because the characteristics which brought success in school might not bring success later in life.

By contrast, the "outies"—those on the intermediate rungs of the status ladder—brood about snubs and slights which "innies" dish out, steel themselves against put-downs, struggle to build substantial accomplishments. In short, the "outies" in high school learn traits which are most likely to be rewarded later in life. So the tables are turned—"outies" become successful later, while "innies" search fruitlessly for an encore, although they typically slip into near-oblivion.

After having amassed a great deal of evidence to support this position about "innies" and "outies," however, Keyes insists that the power of high school society is great enough to define self-images that many students never lose. Although "outies" might not always feel downtrodden, they do exhibit sometimes an overwhelming need to win on the "innies'" terms. "Innies" often retain that ebullient self-confidence far beyond the point where it seems reasonably or justifiably related to other aspects of their lives. Keyes's investigation of lives of the famous and his insights about class reunion interviews bolster not only his "innie"/"outie" theory, but also his idea that people remember so vividly their high school experiences because high school is a time of trauma, even physical danger, for every adolescent. This trauma heightens and intensifies the power to remember and makes us feel intensely alive. For that reason, walking down a crowded secondary school hallway can awaken the painful images of adolescent torments. At times those painful memories re-emerge. Sometimes what might begin as rational conversations between teenagers and their parents triggers the stinging recollection of some unresolved adolescent crisis, and suddenly that crisis re-emerges in all its fury for someone who is now approaching fifty. In such cases what begins as rational dialogue can quickly become much less reasoned.

In short, there is no substitute for this other side of the coin—knowledge of the institution of schooling and its power to socialize. Though Keyes's work begins with entertaining nostalgia, the book also makes serious and scholarly comparisons of his studies with those discussed in other works, such as Gail Sheehy's *Passages,* James Coleman's studies of adolescents, Erik Erikson's theories of development, and Lyn Tornabene's back-to-high-school study, entitled *I Passed as a Teenager.* He also offers superb insights about outbursts of emotion which Thomas Harris in *I'm OK–You're OK* calls "hooking your child." Such outbursts might be likely to occur between a teenage son and his father, but they have also been known to occur between a teenage student and a teacher. Thus, the message is: Know the environment, and know how one fits into it.

There is another aspect about the high school environment and Keyes's advice which we need to examine. Keyes's work shows clearly that the unfortunate power of adolescent peer pressure leads to perpetuation of sex role stereotypes for males and females, although Keyes himself seems not to have set out to make us aware of the traumas associated with sexism. Nevertheless, it is this sexist nature of high school tribalism which undoubtedly accounts for much of what all of us remember so vividly as adolescent trauma. Reminding pre-service and in-service teachers about the power of sexism should be a first step in encouraging teachers to help youngsters move away from the superficial status rewards that Keyes discusses. For instance, an Existentialist teacher might use values clarification to help youngsters see that they do not have to conform to the strictures of traditional male and female roles. An Essentialist teacher can use his or her own behavior as an example of refusing to reward students for slipping into sexist ways of thinking.

Although Keyes's work is useful for the graphic way it exposes the superficiality of peer rewards, one needs to be reminded that the innie/outie theory he has proposed does not always operate negatively. People do reassess their skills, grow, change, and become successful, although they may have enjoyed little status in high school. However, those with high status also might develop positive self-images and go on to greater successes and achievements, even though they might have been high school innies doomed by Keyes to stagnation. Gail Sheehy's *Passages* offers an excellent antidote to Keyes's success theories. Negative aspects of the high school environment do not, despite what Keyes maintains, necessarily relegate one to an unfulfilled existence.

I would like to reduce those phrases about knowing one's self and one's environment to a few specific suggestions. Don't teach unless you know what your style of behavior is asking students to do. This advice implies, of course, that one has reached thoughtful positions on learners, subject matter, and role model choice. It also implies that one understands the dynamics of the hidden curriculum, and, most importantly, that one can let students know one understands. Moreover, be sure to match teaching and testing with appropriate techniques and assumptions. For secondary schools, where anxieties are higher, this translates into specific suggestions about what to read before, during, and after exposure to the setting. Be sure to read the following books: *I'm OK—You're OK* by Thomas Harris, *White over Black* by Winthrop Jordan, *Children of Sanchez* by Oscar Lewis, and *Is There Life after High School?*

## Eclecticism?

We began this volume with the question of teaching as an eclectic, and it seems a fitting point on which to end. We all borrow from all role models, with varying degrees of effectiveness, of course. Nevertheless, we exhibit preferences in our use of divergence or convergence. Suppose, however, one has thoughtfully and conscientiously selected a role model and one also understands thoroughly the teaching environment, what happens if the youngsters themselves, at least in certain classes, are not prepared to respond to the style of teaching one has so carefully developed? What if one has to face head-on the same difficulty the character in Pirsig's novel faced in his rhetoric classes when he wanted to be an Experimentalist and his students couldn't comprehend that role model?

We all know that we have to adapt to the needs of youngsters sitting before us in class. In addition, we usually have a large enough repertoire of teaching behaviors comprising our styles so that we can select different teaching strategies to deal effectively with students, while at the same time not having to violate our behavior preferences. Then it is simply a matter of helping students see expanded possibilities for success, as they respond to the teacher's preferred behaviors and teaching strategies. In short, the teacher must educate students about his or her own teaching methodology, and then show how it can be a valuable aid in learning.

When one does a thorough job of educating one's audience—including students, administrators, and parents—about the benefits of one's role model, as well as other role models, the teacher may then be able to reap the additional rewards of putting to rest some of their anxieties about basic education. There really are a number of ways to be sure kids are learning the basics. If one honors convergence, most people assume one is somehow teaching basic skills, although those basics may be defined and selected from almost infinite variations. But sometimes it is harder for students, administrators, and parents to see clearly the benefits of honoring divergence. It is, of course, not a choice about whether to teach or not teach basic skills, but rather the choice is how the basics are to be taught. If the emphasis is on knowledge—whether received from an authority or created, regrouped, and synthesized through analysis—and if one can actually show what knowledge was gained, through our Experimentalist "catalogue" lesson or through our Reconstructionist and Existentialist lessons, then one can usually put to rest fears about the basics. Once people realize that no reason at all exists for assuming there must be a dichotomy between learning through painful drill on the one hand and non-learning through permissive chaos on the other, they are well on their way to understanding the variety of teaching behaviors. Teaching responsibly and effectively means selecting thoughtfully from among role models and building a style of classroom behavior.

What happens, however, if one's efforts to educate various audiences about the benefits of different role models are unsuccessful? What if, in effect, one must violate one's own teaching style? Knowing about other role models, in addition to the preferred one, will be a valuable aid. However, the teacher may need to be honest with youngsters and tell them he or she prefers to teach in a certain way, although that particular way does not seem appropriate at the moment. The preferred way to teach is something one can explain briefly; the teacher should explain what preparations might be necessary before the desired style is actually implemented. For example, I often began classes in U.S. history with a unit on the possible uses of history, accompanied with an explanation that by mid-year students would be planning with me what and how we would study. That is, I began as an Essentialist problem-solver, but by mid-year had moved into Experimentalist problem-solving. Students were ultimately taught the Great Books system for categorizing questions; then we proceeded along lines outlined for a Core Curriculum in our third chapter.

I am convinced that a teacher will have more success if he or she is honest with students about using techniques which will help them become prepared for responding to the way the teacher likes best to teach. But, of course, if one is an eclectic superteacher, if one has that healthy kind of eclecticism we spoke about earlier in this chapter, then one's chances of exhibiting charisma in any and all types of classroom settings will be greatly increased.

Let's look at this healthy kind of eclecticism for a moment. The true eclectic, who feels equally comfortable with any role model, is likely to think of the different role models as containing various instructional strategies which he or she can use or discard at will, as situations indicate or permit. Then, what we have called role models become for the true eclectic different lesson strategies which can be used equally effectively. I think of this true eclectic as being about as rare among educators as is the singer with "perfect pitch" among musicians. That soloist or instrumentalist with "perfect pitch" doesn't have to stop to analyze and intellectualize about harmony and form. It's all so "natural"—it just flows in a totality of sound and rhythm. These are rare gifts.

The rarity of true eclectics among educators is a reminder that most teachers do exhibit a definite preference for convergence or divergence. This is another way of saying that some teachers are more effective with certain kinds of students, and other teachers do best with certain other kinds of students. Where would this not be quite readily observable—almost self-evident? It was especially self-evident in the school where I taught, which was filled with tensions and challenges strong enough for us all to witness a great many comings and goings of staff members. In that setting, however, teachers quite readily benefitted from being honest with students about many of the items we have been discussing throughout this book. The profession has nothing to lose—among students, administrators, and parents—

by educating others about the rich variations in types of teaching behaviors and the benefits of each? What student would not find it helpful to know a teacher's view of subject matter? Students, of course, want to be reassurred they have many opportunities to be successful.

On the first day of classes a colleague of mine distributed materials similar to the following. The challenges of the particular situation warranted what may seem to be extreme precision and minute attention to detail. As the document is examined, consider what it might indicate about preference for divergence or convergence. Consider also that there must be a workable synthesis between a thoughtfully constructed teaching style and the demands of the environment as a teacher educates students about any preferred way of teaching. Even if one is an eclectic "superteacher," the need to find an appropriate way to be honest with youngsters about teaching behaviors is still present.

---

### Prospectus for History Students

#### *United States and Virginia History*

If the study of history is to be useful on a higher level than the mere accumulation of facts, a class in United States and Virginia History should provide students with the opportunity to evaluate various positions on a relevant issue and to reach their own logical and defensible conclusions. The development of skills in techniques of evaluating printed matter and forming one's own conclusions requires much practice; therefore, each unit will contain printed material by contemporaries of the era under examination and by historians investigating the period. This printed matter will frequently present the student with conflicting interpretations of the period and will allow the student to make up his own mind about historical trends operating during the era under study. In other words, this approach to the study of history allows the student to become his own historian.

Before a student can successfully embark on this adventure of becoming his own historian, however, he needs to learn something about the nature of historical study and the skills necessary for historical investigation. Our first unit, therefore, will help you broaden your understanding of how historical investigation can be a valuable aid in your own personal life.

Consider carefully the following list of units of study and the activities of the introductory unit, which will last approximately two weeks:

I. The Nature of History as an Academic Discipline—Its Uses and Pleasures

II. The Colonial Period (from European and African beginnings to 1763)

III. The American Revolution

IV. *E Pluribus Unum*

  V. The Growth of American Nationalism

  VI. The Age of Andrew Jackson

  VII. Sectionalism and the Civil War

 VIII. Reconstruction

  IX. Industrialism

   X. The Era of Theodore Roosevelt

  XI. The Roaring Twenties

  XII. The Era of Franklin Delano Roosevelt

 XIII. Contemporary Developments
(Current news, Virginia history, and the history of the Black American and others who have made major contributions to our culture are threads to be woven into the fabric of the course.)

*Unit I: The Nature of History as an Academic
Discipline—Its Uses and Pleasures*

A. Required Assignments

1. Write a one-page essay answering the following questions: Who am I? Where am I? What am I? You may be as philosophical in your approach as you wish. Due Wednesday, September 8.

2. Read carefully the handout, "Riddle of the Kensington Stone," and be prepared for a class discussion concerning this article on Wednesday, September 8.

3. Read carefully and be prepared to discuss the article, "The Stone is a Fraud," from *American Heritage*, April 1959. Due Friday, September 10.

4. Each student should have developed his own definition of history (based on ideas exposed in class, as well as your own thoughts) by the end of this unit.

5. Key terms to be learned: history, fact, primary source, secondary source, hypothesis, conclusion, frame of reference (mind set, bias), validation, scientific method, historian, historiography.

B. Optional Individual Assignments

1. A student may wish to investigate archaeological techniques which have been employed in restoring Colonial Williamsburg, *i.e.*, aerial photography, cross-trenching, systematic classification of artifacts, etc., and report his findings to the class. An excellent source is Ivor Noel Hume, *Here Lies Virginia*.

2. To illustrate the failures of scientific history a student may wish to research Henry Ford's statement, "History is bunk," and the "debunking" movement.

3. A student may wish to investigate the history of his own locality and share his research findings with the class.

4. As an illustration of the instructive value of history a student may wish to review for the class John Hershey's *Hiroshima* (Bantam Pathfinder Edition, New York, 1966).

5. To provide added information about ways to predict the future which may or may not be as reliable as the investigation of historical trends a student may wish to review for the class Ruth Montgomery's *A Gift of*

*Prophecy* (about Jeanne Dixon) or Ruth Montgomery's *A Search for the Truth*.

6.   To broaden our ideas of man's place in history and to introduce African contributions to Western culture a student may wish to read and review for the class Robert Ardrey's *African Genesis*.

C.   Helpful Hints for Future Units

1.   At the beginning of each unit students will receive a work sheet giving assignments for that unit. The work sheet will contain lists of optional assignments which students may select because of personal interest or because they may desire to improve their grade average for the six weeks. *Do not be dismayed* if your test scores are not as high as you would like. In a social studies classroom there is always the opportunity for success for the student who is willing to strive. If you do not take tests well, you will have the opportunity to achieve in oral class participation, in a variety of projects, or in keeping a neat notebook of classroom activities and assignments. Notebooks are not required, but it is strongly recommended that each student keep a careful record of classroom activities and assignments since much of this material will *not* be included in the textbook. Students may elect to have notebooks graded to improve their average for each unit of study.

*Every student is assured of successful completion of this course if he is willing to work.*

2.   If you complete carefully the requirements of Unit I you will very probably find historical study more fascinating than you had previously thought. Skills of this unit will be further developed as the year proceeds, and the major project of the second semester will be based on the processes of historical investigation and evaluation learned in Unit I.

3.   Your instructor will do his best to make the study of history enjoyable and challenging. In turn, each student is expected to give his best in the classroom every day in terms of general cooperation, attentiveness, and effort. Each student is to be in his seat and ready to proceed with the day's activities when the tardy bell sounds. In the event of tardiness the student will be asked if he can produce an excuse. If a valid excuse for tardiness is not produced, the student is responsible for making up 30 minutes of detention time after school on the day after tardiness occurs. If a student is absent, the student must present a valid excuse at least by the second day of his return to school in order to make up work missed while the student was away. If the excuse is not presented within the time limit, the student cannot make up any work and must receive a *zero* for assignments due on the days of his absence. *Please* don't lose credit through failure to bring an excuse. It is our job to help you do your very best. *Do not* harm your grade average by absences. Responsibility for making up work missed during absences must lie with the student. *Always* ask about activities you missed during an absence.

This agreement between instructor and students follows the principle of John Locke's social contract idea, which will be studied in connection with the American Revolution. I pledge my best efforts to make the course enjoyable and challenging. Students pledge to give their best in terms of co-operation, attentiveness, and effort. If students remember this agreement and practice it, successful completion of the course is assured. For those students who need occasional reminders of our social contract the demerit system will be followed. One demerit for any given day is a friendly reminder, but the second demerit for any given day means the student has the responsibility to make up 30 minutes of detention after school on the day after a second demerit has been received.

4.   Even though I enjoy teaching history and sometimes get very involved in any particular topic, no history subject matter is as important in this classroom as you, the student. *Please* tell me about your particular problems with assignments. *Never* hesitate to inform me of your difficulties with the course, for I assure you these difficulties can be remedied. If you have problems involving schoolwork in general, please let me be of service. We are all here to learn something about history, but we must work co-operatively to make the experience meaningful and useful to each individual. Best wishes to each of you for a very successful year at Central High. Always remember that *effort assures success.*

---

### The Last Word?

When I was finalizing materials for this chapter, the article on page 267 appeared in *The Washington Post* for April 23, 1979. Its timeliness will, I think, be quite evident in view of the topics we have just examined and because we all worry about teachers' effectiveness and competence. The solution proposed seems logical, yet simple. I hope they decide to use several different lists which "hang together" logically, which show characteristics that "cluster"—somewhat like our role models, perhaps? At any rate, I do hope various viewpoints are represented in the list-making to emphasize the fact that there is never one best way to teach.

### ITEMS FOR ANALYSIS

Try your analytical skills with these items. Assume each situation represents the teaching style for the instructor involved. Assign one of the following labels to each—Essentialism, Experimentalism, Reconstructionism, Existentialism, Perennialism, Behaviorism—and justify your use of the label. (Consult Appendix B for preferred answers.)

A.   Mrs. Imano decided to introduce a unit on immigration by having her eighth graders participate in a simulated classroom setting, as if they all were the most recent immigrants to another country. Before beginning the simulation she asked them to think carefully about their feelings and mood

*William Raspberry*

# Tougher Standards for Teachers?

In 1957, the president of the D.C. Board of Education was railing against the "absurdly excessive requirements" for teaching in the local schools.

In 1979, the superintendent of schools is calling for a toughening of standards for new teachers.

The natural inference is that the local school authorities, having observed a link between teacher standards and pupil achievement, are about to raise standards to boost achievement.

Well, maybe.

There can be no doubt that it's a lot easier than it used to be to win certification for a teaching job in the D.C. schools. A review of newspaper clips of the 1950s uncovers not only Board President Walter N. Tobriner's complaint of "absurdly" high standards, which, he said, made it difficult to recruit for the local system, but also a news account of a 1954 examination failed by 91 of 248 teacher candidates.

Those were the days of the "Franklin Test," so called because it was given in the Franklin Building, which housed the school system's administrative offices. Teacher applicants spent all day taking written examinations—a morning session covering their major subjects and an afternoon session on their minors.

If they got by that rigorous process, they then had to stand for an oral examination. Only then could they be hired—for a two-year probationary period.

Then, in the late 1950s, the local authorities switched to the National Teachers Examination, another tough test battery.

Some 10 years ago, testing was dropped altogether, except for such specialties as foreign-language instruction.

And that, you might conclude, is where the local schools started their academic plunge.

Well, it ain't necessarily so.

Solomon Kendrick, chief examiner for the local school system, was around for a good deal of that time, and his considered opinion is that the ups and downs of teacher certification requirements have had very little to do with the ups and downs of pupil test scores.

In the old, tough days, applicants who passed the written and oral examinations were hired as regular, permanent teachers. But because too few of the applicants passed, many of those who failed were hired as temporaries.

"That gave us a chance to look at the validity of the examination results," Kendrick said, "and what we observed was that many of the applicants who passed the test turned out to be poor teachers while many of those who failed the test turned out to be excellent teachers."

There was, he said, "no correlation" between test results and teacher competency.

Since 1969, he said, certification has been based on paper qualifications, together with references and college transcripts.

"The part of the examination that dealt with subject matter seemed valid enough," he said, "but so far as the general part, the aptitude part, which was supposed to tell us something of the applicant's ability to teach, it told us nothing."

The inability to show a correlation between test scores and competence led, in 1969, to certification based on paper qualifications. "The tests simply didn't tell us what we wanted to know," Kendrick said.

Still, the chief examiner recognizes the need for some device to rank applicants for teaching positions. He thinks he has come up with it in his proposal for competency-based certification.

"The idea—and [Superintendent Vincent E.] Reed has bought it—is to take the best teachers, people recognized as outstanding by their principals, their peers and their students, and use them as guinea pigs.

"We will try to see what makes them outstanding, then we will try to determine methods of ascertaining those qualities in candidates. Based on what we learn, we will then administer written, oral and performance examinations, with the ratings to be done by the outstanding teachers themselves rather than the board of examiners.

The written examinations, he said, will be standardized on the outstanding local teachers, rather than on national norms, and will stress written and oral English.

The new examinations will apply only to newly hired teachers, of which there are very few, but that doesn't bother Kendrick.

"For the most part, we have very good teachers out there," he said. "Our teachers are under the microscope more than others, but they compare quite favorably with those in the [surrounding] counties. In fact the [suburban] teachers, and even those in the local private schools, can't touch our teachers.

"The difference is that ours have to deal with students who have more problems."

Kendrick may be right. But if he is, then there's no reason to expect much improvement in local school achievement, even under Kendrick's impressively sensible new certification plan.

changes while the simulation was proceeding, so that they might be able to describe these feelings accurately after the lesson. She then began immediately to conduct her lesson in Italian because she knew none of the students spoke or understood that language. Youngsters were able to realize that she was giving them a greeting and calling the roll; however, her pronunciation of their names carried a definite Italian accent. She then asked students to repeat after her the Italian equivalents to their Anglicized names until she was satisfied with the voice inflection and intonation. When she

finished the simulation, students were asked to respond briefly in writing to
the following questions:

1. What emotions did you feel as you participated in the simulation? Describe each emotion in one sentence, and be sure you
   are dealing only with the way you felt rather than with what
   you think the teacher might have felt.
2. Do you believe the teacher treated you unfairly? If not, why not?
   If so, in what way or ways did the teacher seem to be unfair?

Students were told not to sign their names to responses. When the papers
were collected, Mrs. Imano informed youngsters that she would, for tomorrow, use their responses to begin discussions about what it may mean to live
in a country where both customs and language are totally unfamiliar.

B.   Ms. Numis has decided to introduce a brief unit, "America's
Changing Money Market," by asking her eleventh grade United States
history students to examine six varieties of coins. She has asked her students
to work in groups of five. Ms. Numis has just distributed six coins to each
group: an Indian-head penny (1906), a buffalo nickel (1930), a "Mercury"
dime (1944), a Franklin half-dollar (1951), a Washington quarter (1969), and a
Bicentennial quarter (1976). Each group is to develop four generalizations
about the people who minted these coins and four generalizations about
changes in America's money market. All generalizations must be supported
by their observations of the coins. For the rest of today's class students will
observe the coins carefully, take notes, and discuss their findings. Tomorrow
each group will finalize its lists of generalizations.

C.   Mr. Boyer has just finished setting up a "lab practical" for his
tenth grade biology students. The first examination problem involves having
youngsters look at five slides of bacteria under microscopes in order to categorize the bacteria according to shape—bacillus (rod-shaped), coccus
(spherical), and spirillum (spiral).

D.   "Gang, we are going to learn all the songs on this record," I said.
"And I just thought of a good reason for doing it. Because you are going to
look like geniuses when you know these songs. People are going to come to
this island to revel in stupidity and poverty. I am going to switch on the
record player and you are going to look at these people and exclaim with
British accents, 'Pahdon me, suh. Are you perchance familiar with Rimsky-
Korsakov?' We can knock their behinds off. Now, an important question: do
you guys and gals think you can learn these songs and who wrote them? You
already know three of them. You know Beethoven's Fifth, 'The Flight of the
Bumblebee' by Rimsky-Korsakov and Brahms' Lullaby. You learned three
of them without even trying. Can you learn a whole mess of them?"

"Yeah," everyone shouted.

"I believe you."

So we did it. That night I chose twenty of the most impressive titles
written by the most impressive composers. For the next two months a
portion of each day was set aside for the consumption, memorization, and

enjoyment of this top twenty. On a weekend I purchased a huge poster of Beethoven, and hung his shaggy-maned visage on the bulletin board. It tickled me to think of Big B's reaction to his celebration on an island as remote as Yamacraw. In a short time he became "Bay-Toven the Fifth" and no matter how earnestly I tried to explain that the Fifth was not an addendum to his name, so it remained. It gave an incredible feeling to put the needle down, to hear Tchaikovsky swing into the room, then watch the hands shoot up. . . .*

E. "I am not here tonight for the love of the school board. I have been on the island and have seen the conditions there. You have been presiding over an educational desert. Children who grow up on that island don't have a prayer of receiving an adequate education. They grow up without hope. They leave the island without hope. They drift into the big cities of the East Coast and rot in some tenement slum—without hope. They are not taught to read, to write, to speak, or to be proud of themselves or their race. Their parents are not influential, literate, or vocal, so this educational system is perpetuated. If these parents were white and important, their school would be as fine as any school in the county. If their parents were white, the question of a gas bill and maintenance bill would never come up—even if I were driving a battleship to work. But the school is black. The people on the island are black. And, my God, the hopelessness of teaching in a black school, cut off from society by water, is an agony few people have experienced. Yamacraw requires sweeping reform of your thinking. It demands for a brief moment that you forget about money and budgets and balanced books. Forget about your building plans, ordering new volleyballs for the high school, and how many tractors to purchase next year. Think instead about children. People. Human beings. Feel for once that education is about people—not figures." . . . During the entire period of my banishment and trial, I wanted to tell Piedmont and Bennington that what was happening between us was not confined to Beaufort, South Carolina. I wanted to tell them about the river that was rising quickly, flooding the marshes and threatening the dry land. I wanted them to know that their day was ending. When I saw them at the trial, I knew that they were soldiers of the rear guard, captains of a doomed army retreating through the snow and praying that the shadows of the quick, dark wolves, waiting in the cold, would come no closer. They were old men and could not accept the new sun rising out of the strange waters. The world was very different now.*

F. Ms. Ryder's health education class, as part of a unit on human relationships in the family, was asked to read an article titled "A New Look at Living Together" (*Psychology Today*, December 1977). After discussing results of studies reported in this article—that cohabiting couples are not likely to get married and that cohabitation is not on the way to replacing marriage—youngsters have just been asked to volunteer to role play a scene between two parents, their daughter and her boyfriend who wish to live together before deciding whether to marry. The situation for role playing involves the daughter and her boyfriend sitting down to inform her parents of their decision to live together. Both the daughter and her boyfriend are 21, and the parents are in their late 40's. The parents have no knowledge of what their daughter is about to tell them.

As a follow-up activity, Ms. Ryder plans to have students write paragraphs about how they would react if a son or daughter were to inform them of a decision to live with someone of the opposite sex before marriage. These paragraphs are to include comments about whether they agree or disagree with the "parents" in the role-playing exercise, why they agree or disagree (to include a philosophical moral rationale), and how the studies they have read about in several articles may be used to support their positions.

G.   An eleventh grade United States history class has completed a study of the effects of industrialization on minority ethnic groups. The teacher has just shown the film *Geronimo Jones,* in which a white man at a local trading post "cons" a twelve-year-old Indian lad out of a highly prized amulet presented to him by his grandfather. Students have been asked to describe what they consider to be the three most important choices this Indian youngster will face in life, and advise him about those choices on the basis of what they have just learned during their study of industrialization's effects on minority ethnic groups.

H.   Ms. Rossi's first grade class has been studying number patterns and addition. She has just designed a game which uses large cardboard signs that look like dominoes and is quite anxious to have her students play it. The class will be divided into two teams and will participate in pairs. Each pair of students will have to run and attempt to be first to touch the domino when Ms. Rossi gives a signal. The first student to touch the domino has the first chance at identifying the number pattern on each half of the domino and at giving the sum of the two numbers represented.

I.   Ninth graders in Mr. Quillen's English class were asked to write one paragraph about what it is like to be a parent. After youngsters had an opportunity to discuss duties and responsibilities of parenthood mentioned in their compositions, Mr. Quillen required each child to think of a plant like a parent and describe that plant. After making responses like "redwood, because it's something big that you look up to," and "rosebush, because its thorns protect you," youngsters were then asked to enlarge their descriptions of the rosebush until they could think of words that seemed like opposites. After talking about the pairing of "beautiful" and "thorny," Mr. Quillen told youngsters to list items which were beautiful and thorny at the same time. "Some girls," "a book," "coral," and "oven" were examples of the many student responses.

Mr. Quillen then required students to go back to the original task and write another paragraph about being a parent. This time they had to use as many as possible of the words and phrases they had mentioned which related to being both beautiful and thorny. Responses were collected so that students could, in a later lesson, analyze the differences between their first and second paragraphs for use of descriptive words.

J. Students in Mr. Drucker's sixth grade class had decided they wished to go to Colonial Williamsburg on their field trip. Mr. Drucker gave a planning committee the task of finding the shortest route to Williamsburg (using only primary roads) and of determining how long it would take their bus to travel the distance if its average speed were 35 miles per hour.

K. A group of senior high school English students have read excerpts from Elizabeth Kubler-Ross's book, *On Death and Dying,* in which the psychological stages of dying were explained. Next these students saw a videotape of John Gunther's *Death Be Not Proud.* The teacher has just asked them to write a paper in which they attempt to apply Dr. Kubler-Ross's "stages" to the thought processes the main character in the play went through before he could accept the fact of his terminal illness. Students must justify why they used the name of each stage and what portion of the main character's action would be included in that stage.

# APPENDIX A

## INTERPRETATION OF "S-C TEACHING INVENTORY"

The first 20 items represent student-oriented responses, and the second 20 items represent content-oriented responses. As you review your responses, give yourself one "point" on the student-orientation axis each time one of your "answers" matches a response listed below. Follow the same procedure for content-oriented responses. For example, if you received 15 "points" on the "S" axis, count up to line "15" and trace your pencil over that horizontal line in the grid on the Summary Sheet. If you received 15 "points" on the "C" axis, count across to line "15" and trace your pencil over that vertical line in the grid on the Summary Sheet. Where your pencil lines intersect should be matched with the grid showing models. Notice that if this intersection falls in the top two quadrants, you are probably Experimentalist/Existentialist. If the intersection falls within the bottom two quadrants, you are probably Esentialist/Perennialist. (Note: Strategies outlined on the grid are meant to represent extremes because they are near the "edges." Those descriptions do not match directly the more median or responsible role models we have examined.)

| "S" Responses | "C" Responses |
|---|---|
| 1. A | 21. B |
| 2. A | 22. B |
| 3. B | 23. A |
| 4. B | 24. A |
| 5. B | 25. B |
| 6. A | 26. A |
| 7. B | 27. A |
| 8. A | 28. A |
| 9. B | 29. B |
| 10. B | 30. B |
| 11. A | 31. B |
| 12. B | 32. A |
| 13. A | 33. B |
| 14. A | 34. A |
| 15. B | 35. A |
| 16. A | 36. B |
| 17. A | 37. A |
| 18. B | 38. A |
| 19. A | 39. B |
| 20. B | 40. B |

## S-C TEACHING INVENTORY
## SUMMARY SHEET

Name _____ Date _____

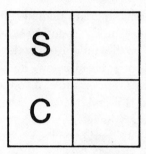

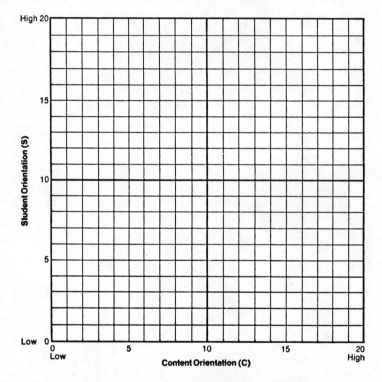

*Reprinted from Pfeiffer, J. W. and Jones, J. E. (Eds.) *The 1974 Annual Handbook for Group Facilitators* (La Jolla, CA.: University Associates, 1974.) Used with permission.

**Models of Teaching Strategies**

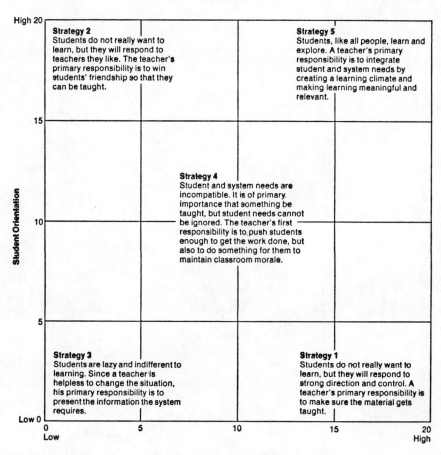

High 20

**Strategy 2**
Students do not really want to learn, but they will respond to teachers they like. The teacher's primary responsibility is to win students' friendship so that they can be taught.

**Strategy 5**
Students, like all people, learn and explore. A teacher's primary responsibility is to integrate student and system needs by creating a learning climate and making learning meaningful and relevant.

15

**Strategy 4**
Student and system needs are incompatible. It is of primary importance that something be taught, but student needs cannot be ignored. The teacher's first responsibility is to push students enough to get the work done, but also to do something for them to maintain classroom morale.

10

5

**Strategy 3**
Students are lazy and indifferent to learning. Since a teacher is helpless to change the situation, his primary responsibility is to present the information the system requires.

**Strategy 1**
Students do not really want to learn, but they will respond to strong direction and control. A teacher's primary responsibility is to make sure the material gets taught.

Low 0

Student Orientation

0    5    10    15    20
Low                      High

Content Orientation

# APPENDIX B

## PREFERRED ANSWERS TO PRACTICE ITEMS*

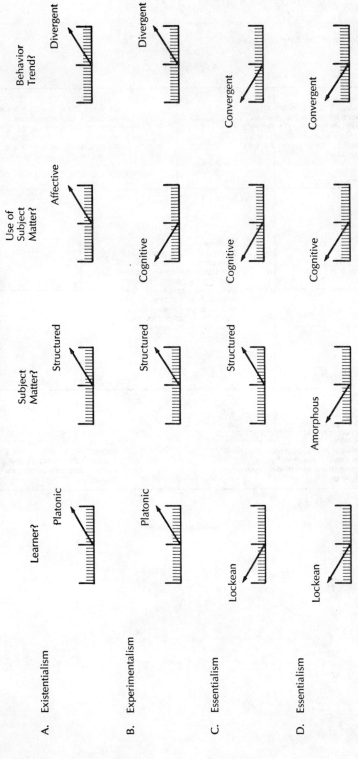

A. Existentialism

B. Experimentalism

C. Essentialism

D. Essentialism

*Note: Perennialism is not included here because, as explained in Chapter 4, it is not susceptible to analysis simply through collecting data on classroom behavior. One must question the teacher about assumptions regarding the dialectic and truth before using the Perennialist label. That means this role model can be analyzed in real life, but not on paper for items such as those listed above. Behaviorism has not been included, since behavior modification systems employed in a classroom would be self-evident.

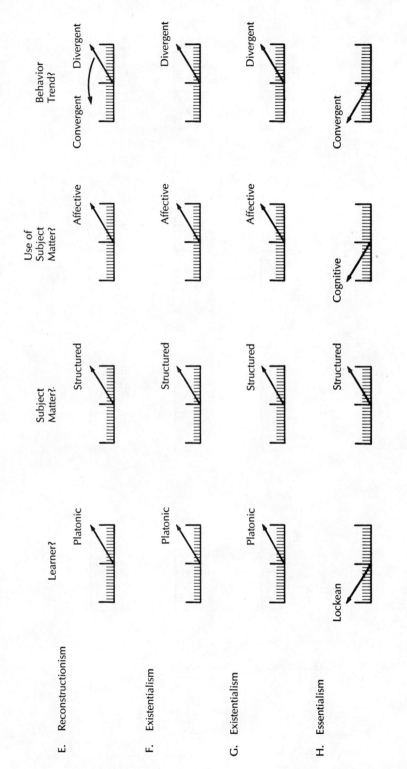

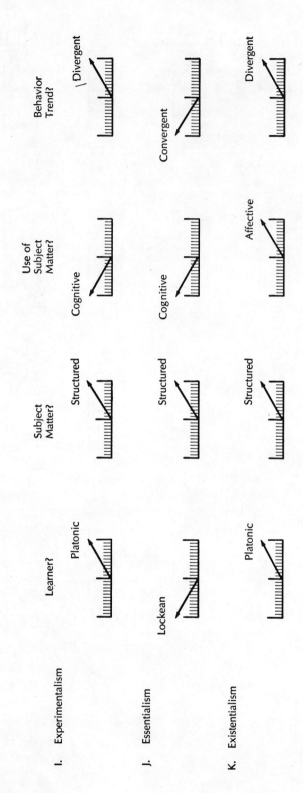

# APPENDIX C

## BIBLIOGRAPHIC ESSAY

What follows is a personal view of sources that influenced me in developing this book. I am especially indebted to Marie Wirsihg, *Teaching and Philosophy: A Synthesis* (Boston: Houghton Mifflin, 1972) and to George F. Kneller, *Introduction to the Philosophy of Education*, 2nd ed., rev. (New York: John Wiley and Sons, 1971). These two texts provided the philosophical groundwork for my particular perspective in *Teaching with Charisma*.


## Chapter One:
## The Heart of the Matter, An Analytical Tool

In using the terms "Lockean" (to denote passive learners) and "Platonic" (to denote active learners) I have tried to connect current classroom practice and attitudes with the history of educational thought before the nineteenth and twentieth centuries. *Locke Selections* (New York: Charles Scribner's Sons, 1956), edited by Sterling Lamprecht, contains insightful introductions and commentary which proved especially useful for interpreting Locke's "Essay Concerning Human Understanding." In using the term "Lockean" for one end of a continuum I am not denying the concept of what Locke calls "complex knowledge," derived from mental operations a perceiver/learner performs upon that which he perceives. I am saying, however, that Locke's concept of *tabula rasa* embodies a "passive" learner whose main duty is seen as absorbing information.

The term "Platonic," on the contrary, denotes an active learner; in essence, this is as close as I could get before the writings of late nineteenth and twentieth century thinkers to the view of an active learner who creates knowledge, while interacting with the environment. Plato's search for Truth through the dialectic was viewed as leading ultimately to convergence. Nevertheless, Plato's dialectician often resembled the learner who creates knowledge through his or her own activity because convergence was delayed for an extended period of time. In the short run, the process of dialectic might look as though divergence were being sought. See Chapter 6 in the text for refinements on these ideas. See also James Bowen, *A History of Western Education*, 2 vols. (New York: St. Martin's Press, 1972) for an excellent treatment of Plato's dialectic and the doctrine of reminiscence. Read Plato, *The Republic and Other Works*, trans. B. Jowett (Garden City, N.Y.: Doubleday and Co., 1960) for a sense of the long-delayed convergence on Truth which philosopher-rulers were supposed to achieve. See Plato's *Memo* in Harry S. Broudy and John R. Palmer, *Exemplars of Teaching Method* (Chicago: Rand McNally, 1965) for a conversation about the Pythagorean theorem which illustrates short-term convergence on Truth.

Jerome Bruner, *The Process of Education*, rev. ed. (Cambridge: Harvard University Press, 1977) provides an excellent treatment of the concept of structure regarding academic disciplines. Since *Teaching with Charisma* attempts to integrate current practices regarding styles of teaching with practices employed throughout most of educational history, it was deemed appropriate to use the term "amorphous." That is, a continuum on the nature of subject matter should record not only how ideas, facts, and concepts relate to each other within a discipline, but also how some teachers have emphasized rote memory, at the expense of understanding. For example, Upton Sinclair, *The Goose-Step* (published by the author at Pasadena, Calif., 1923) and Upton Sinclair, *The Goslings* (Published by the author at Pasadena, Calif., 1924) offer entertaining insights into conservatism in higher education and in public school establishments just after World War I. Sinclair wrote arrestingly about the power of rote memorization. These volumes are, unfortunately, out of print and difficult to obtain, but superbly reward the researcher's time and effort. In addition, Pat Conroy, *The Water Is Wide* (New York: Dell Publishing Co., 1972) offers a charming description of an "amorphous" view of subject matter, when he described children attempting to memorize musical selections. It is difficult today to find an instructor who deliberately emphasizes rote memorization and disregards any understanding of a discipline's structure. However, in nineteenth century American education this "amorphous" approach was decidedly prolific.

Louis Rubin, *Curriculum Handbook* (Boston: Allyn and Bacon, 1977) gives an excellent brief overview of curriculum projects; this book emphasizes each discipline's structure and describes how those projects have evolved during the last three decades. He traces admirably the influence of Bruner's *Process of Education* and the Wood's Hole Conference on views about the manner in which disciplines should be taught in public schools. As Rubin shows in his extensive bibliographies for each discipline, history and the social sciences have evolved markedly, largely because their supporters in public schools have culled from the sciences and mathematics to emphasize the "structure-of-the-discipline" concept. Both Allan Nevins, *The Gateway to History*, rev. ed. (Garden City, N.Y.: Doubleday and Co., 1962) and A. L. Rowse, *The Use of History*, rev. ed. (New York: Collier Books, 1963) are pacemaking works that emphasize creative possibilities for using history's methodological structure as a means for broadening the scope of social science knowledge. Kenneth A. Lockridge, *A New England Town: The First Hundred Years* (New York: Norton and Co., 1970) is a graphic example of one historian's emphasis on the structure of a discipline that transcends the concepts promulgated by Nevins and Rowse. Lockridge borrowed from mathematics and from sociology in applying statistical analysis to colonial records. Lockridge's use of new methodology to gain insights from old, long-exposed data illustrates a major point in Kenneth Clark, *Civilisation: A Personal View* (New York: Harper and Row, 1970); in effect, the late nineteenth and twentieth centuries have increased fascination with the powers inherent in the fields of mathematics, technology, and engineering.

By the same token, Clark's personal view of civilization, which seeks to use art as a major means for reconstructing the flow of intellectual history, illustrates an almost opposite trend in the social sciences—the trend of ignoring the methodologies associated with science, while at the same time concentrating on literature and the fine arts to reap new insights about social evolution. This trend is also well illustrated in Michael Kammen, *People of Paradox: An Inquiry Concerning the Origins of American Civilization* (New York: Knopf, 1972). Kammen looks at the entire scope of American letters before deciding that social dynamism has burgeoned in this country because our society harbors extreme intellectual tensions. These tensions he views as a "tryptych: a picture in three compartments side by side, commonly hinged so that the two lateral scenes may fold in toward the central one." He sees one lateral frame of the tryptych representing Americans' search for legitimacy in government and institutions generally; this involves efforts to forge a *raison d'être* totally separate from European society. The problem of excessive pluralism, which he sees as the other side of the tryptych, made it difficult to build national feeling into a rapidly evolving United States. For the central panel, he uses the concept of biformity, which includes our fascination with apparent opposites; for example, the concept of freedom which might, on the one hand, represent liberty within a structure, or, on the other hand, it might signify the potential chaos of anarchy. From this tryptych of peculiarly volatile ideals has come American dynamism, according to Kammen. Precedents for ideas discussed by Clark and Kammen appear in the following sources: Vernon L. Parrington, *Main Currents in American Thought* (New York: Harcourt, 1930); and Van Wyck Brooks, *The Flowering of New England* (New York: E. P. Dutton and Co., 1952).

Though works by Kammen and Clark are characteristic of intellectual history, these works do not adopt an "amorphous" view of academic disciplines. In fact, their relatively new attempts at methodology simply create novel structures within disciplines, an approach which reminds us that problem-solving techniques culled from mathematics and the sciences are not the only ways to proceed in academia. They do, of course, offer new tools for understanding how disciplines are structured. Nevertheless, the methods they illustrate have created enough tension in academia to make scholars search for new definitions of disciplines, in addition to the "amorphous" versus "structured" continuum. One excellent example is Robert D.

Barr, James L. Barth, and Samuel Shermis, *Defining the Social Studies: Bulletin 51 of National Council for the Social Studies* (Arlington, Va.: National Council for the Social Studies, 1977) which tries to salvage a curriculum area that seems to be splintering. In recent years the most well attended sessions at NCSS annual meetings have been those which deal directly with the question of structure.

In relation to our third continuum in the analytical tool—the "cognitive" versus "affective" dilemma—I have relied heavily on Benjamin Bloom et al., *Taxonomy of Educational Objectives: Cognitive Domain* (New York: D. McKay Co., 1956). It is noteworthy that our definition of affective involves only levels three through five in David Krathwohl et al., *Taxonomy of Educational Objectives: Affective Domain* (New York: Longman, 1964). I also referred to a concept for "personalizing" learning along the "cognitive" versus "affective" continuum, known as the "cone of experience," and set forth in Edgar Dale, *Audiovisual Methods in Teaching*, 3rd ed., rev. (New York: Dryden Press, 1969). Those interested in looking deeper into the controversial and affective nature of the examples on evolution might wish to consult the three following sources: Stephen Jay Gould, *Ever Since Darwin: Reflections on Natural History* (New York: Norton and Co., 1977); B. Ann Slate and Alan Berry, *Bigfoot* (New York: Bantam Books, 1976); and Richard Hofstadter, *Social Darwinism in American Thought*, rev. ed. (Boston: Beacon Press, 1955). The trend toward potentially affective topics, such as "death education," is well documented in Louis Rubin, *Curriculum Handbook* (Boston: Allyn and Bacon, 1977) for social science and humanities curriculum areas. One might also profitably consult Maurice Hunt and Lawrence Metcalf, *Teaching High School Social Studies: Problems in Reflective Thinking and Social Understanding* (New York: Harper and Row, 1968) for dealing with what they have termed the "closed areas." See also Elisabeth Kübler-Ross, *On Death and Dying* (New York: Macmillan Co., 1969), as well as John Gunther, *Death Be Not Proud: A Memoir* (New York: Harper, 1949); both of these books offer perspectives applicable to classes in "death education."

The framework for terminology about facts, concepts, generalizations, hypotheses, beliefs, and values included in the section relating to a teacher's planning notebook is taken primarily from Edwin Fenton, *Teaching the New Social Studies in Secondary Schools: An Inductive Approach* (New York: Holt, Rinehart and Winston, 1966). For planning notebook ideas about a favorable balance of trade, including this concept's meaning throughout history, consult Robert L. Heilbroner, *The Making of Economic Society* (Englewood Cliffs, N.J.: Prentice-Hall, 1962) and Howard J. Ruff, *How to Prosper During the Coming Bad Years* (New York: Times Books, 1979). Concepts of the struggle between good and evil in Massachusetts Bay in the seventeenth century are discussed in the following books: Emery John Battis, *Saints and Sectaries: Ann Hutchinson and the Antinomian Controversy in the Massachusetts Bay Colony* (Chapel Hill, N.C.: University of North Carolina Press, 1975); and, Chadwick Hansen, *Witchcraft at Salem* (New York: G. Braziller, 1969). The power of the so-called "Puritan work ethic" is amply treated in the following three works: Perry Miller, *Errand into the Wilderness* (New York: Harper and Row, 1956); Edmund S. Morgan, *The Puritan Family*, rev. ed. (New York: Harper and Row, 1966); and, Alan Simpson, *Puritanism in Old and New England* (Chicago: University of Chicago Press, 1967).

All of the sources cited above will guide students who wish to examine in depth the foundation on which the analytical tool is based. The analytical tool's most important continuum—the "convergence" versus "divergence" continuum—is fully summarized and analyzed in terms of observation and measurement in the following two sources: Ned Flanders, *Analyzing Teaching Behavior* (Reading, Mass.: Addison-Wesley, 1970); Ned Flanders and Edmund J. Amidon, *The Role of the Teacher in the Classroom: A Manual for Understanding and Improving Teacher Classroom Behavior*, rev. ed. (Minneapolis, Minn.: Association for Productive Teaching, 1971). See also Lee Ehman, Howard Mehlinger, and John Patrick, *Toward Effective Instruction in Secondary Social Studies* (Boston: Houghton Mifflin, 1974) for an assessment of convergence and divergence in testing.

## Chapter Two:
## The Essentialist Teacher as Problem-Solver

Sources for those who wish to examine Essentialism are prolific and readily available, so it is not my purpose here to provide an extensive bibliography. In fact, the topic is almost impossible to avoid and runs throughout educational literature, from the writings of the Sophists in Ancient Greece to the latest publications from the Council for Basic Education. One should be prepared, however, to find the tenets of Essentialism advanced under various names. Sometimes, as with Kneller, it is known as Essentialism, a name which I prefer. Sometimes, as with Wirsing, it is called Logical Positivism. At other times, as with Morris and Pai, it is referred to as embodied in the root philosophy of Realism. Any of the following volumes provide excellent summaries and have more than adequate bibliographic references: George F. Kneller, *Introduction to the Philosophy of Education*, 2nd ed., rev. (New York: John Wiley and Sons, 1971); Marie Wirsing, *Teaching and Philosophy: A Synthesis* (Boston: Houghton Mifflin, 1972); Van Cleve Morris and Young

Pai, *Philosophy and the American School,* 2nd ed., rev. (Boston: Houghton Mifflin, 1976).

The general point of departure for our Essentialist lesson is based in part on ideas from Edwin Fenton, *Teaching the New Social Studies in Secondary Schools: An Inductive Approach* (New York: Holt, Rinehart and Winston, 1966). Fenton also made use of Thomas R. Henry, "The Riddle of the Kensington Rune Stone," *Saturday Evening Post,* August 21, 1948. For those interested in probing more deeply the Kensington Stone controversy (especially teachers who may wish to use additional materials in order to create an Experimentalist lesson), the following sources are quite rewarding: Erik Wahlgren, "The Case of the Kensington Rune Stone," *American Heritage,* April 1959; and Gwyn Jones, *A History of the Vikings* (London: Oxford University Press, 1968).

The style of Essentialism represented by our "Kensington Stone" lesson first began to be popular in the late 1950s and early 1960s. Such efforts in the social sciences were based primarily on the "structure-of-the-disciplines" movement so thoroughly applied in the sciences, in part because of a general malaise about education in this country which began after the U.S.S.R. launched Sputnik. For the history and current status of such projects as *Chem Study, Harvard Project Physics, SRSS (Sociological Resources for the Secondary School), Man: A Course of Study,* and others which date from this general period, consult the following volumes: Louis Rubin, *Curriculum Handbook* (Boston: Allyn and Bacon, 1977); Dwight W. Allen and Eli Seifman, eds., *Teacher's Handbook* (Glenview, Ill.: Scott, Foresman and Co., 1971); and Joel Spring, *The Sorting Machine: National Educational Policy Since 1945* (New York: David McKay Co., 1976).

The most vehement Essentialist writings of the 1950s and 1960s are quite similar in intensity to those of some romantic critics, Reconstructionists, and deschoolers of the 1960s and 1970s. Excellent examples include the following: Max Rafferty, *What They Are Doing to Your Children* (New York: New American Library, 1964); Max Rafferty, "Should Gays Teach School?" *Phi Delta Kappan,* October 1977; and Mara Wolynski, "Confessions of a Misspent Youth," *Newsweek,* August 30, 1976. Other noteworthy examples which have become minor classics include: Mortimer Smith, *The Diminished Mind: A Study of Planned Mediocrity in Our Schools* (Chicago: H. Regnery Co., 1954); Rudolph Flesch, *Why Johnny Can't Read—and What You Can Do About It* (New York: Harper, 1955); Arthur S. Trace, *What Ivan Knows that Johnny Doesn't* (New York: Random House, 1961); and Arthur S. Trace, *Reading without Dick and Jane* (Chicago: H. Regnery Co., 1965). Though their philosophic perspective is quite different from Reconstructionist reformers and deschoolers, the rhetoric of Essentialists equals the force and tone of many radical reformers.

For a slightly different Essentialist critique of the educational establishment, see James B. Conant, *The Education of American Teachers* (Boston: Houghton Mifflin, 1963). Moreover, an earlier Essentialist position is articulated in Jacques Barzun, *Teacher in America* (Garden City, N.Y.: Doubleday Anchor Books, 1955). Barzun's work, first published in 1945, lacks the Cold War and post-Sputnik urgency of many of the other volumes mentioned above.

Two excellent sources for the Sophists' brand of "Essentialism" and for treatment of the Sophistic ideal for learning, as it was copied in the Middle Ages, are: H. I. Marrou, *A History of Education in Antiquity* (New York: Mentor Books, 1964); and James Bowen, *A History of Western Education*, 2 vols. (New York: St. Martin's Press, 1972). This lengthy evolution of the Essentialist position has taken on new meaning because of the current "back-to-basics" furor. Worries about declining standardized test scores and many other concerns have produced a market glutted with articles calling for change along Essentialist lines. A useful source which provides Essentialist commentaries on non-Essentialist learning modes is Mortimer Smith, Richard Peck, and George Weber, *A Consumer's Guide to Educational Innovations* (Washington: Council for Basic Education, 1972).

A superb satire on the conflict between Essentialism and Experimentalism is J. Abner Peddiwell, *The Sabre-Tooth Curriculum* (New York: McGraw-Hill, 1939). This work about the "old guard" in Paleolithic society attempting to maintain their traditional curriculum for hunting sabre-tooth tigers, after such tigers have become extinct, is entertaining and insightful.

## Chapter Three:
## The Experimentalist Teacher as Problem-Solver

Students should consult the three basic sources referred to previously— Kneller, Morris and Pai, and Wirsing—for an overview of Experimentalism and for bibliographic guidance. It is again helpful to remember that more than one term is commonly used to describe the philosophical underpinnings of our catalogue lesson. In works by Morris and Pai and Wirsing "Experimentalism" denotes the educational philosophy, and "Pragmatism" denotes the root philosophy. Kneller uses the term "Progressivism" as the contemporary label for the philosophy underlying our catalogue lesson. For reasons stated in the text, however, I prefer to use the word "Progressivism" in an historical, rather than in a contemporary, context.

Our use of reprints from the 1908 *Sears, Roebuck Catalogue No. 117* (Chicago: Follett, 1969) exemplifies a new impetus for infusing economic concepts into elementary and secondary school curricula. This impetus spearheaded mostly by the Joint Council on Economic Education,

1212 Avenue of the Americas, New York, N.Y. 10036, and the increased use
of their Test of Economic Literacy as a diagnostic instrument, can be appreciated more fully by examining the following sources: Daniel A. McGow-
an, *Consumer Economics* (Chicago: Rand McNally, 1978); Elbert V. Bow-
den, *Economics: the Science of Common Sense* (Cincinnati: South-Western
Publishing Co., 1978); and Lucille G. Ford, *University Economics: Guide
for Education Majors* (Cleveland, Ohio: Martha Holden Jennings Foundation, 1979). Nevertheless, the concerns of an unstable economy have made a
balanced approach, such as the one in John Kenneth Galbraith, *The Age of
Uncertainty* (Boston: Houghton Mifflin Co., 1977), necessary to help us keep
a perspective on the more startling ideas portrayed in other books, such as
Howard J. Ruff, *How to Prosper During the Coming Bad Years* (New York:
Times Books, 1979). Since economic concepts have often been accused of
raising as many fears among teachers and the general public as the now
famous "math anxiety," the following compendia of teaching strategies serve
as comforting references: Donald G. Davison, ed., *Strategies for Teaching
Economics–Primary Level* (New York: Joint Council on Economic Educa-
tion, 1977); Marilyn Kourilsky, ed., *Strategies for Teaching Economics–
Intermediate Level* (New York: Joint Council on Economic Education, 1978);
James F. Niss, Judith Breneke, and John Clow, eds., *Strategies for Teaching
Economics–Basic Business and Consumer Education (Secondary)* (New
York: Joint Council on Economic Education, 1979).

Our catalogue lesson is also aptly suited to highlight the anxiety and
potential "management-of-resources" problem which causes fatigue and may
ultimately lead to "burn-out." Such difficulties are more often associated
with teaching styles which emphasize divergence, rather than with those
which stress convergence. Particularly helpful sources for understanding respectively the physiological and emotional aspects of "burn-out" are: Walter
McQuade and Ann Aikman, *Stress—What It Is, What It Can Do to Your
Health, How to Fight Back* (New York: Bantam Books, 1974); and Thomas
Anthony Harris, *I'm OK—Your're OK* (New York: Avon Press, 1973). Harris'
explanation of "triggering the child" is particularly relevant to manifestation
of stress in classrooms. Herbert L. Foster, *Ribbin', Jivin', and Playin' the
Dozens: The Unrecognized Dilemma of Inner City Schools* (Cambridge,
Mass.: Ballinger, 1974) offers a particularly powerful picture of the special
stresses associated with schools which serve explosive ethnic and socioeconomic mixtures of students. What can happen in human service professions to bring on "burn-out" is graphically told by Christina Maslach, "Helping the Troubled," *Washington Post,* September 19, 1976, as well as by Joan
McQueeney Mitric, "Diary of a Fed-Up Teacher," *Washington Post,*
January 26, 1980. Learning to enjoy the challenges of stress (if such a feat is

possible given an individual's emotional and psychological profile) and disciplining oneself to set aside some time each day for a change-of-pace activity and a definite time to do absolutely nothing can go far in safeguarding against "burn-out."

In connection with the "management-of-resources" problem, teachers may also find two other sources especially helpful in keeping some potential pitfalls of Experimentalist problem-solving in perspective. Alice Kaplan Gordon, *Games for Growth: Educational Games in the Classroom* (Palo Alto, Calif.: Science Research Associates, 1970) offers guidance in selecting commercially produced simulations for the classroom; many of her suggestions use Experimentalist problem-solving as their foundation. For those interested in teaching social sciences and humanities disciplines, Barry K. Beyer, *Teaching Thinking in Social Studies: Using Inquiry in the Classroom*, 2nd ed., rev. (Columbus, Ohio: Charles E. Merrill, 1979) investigates the advantages and disadvantages of Essentialist problem-solving, which he calls the "discovery" approach, and Experimentalist problem-solving, which he calls the "open" approach.

Although there are many excellent references regarding antecedents for current Experimentalist problem-solving strategies, Lawrence Cremin, *The Transformation of the School: Progressivism in American Education, 1876–1957* (New York: Random House, 1964), as well as Rush Welter, *Popular Education and Democratic Thought in America* (New York: Columbia University Press, 1962) are among the best in providing a general overview of the movement's historical development. Two books by Daniel Boorstin—*The Americans: The Colonial Experience* (New York: Random House, 1958), and, *The Americans: The National Experience* (New York: Random House, 1965)—offer a convincing argument that the Pragmatism of William James represents a natural outgrowth for our culture. Among the most useful sources for the philosophy of James are the following: *Principles of Psychology* (New York: H. Holt and Co., 1890); *The Will to Believe* (New York: Longmans, Green and Co., 1896); *Talks to Teachers on Psychology and to Students on Some of Life's Ideals* (New York: Dover Publications, 1899); *The Varieties of Religious Experience* (New York: Longmans, Green and Co., 1902); and *Pragmatism, A New Name for Some Old Ways of Thinking* (New York: Longmans, Green and Co., 1907). The introduction and notes in John K. Roth, ed., *The Moral Philosophy of William James* (New York: Crowell, 1969) offer helpful insights and perspectives.

It is impossible to treat fully, in an introductory volume such as this, the manner in which John Dewey's thinking builds on William James's Pragmatism. Dewey and his Progressive followers have left an astonishingly large legacy in print. Major works by John Dewey are: *The Child and the Cur-*

*riculum* (Chicago: University of Chicago Press, 1902); *The School and Society* (New York: McClure, Phillips and Co., 1907); *My Pedagogic Creed* (Chicago: A. Flanagan Co., 1910); *Democracy and Education: An Introduction to the Philosophy of Education* (New York: Macmillan Co., 1916); *The Way Out of Educational Confusion* (Westport, Conn.: Greenwood Press, 1970), based on a lecture presented in 1931; *How We Think: A Restatement of the Relation of Reflective Thinking to the Educative Process* (Boston: D. C. Heath, 1933); *Logic: The Theory of Inquiry* (New York: H. Holt and Co., 1938); *Freedom and Culture* (New York: G. P. Putnam's Sons, 1939); *Experience and Education* (New York: Macmillan Co., 1949); *Experience and Nature* (LaSalle, Ill.: Open Court Press, 1958); and *Reconstruction in Philosophy* (Boston: Beacon Press, 1957). The following volumes by William Heard Kilpatrick are particularly helpful for their insights into Kilpatrick's role as a popularizer of Dewey's work: *Group Education for a Democracy* (New York: Association Press, 1940); and *Education for a Changing Civilization* (New York: Arno Press, 1971), copyrighted in 1926.

Hegel's influence on Dewey's thought may be assessed by consulting: Georg Wilhelm Friedrich Hegel, *Hegel: Texts and Commentary*, trans. and ed. Walter Kaufman (Garden City, N.Y.: Anchor Books, 1966); and Hans-Georg Gadamer, *Hegel's Dialectic*, trans. Christopher Smith (New Haven: Yale University Press, 1976). Although Plato, Hegel, and Dewey all relied on a dialectical process of thinking, there are important differences in conception and application. Plato regarded the dialectic as the way back to Truth. Hegel saw dialectic as the rational force behind events in history—a rationality which brought about progress through the sweep of events. Dewey's use of dialectic was similar to Plato's in that ideas and conflict among ideas were emphasized; however, Dewey's thinking did not include a belief in changeless Truth. See Jesse Glenn Gray, *Hegel and Greek Thought* (New York: Harper and Row, 1968).

I have attempted to be consistent with the spirit of Dewey's educational synthesis in the section on the "updated" core curriculum. That is, Dewey used the dialectic as a way of resolving conflicts that were cognitive and affective. I have attempted to do the same with the "updated" core so that it contains elements which can be regarded as Experimentalist, Reconstructionist, and Existentialist. The following volumes offer a wealth of insights to any student who wishes to understand the massive effort put into the Progressive Education Association's Eight-Year Study: Wilford Aikin, *Adventure in American Education, Vol. I: The Story of the Eight-Year Study* (New York: Harper and Brothers, 1942); H. H. Giles, S. P. McCutchen, and A. N. Zechiel, *Adventure in American Education, Vol. II: Exploring the Curriculum* (New York: Harper and Brothers, 1942); Eugene R. Smith and

Ralph W. Tyler, *Adventure in American Education, Vol. III: Appraising and Recording Student Progress* (New York: Harper and Brothers, 1942); Dean Chamberlin, Enid Chamberlin, Neal E. Drought, and William E. Scott, *Adventure in American Education, Vol. IV: Did They Succeed in College?* (New York: Harper and Brothers, 1942); and Progressive Education Association, *Adventure in American Education*, Vol. V: *Thirty Schools Tell Their Story* (New York: Harper and Brothers, 1943). See also H. H. Giles, *Teacher-Pupil Planning* (New York: Harper and Brothers, 1941) for insights into Progressive ideas on cooperative curriculum-building efforts. See also my own article, "Pupil-Teacher Planning in Open-Space Secondary Schools," *Education*, March-April, 1978, for a more complete treatment of ideas on "updating." See also the Great Books Foundation, *A Manual for Co-Leaders* (Chicago: Great Books Foundation, 1965) for the discussion technique. In addition, see Louis E. Raths, Merrill Harmin, and Sidney B. Simon, *Values and Teaching*, 2nd ed., rev. (Columbus: Charles E. Merrill Co., 1978) for ideas on values clarification.

The following volumes, because they embody utopian schemes, refer to the Reconstructionist elements within Dewey's educational synthesis and contain the more controversial reformist sentiments in the proposed "updated" core: Plato, *The Republic and Other Works*, trans. B. Jowett (Garden City, N.Y.: Doubleday and Co., 1960); Thomas More, *Utopia*, trans. Peter K. Marshall (New York: Washington Square Press, 1965); Edward Bellamy, *Looking Backward, 2000-1887* (New York: New American Library, 1960); B. F. Skinner, *Walden II* (New York: Macmillan Co., 1976); George Orwell, *1984: Text, Sources, Criticism*, ed. Irving Howe (New York: Harcourt, Brace, and World, 1963); Aldous Huxley, *Brave New World* and *Brave New World Revisited* (New York: Harper, 1965); and Alvin Toffler, *Future Shock* (New York: Random House, 1970). Because these works are all reformist and Reconstructionist in character, they are also appropriate sources for further reading after Chapter 4, "The Reconstructionist Teacher as 'Experimentalist-Turned-Reformer.'"

This tendency to draw students into Reconstructionist schemes was a typical outcome of the core curriculum as practiced in the 1930s and of Dewey's classroom democracy in general. See Kenneth L. Heaton, William G. Camp, and Paul B. Diederich, *Professional Education for Experienced Teachers: The Program of the Summer Workshop* (Chicago: University Press, 1940) for an assessment of this tendency. See also Karl Marx and Friedrich Engels, *The Communist Manifesto*, ed. Samuel H. Beer (New York: Appleton-Century-Crofts, 1955) to assess Marxian Socialist use of the Hegelian dialectic. Controversies linking Marxian Socialism, democracy's distress in the 1930s, and McCarthyism were well analyzed by a CBS-TV documentary report in the fall of 1977. The same program offered insights and information into Senator McCarthy's charges and proposed charges against Lillian Hellman and Lucille Ball.

Controversies inherent in the old Progressive synthesis provided the philosophic wedge whereby Theodore Brameld, George Counts, and Harold Rugg could forge the Reconstructionist world view. See Theodore Brameld, *Toward a Reconstructed Philosophy of Education* (New York: Dryden Press, 1956); Theodore Brameld, *The Use of Explosive Ideas in Education* (Pittsburgh: University of Pittsburgh Press, 1965); Harold O. Rugg and Ann Schumaker, *The Child-Centered School* (New York: Arno Press, 1969), copyrighted in 1928; Harold Rugg, *The Teacher of Teachers: Frontiers of Theory and Practice in Teacher Education* (Westport, Conn.: Greenwood Press, 1970), copyrighted in 1952; Harold Rugg, *Democracy and the Curriculum: First Yearbook of the John Dewey Society* (New York: Harper and Brothers, 1937); George Counts, *The American Road to Culture: A Social Interpretation of Education in the U.S.* (New York: Arno Press and the New York Times Co., 1971), originally published in 1930; George Counts, *Dare the School Build a New Social Order* (New York: Arno Press, 1969), copyrighted in 1932; and George Counts, *Education and the Foundations of Human Freedom* (Pittsburgh: University of Pittsburgh Press, 1962).

## Chapter Four:
## The Reconstructionist Teacher as "Experimentalist-Turned-Reformer"

Since we are examining in this chapter a philosophy which has developed from the Progressive synthesis and is closely related to Experimentalism, we need to remember that the Reconstructionist position is implicit in most of John Dewey's works. Therefore, for additional insights, refer to bibliographic references in the preceding section. See all references by Dewey, George Counts, Harold Rugg. See all references regarding the Progressive Education Association's Eight-Year Study, the H. H. Giles work on teacher-pupil planning, and the Heaton, Camp, Diederich assessment of in-service teacher education. Moreover, the utopian works by Plato, More, Bellamy, Skinner, Orwell, Huxley, and Toffler contain the spirit of what some Reconstructionists have tried to accomplish and continue to press for. The following works by Theodore Brameld are pace setting: *Toward a Reconstructed Philosophy of Education* (New York: Dryden Press, 1956); *Education for the Emerging Age: New Ends and Stronger Means* (New York: Harper, 1961); *The Use of Explosive Ideas in Education* (Pittsburgh: University of Pittsburgh Press, 1965). George F. Kneller, as well as Morris and

Pai, give helpful perspectives and provide an overview of Reconstruction-ism's evolution.

Our Reconstructionist lesson begins from an attitude of near panic about economic uncertainty in the day of energy crises. Its perspective, especially in regard to the sobering predictions of Club Rome scientists, is basically that of Grenville Clark and Louis Sohn, *World Peace through World Law* (Chicago: World Without War Publications, 1973) because the em-phasis is on the absolute necessity for congruent world solutions to problems of worldwide scope and intensity. See also Michael Kernan, "Forecasting the Future," *The Washington Post*, July 8, 1976. Students who wish to probe this issue more deeply might also consult R. Buckminster Fuller, *Utopia or Ob-livion: The Prospects for Humanity* (New York: Bantam Books, 1969). The down-to-earth approach to economics in the lesson seems to contain a com-bination of insights from John Kenneth Galbraith, *The Age of Uncertainty* (Boston: Houghton Mifflin Co., 1977); Howard J. Ruff, *How to Prosper dur-ing the Coming Bad Years* (New York: Times Books, 1979); and Sylvia Por-ter's *Money Book* (Garden City, N.Y.: Doubleday, 1975). An interesting cor-rective to the emphasis on economic doom is offered by an editorial, "Prophecy and Pessimism," *Saturday Review*, August 24, 1974.

Though our Reconstructionist lesson focuses on world government and the potential for using classroom situations to convince students of its merit, I have included in this chapter references to Reconstructionist reformers as if they were on a continuum. That is, reformers who feel they can work through the public education establishment are included, as well as those who are so angry and frustrated that they prefer some form of alternative schooling, or perhaps no formal schooling at all, as the appropriate means for accomplishing their goals. This continuum is indicated generally by sampling works such as the following: Edgar Z. Friedenberg, *Coming of Age in Amer-ica: Growth and Acquiescence* (New York: Vintage Books, 1963); Neil Post-man and Charles Weingartner, *Teaching as a Subversive Activity* (New York: Delacorte Press, 1969); John Holt, *How Children Fail* (New York: Dell Pub-lishing Co., 1964); Paul Goodman, *Growing Up Absurd: Problems of Youth in the Organizational System* (New York: Vintage Books, 1960); Paul Good-man, *Compulsory Miseducation and the Community of Scholars* (New York: Vintage Books, 1966); Pat Conroy, *The Water Is Wide* (New York: Dell Pub-lishing Co., 1972); Jonathan Kozol, *Death at an Early Age* (Boston: Houghton Mifflin Co., 1967); Jonathan Kozol, *The Night Is Dark and I Am Far from Home* (New York: Bantam Books, 1977); Ivan Illich, *Deschooling Society* (New York: Harper and Row, 1970); Paulo Freire, *Pedagogy of the Oppressed* (New York: Herder and Herder, 1970). Interesting insights can be gained from comparing Postman and Weingartner's earlier book with Neil Postman, *Teaching as a Conserving Activity* (New York: Delacorte Press, 1979). The section on the "romantic critics" in Henry J. Perkinson, *Two Hundred Years of American Educational Thought* (New York: David McKay Co., 1976) is especially useful for its succinct overview.

Another useful work on the history of Reconstructionist thought, and particularly on the "Reconstructionist question" of reform, is Michael B. Katz, *The Irony of Early School Reform* (Cambridge, Mass.: Harvard University Press, 1968). Katz's interpretation of the role of Horace Mann in beginning the free school movement is interesting for its searching analysis of motives and for its suggestion that Mann's motives were not entirely altruistic. Students who wish to probe issues represented by our graph of the flow of ideas regarding the use of schools to effect reform should consult the following sources: Peter Schrag, "End of the Impossible Dream," *Saturday Review*, September 19, 1970; Andrew Carnegie, *The Gospel of Wealth and Other Timely Essays*, ed. Edward C. Kirkland (Cambridge, Mass.: Belknap Press, 1962); William Graham Sumner, *What Social Classes Owe to Each Other* (New York: Harper and Brothers, 1883). As a follow-up to Sumner's view of societal struggle, Edward Bellamy, *Looking Backward, 2000–1887* (New York: New American Library, 1960) contains a particularly graphic description of society as a coach containing seats of various degrees of comfort and pulled by a team. His description reveals how Spencer's world view might have been interpreted by the masses, as do the many Horatio Alger novels which involve struggle and emphasize the importance of being in the right place at the right time. See John Tebbel, *Horatio Alger—From Rags to Riches* (New York: Macmillan Co., 1963).

For those who need a brief overview of differences between Emersonian views of reform and the societal view of Sumner, the three following works are helpful: David Brion Davis, ed., *Ante-Bellum Reform* (New York: Harper and Row, 1967); Richard Hofstadter, *Social Darwinism in American Thought*, rev. ed. (Boston: Beacon Press, 1955); George M. Frederickson, *The Inner Civil War* (New York: Harper and Row, 1965). The Frederickson work focuses on intellectual struggles which reached a peak during our Civil War era and which markedly changed popular conceptions of reform and charity. Frederickson's analysis of the career of George Bellows, head of the U.S. Sanitary Commission, is an excellent case study in changing attitudes.

Henry J. Perkinson, *The Imperfect Panacea: American Faith in Education, 1865–1976*, 2nd ed., rev. (New York: Random House, 1977) gives a pertinent overview of ideas about educational reform. His analyses help put into perspective Upton Sinclair's electrifying prose style in *The Goose-Step* (published by the author at Pasadena, Calif., 1923) and *The Goslings* (published by the author at Pasadena, Calif., 1924). I also consider the Perkinson volume indispensable for its clear analysis of events in public education since the publication of James S. Coleman et al., *Equality of Educational Opportunity, Report of the Office of Education to Congress and the President* (Washington, D.C.: U.S. Printing Office, 1966). See also Elizabeth Leonie Simpson, *Democracy's Stepchildren* (San Francisco: Jossey-Bass Co., 1971). Margaret Mead, *Culture and Commitment* (Garden City, N.Y.: National History Press, Doubleday, 1970) offers a forceful description of recent Reconstructionist dilemmas. What does society do when change is occurring so rapidly that the young must teach themselves and their elders? Mead felt we have almost reached this state of affairs, which she called a "pre-figurative" society. For the time being at any rate, before change overwhelms us, an excellent source for those interested in putting Reconstructionist strategies into action in the classroom is Miriam Wolf-Wasserman and Linda Hutchinson, *Teaching Human Dignity: Social Change Lessons for Every Teacher* (Minneapolis, Minn.: Education Exploration Center, 1978).

## Chapter Five:
## The Existentialist Teacher as Inquirer into Human Nature

Existentialist teaching strategies burgeoned in this country during the 1960s and 1970s, especially after educators realized that something had to happen to personalize learning in an age when students could routinely bombard themselves with the most sophisticated, stimulating, and entertaining media. How could teacher and classroom ever hope to compete? Out of these efforts to personalize curricula at all levels have come two phrases which are generally associated with Existentialist teaching styles: humanistic education and values clarification. Courtney D. Schlosser, ed., *The Person in Education: A Humanistic Approach* (New York: Macmillan Co., 1976) offers a probing collection of material which attempts to synthesize and analyze antecedents for humanistic education and values clarification, especially those derived from Existentialism. Please also consult sections on Existentialism in Kneller, Morris and Pai, and Wirsing. Two other helpful sources which give a brief overview are: Van Cleve Morris, *Existentialism in Education* (New York: Harper and Row, 1966); and Rollo May, ed., *Existential Psychology* (New York: Random House, 1961).

Our Existentialist lesson is based on the concept known as the "death dread." For students interested in investigating issues mentioned in the classroom dialogue, it would be helpful to begin with the following sources: Marshall Kilduff and Ron Javers, *The Suicide Cult: The Inside Story of the People's Temple Sect and the Massacre in Guyana* (New York: Bantam Books,

1978); Albert Camus, *L'Étranger*, trans. Stuart Gilbert (New York: Random House, 1946); Roselle Chartock and Jack Spencer, eds., *The Holocaust Years: Society on Trial* (New York: Bantam Books, 1978); and Winthrop Jordan, *White Over Black: American Attitudes Toward the Negro, 1550-1812* (Chapel Hill, N.C.: University of North Carolina Press, 1968).

Perhaps among the most important of recent stimuli for using Existential teaching styles which focus so directly on the "death dread" are the writings of Dr. Elisabeth Kübler-Ross and her determination to research the difficulties of preparing health service professionals to work with terminally ill patients. Dr. Raymond A. Moody, *Life after Life: The Investigation of a Phenomenon, Survival of Bodily Death* (New York: Bantam Books, 1976) is another work resulting from a physician's investigation of death; this book follows in the tradition of Dr. Kübler-Ross's, but it has perhaps created even greater popular interest because it focuses clearly on an afterlife. However, there are many additional evidences of Existential modes of thought in literature and philosophy which pre-date the twentieth century. Students can profitably consult H. I. Marrou, *History of Education in Antiquity* (New York: Mentor Books, 1964) for a treatment of the Sophistic dictum of man as the measure of all things, as the creator of his own social and cultural milieu.

Many students are already familiar with Existentialist views expressed in great works of literature, but they are perhaps less well acquainted with Existential theological treatises. The following literary works are among the best known for their Existential character: Albert Camus, *The Plague*, trans. Stuart Gilbert (New York: Modern Library, 1948) and *The Myth of Sisyphus and Other Essays* (New York: Vintage Books, 1959), in addition to *The Stranger* discussed in the text; Jean-Paul Sartre, *Being and Nothingness*, trans. Hazel E. Barnes (New York: Citadel Press, 1968); André Gide, *La Symphonie Pastorale* (Paris: Gallimard, 1925); Fyodor Dostoevsky, *Crime and Punishment*, trans. Constance Garnett (New York: Vintage Books, 1950); John Gunther, *Death Be Not Proud: A Memoir* (New York: Harper, 1949). The following volume, first published in 1939, represents the most avidly Existential and vehement anti-war novel I know: Dalton Trumbo, *Johnny Got His Gun* (New York: Bantam Books, 1970). Trumbo's work portrays the struggles of a totally immobile, mangled soldier who must entirely reconstruct his existence; it is far more angry in tone than Erich Maria Remarque, *All Quiet on the Western Front* (Greenwich, Conn.: Fawcett Publications, 1965), for instance. Please also see Judith Ish-Kishor, *Tales from the Wise Men of Israel* (Philadelphia: J. B. Lippincott Co., 1962) for the charming re-telling of "King Solomon's Ring."

One of the most pacemaking theological works in the Existential mode was first published in German in 1923—Martin Buber, *I and Thou*, trans. Ronald Gregor Smith (New York: Charles Scribner's Sons, 1958). Buber analyzes the means whereby God may be found in relationships with other human beings who are to be met as individuals and treasured for their uniqueness. See also Paul Tillich, *The Courage To Be* (New Haven, Conn.: Yale University Press, 1952), and Bishop John A. T. Robinson, *Honest to God* (Philadelphia: Westminster Press, 1963). Another work that is almost theological in its stirring attempts to show love as the only sustaining human reality through a nightmare of suffering inside Nazi concentration camps is from a psychiatrist: Victor Frankl, *Man's Search for Meaning* (New York: Washington Square Press, 1963). This volume is a unique blend of theology and psychology.

The ideal human relationship, one born of mutual respect and a sharing of unique personal qualities, offers quite a challenge when we think of the timeworn advice to teachers about "building rapport" with their students. It is because this "Existential" relationship with students is such a compelling ideal, whatever one's teaching strategy and philosophy might be, that teachers should weigh it against several approaches to classroom management. Any classroom management scheme will have natural strengths and weaknesses, so students should think carefully about which might help them get closest to the Existential ideal. The following volumes are especially noteworthy in exposing teachers and prospective teachers to a basic range of alternatives: Thomas Gordon, *Teacher Effectiveness Training* (New York: Peter Wyden, Publisher, 1974); Rudolph Dreikurs, *Children: The Challenge* (New York: Hawthorn Books, 1964); Haim G. Ginott, *Teacher and Child* (New York: Macmillan Co., 1972); Thomas Harris, *I'm OK–You're OK* (New York: Avon Press, 1973); William Glasser, *Reality Therapy* (New York: Harper and Row, 1965); Judith Worell and C. Michael Nelson, *Managing Instructional Problems: A Case Study Workbook* (New York: McGraw-Hill Co., 1974); and James Dobson, *Dare to Discipline* (New York: Bantam Books, 1970). Because it is typical for many writers on classroom management to assume students will always be aged twelve or younger, rather than teenagers whose size can more easily intimidate, I have found the following volume to be exceedingly useful: Thomas J. Brown, *Student Teaching in a Secondary School* (New York: Harper and Row, 1960). Brown's most outstanding chapter, "Discipline and Teaching," makes the point that it is not the technique a teacher uses to attempt discipline that bring success; instead, it is the expectation a teacher has, an expectation which he or she communicates verbally and nonverbally that students will indeed wish to cooperate. Another volume which is helpful in providing an overview, but which I personally dislike because it includes medieval methods of humiliation, is William J. Gnagey, *Maintaining Discipline in Classroom Instruction* (New York: Macmillan Co., 1975).

There are many sources to guide teachers in attempts to have learning involve students' emotions, after a classroom environment approaching the Existential ideal of mutual respect has been established. I consider the following sources to be among the best because of their sound advice and careful coupling of theory with technique: Louis E. Raths, Merrill Harmin, and Sidney B. Simon, *Values and Teaching*, 2nd ed., rev. (Columbus, Ohio: Charles Merrill Co., 1978); Sidney B. Simon, Leland Howe and Howard Kirschenbaum, *Values Clarification: A Handbook of Practical Strategies* (New York: Hart Publishing Co., 1972); Lawrence Metcalf, *Values Education: 41st Yearbook of National Council for the Social Studies* (Washington, D.C.: National Council for the Social Studies, 1971); Howard Kirschenbaum, *Advanced Value Clarification* (LaJolla, Calif.: University Associates, 1977). Please also consult the following works on moral education for a slightly more conservative approach to the study of values: Lawrence Kohlberg, *Collected Papers on Moral Development and Moral Education* (Cambridge, Mass.: Moral Education and Research Foundation, 1973); Lawrence Kohlberg, *Essays in Moral Development* (Cambridge, Mass.: Harvard University Center for Moral Education, 1978); Richard Hersh, Diana Pritchard Paolitto, and Joseph Reimer, *Promoting Moral Growth: From Piaget to Kohlberg* (New York: Longman, 1979); and Thomas Lickona, "How to Encourage Moral Development" in *Learning, The Magazine for Creative Teaching*, March 1977.

It is quite obvious from consulting the above examples of values clarification theories and strategies that some of the suggested techniques "slide" into procedures for individual or small group counseling. Perhaps nowhere is this tendency better illustrated than in the story of Summerhill: A. S. Neill, *Summerhill: A Radical Approach to Child Rearing* (New York: Hart Publishing Co., 1960). One could not leave this topic without showing the strong relationship between Existentialism in education and Existentialism in psychology. The ASCD Yearbook for 1962 is an indispensable compendium of insights by educators and psychologists relating to what was then known as the "third force" in psychology: Arthur W. Combs, ed., *Perceiving, Behaving, Becoming* (Washington, D.C.: National Education Association, 1962). This "third force" or "Existential" psychology was seen as totally separate from Freudianism and Behaviorism. See Calvin S. Hall, *A Primer of Freudian Psychology* (New York: Mentor Books, 1955), and B. F. Skinner, *Beyond Freedom and Dignity* (New York: Alfred A. Knopf, Publishers, 1971) for comparisons. See also the following pacemaking works in "third force" psychology: Gordon Allport, *Becoming* (New Haven, Conn.: Yale University Press, 1955); Abraham H. Maslow, *Toward a Psychology of Being*, 2nd ed., rev. (New York: D. Van Nostrand and Co., 1968); Carl Rogers, *On Becoming a Person* (Boston: Houghton Mifflin Co., 1961). It is noteworthy that Robert Coles, *Children of Crisis*, 5 vols. (Boston: Little, Brown, and Co., 1964–1978) is also in this tradition.

For those interested in probing more deeply into the evolutionist and religious fundamentalist controversies mentioned in this chapter, please consult Hal Lindsey, *The Late Great Planet Earth* (Grand Rapids, Mich.: Zodervan Publishing House, 1977); B. Ann Slate and Alan Berry, *Bigfoot* (New York: Bantam Books, 1976); and Werner Keller, *The Bible as History*, trans. William Neil (New York: Bantam Books, 1956). The Scopes trial is respectively reported and dramatized in the following works: Frederick Lewis Allen, *Only Yesterday: An Informal History of the 1920s* (New York: Harper and Row, 1964); and Jerome Lawrence and Robert E. Lee, *Inherit the Wind* (New York: Bantam Books, 1975). See also Jacques Barzun, *Darwin, Marx, Wagner: Critique of a Heritage*, 2nd ed., rev. (Garden City, N.Y.: Doubleday and Co., 1958). To update the controversy, students can profitably consult the Phi Delta Kappa "fastback" series, Franklin Parker, *The Battle of the Books: Kanawha County* (Bloomington, Ind.: Phi Delta Kappa Educational Foundation, 1975). An examination of one of the offending textbooks might also prove instructive: Robert Weinberger and Nathan S. Blount, eds., *Responding: Basic Sequence Three* (Lexington, Mass.: Ginn and Co., 1973).

For those who wish to continue in the tradition of Existential teachers the following two sources are excellent references because they cut across so many subject areas and age levels: Harry Morgan, *The Learning Community: A Humanistic Cookbook for Teachers* (Columbus, Ohio: Charles E. Merrill Co., 1973); and Gene Stanford and Deborah Perry, *Death Out of the Closet: A Curriculum Guide to Living with Dying* (New York: Bantam Books, 1976).

## Chapter Six:
## The Perennialist Teacher as Inquirer into Human Nature

Although there is a considerable crossover of methodology between Existentialism and Perennialism, the philosophic foundation of each is quite separate. This crossover, however, comes from an interesting parallelism between the Existential psychologist's concept of inner nature and the Perennialist's view of inner nature. Please consult Morris and Pai on Neo-Thomism and Idealism, Kneller on Perennialism, and Wirsing on Transempiricism. In addition to the terms listed above to designate what we have called Perennialism, sometimes one also finds the names Classical Realism, Classical Humanism, and Neoplatonism used almost interchangeably with any of the previous expressions—all of which indicate philosophical positions closely related to Plato's position.

I have stressed the Great Books Foundation, *A Manual for Co-Leaders* (Chicago: Great Books Foundation, 1965) as embodying what is perhaps the most faithful contemporary rendering of Plato's dialectic. I have also chosen to emphasize the St. John's College curriculum as it adapts the Great Books Foundation's principles. See St. John's College Catalogue for 1972–1973, as well as Kenneth Turner, "Civilization and St. John's," *Potomac* magazine, May 4, 1975.

Students who wish to probe more deeply into issues for our Perennialist lesson should consult William Sidney Drewry, *The Southampton Insurrection* (Washington, D.C.: Neale Co., 1900), and the fictionalized treatment in William Styron, *The Confessions of Nat Turner* (New York: Random House, 1966). Styron has used Thomas Gray's account as the takeoff point for his plot lines. What I have tried to accomplish by using Gray's primary source material, rather than by drawing from a great work of literature, is to show that the Great Books strategy for discussion is applicable to a wide array of materials used in classrooms everywhere and is not just for analyzing a "great book." It also appeared helpful to use this sensationalist account of the insurrection to emphasize the amount of rationality and how matter-of-factly a discussion leader from the Great Books tradition would conduct himself or herself. Students of slave insurrections in this country will get additional insights about the theory of black revolt from Carter G. Woodson, *The Negro in our History*, 12th ed., rev. (Washington, D.C.: Associated Publishers, 1972); *The Education of the Negro Prior to 1861* (New York: G. P. Putnam's Sons, 1915); and John Hope Franklin, *From Slavery to Freedom*, 3rd ed., rev. (New York: Vintage Books, 1969). See also U. B. Phillips, *American Negro Slavery* (New York: Peter Smith, 1959); Stanley Elkins, *Slavery*, 2nd ed., rev. (Chicago: University of Chicago Press, 1968); Eugene Genovese, *The Political Economy of Slavery* (New York: Pantheon Books, 1965); and Kenneth M. Stampp, *The Peculiar Institution* (New York: Vintage Books, 1964).

For antecedents to the Perennialist school of thought and for insights into our role model analysis, students should consult: H. I. Marrou, *History of Education in Antiquity* (New York: Mentor Books, 1964); James Bowen, *A History of Western Education*, 2 vols. (New York: St. Martin's Press, 1972); and E. B. Castle, *Ancient Education and Today* (Baltimore, Md.: Penguin Books, 1965). It is especially unfortunate that the Castle volume is out of print because of its exceptionally helpful analysis of the Greek concept *paideia*, the ideal for educational excellence. J. Glenn Gray, *Hegel and Greek Thought* (New York: Harper and Row, 1968) is also an indispensable aid in comparing Plato's use of dialectic with Hegel's concept of the same process. See also Plato, *The Republic and Other Works*, trans. B. Jowett (Garden City, N.Y.: Doubleday and Co., 1960), and Plato's *Meno* in Harry S. Broudy and John Palmer, *Exemplars of Teaching Method* (Chicago: Rand McNally, 1965). A good sampling of the work of one of the guiding lights of Perennialism in this century can be obtained in Robert Maynard Hutchins, *The Higher Learning in America* (New Haven, Conn.: Yale University Press, 1970), first published in 1936.

For those who wish to probe possible comparisons between the concept of inner nature as viewed by Existentialists and Perennialists, please refer again to all references in the previous section of this essay regarding Arthur W. Combs, Abraham Maslow, and Carl Rogers. Also Lloyd deMause, ed., *The History of Childhood* (New York: Harper and Row, 1975) is useful for perspectives on different attitudes held in different time periods toward the young, and appropriate forms of education for them. This source is especially helpful in reminding us that some of the clientele in Alcott's Temple School resembled Little Eva from Harriet Beecher Stowe, *Uncle Tom's Cabin* (New York: E. P. Dutton, 1970) in terms of temperament and skill development.

Please consult my own article, "Bronson Alcott, Abraham Maslow, and 'Third Force' Psychology," *Education*, Winter 1977, for a more complete treatment of parallels between the Existentialist and Perennialist view of inner nature than was appropriate for this text. Van Wyck Brooks, *The Flowering of New England* (New York: E. P. Dutton, 1952) is a superb source for giving highlights of the mood in Transcendentalist New England. Also the following three sources are extremely helpful for general historical background and for putting into perspective a number of trends in intellectual history: Alice Felt Tyler, *Freedom's Ferment: Phases of American Social History from the Colonial Period to the Outbreak of the Civil War* (New York: Harper and Row, 1962); David Brion Davis, ed., *Ante-Bellum Reform* (New York: Harper and Row, 1967); Michael Kammen, *People of Paradox: An Inquiry Concerning the Origins of American Civilization* (New York: Knopf, 1972).

The journals of Bronson Alcott are exceptionally rewarding for their nearly poetic style and for the insights they reveal into this Transcendentalist's view of education. See Odell Shepard, ed., *The Journals of Bronson Alcott* (Boston: Little, Brown and Co., 1938). See also Alcott's superintendent's reports in Walter Harding, ed., *Essays on Education* (Gainesville, Fla.: Scholars' Facsimiles and Reprints, 1960). Elizabeth Peabody, *Record of a School* (Boston: James Munroe and Co., 1835) offers a rare opportunity for study and analysis, as do the two succeeding revised editions, one in 1836 by Boston's Russell, Shattuck, and Company, and another in 1874 by Boston's Roberts Brothers. See also A. Bronson Alcott, *Conversations with Children on the Gospels*, 2 vols. (Boston: James Munroe and Co., 1836) and Ralph Waldo Emerson, *Nature*, ed. Warner Berthoff (San Francisco: Chandler Publishing Co., 1968). The following sources offer myriad evaluations of Bronson Alcott's work as an educator and illustrate the controversy his life provoked: Odell Shepard, *Pedlar's Progress: The Life of Bronson Alcott* (Boston: Little, Brown and Co., 1937); George E. Haefner, *A Critical Estimate of the Educational Theories and Practices of A. Bronson Alcott* (New York: Columbia University Press, 1937); Dorothy McCuskey, *Bronson Alcott, Teacher* (New York: Macmillan Co., 1940); and Charles Strickland, "A Transcendentalist Father: The Child-Rearing Practices of Bronson Alcott," *History of Childhood Quarterly*, Summer 1973. Students may also find it profitable to compare Alcott's terminology with that of Arthur T. Jersild, *When Teachers Face Themselves* (New York: Columbia University Bureau of Publications, 1956).

For those interested in pursuing references regarding attempts to update an English history text at the close of the chapter, the sources are: Edward P. Cheyney, *A Short History of England*, rev. ed. (Boston: Ginn and Co., 1960); Walter Phelps Hall, Robert Greenhalgh Albion, and Jennie Barnes Pope, *A History of England and the Empire-Commonwealth*, 4th ed., rev. (Waltham, England: Blaisdell Publishing Co., 1969).

## Chapter Seven:
## Toward Teaching with Charisma: Role Models, Philosophy, and Individual Preference

In taking the final look at our role models and in encouraging teachers and prospective teachers to build viable teaching styles from them, I am especially indebted to Marie Wirsing, *Teaching and Philosophy: A Synthesis* (Boston: Houghton Mifflin, 1972) regarding philosophical "camps" and to Charles Dennis Marler, *Philosophy and Schooling* (Boston: Allyn and Bacon, 1975) for an approach to eclecticism. See also Morris and Pai on Behaviorism and Charles Marler on behavior modification. B. F. Skinner, *Walden II* (New York: Macmillan, 1976); B. F. Skinner, *Beyond Freedom and Dignity* (New York: Knopf, 1971); and Aldous Huxley, *Brave New World* and *Brave New World Revisited* (New York: Harper, 1965) are major expressions of Behaviorism. Joseph Wint and Dennis Van Avery, "Contrasting Solutions to School Violence," *Phi Delta Kappan*, November 1975, offers interesting insights into administration of schools which can profitably be compared and contrasted with Behaviorism. Work in the area of "metaphoric thinking" contained in the following sources should also be evaluated in terms of traditional expressions of Behaviorism: Bob Samples, "Mind Cycles and Learning, *Phi Delta Kappan,* May 1977, and Philip Miele, "The Power of Suggestion," *Parade,* March 12, 1978. One of the foremost proponents of suggestopaedia in foreign language instruction is Dr. Georgi Lozanov. Dr. Lozanov's work is described in the *Parade* article mentioned above. See also Gabriel Racle, *Suggestopaedia—Canada* (Ottawa: Public Service Commission of Canada, 1977), available from Suggestopaedia-Canada, 1725 Woodward Drive, Room 420, Aselford-Martin Building, Ottawa, Ontario K1A OM1, Canada.

The perspective for analyzing testing, and the development of test items appropriate for each role model, comes basically from the entire question of evaluation as presented in Robert Pirsig, *Zen and the Art of Motorcycle Maintenance* (New York: Bantam Books, 1974), and Lee Ehman, Howard Mehlinger, and John Patrick, *Toward Effective Instruction in Secondary Social Studies* (Boston: Houghton Mifflin, 1974). Since the question of divergent thinking as facilitated by "open-space" floor plans surfaces in this discussion, students may wish to consult Herbert R. Kohl, *The Open Classroom: A Practical Guide to a New Way of Teaching* (New York: New York Review, 1969), and Fred M. Hechinger, "Where Have All the Innovations Gone?" *Today's Education,* September/October 1976. See also Robert Mager, *Preparing Instructional Objectives* (Palo Alto, Calif.: Fearon Publishers, 1962); Norris Sanders, *Classroom Questions: What Kinds?* (New York: Harper and Row, 1966); and Marie Wirsing on behavioral objectives, cognitive/affective objectives, and evaluation. Sample test items in this section refer to Lewis Paul Todd and Merle Curti, *Rise of the American Notion —Tests* (New York: Harcourt, Brace and World, 1966); Upton Sinclair, *The Jungle* (New York: New American Library, 1905); and, J. Howard, "Canned Menace Called Botulism," *Life,* September 10, 1971. For the self-assessment variety of "testing" with the "S-C Teaching Inventory," see pages 113–122 of J. W. Pfeiffer and J. E. Jones, eds., *The 1974 Annual Handbook for Group Facilitators* (La Jolla, Calif.: University Associates, 1974). Morris Spier used a five-member committee to generate "several hundred statements reflecting the kinds of experiences that might be encountered in the real world of teaching." Then the committee sorted statements into four categories represented by each half of the axes on the grid. Then every statement in the first two categories was paired with every statement in the second two categories, and those statements not belonging to any of the categories below were discarded.

*Category I*
Statements which reflect a teacher's willingness to share classroom authority and responsibility with students.

*Category II*
Statements which reflect a teacher's tendency to centralize classroom authority in his or her own hands.

*Category III*
Statements which reflect a teacher's concern for the content of the job, *i.e.*, the performance of task activities, including planning and scheduling course content and evaluating student progress.

*Category IV*
Statements which reflect a teacher's concern for "role attributes" of the job, including having the respect of students and colleagues, being an expert, or modeling behavior for students to evaluate.

Spier adapted his "scoring" graph from R. Blake and J. S. Mouton, *The Managerial Grid* (Houston: Gulf Publishing Co., 1964), and the "scoring" procedure he developed parallels the philosophical "camps" which we have used in this volume.

In trying to put this self-assessment into perspective across the sweep of educational history in this country—see Michael Katz, *The Irony of Early School Reform* (Boston: Beacon Press, 1968)—I keep adding to the list of my favorite volumes to be read before a prospective teacher begins professional life. Very high on my list are Robert Pirsig, *Zen and the Art of Motorcycle Maintenance* (New York: Bantam Books, 1975); Ralph Keyes, *Is There Life after High School?* (New York: Warner Books, 1976); Gail Sheehy, *Passages: Predictable Crises of Adult Life* (New York: Bantam Books, 1977); Lyn Tornabene, *I Passed as a Teenager* (New York: Simon and Schuster, 1967); Hershel Thornburg, *The Bubble Gum Years: Sticking with Kids from 9–13* (Tucson, Ariz.: H.E.L.P. Books, 1978). But then there is Thomas A. Harris, *I'm OK–You're OK* (New York: Avon Books, 1973); Winthrop Jordan, *White Over Black* (Baltimore, Md.: Penguin Books, 1968); and Oscar Lewis, *Children of Sanchez* (New York: Random House, 1961). Students could also profit by examining Oscar Handlin, *The Uprooted*, 2nd ed., rev. (Boston: Little, Brown and Co., 1973); John Higham, *Strangers in the Land* (New York: Atheneum, 1965); and Maldwyn Allen Jones, *American Immigration* (Chicago: University of Chicago Press, 1960).

The following sources which might be of general interest to students and which have not been given previously in this volume come from the sample "U.S. history prospectus": Ivor Noel Hume, *Here Lies Virginia*

(New York: Knopf, 1963); John Hersey, *Hiroshima* (New York: Bantam Books, 1966); Ruth Montgomery, *A Gift of Prophecy* (New York: Bantam Books, 1966); Robert Ardrey, *African Genesis* (New York: Dell Publishing Co., 1961).

And then the article which seems to summarize so well the need for self-assessment of teaching styles and professional development: William Raspberry, "Tougher Standards for Teachers?" *The Washington Post*, April 23, 1979.

For those who wish to probe more deeply items for analysis, the following sources may be informative. See Ronald Hyman, *Ways of Teaching*, 2nd ed., rev. (Philadelphia: J. B. Lippincott Co., 1974) for situations similar to those in Item *B*. See James Hassett, "A New Look at Living Together," *Psychology Today*, December 1977, as referred to in Item *G*. See Marsha Weil, Bruce Joyce, and Bridget Kluwin, *Personal Models of Teaching* (Englewood Cliffs, N.J.: Prentice-Hall, 1978) for situations similar to those in Item *I*. Sources for other items are indicated in the text and have been cited elsewhere in this volume.

# INDEX

**309**

311